SWNHS
WX138
(3)
D0270013

ECONOMICS OF HEALTH CARE FINANCING

The Visible Hand

UNIVERSITY OF PLYMO
LIBRARY SERVICE

Cam Donaldson and Karen Gerard

with

Stephen Jan, Craig Mitton and Virginia Wiseman

Second Edition

palgrave
macmillan

© Cam Donaldson and Karen Gerard 2005

All rights reserved. No reproduction, copy or transmission of this publication may be made without written permission.

No paragraph of this publication may be reproduced, copied or transmitted save with written permission or in accordance with the provisions of the Copyright, Designs and Patents Act 1988, or under the terms of any licence permitting limited copying issued by the Copyright Licensing Agency, 90 Tottenham Court Road, London W1T 4LP.

Any person who does any unauthorised act in relation to this publication may be liable to criminal prosecution and civil claims for damages.

The authors have asserted their rights to be identified as the authors of this work in accordance with the Copyright, Designs and Patents Act 1988.

First published 2005 by
PALGRAVE MACMILLAN
Houndmills, Basingstoke, Hampshire RG21 6XS and
175 Fifth Avenue, New York, N.Y. 10010
Companies and representatives throughout the world

PALGRAVE MACMILLAN is the global academic imprint of the Palgrave Macmillan division of St. Martin's Press, LLC and of Palgrave Macmillan Ltd. Macmillan® is a registered trademark in the United States, United Kingdom and other countries. Palgrave is a registered trademark in the European Union and other countries.

ISBN 0–333–98431–5

This book is printed on paper suitable for recycling and made from fully managed and sustained forest sources.

A catalogue record for this book is available from the British Library.

Library of Congress Cataloging-in-Publication Data

Donaldson, Cam.
    Economics of health care financing / Cam Donaldson and Karen Gerard ;
with Stephen Jan, Craig Mitton, and Virginia Wiseman—2nd ed.
        p. cm.
    Includes bibliographical references and index.
    ISBN 0–333–98431–5 (pbk.)
        1. Medical economics. 2. Medical care—Finance. I. Gerard, Karen.
    II. Title.

RA410.D66 2004
338.4'33621—dc22   2004052091

10 9 8 7 6 5 4 3 2 1
14 13 12 11 10 09 08 07 06 05

Printed and bound in China

CONTENTS

Contents

LIST OF FIGURES AND TABLES

FIGURES

TABLES

NOTES ON AUTHORS

Cam Donaldson holds the Health Foundation Chair in Health Economics at the University of Newcastle upon Tyne, where he is based in the Centre for Health Services Research and jointly appointed to the School of Population & Health Sciences and the Business School (Economics). He is a Public Service Fellow in the ESRC Advanced Institute of Management Research (AIM) (for 2003–04) and Research Professor at the University of Calgary. Cam has also held the Svare Chair in Health Economics at the University of Calgary, where he was a Canadian Institutes of Health Research Senior Investigator and Alberta Heritage Senior Scholar, and has been a professor at the University of Aberdeen in the UK, from where he obtained his PhD in Economics. He has published widely on his research interests of financing and organisation of health care, measuring the benefits of health care, economic evaluation and using economics in health care priority setting. He sits on the editorial boards of *Health Economics* and *Health Policy* and is an advisory editor for *Social Science and Medicine*.

Karen Gerard holds the positions of Senior Lecturer in the Health Care Research Unit, Faculty of Medicine, Health and Life Sciences at the University of Southampton and Senior Visiting Fellow, Health Economics Research Centre at the University of Oxford. She has published widely, her main research interests relating to: health care financing systems; economic evaluation methods and applications; using economic information to promote efficient and equitable decision-making at patient and societal levels; and measurement and valuation of economic outcomes, especially stated preference choice modelling techniques. She has applied a number of these interests in a variety of contexts, most recently in primary care and chronic disease. Karen also leads the health economics programme of research and education at the University of Southampton.

Stephen Jan is a Lecturer in the Health Economics and Financing Programme, Health Policy Unit, London School of Hygiene and Tropical Medicine and a member of the Social and Public Health Economics Research (SPHERe) Group at Curtin University of Technology. He completed his PhD at the University of Sydney examining institutionalist economic approaches in the analysis of health sector decision-making and evaluation – an area in which he has since published quite extensively. His other research interests include the economics of health sector regulation, dual job holding amongst medical practitioners in low- and middle-income countries, equity in resource allocation and Aboriginal health.

Craig Mitton is a Research Scientist in the Centre for Healthcare Innovation and Improvement in the British Columbia Research Institute for Children's and Women's Health and Assistant Professor in the Department of Health Care and Epidemiology at the University of British Columbia. From 2001–03, Craig held a post-doctoral fellowship, funded by the Canadian Health Services Research Foundation and based jointly in the Centre for Health and Policy Studies at the University of Calgary and the Division of Health Sciences at Curtin University, Perth, Australia. The focus of his research is in the application of health economics to impact real-world priority setting activity in health organisations, an area in which he is widely published.

Virginia Wiseman is a Lecturer in Health Economics in the Gates Malaria Programme and Health Policy Unit at the London School of Hygiene and Tropical Medicine. She is also a member of the Social and Public Health Economics Research (SPHERe) Group based at Curtin University in Perth, Western Australia. Her research interests include equity, the role of community preferences in priority setting and the financing and delivery of heath care programmes in low- and middle-income countries. Virginia has recently received a grant from the Gates Malaria Partnership to investigate the social and economic determinants of demand for malaria treatment and prevention in East and West Africa.

ACKNOWLEDGEMENTS

There are many people to thank for their help in preparing this book.

First, we would like to thank those who were involved in advising us on the first edition, as their stamp is still impressed on the contents of this version. Also, it would not have been possible to produce the book had we not had such wonderful experiences and colleagues at the various institutions at which we have worked previously: the Centre for Health Economics at the University of York, the Department of Public Health and Community Medicine at the University of Sydney, the Centre for Health Economics Research and Evaluation at Sydney University of Technology, the Health Economics Research Unit at the University of Aberdeen, the Department of Epidemiology and Public Health, University of Newcastle upon Tyne, the Departments of Economics and Community Health Sciences and Centre for Health and Policy Studies at the University of Calgary.

This time around, we received additional and valuable help from colleagues about health care financing in particular countries: Jane Hall (Australia), Ivar Kristiansen (Norway) and Joe Newhouse (US). John Cullis, from the University of Bath, kept us on the straight and narrow with respect to our explanations and definitions of a market. Diane Lorenzetti (University of Calgary) and Fiona Renton (University of Newcastle upon Tyne) provided invaluable support with respect to literature searching and information provision. Warm thanks are also due to Lindsay Bradshaw (University of Calgary), Eileen Coope and Anita Tibbs (University of Newcastle upon Tyne) and Nicola Boulton (University of Oxford) for their tremendous administrative support and patience.

Finally, although all remaining errors are ours, we could not sign off without putting some of the blame for the very existence of this book on Tony Culyer of the University of York and Gavin Mooney of Curtin University in Perth, Western Australia! Basically, the first edition would not have been written without their inspiration and support. Tony brought two of the authors (CD and KG) into the field of health care financing through some work undertaken for the Institute of Health Services Management prior to the UK health service reforms of the early 1990s. Gavin took up the running and made us believe we could write a book in the first place and, since then, has influenced us all. Little did he know he'd get a second edition to plough through!

PART I

MARKETS AND MARKET FAILURE IN HEALTH CARE

HEALTH CARE FINANCING REFORMS: MOVING INTO THE NEW MILLENIUM

INTRODUCTION

During the 1990s, many governments changed their methods of financing health services. These changes have often been, in part, based on political ideology but are also, it is claimed, results of economic or financial pressures. Implicit in many of the changes has been a genuine desire to do better with the health care resources at the disposal of nations. But do these reforms actually work out like this?

Despite involving large amounts of public and private money and resources, as well as potentially affecting the welfare of large numbers of the population, it is often the case that scant regard is paid to the economic principles and economic evidence on the costs and effects of such change. Since publication of the first edition of this book the body of literature on the economics of health care financing has grown even larger but without necessarily becoming any more accessible or easier for any interested person to draw together. Hence, the main aim of this revised edition is the same; that is to allow such individuals to gain easier access to the economic literature and principles on health care financing. A subsidiary aim is to keep up with developments and new empirical findings in this rapidly changing field. In meeting these aims there are four strands. First, we set out the economic principles of markets and market failure which underpin different methods of financing health care. Second, we outline different methods of funding health care and review the efficiency and equity objectives of these methods. In the third part of the book we assess the evidence from economic studies of the different methods in light of efficiency and equity objectives. Finally, we examine some future challenges for research and policy making regarding health care financing.

In introducing the rest of the book, in this chapter, we focus on two issues. First, changes in financing arrangements which have taken place in different regions of the world are highlighted. The reader should note that it is not the intent here to review the arrangements *per se* or to be comprehensive, but, rather, to focus on change. The nature of such change sets an agenda for the remainder of the book. Thereafter, we indicate how each chapter contributes to the overall assessment of the changes that have been, and are, going on.

THE CHANGING WORLD OF HEALTH CARE FINANCING

Western Europe

In Western European health care systems, the basic funding arrangements have traditionally been of two main sorts: directly from tax revenues (such as in Denmark, Norway, Sweden and the UK) and funding from social insurance contributions (such as in France and Germany) (Jonsson, 1989).[1] Some systems, like those in Italy and Spain, use a mixture of the two, although the trend in Spain in recent years has been towards the former (Taroni *et al.*, 1998; Puig-Junoy, 1999). The Dutch system is slightly different again, relying not only on social insurance but also on a large degree of private insurance for routine care for those over a certain level of income.

So, even within a small geographical area of the world, basic funding arrangements differ. In Western Europe these reflect not only economic considerations but also cultural differences and the history of health care financing in the countries involved. Of more recent importance, however, are the changes in financing arrangements which these countries have made and whether these will make things better or worse for their populations.

Some of these changes are at a system level (i.e. changing the funding arrangements by trying to introduce more competition) and can be evaluated with varying degrees of difficulty. Others are at a micro level (e.g. considering different ways of paying providers, but still remaining within the basic system of fund raising). For many micro-level changes, such as patient charges, a great deal of information exists which can help in determining whether or not such changes are for the better.

Regarding basic-system changes, the governments of both Italy and Spain made commitments to move towards systems funded mainly from taxation (Italian Ministry of Justice, 1978; Ministerio de Sanidad y Consumo, 1989). Progress towards this has been made in both countries. About 51 per cent of funding in Italy is still dependent on social insurance, with about 46 per cent of funding coming from general taxation (Taroni *et al.*, 1998). In Spain, about 20 per cent of funding is accounted for by private insurance and charges, with the remainder financed from general taxation (Puig-Junoy, 1999). Meanwhile, although the Greek Government introduced legislation in 1983 in an attempt to expand the role of the public sector, private sector financing has increased in importance there (Liaropoulos and Tragakes, 1998).

Other major reforms, but not involving the basic systems of raising finances, nevertheless included attempts to inject more competitive elements into health care financing and provision, most notably in the Netherlands, Sweden and the UK (van de Ven, 1989; Hakansson, 1994; Secretaries of State, 1989). In these countries, the main reform has been to introduce competition in health care provision rather than in financing. Thus, 'purchasers' (sickness funds in the Netherlands, counties in Sweden, and, until recently, district health authorities in the UK) were encouraged to play the role of contracting for care on behalf of the communities they serve. Generally, this care could be purchased from either public or private providers, the aim being for providers to compete for funds on the basis of the cost and quality of services they provide. Such reforms have spread to other countries, such as Finland (Linna, 2000), and even Denmark is now proposing to let publicly funded patients choose between public and private providers for surgical procedures (Csillag, 2001). In France, in 1997, regional agencies were given powers to contract with providers, although this reform has still to be implemented in any meaningful way (Segouin and Thayer, 1999). Likewise, the Greek Government has announced, but not yet implemented, a move to a purchaser–provider arrangement for health care (Tountas *et al.*, 2002). Germany, too, now encourages selective contracting since the introduction of competition amongst its sickness funds, the latter being the bodies that administer insurance funds (European Observatory on Health Care Systems, 2002).

Also, in some systems, reforms based on the US health maintenance organisation (HMO) model were introduced. For instance, in the UK, during the 1990s, many general practitioners (GPs) were allocated budgets with which to purchase certain types of hospital care on behalf of those on their lists (Secretaries of State, 1989), a reform which was recently modified by the Labour administration there (Her Majesty's Government, 1999). Meanwhile, the Netherlands has struggled throughout the 1990s to introduce a system of competition amongst the sickness funds whereby consumers pay a flat rate which is risk-adjusted via a government subsidy (van de Ven and Rutten, 1994; van Doorslaer and Schut, 2000). Despite this, other countries, such as Switzerland and Germany, have tried to implement similar reforms (Zweifel, 2000; European Observatory on Health Care Systems, 2002). Of course, the main challenge of such reforms has been to guarantee that the risk-adjustment component can compensate for most of the variation in health expenditures amongst enrolees, thus ensuring a fair distribution of funds and prevention of risk selection.

There are many more micro-level changes which have been taking place in Western European countries. Patient charges for health care are substantial in many countries, such as Spain. In Norway, such charges are levied for visits to GPs, patients paying 100 per cent for a visit of less than 15 minutes without any additional services, with the additional services (e.g. laboratory tests) paid by government. This is similar to Sweden, although in the latter country there is a maximum annual outlay (Kristiansen and Pedersen, 2000). Belgium too has substantial out-of-pocket payments (up to 40 per cent of agreed fees), although some of these (for hospitalisations) can be recovered through private insurance (van Doorslaer and Schut, 2000). In France, about 13 per cent of health care costs are borne directly by patient payments (Poullier and Sandier, 2000). In Germany, there is a small daily charge (of 9 Euros, in 2002 prices) for the first 14 days in hospital, although various exemptions apply (European Observatory on Health Care Systems, 2002). Even in Sweden, perceived as one of the most egalitarian societies, user charges have played an uncontended role in health care financing ever since health care was socialized in 1970, before which patients paid out-of-pocket for a large proportion

5

of services (Hjertqvist, 2002). Most countries operate systems of charging patients (at least in part) for GP drug prescriptions as well as other elements (such as medical aids, dental care, physiotherapy and spectacles) which now seem to be regarded as 'supplementary'.

Specifically on payment of doctors, there are various arrangements across Western Europe. In most cases, hospital doctors are salaried, although in France (private hospitals), Belgium and Luxembourg, the system is based on fee-for-service (FFS) (Directorate General for Research, 1988). GPs are reimbursed in a mixture of ways; totally FFS in Germany, but with a recent introduction of a cap on total spending (Henke *et al.*, 1994), some salaried and some FFS, as was the case in Norway (Kristiansen, 1989) before switching to capitation combined with FFS, as exists in countries such as Italy and the UK, sometimes in combination with further allowances for achieving particular objectives (Directorate General for Research, 1988; Donaldson and Gerard, 1989a), and HMO-style arrangements in the UK (now for most practices) and the Netherlands as mentioned above.

Hospital funding also varies and some recent changes have been observed. In Denmark, Italy and Spain, hospitals can receive most of their revenues through a block grant from the central pool of funding, be it taxation or social insurance (Jonsson, 1989). Recent innovations, however, have included more competition between providers to attract funds (as in the Netherlands and the UK), experiments with clinical budgeting (also in the Netherlands and the UK) and the proposals and experiments with diagnosis-related group (DRG) funding in Austria, Germany and Norway (Magnussen and Solstad, 1994; Sommersguter-Reichmann, 2000; Scholkopf, 2000). Once again, in many countries, attempts have been made to cap hospital expenditure by making grants prospective.

In most countries during the 1990s, there have been important moves to curb the growth of drug expenditures. In many cases, for example, France and Germany, this simply involves placing a cap on such expenditures, usually in the general practice setting, whilst introducing an element of financial risk for providers by having overspends (or a proportion of them) deducted from the following year's allocation (Kamke, 1998; Segouin and Thayer, 1999). Reference-based pricing has also been introduced in Germany (Kamke, 1998). Under this scheme, drugs are classified into therapeutic categories, and the sickness funds reimburse pharmacies the cost of the lowest drug price in the respective category. The additional cost of any other drug in the category is the responsibility of the provider or patient, depending on the scheme.

Eastern Europe

Pre-1989, the health care systems of Eastern Europe were based on the principle of 'free' access, financed by monies from general revenues of governments. Since then, however, the health care systems of this region of the world have undergone substantial reforms, in many cases trying to move from tax-based financing to social insurance (Ensor and Thompson, 1998). Pre-reform, general revenues were devolved to more local levels, and this has largely remained the case under moves to social insurance. Through restructuring and openness it became clear that Eastern European health care faced many problems: perverse incentives (such as hospital funding being based on bed days and, in primary care clinics, on attendances), shortages of supplies and equipment, and duplication of services between primary care clinics and hospitals. With economic restructuring leading to falling government revenues, in many cases, like that of nations comprising the former Soviet Union, the intention was to use social insurance to increase or maintain previous levels of health care funding, along with reforms aimed at increasing the 'flexibility' of the system. In many countries (such as Bulgaria), control of funds remains with the Ministry of Health, whilst in others (such as Georgia), this control is exercised by a body at arms length from the Ministry. Yet other countries, such as Poland, are considering going further, by having sickness funds administered by private insurance companies (Tymowska, 2001). In all cases, payments from taxation (or by top-slicing social insurance monies) still have to be made to sickness funds in order to account for differences in risk levels of enrolees.

In most systems in Eastern Europe, the role of the private sector in financing and provision has increased, as even social insurance has struggled to get off the ground due to economic recession and consequent problems in raising funds from employers (Ensor and Thompson, 1998).

In Poland, recent reforms discussed have included provision of a limited health package by the state plus a system of voluntary health insurance for services beyond the basic package (Indulski *et al.*, 1989). Whilst the state struggles to maintain the basic package, the use of private sources of finance grows, with up to 40 per cent of health care expenditures estimated to come from this source (Tymowska, 2001). Such a phenomenon has also been observed in other countries, such as Bulgaria (Delcheva *et al.*, 1997) and Russia (Twigg, 1999).

In the Russian Federation, an important innovation in the late-1980s was the experiment in primary care clinics (or polyclinics) and hospital funding taking place in St Petersburg, Samara and Kemerovo (Siberia) (Hakansson *et al.*, 1988). Hitherto, hospital budgets went from the Ministry of Health to the hospitals and polyclinics separately. In the experiment, however, polyclinics held the budget, the hospital being paid by the polyclinic for services carried out on the polyclinic's patients. The polyclinics received a fee for each patient registered, and so had an incentive to attract patients. Polyclinics and hospitals retained surpluses. The aim was to achieve greater efficiency in health care, in particular to reduce length of stay which had been rising. Subsequent to economic collapse in the early 1990s, this experiment collapsed, due to difficulties in making payments (Isakova *et al.*, 1995). Further reforms were, however, based on similar principles. Now, each territory in the Federation has its own social insurance plan, the main difference from other countries mentioned above being that territorial governments contract with insurers who then act as intermediaries with providers. Thus, there is an element of competition amongst insurers in attracting public funds. But, similar to most of the other countries using social insurance, there is also an element of competition on the supply-side, with providers attempting to win contracts from funders (or the intermediaries). The extent to which such reforms have been implemented within the Russian Federation varies, which makes for some interesting comparisons and, thus, assessment of these reforms (Twigg, 1999).

Most of the above reforms also require micro-level change in order to eliminate perverse incentives, thus allowing such reforms to have maximum impact. Therefore, it has been the case, for example, in the Russian Federation, that different schemes for reimbursing hospitals have been tried or are being discussed. These include global budgets and DRG-style forms of reimbursement (Isakova *et al.*, 1995; Twigg, 1999). However, it is fair to say that, generally, such changes have not been fully implemented.

North America

The Canadian health care system has been relatively stable over the last 30 years, since the introduction of public health care insurance. The most frequent debates have been about the introduction or extension of patient charges (Barer *et al.*, 1979; Evans, 2000). The switch in Canada, from a US-type system to public insurance, provides some useful comparisons at the global level, with extremely large sample sizes (about 30 million people in the Canadian group versus about 250 million in the US!). Despite apparent stability, there have been significant micro-level reforms within the Canadian system, the most notable being the move to regionalisation in most of the provinces; now provincial governments, who are responsible for health care in Canada, allocate budgets to geographically defined health authorities on the basis (at least in part) of needs-based formulae (Province of Alberta, 1994). These authorities are meant to plan services for their local populations. Other innovations in the Canadian system have been the introduction of reference-based pricing, notably in British Columbia, and giving health authorities the option of applying to the Minister of Health for permission to contract out services to private providers (Alberta Health and Wellness, 1999). One further trend (rather than reform) which has taken place within Canada has been the growth in the share of total health care spending derived from private sources, having risen from around 25 to 30 per cent over the period 1990 to 1999 (Evans, 2000), although this trend has been reversed slightly in recent years.

The US is one of the few countries in the Organisation for Economic Cooperation and Development (OECD)[2] which does not have universal (or close to universal) coverage of its population, whether through tax-funded schemes or private health care insurance (see Table 9.4 in Chapter 9). In the US, the public health care system is in two main parts (although this varies slightly from state to state): Medicaid for low-income persons and financed from federal and state general taxation revenue; and Medicare for those aged over 65 years, those on renal dialysis and those who are permanently disabled (financed by a combination of pay-roll taxes on earnings up to a ceiling, premiums paid by elderly people and general revenues) (Ginsburg, 1988). Medicare also requires direct charges from patients for doctors' bills and hospitalisations (often in the form of a deductible with a percentage user charge thereafter). Within the US Medicare system a prospective pricing system for hospital episodes was introduced in 1983. DRGs have been used to fix prices paid by Medicare for hospitalisation, price being determined by the patient's diagnosis. This innovation has been well studied and has also spread to other countries (see above and below).

The greatest change in the US health care market over the past two decades, however, has been the move in the private sector from domination by private health care insurance to 'managed care', as embodied most notably in the proliferation of HMOs and preferred provider organisations (PPOs) (Churchill, 1999). Managed care embodies several features, such as: greater competitiveness amongst funders in attracting enrolees; more active 'management' of providers by these funders (through the use of protocols and negotiation of lower fees and prices); and some might say, greater restrictions on the range of services, providers and other aspects of care made available. Both Medicare and Medicaid programs have also made substantial use of managed care (Freund and Hurley, 1995). Managed care potentially affects both hospital financing and doctor reimbursement. Payment of doctors in the US, however, remains dominated by FFS and many policies still require substantial out-of-pocket payments from enrolees.

Despite recent developments, mostly aimed at cost containment, the percentage of the non-elderly population uninsured reached a high of 18.4 per cent in 1998 (Gold *et al.*, 2001). This used to lead to calls for a system of universal health care insurance (Enthoven and Kronick, 1989a,b; Navarro, 1989). However, more recently it seems that states are resigned to trying to improve coverage within the current Medicaid system, with some, such as Oregon and Tennessee, having achieved limited success (Gold *et al.*, 2001).

Latin America

Latin America is dominated by social insurance systems (Akin, 1988). Workers usually pay a fixed percentage of wages to the system and most are self-financing. Sixteen Latin American countries use such systems, with varying degrees of success regarding coverage: as high as 87 per cent of the population being covered in Chile and as low as 7 per cent in the Dominican Republic (Pan American Health Organisation, 1998).

Despite good rates of coverage, many governments have aimed to expand this. Combined with fiscal crises during the 1990s and recognition of fragmentation and 'overconsumption' in various systems, many countries have instituted substantial reforms. Two-tier systems exist in all countries, with more wealthy members of society receiving access to better facilities through private health insurance. Generally, however, most funds derived from payroll and other taxes are placed with financial intermediaries (e.g. obras sociales in Argentina). Differing degrees of redistribution from richer to poorer intermediaries takes place, depending on country. In countries such as Argentina, Chile and Colombia, these intermediaries have been encouraged to compete more with each other to attract enrolees and to, in turn, encourage competition amongst providers (Jack, 2000). This has also led to a range of payment mechanisms for providers. Columbia has the most extensive experience of such managed competition (Hsiao, 1995; Plaza *et al.*, 2001). While the increased enrolment of a large number of poor people is cited as a key achievement of the subsidised system, a series of constraints undermining both utilisation and access were identified (Plaza *et al.*, 2001). Uruguay has also been at the forefront of experimentation with prepaid health care plans, such as HMOs, whilst Brazil has recently introduced a DRG system for funding hospital care.

Australasia

Up to 1990, the stability of the Australian and New Zealand health care systems contrasted greatly. The New Zealand health care system, the first to establish a National Health Service, had remained very stable, whilst the Australian health care system, on the other hand, was (and remains) a constant source of political debate, having been subject to many fundamental changes since 1945.

In 1984, a universal public health insurance system (Medicare) was reintroduced in Australia. A previous version (Medibank) had operated for 12 months in 1975–76, but had been gradually dismantled under Liberal administrations until the return of a Labour Government in 1983. In the system prior to Medicare, private insurance was widespread as was use of patient charges. Elderly people and some poor people were covered by the public sector, but many people remained uninsured (Deeble, 1982; Palmer and Short, 1989). In opposition since 1983, Liberal Party policy had advocated a return to the previous system along with assurances that it would not be more costly and that universal coverage would be maintained. However, since being in government from 1996, the Liberal Party has maintained Medicare with some erosions at the edges, such as the encouragement of private insurance through subsidies and tax incentives in order to arrest the decline in its uptake (Deeble and Smith, 2000), most notably the introduction of 'lifetime community rating' insurance to take account of individuals' life time risks averaged over the lifetime of enrolment (Willcox, 2001). Australia has also become a major user of DRGs (Braithwaite *et al.*, 1998).

It now seems that it is the New Zealand system which is more subject to change. The early 1990s saw the introduction of provider competition, as in the UK and The Netherlands. Four new regional health authorities (RHAs) were created to purchase care on behalf of their populations (about 800 000 people each) from competitors in public, private and voluntary sectors. People could opt out of RHA cover to a private sector plan, taking a weighted cash allocation with them, so there was also some competition in financing. Second, patient charges were introduced for outpatient visits and inpatient stays, thus increasing the proportion of funding which comes from private sources (Hopkins and Cumming, 2001). A change of government in 1996 has resulted in abandonment of the internal-market-style reforms, with the four RHAs amalgamated into one, removal of the profit motive from public hospitals and greater emphases on longer term contracts, cooperation and openness (Krieble, 2000). However, the private sector will continue to compete for those wishing to supplement access to public services. Furthermore, out-of-pocket expenditures, largely user charges, have increased and now account for 16 per cent of health care costs (European Observatory on Health Care Systems, 2002).

Lower income countries

Financing reforms in the health sectors of many low- and middle-income countries can be grouped under three broad, and related, themes. The first is the diversification of funding patterns away from tax revenues to fund public health services and the second is the formalisation of relationships between public and private sectors (Mills *et al.*, 2001). A third theme is that of reforming the role of consumers and citizens in the financing and planning of health services. Initiatives under each theme can also be characterised by the actors involved (Mills, 2000).

Poor economic trends in many lower income countries have motivated policy-makers to consider cost recovery in the health sector, a mechanism whereby users pay part or all of the cost of care in a public facility as a means of generating additional funds. A number of innovative schemes have been, and continue to be, explored in low- and middle-income countries. Two reform options available to health care planners include payment by the service users only (e.g. fee for service payment or payment per episode of sickness or risk) and payments based on risk-sharing schemes through the contributions of potential users (Noterman *et al.*, 1995).

User fees have been a very common component of reform packages, especially in Africa (Gilson and Mills, 1995; Mills, 2000; Mills *et al.*, 2001). While they are becoming more widely accepted, there is still a long way to go both in terms of understanding and responding to the welfare implications of this type of cost recovery strategy (Diop *et al.*, 1995) and in delivering the improvements in access and quality that are expected to accompany the introduction of fees (McPake, 1993). In many countries, strengthening the participation of health care users in decision-making has been an important component of health sector reform (Broomberg, 1994; Twaddle, 1996; Mosquera *et al.*, 2001). Such community participation is often cited as a key principle underlying the implementation of user fees. In the case of Zambia, it was argued that under a cost-sharing policy the 'dependency syndrome' would be broken into active involvement and a greater sense of 'ownership of public health care' (van Der Geest *et al.*, 2000).

Risk sharing is based on the assessment of the probability that a particular event or use of an intervention will occur over a given time-span (Noterman *et al.*, 1995). The cost of this intervention will be supported by the contributions of people who subscribe to the scheme. A number of lower income countries have experimented with voluntary risk-sharing strategies in rural areas (Creese and Bennett, 1997; McPake, 2000).

A variety of public–private mix practices have been implemented in low- and middle-income countries to encourage efficiency. One practice that has received considerable attention has been the contracting out of clinical and non-clinical services. Experience with managed competition in the developing world is relatively limited (Tollman *et al.*, 1990; Ron, 1999; Mills *et al.*, 2001), the most extensive experience being that in Colombia, referred to above (Hsiao, 1995; Plaza *et al.*, 2001).

Specific hospital reforms include the use of 'cost recovery beds' in public hospitals. Allowing public hospitals to invest in and operate a system of higher charges for commercial beds, enabling them to compete for those users who are willing to pay for better quality hospital amenities, is one recent type of reform in developing countries, Indonesia providing a good example (Suwandono, 2001).

South Africa provides an interesting case, whereby, since democracy was introduced, reforms have involved a mix of the egalitarian (i.e. attempting to differentiate contributions for a package of benefits only on the basis of income) to more regressive financing (such as continued user charges and the introduction of medical savings accounts, or MSAs) aimed at controlling consumer behaviour more directly and giving physicians some freedom as to whom they treat and for what price (van Der Heever, 1998). The last of these reforms, MSAs, have also been introduced in China and in more developed countries such as Singapore and (in a small way) in the US.

As will be seen, there is a growing literature describing and comparing the types of health sector reforms being undertaken in low(er) and middle-income countries. However, the political challenges associated with the adoption and implementation of health reform proposals are greater in these environments. The design and implementation of new health reforms occurs through an interaction between various international lending agencies and national government bodies, each with their own political agenda (Glassman *et al.*, 1999). This makes it difficult to pin down causes and effects.

OUTLINE OF THE BOOK

The first part of the book, Chapters 2 and 3, deals with the economic reasoning behind the health care systems which different countries have. Some commentators have claimed that government intervention in health care financing should be far less than it is today (Logan *et al.*, 1989; Zelder, 2000), with more being left to market forces. Indeed, no matter what system of financing is in operation, market forces will always exist. How they operate will depend on the structure of the basic financing system. Therefore, as market forces can never be ignored in the health care financing debate, in Chapter 2 we deal with the issue of defining 'markets'. Before discussing market failure and building in major modifications, such as government intervention, it is useful to strip markets bare and describe how they would work in ideal conditions.

Towards the end of Chapter 2, and more fully in Chapter 3, the reasons for the failure of markets in health care financing are outlined. It will be seen that government intervention in health care financing is not only inevitable but also to the benefit of the community. The main problems with which financing systems and, therefore, governments have to deal come to light explicitly in this chapter, devising financing mechanisms which avoid: 'moral hazard', whereby, as a result of being insured (publicly or privately), the attitudes of consumers and providers of health care change so that they have no incentive to moderate 'overuse' of services 'because the insurer will pay'; 'adverse selection' and the problem of ensuring access to care for less-well-off groups in need; judging how much societies care about the access of less-well-off-groups; and problems of asymmetry of information which leads to consumer ignorance of much health care and puts the doctor in a particularly powerful position in the health care market.

Government intervention does not necessarily imply that the form of intervention will be uniform across different countries. The different basic systems of health care financing and their objectives are, therefore, outlined in Part II which encompasses Chapters 4 and 5. It will be seen that within the different systems outlined in Chapter 4 many micro-level type arrangements exist. These arrangements are not exclusive to one type of system; for instance, patient charges can be tried in public as well as privately orientated systems. The objectives of health care systems against which changes in financial arrangements should be measured are outlined in Chapter 5. These objectives cover efficiency and equity, and it will be seen that there is a greater consensus over defining the former rather than the latter type of objectives.

The evidence on different arrangements in dealing with the main problems of financing is dealt with in Part III of the book. As moral hazard is the area of concern here which is most well researched by economists and others, it is dealt with in Chapters 6–8. In Chapter 6 different ways of dealing with moral hazard on the part of the consumer are examined. Chapters 7 and 8 concentrate on the supply side of the market; examining mechanisms for countering moral hazard amongst doctors and in hospitals respectively.

The challenges of adverse selection and achievement of equity are returned to in Chapter 9. Different financing systems obviously have implications for equity as well as efficiency.

Part IV looks to the future. In Chapter 10 we ask 'given the financing arrangements that exist, how can economics techniques be used in the future to improve things?' The chapter is thus about using approaches which take account of costs and benefits in order to set the budget for health care and allocate resources within health care; the approaches are based on principles of economic evaluation and examining determinants of health (of which more details follow later).

Finally in Chapter 11, we conclude on the state of current evidence. No hard and fast answers are given, but much more can be concluded than was the case 12 years ago, when the first edition of this book was published. But, the following questions will be addressed:

- How will funds be raised and what does this mean for the nature of the financial intermediary that stands between the consumer and the provider and the principles on which the 'insurance premium' will be based?

- What is the role of out-of-pocket payments made by the consumer at the point of use? Can other forms of reliance on consumer preferences, such as MSAs, be used?
- How are professional providers to be paid?
- How are institutions to be reimbursed?
- How will the 'market' be organised and to what degree will competition be used within this?

In answering these questions, financing arrangements are judged in terms of efficiency and equity. Some arrangements are judged less desirable than others and future areas for health economics research identified.

2 MARKETS AND HEALTH CARE: INTRODUCING THE INVISIBLE HAND

INTRODUCTION

Free (i.e. unregulated) markets in health care are rare, almost all health care systems in the world operating with some level of government intervention. Yet, market forces were not 'invented'. They have always existed and will continue to do so. This can be either in an unregulated form or in an adjusted form based, in turn, on the regulatory framework imposed upon them. These are significant observations because they mean current debates and proposed 'solutions' to questions concerning optimal ways of financing and allocating health care must inherently consider the applicability and shortcomings of 'market' forces.

Free market solutions are often upheld as being efficient. By this, it is meant (in economics language) that benefits to the community[1] are maximised. The reality, of course, is that they do not work as well for some economic goods and services as for others. Notwithstanding, the free market is an important concept and starting point in economic analysis. It contributes to the understanding of exchange and distribution of resources within any sector of an economy. Thus, it is appropriate to commence this book with due consideration of how well markets work in the case of financing and allocating health care resources. In particular, we begin with an analysis of the perfect market system (also referred to as 'perfect competition') for health care. It is important to give serious consideration to the theory underlying perfect markets for four main reasons:

(1) The perfect market system is one which would unequivocally work best for health care, but only under certain ideal and strong assumptions. A perfect market delivers the highly desirable outcome of maximum consumer satisfaction or well-being (also referred to as 'utility') with the resources available to society. How such an outcome arises will be explained below. The usefulness of this model of perfect competition is that, even if it cannot be attained, it serves as a standard against which the success or failure of alternative financing mechanisms, whether market- or public-orientated, can be measured. The question then becomes one of how close other systems come to achieving this standard.

(2) There have always been economists who are of the view that all health care should be financed through competition, except for public health interventions (e.g. immunisation programmes) and subsidisation for the poor (Lees, 1961, 1962; Green, 1986; Logan *et al.*, 1989; Skidelsky, 1996).[2] Therefore, it is important to be aware of the economic theory upon which such arguments are based so as to be able to construct arguments either in favour of or against such a mode of financing.

(3) Market theories of demand and supply are fundamental building blocks of microeconomics theory. Even if one doubts the usefulness of market forces in the financing and allocation of health care, it is important to know how a perfect market would work, as economic theories of why some markets (including health care) fail to work stem from that very knowledge.

(4) Some health care systems may rely on a mixed economy, including elements of both government intervention and competition. So it is conceivable that market forces can play a part in the allocation of some health care resources, even where government intervention is present.

The aims of this chapter are, first, to explain what a market is and how a perfect market for health care would work under its ideal, and strong, assumptions and, second, to make clear what these assumptions are. This will then lead into the third chapter which examines the possible consequences of breakdowns in, or failure of, these ideal conditions.

WHAT IS A MARKET AND HOW DOES IT WORK?

In mainstream economics, individuals are the units of analysis. Individuals are seen as sovereign; that is they have preferences, evaluate choices and act. Markets are the fora for interaction of such individuals and producers.[3] We can examine what markets are and how they work using the economic concepts of demand and supply. Markets are made up of a demand side and a supply side with individual consumers acting on the demand side and individual producers acting on the supply side. The terms 'consumer' and 'producer' are simply used by economists to distinguish between individuals acting on different sides (i.e. demand and supply sides) of the market. A market is simply an adjustment mechanism for supply and demand which permits the exchange of goods and services between consumers and producers without the need for government intervention. Markets adjust using price and quantity signals. At the given market price, producers offer their products for sale and consumers spend their (disposable) income according to their preferences (wants and desires). In a perfect market situation this will mean no producers or consumers are left unsatisfied by the resultant exchange and distribution; at the given market price producers are able to sell all that they want (securing a normal return, or profit, on the resource inputs they employ) and consumers are able to purchase all they wish (so maximising their utility). Economists refer to this outcome as 'a cleared market' or 'market equilibrium'. Equilibrium is a stable position which will be maintained unless something happens to change the underlying factors which determine supply and demand.

Thus, if market forces lead to the achievement of (or close approximation to) the utility maximisation of all the individuals participating in market transactions, it would be desirable to leave markets unfettered by government intervention. As government intervention in administering the allocation of resources to different groups of individuals is not costless in itself, it is better that such intervention be avoided and those freed up resources put to some other desirable use.

If the right kind of information is conveyed between consumers and producers then these market signals avoid the need for resources being taken up in such administration. These signals help to ensure that the optimum solution (cleared markets) is found. In other words, if markets do not clear (i.e. quantity supplied is greater than quantity demanded at a given price, or vice versa), the mechanism of market signals is activated so as to move the market from disequilibrium to equilibrium. The right kind of information for market signals are (1) the prices per unit of the goods or services being traded and (2) the quantities of goods and services demanded and supplied at each price per unit in the economy. For example, if the quantity supplied is greater than the quantity demanded at a given price, this reveals that not enough consumers have a valuation of the good or service that equals or exceeds the price to allow the market to clear, that is, there is excess supply. Thus, the producer can be expected to respond to a quantity signal (i.e. unsold goods) by reducing prices, which will also lead to cutbacks in production (as it is less attractive to produce the good, with less of a return on it) and lower costs (so that falling prices still cover costs). When the price of the good falls, quantity demanded per period will expand. This process of falling supply and increasing demand will continue until the two converge, and quantity supplied is equal to the quantity demanded at a given price, that price being the so-called equilibrium price.

In this situation consumers have responded to price signals initially by not buying all of the good on offer at that price and then by making more purchases per period as prices fall. The producer responded to a quantity signal (i.e. unsold goods) by reducing prices and the levels of production and costs incurred. In perfect competition, the price of the good reflects the minimum cost of producing an additional unit of output per period (see below). The picture is about flows of production and consumption and flows have to be measured per unit of time (e.g. per week, per year or whatever). In some circumstances, it may be a stock that is being traded, so that no additional production is possible within the time period considered. Generally, however, rising relative prices for a good will induce suppliers to produce more per period and vice versa. Price signals are the core of the costless mechanism of the market. This 'invisible hand' theorem was one of the insights of the renowned eighteenth-century economist, Adam Smith, put forward in his famous publication, *The Wealth of Nations* (Smith, 1776). Through the invisible hand, consumers maximise their satisfaction by freely spending their money on goods which, presumably, contribute more to their utility than any others at that point in time. Through the same process, producers sell their products, striving to cover all their costs, including a normal rate of return on capital, which can be termed profit.

In perfectly competitive markets, all such transactions would be desirable. This is because, in perfect markets, such transactions take place under certain ideal and strong assumptions, some of which will now be introduced. In the above description, producers have to lower prices in order to sell their products. This means that such producers are inadvertently competing with other producers on whose products consumers could have spent their money. In the theory of perfect competition, it is assumed that all producers seek to maximise their profits. Each producer is so small, and one of so many, that, individually, s/he cannot exercise control over any aspect of the market except for his or her own costs of production. Without the possibility of collusion with others, producers are forced to compete with each other on the basis of price.

Another basic assumption of this 'classical' model of economic behaviour is that consumers are fully informed and knowledgeable and will, therefore, possess the ability to seek out producers with the lowest prices.[4] This situation results in producers having an incentive to operate at minimum cost so as to be able to set prices low enough to attract as many consumers as possible. Producers not operating at least cost will have this reflected in higher prices, to which consumers will respond by switching their demands elsewhere. High cost producers will go out of business. Those remaining in business will be technically efficient in their production either by maximising output for a given cost or by minimising costs for a given level of output.

Applying this model to the health care market means that, by definition, fully informed and knowledgeable consumers will weigh up the costs and benefits of health care relative to other goods. They will spend that amount of money on health care which maximises their well-being. This will result in the appropriate amount of resources being allocated to health care overall and to different types of health care (what is termed in economics language allocative efficiency). At the same time, health care producers, seeking to maximise profits, will produce consumers' most highly valued types of health care at least cost, so behaving in a technically efficient manner. This combination of technical and allocative efficiency (which will be discussed at greater length in Chapter 5) ensures that consumers' well-being is maximised at least cost to society.

Thus, self-interest is the basis of the market; consumers seek to maximise utility and producers seek to maximise profit. So, it seems that, under certain conditions, the pursuit of self-interest is not necessarily a bad thing; the market delivering maximum utility from the resources available to society. Many of the assertions of Smith (1776) reflect this. The following are two such assertions which have been quoted by ten Have (1988) and Culyer (1985) respectively to demonstrate the economic view of how markets function.

Assertion 1
In almost every other race of animals, each individual, when it is grown up to maturity, is entirely independent, and in the natural state has occasion for the assistance of no other

living creature. But man has almost constant occasion for the help of his brethren, and it is in vain for him to expect it from their benevolence only. He is more likely to prevail if he can interest their self-love in his favour, and to show them that it is to their own advantage to do for him what he requires of them … It is not from the benevolence of the butcher, the brewer, or the baker that we expect our dinner, but from their regard for their own self-interest. We address ourselves, not to their humanity, but to their self-love, and never talk to them of our own necessities, but of their advantages.

Assertion 2

But it is only for the sake of profit that any man employs a capital in the support of industry; and he will always, therefore, endeavour to employ it in the support of that industry of which the produce is likely to be of the greatest value, or to exchange for the greatest quantity either of money or of other goods … As every individual, therefore, endeavours as much as he can … so to direct that industry … every individual necessarily labours to render the annual revenue of the Society as great as he can. He generally, indeed, neither intends to promote the public interest, nor knows how much he is promoting it … He is in this, as in many other cases, led by an invisible hand to promote an end which was no part of his intentions … I have never known much good done by those who affected to trade for the public good. It is an affectation, indeed, not very common among merchants, and very few words need to be employed in dissuading them from it.

Remember that these assertions rest on two value judgements, one of which we have already introduced: that consumers are fully knowledgeable and informed and, therefore, are the best judges of their own well-being; and that the prevailing distribution of income is fair enabling consumers to be appropriately empowered by their prevailing level of disposable income. The latter judgement does emphasise the fact that the distribution of resources in markets is a result not only of consumers' willingness to pay but also of their ability to pay. Demand is about what individuals can and will do, not about what they would like to do if their incomes were higher.

Even given these restrictions, Smith's insight is remarkable in that consumers' utility can be maximised without any need to expend real resources on some kind of centralised planning mechanism organised by government. On the issue of the distribution of income, it may be possible to redistribute income and still rely on the invisible hand of the market to allocate resources efficiently (Arrow, 1963).

It is because of assertions like those above that Smith is often seen as the champion of self-interest. After all, the self interest of suppliers matched by the self-interest of consumers leads to an optimal outcome for society as 'man is led, as if by an Invisible Hand, to promote ends which were no part of his original intention' (see also Skinner, 1986, p. 40). However, Smith merely observed self-interest to be characteristic of people rather than a virtue, and, as such, is often misquoted. This paradox of private gain yielding social good can only work under certain ideal conditions, to which we will return later in the chapter. Smith also recognised this limitation, which make his insights even more remarkable in terms of their relevance to the modern day. Therefore, two more of his observations are discussed, one later in this chapter and the other in Chapter 3.

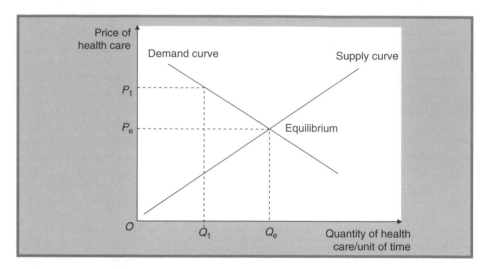

Figure 2.1 Demand for and supply of health care

In the meantime, a more formal analysis of how a perfect market in health care works can be described with reference to Figure 2.1. In this figure supply and demand are described in terms of their relationship to price per unit and quantity per unit of time. The price of a unit of health care is represented on the vertical axis and the quantity of health care demanded and supplied per unit of time (say, per annum) is represented on the horizontal axis. The demand for health care is expressed as a downward sloping curve. This reflects the general view that as the price of a good falls, more of that good will be demanded per period. The underlying assumption is that all other things, such as consumers' preferences, income and the prices of other goods, remain constant. Each point on the demand curve, therefore, represents how much health care consumers want to buy at each price, given their preferences, incomes and the prices of other goods. Looked at another way, it represents how much consumers are willing to pay for different quantities of health care. At Q_e, consumers are willing to pay only P_e for one more unit of health care, whereas, at the level of provision of Q_1, consumers would have been willing to pay a higher price, P_1, for one more unit of health care as a result of it being more scarce. This is reflected in the negative slope of the demand curve or in the language of economics the decreasing marginal valuation of successive units per period.

The use and exchange of many goods can be characterised in the above fashion. In most cases, the consumer judges the value they would obtain from using the good (value in use). If the good can be traded in the market, it has value in exchange which will be determined in part by consumers' values in use. This is where we meet the first problem with health care, as it can be argued that health care itself is not a 'good'. Rather, the demand for health care is derived from a demand for health improvements or health maintenance. In contributing to a consumer's utility, health improvements and health maintenance have value in use. Health per se cannot be traded, however, neither between individuals nor by a single individual over different points in time. Nevertheless, health contributes to utility. As health itself cannot be traded (or exchanged) in the market place for other goods, it has no value in exchange. Health care normally has no value in use (unless people like being operated on for reasons other than to lengthen, or enhance the health-related quality of, their life!). However, it can be traded and, when leading to health improvement or health maintenance, has value in exchange.

This is important because, if we are to assume the existence of a fully informed consumer, then the implication is that the consumer has perfect knowledge of the relationship between health care and its contribution to health improvements or maintenance of health and, therefore, has the ability to judge value in exchange of health care as well as the value in use of health.

The supply curve for health care slopes upwards from the bottom left of Figure 2.1 to top right. This is because, normally, increasing the amount supplied to any market per period involves an increasing cost for an additional unit of output (so-called increasing marginal cost), and, consequently, the price has to be higher to cover marginal cost. The higher the price the more will be supplied per period. In considering the consequences of a change in market circumstances, a distinction has to be made between producing over the short run and the long run. If demand, for some reason (such as change in preferences), increases (the demand curve shifts to the right) putting upward pressure on prices in the market, then producers will respond. In the short run they will expand output along their upward sloping supply curves and, as they were covering all costs at the initial price, this must result in existing producers receiving greater than normal returns at the new raised price. In the long run however this is not sustainable. New entrants (i.e. more producers) will be attracted to that market and the industry supply curve will shift to the right putting downward pressure on prices until only normal returns are once again secured by all producers. Each point on the supply curve represents how much health care producers are willing and able to supply per period at each price given technology, the prices they have to pay for inputs (e.g. wages of labour) and levels of government regulation.

The market 'clears' where demand is equal to supply. This is at the point of equilibrium in Figure 2.1 where price is equal to P_e and quantities demanded and supplied per period are equal to Q_e. As the quantity of health care supplied to the market by producers is equivalent to the quantity demanded by consumers, there is no waste.

Given all the assumptions built in above, competitive forces would always ensure that equilibrium is reached in the long run. To illustrate this, take the situation in Figure 2.2 at price P_1 where supply is greater than demand. Suppliers of health care will notice that this is the case as they will have produced health care which remains unsold or will have staff and equipment which are idle. In such a situation, suppliers will respond to this excess quantity signal by lowering prices,

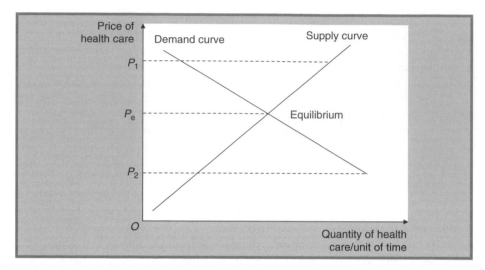

Figure 2.2 Long-run market equilibrium

thus enticing consumers to expand their demand for the unused health care. In the face of falling prices, consumers will expand their demand for health care. Demand will continue to expand and supply will contract until the two are equal at the point of equilibrium. If, at the equilibrium price, producers cannot cover all their costs, then some will go out of business, decreasing supply until the price rises just enough for all costs to be covered. At P_2 in Figure 2.2, a situation of excess demand prevails. In this situation, consumers respond by bidding up prices. This results in an expansion in the supply of health care and a contraction in demand (through movements along these curves) as some consumers are bid out of the market. Again this process continues until demand is equal to supply. In some markets, intermediaries emerge to lower the costs of information acquisition. The housing market is an interesting case in which this is done by the transfer of price and quantity information via estate agents/realtors, newspaper columns and, of course, the internet. As suggested, these modes of transferring information develop because the cost to individual consumers of collating data on the availability and prices of housing would otherwise be too great. Thus, where the market fails in transferring signals from sellers to buyers, another market develops to fulfil that function.

Until the growth of private health insurance in developed countries during the 1930s and 1940s, much health care was provided in the fashion of markets described above. Arms-length transactions took place between doctors and patients and those who could pay the market price got care whilst those who could not did not receive care. Of course some less well-off people (usually working-class males) were covered by government insurance schemes and others gained access to care through charitable organisations. However, even today many people (often the better off in societies) pay for health care via market transactions.

MARKETS: THE PANACEA FOR HEALTH CARE ILLS?

Should health care be organised in this way? If markets worked perfectly, in the way described above, the answer to this question would be an unqualified 'yes', provided that any problems of equity in the distribution of income could be overcome (e.g. through progressive taxation, through which taxation takes an increasing proportion of income as income rises, to redistribute income to the poor). No alternative system would achieve the same level of utility from health care, or, if it did, it could only be done at greater cost. For this reason the perfect market is regarded as the 'gold standard' of transaction mechanisms.

The problem is that, when examining the realities of markets, the answer to the question, 'should health care be organised using the market mechanism?' is not so clear cut. This is because perfectly functioning markets require a number of crucial, strong assumptions to hold true, the reality being that there is no market in which all of the assumptions do hold true. The relevant questions then become:

(1) How many of these assumptions break down in health care relative to other goods?
(2) To what extent do the assumptions break down?
(3) Once one or more of the assumptions break down, should the market remain unregulated, or is there a way of 'helping' markets to work?
(4) Is there an alternative way of financing and organising health care which is more likely to meet the objectives of individuals than an unregulated market, whatever these objectives may be?

The first two of these questions are dealt with in the following chapter in which the issue of market failure is discussed at some length. The third and fourth are dealt with throughout the remainder of the book: by considering how complete market failure in health care might be; in Part II, by describing alternative methods of financing health care and considering some possible objectives for health care; and then, in Part III, by comparing how different health care financing mechanisms perform in the pursuit of these objectives. The implication of the third question is that, although there is no commodity which meets all of the assumptions required of a perfect market, an unregulated or regulated market may still be the preferred mode of exchange as it approximates the objectives of utility maximisation at least cost better than any alternative mode.

Before addressing the extent to which the assumptions of perfect markets break down, we need to know exactly what the crucial assumptions of the perfect market are. Two of these have already been introduced in the previous section, but an explicit listing and brief discussion would be more helpful in structuring the detailed arguments to follow in the next chapter. It is this to which we now turn.

THE CRUCIAL ASSUMPTIONS

In order to achieve the optimal outcomes of utility maximisation at least cost, perfect markets require five main conditions to hold true: sufficient suppliers to promote genuine competition and, therefore, prevent collusion; perfect knowledge on the part of the consumer; certainty; no externalities; and consumers to act free of self-interested advice from suppliers. Each of these assumptions is discussed in more detail below. In order to set up the arguments to be presented in detail in the following chapter, a brief counter-argument to each assumption is presented here.

Numerous, small producers with no market power

As mentioned earlier, in perfect markets it is assumed that the number of producers is sufficient to make each think they do not individually have any market power (the actual number for this to be the case may not be that large). This phenomenon is referred to as price-taking behaviour; they compete with each other only on the basis of price. Without the possibility of collusion and in order to attract consumers, producers have to keep prices as low as possible. Thus, the costs of commodities, including health care, are minimised. This process breaks down in health care because the need for experts to advise patients (and commit resources) results in the requirement for licences (medical and other health-related qualifications) to permit doctors and other health care professionals to practise. In a position of being able to grant licensure to prospective colleagues, doctors are empowered with a degree of market control which permits them to restrict entry to their profession and, therefore, restrict the competitive forces which act to minimise health care costs. If entry to the profession is limited then the amount of health care provided will be less than would otherwise have been the case because there are fewer doctors. With supply limited the price of health care will be higher than it would have been.[5] Despite this, it is argued that licensure is required in order to maintain standards. Possible ways out of this seeming dilemma may be to remunerate doctors in a way that encourages provision of good quality care at low cost and to involve governments (as representatives of consumers) in negotiating with doctors on the numbers of qualified staff required.

Perfect knowledge

The assumption of perfect knowledge on the part of the consumer infers that the consumer of health care is fully informed and knowledgeable and will possess the ability to seek out producers with the lowest prices. It also infers that the consumer is aware of her or his health status and all the options available to contribute to an improvement in health. Equally important is the assumption that the consumer knows how each of these options will contribute to better health and is able to judge the relative quality of each (i.e. the consumer has knowledge of the technological relationship between health care and health improvements or health maintenance).

Again, it may well be the case for many minor common ailments and also some chronic conditions, that consumers are aware of not only their health status but also the treatment options available. However, this is unlikely to be the case for more serious and infrequently occurring conditions, such as breast cancer or appendicitis. Even in the case of minor and chronic ailments, information on new developments in treatment may get through to health care providers long before it does to consumers.

The accumulation of knowledge is also determined by the regularity with which one uses the market. Again, consumers of health care are less likely to make regular use of the market than consumers of foodstuffs. Furthermore, some element of knowledge accumulation is determined by 'learning from mistakes'. Given the technological relationship between health care and health and without chances to make regular use of the health care market or to learn from mistakes, consumers may often be in a position from which they cannot judge what life would be like either in the absence of health care or if health care is consumed (Weisbrod, 1978). When in the position of considering whether or not to purchase health care, it is the difference between these two states of the world which is of importance to the consumer. In such situations, the advice of a more qualified and knowledgeable 'expert' who is familiar with the market, in this case a doctor, is required. The need for an expert is further enhanced by the nature of the decision faced by the consumer: with many commodities, making the wrong decision does not have drastic consequences and the choice can often be repeated and rectified at very little cost, whereas, with health care, errors in decision-making may have serious consequences and the choice may not be repeatable!

Certainty

The assumption of certainty is built into the perfect market, that is that consumers know exactly what they want, when they want it and where they can get it. This means health care consumption can be planned in the same way as one's weekly consumption of foodstuffs. Clearly the consumption of some items of health care can be planned in this way. Once a person knows s/he is shortsighted, s/he may be able to plan how often s/he will have her or his eyes checked and when s/he will purchase her or his next set of contact lenses. However, it is also clearly the case that many items of health care consumption (such as an emergency visit) cannot be planned in this way. This is because deteriorations in health are often sudden and/or unexpected. In addition, the health care required to offset such health problems may be expensive and unaffordable either in a one-off payment or, if the condition persists, over a period of time. In such situations, health insurance markets are likely to develop to counter the financial burdens of the uncertain effects of ill-health. Such markets experience some problems which are similar to publicly financed health services and other problems in addition to those arising in publicly financed services, the latter giving rise to the need for some government regulation. The nature of these problems will be discussed in the following chapter.

No externalities

Externalities are spillovers from other people's production or consumption of commodities which affect an individual in either a negative or a positive way but which are uncompensated for in the market. The costs and benefits of such spillovers will not be accounted for in market transactions because, when such transactions take place, narrowly self-interested consumers and suppliers only consider costs and benefits to themselves. A commonly used example of an externality is a neighbour's beautiful garden from which one reaps benefits without having to contribute to the costs of producing such benefits. If the supplier of a positive externality does not reap the full rewards from production of their commodity, then that commodity will tend to be underproduced. The gardener in question would have produced an even more beautiful garden or helped others in enhancing their gardens if payment could have been received for doing so. The most obvious example of a negative externality which exists in modern economies is that of ozone depletion. If producers of commodities leading to negative externalities do not have to bear the costs of such externalities, too much of these commodities will be produced. Without producers and consumers bearing the cost of repair or prevention of ozone depletion, too many ozone-depleting commodities will be produced and consumed. The extent of policy-relevant externalities is disputed. Note the constant haggling over implementation of the Kyoto Protocol to the United Nations Framework Convention on Climate Control, some of the haggling being about who should pay and some of which is about the extent of the damage (or, at least, whether or not any damage is part of a natural cycle). An individual who has a cost imposed on them will seek compensation and an individual who confers a benefit will also seek compensation. If compensation takes place, the externality is said to be 'internalised' and the result deemed efficient.

In health care, there may be various forms of positive externalities. For example, some people may benefit from other people's consumption of needed health care. An obvious example here is vaccination, which has direct effects on risks to one's own health. Benefit may also arise from knowing that someone else is receiving needed health care even if this does not impact on one's own health status. As unregulated markets may not account for externalities, such markets may lead to underproduction of health care. On the other hand negative externalities in health care include iatrogenic illness. In this case market transactions could lead to overproduction of health care.

Consumers act free of self-interested 'advice' from doctors

Following on from the assumption of perfect knowledge, consumers can act freely in their own interest when making decisions about what to consume and what not to consume. Suppliers, acting in their own interest, provide commodities most highly valued by consumers relative to their prices. But, given a lack of perfect knowledge on the part of consumers of health care, doctors are often placed in the position of providing expert advice to consumers about care to be provided by themselves or their colleagues. Thus, the supplier of care is able to influence substantially demand for that care. Placed in such a situation it is asking a lot of doctors to act simultaneously on behalf of their own and their patients' interests. For instance, there may be situations in which doctors actually have an incentive, financial or otherwise, to provide care of no value or of little value relative to its cost.

CONSUMER IS SOVEREIGN?

If all of the above assumptions held true, there would be very little acrimony over the issues of how many resources should be devoted to health care overall or about levels of spending on different types of health care. This is because, as pointed out by McGuire *et al.* (1988), consumers of health care will:

(1) have to judge the cost of health care;
(2) bear the cost of health care;
(3) have to judge the benefits of health care;
(4) receive the benefits of any health care consumed;
(5) make decisions, as a rational and knowledgeable consumer will only purchase health care whose benefits are greater than its costs.

Armed with knowledge and the ability to switch demands from one provider to another, consumers determine the appropriate level of price at which supply will equal demand. At that level of supply and demand the size of the health care sector is determined. With rationing by price, there will be no queues for care. There can be no (justified) complaints when the level of spending on health care and its quality are dictated by the preferences of fully knowledgeable consumers. If some people are denied access to care, and this is thought to be unjust, the solution is to redistribute income and let the market do the rest, once again relying on fully knowledgeable consumers.

This dominance of consumers' preferences is known as consumer sovereignty. Whether consumer sovereignty is widespread is open to debate. It is not known whether consumers actively or passively accept many of the products which are available in the market place. Perhaps consumer sovereignty enters the decision-making process at an early stage when marketing experts are assessing the potential of a product. Often quoted examples of the power of consumers to dictate to producers are the failures of the Ford Edsel motor car in the 1950s and New Coke in the 1980s, both in the US. Consumers did not take to these products and they were subsequently, and quickly, withdrawn from the market. In the latter case, the original Coke (or what became known as Classic Coke) was reintroduced, as it was supposedly of greater utility to consumers. Despite such famous occurrences, it should be noted that examples of such consumer power are few and far between. They demonstrate that consumers can be powerful but not that consumer sovereignty is widespread.

CONCLUSIONS

We have attempted to demonstrate in this chapter how markets for health care would work under idealised conditions. But these rely on strong assumptions. The reality, of course, is that no market works under such idealised conditions and that market processes are not fully understood. The nearest to an ideal market might be thought to be an asset market like the stock market. These markets appear to have all the characteristics that are much admired in neoclassical economics. The participants can be viewed as *homo economicus* (rational, self-interested, with a self-interest that is primarily wealth or income motivated). The context is one of rapid response to changing information sets. Asset markets are, in short, quintessential markets in which both sellers and buyers are armed with good knowledge of the world market in shares, kept up to date by computer technology. In such markets, consumers can be relied upon to judge cost and quality and producers to minimise costs. However, there are serious economists who challenge this view almost completely. They see the operation of the stock market as a process driven by fads and fashions and, therefore, account for the recent long bull run in the markets of many countries and their recent collapse in terms of psychological concepts (Shiller, 2000).

Closer inspection of any issue always reveals disputes and different interpretations. As we have already hinted, idealised conditions seldom, if ever, exist in health care. This does not, of itself, necessitate government intervention in the health care market. Many commodities are traded in markets which are not perfect but, equally, remain free of government 'interference'. On the demand side of many markets, including food, income subsidies are provided to certain groups of people to give them the capability to purchase the basic necessities of life. On the supply side, farming subsidies and food inspectorates are employed to monitor and maintain standards[6] and there is regulation with respect to monopolies and mergers. But, for the most part government intervention does not go beyond these levels. In the case of food, once consumers have been subsidised and producers' standards monitored, these groups are free to enter into transactions with one another in a relatively unregulated environment. The question, then, is the degree of imperfection. The following chapter explores in more detail the failure of the crucial assumptions of perfect markets in health care and introduces possible policy responses to such failures. If such imperfections are accepted, extensive government intervention in health care is difficult to avoid if maximisation of the societal welfare is the objective of such care. Hence, the notion of the 'Visible Hand' which is what the remainder of this book is about.

3

MARKET FAILURE IN HEALTH CARE: JUSTIFYING THE VISIBLE HAND

INTRODUCTION

It would take but a moment's thought to realise that not many markets possess all of the ideal characteristics outlined in the previous chapter. Thus, many commodities are not traded in perfect markets. As discussed previously, even in the most market-orientated economies a common, everyday commodity like food is subjected to some limited level of government intervention in its financing (e.g. farming subsidies) and sometimes in its provision (e.g. food standards inspectorate).

For the most part, government intervention in markets does not go beyond these levels. In the case of foodstuffs, once consumers have been subsidised and producers inspected, they are free to make transactions between one another in a largely unregulated environment. It is assumed that consumers are the best judges of their own welfare. However, in health care, government intervention is much more extensive than this. Intervention in the health care market often involves governments in purchasing care on behalf of consumers and even providing such care.

The aim of this chapter is to introduce the economic arguments which are used to justify such extensive government intervention in health care. This involves examining why the market in health care fails. Although no markets work perfectly (according to the ideal assumptions outlined in the previous chapter), it may still be that leaving the resource allocation process to be determined by market forces remains the best way of getting as close as possible to the ideal outcomes of the perfect market. Many imperfect markets remain fiercely competitive, which may be of benefit to consumers. The basic reasoning underlying *extensive* government intervention in health care, however, is that *none* of the ideal assumptions of perfect markets works in the case of health care. Thus, market failure in the allocation of health care is so complete that extensive government intervention is more likely to result in the achievement of societal objectives than are market forces supplemented by minimal government intervention.

The implication of this is that there are important, and sometimes distinctive, characteristics of the commodity health care which render it more susceptible than other commodities to government intervention, making it more *efficient* as well as more equitable to provide and finance through extensive government intervention.[1] These characteristics, and their consequences, are outlined later in this chapter. They are as follows:

- Risk and uncertainty associated with contracting illness which, in an unregulated market, will lead to the development of voluntary insurance markets and the consequent problems of diseconomies of small scale, moral hazard and adverse selection;
- Externalities;
- Asymmetrical distribution of information about health care between providers and consumers combined with problems of professional licensure.

This taxonomy of the characteristics of health care which lead to market failure in its financing and (sometimes) provision follows that of Arrow (1963), Culyer (1971), Cooper and Culyer (1971) and Culyer (1976), brought together in detail by Evans (1984) and McGuire *et al.* (1988), to whom the reader is referred for a more comprehensive and technical discussion. Although one may recognise each of the above characteristics in other commodities, it is our contention that health care is unique in that it possesses all of these characteristics. One (or even two) of these characteristics existing in a commodity may not justify extensive government intervention. However, it is argued in this chapter that all of these characteristics occurring in one commodity would render market failure so complete as to result in government intervention being the optimal solution for its financing, though not necessarily its provision.

Of course, one might ask why do these arguments require restating? One possible response is that the question of the extent to which governments should intervene in the financing and provision of such commodities fits with the current context of debates about public sector reform and the 'Third Way', which involves consideration of 'the state doing less and regulating more' (Barr, 1998). Furthermore, the world has moved on since the market-failure arguments were made and many influential economists, such as Skidelksy (1996), are of the belief that market forces should play a more prominent role in the financing and delivery of health services:

> The main argument for our own tax-based National Health Service, 'free at the point of use', is that it is cheaper to run than insurance-based systems because the government can control costs. But cost control achieved by screwing down public sector pay and rationing custom by queue or exclusion undermines its morality and legitimacy. In any case, people should be left free to spend as much on health care as they want, with reforms being directed to making the market in health care as efficient as possible. The best way to reform the National Health Service is through a mixture of access charges, encouragement of private health insurance and private finance for capital development within a context of greater producer independence and competition in supply. (Skidelsky, 1996)

In countering proposals of the sort that Skidelsky puts forward, Evans (1997) states,

> ... advocates of private markets tend to make their arguments as if the last forty years has never occurred. The issues that were contentious in the 1950s and 1960s are being dragged out again, with all sorts of old a priori arguments being dusted off, repainted, and presented as new thinking about the role of the private sector.

MARKET FAILURE AND THE UK NHS: WILLIAMS' TALE OF THE DUCK-BILLED PLATYPUS

The discerning reader will also have spotted that many of the world's health care systems were already in place by the time the arguments of Arrow (1963), Cooper and Culyer (1971), Evans (1984) and McGuire *et al.* (1988) were well formulated. However, it could be argued that much health and social policy had been formulated using less well-defined arguments which were, nevertheless, along the same lines; for example, the establishment of the UK NHS (A National Health Service, 1944; Foot, 1973), the altruism underlying the existence of voluntary blood donations systems (Titmuss, 1970), the second Australian universal public insurance system, Medicare (Blewett, 1988; Palmer and Short, 1989), and the Medicare system in Canada (Evans, 1987).

In the UK, the arguments became further refined in the 1960s when the issue of the efficiency of such extensive government intervention was questioned by authors like Lees (1961, 1962). Lees pointed out that other commodities also bore similar characteristics to health care, but that such commodities were not subjected to the same amount of government intervention as health care: food, clothing and shelter are just as necessary as health care; there are unpredictable and large losses associated with things like fire risk, motor car damage and losses at sea; in other areas, such as the law, we have to rely on experts to diagnose a problem and advise on a 'cure'; that it is as equally wrong to withhold care from the poor as it is food and shelter is a case for means testing and not free provision; and that externalities apply to only a small fraction of health care activities.

Although one may recognise each of the above characteristics in other commodities, it is the contention of this chapter that health care is unique in that it possesses *all* of these characteristics. In an article written to celebrate the 25th anniversary of the Health Economists' Study Group in the UK, Williams (1998) illustrates how he made precisely this point in a letter to Lees in November 1961:

> The method of reasoning that you employ here is not adequate to sustain the conclusions that you draw, in fact the conclusion is itself a non sequitur. What you do is consider various characteristics of medical care ... and you show that each of these in turn is to be found in some other (non-collective) good or service. You then draw the quite unwarranted conclusion that medical care is not markedly different ... This conclusion is unwarranted because what you need to show ... is that there are 'other goods in the market' each

of which exhibits all of these characteristics. Let me illustrate my point by analogy. What is peculiar about the duck-billed platypus? It has a duck-type bill, a furry body like a mole, it lays eggs, and it suckles its young! Now the type of analysis you have employed would run as follows ... many birds have duck-type bills, and lots of animals have furry bodies, and as for laying eggs, this is common among birds and reptiles, and all mammals suckle their young, therefore the duck-billed platypus 'would appear to have no characteristics which differentiate it sharply from other ...' etc. I hope my point is clear.

In the following three sections, the main sources of market failure, to which Williams refers as characteristics, are outlined in more detail. Throughout the chapter, possible policy responses to market failure will be introduced and some discussion of their relative merits may take place. However, for the most part, these responses are discussed in detail in forthcoming chapters. After discussing the various aspects of market failure in health care, data on the extent of government involvement in the financing of health care will be presented. It will be seen that, even in the most market-orientated economies, a substantial proportion of health care is publicly financed. However, government financing of health care can take many different forms and, depending on the amount of government intervention, markets in health insurance may also develop. The different kinds of health care systems which may develop as a result of government intervention are described in the following chapter.

RISK, UNCERTAINTY AND THE FAILURE OF VOLUNTARY HEALTH CARE INSURANCE

Uncertainty and the demand for insurance

For the individual, illness is unpredictable. In general terms it may be possible to predict the prognoses associated with various chronic conditions and to predict in probabilistic terms how people of varying ages, circumstances and pre-existing conditions will fare in terms of their future health status. But, at the level of the individual, future health status is likely to be uncertain.

It follows from this that one cannot plan one's future consumption of health care in the way that one could do so for commodities like food. As a result of this inability to plan when a future event will occur, an unregulated market would respond by developing insurance mechanisms whereby an individual, or family, could make payments to some risk-pooling agency (usually an insurance company) for guarantees for some form of financial reimbursement in the event of illness leading to the insured person incurring health care expenses. Some insurance against loss of income may be taken out by the consumer, but, despite the desirability of doing so, it is difficult to insure against anxiety, pain and suffering resulting directly from illness. This is because of difficulties in valuing anxiety, pain and suffering in monetary terms and because insurance companies could never obtain reliable and objective estimates of how much anxiety, pain and suffering an illness leads to.[2] On the other hand, health care expenditures incurred are a fairly reliable signal that an illness has occurred and they are more readily quantifiable. Therefore, it is *health care* insurance which is mostly taken out by insured people, although it is commonly referred to as health insurance (Evans, 1984). People cannot insure against ill-health itself but rather the financial costs of ill-health. Thus, health care insurance embodies the wider concept of income maintenance.

If insurance policies are actuarially fair, premiums paid will equal health care expenditure incurred. However, this assumes that insurance companies make no profit and incur no administration costs. These assumptions do not hold, but people still take out (actuarially unfair) insurance; paying premiums which are 'loaded' so as to cover administration and profit. The reason for this is that, in general, people are risk averse; they do not like risk and gain utility from covering the uncertainty of large financial losses. This is a utility gain for which they are willing to pay.

For example, in a community of ten people it might be known that each person has a one in ten chance of incurring health care expenditures of £1000 per annum. If all are risk averse, each would take out an insurance policy, paying £100 per annum each if it were actuarially fair. However, if administrative costs were £10 per annum, would each person be willing to pay the actuarially unfair premium of £101 each? The answer is probably 'yes'.

People are also more likely to insure against larger losses which are unpredictable than against smaller losses which occur more regularly and, therefore, more predictably. For instance, of those people who visit a dentist every six months for a check-up, some may not find it worth their while insuring against the predictable and inexpensive check-up itself, but would rather insure against the unpredictable and more expensive consequence of requiring treatment subsequent to the check-up. This does not mean, of course, that no one will insure against relatively small potential losses; many people do insure against such losses. The reason for this may be related not only to uncertainty itself, but anxiety associated with incurring financial costs. However, as one would expect, the value of insurance is in providing cover against the uncertainty of financial losses – especially large losses.

From the foregoing, it is apparent that insurance is a sensible institutional response to the problem of uncertainty in the incidence of large health care expenses. How, then, do health care insurance markets fail and why should the public sector intervene in such markets? Such market failure arises from three sources: diseconomies of small scale; moral hazard; and adverse selection.

Diseconomies of small scale

Before explaining the term 'diseconomies of small scale', it is best to explain the converse term, 'economies of scale'. At issue is the relationship between fixed cost and output. The bigger an organisation, the easier it becomes normally for that organisation to distribute a fixed cost across its products, so reducing both the fixed and total cost per unit produced. This is an example of an economy of scale. However, in some situations, organisations can become too large, at which point unit costs of production begin to increase again. Likewise, if an organisation is too small, its unit costs may also begin to rise. So, conventionally, a U-shaped relationship between costs and output is portrayed (i.e diseconomies set in when scale is too small or too large). In health care insurance, an example of an economy of scale is marketing costs which may amount to the same total figure no matter how many people are insured with a particular company. Thus, the more people covered the smaller will be the marketing costs per person which may then be fed back to consumers in reduced premiums. The same may be true for administrative tasks such as processing of bills and premium collection.

Diseconomies of small scale arise in markets with several competing insurance companies, each with its own administrative and marketing costs. In a large company such administrative costs would be reduced as they would be spread over more customers. However, a large monopoly insurer may be exploitative. An alternative policy response would then be to have a public monopoly so that low costs are maintained without the risk of exploitation. Some costs, such as those for marketing, for checking for eligibility of rebates and for the cost of premium collection, may be drastically reduced or cut out altogether if premium collection is 'piggybacked' on to the taxation collection system.

Diseconomies of small scale result in market failure because it is conceivable that a person would not be willing to pay for insurance which is inflated by the cost of small-scale competition or by an exploitative monopolist, but would be willing to vote for a system involving the collection of premiums through some public mechanism, such as taxation. One of the reasons why market mechanisms are often thought to be better than some form of government intervention is that neoclassical theory assumes such costs are zero or at least very small. The cost of producing the information to make the market work is ignored.

The more privately orientated US health care system does appear to be more administratively costly than the system in Canada. A 1993 estimate of administrative costs in the US is 24.7 per cent of total health care expenditure, a figure which is rising (Himmelstein and Woolhandler, 1986; Woolhandler and Himmelstein, 1991; Hellander *et al.*, 1994). Twenty seven per cent of total employment in the US health care system is taken up by administration (Himmelstein *et al.*, 1996). More recently, the cost of administering US hospitals has been estimated at 26 per cent of total hospital costs in 1994, compared with an estimate of 2–6 per cent for general and senior management costs in the UK NHS (Audit Commission, 1995; Woolhandler and Himmelstein, 1997). There is now considerable debate in the US on the issue of how to measure administrative costs (Thorpe, 1992). However, the activities of the 1980s involving the introduction of more competition into the US health care system is itself thought to have resulted in increased administrative costs as a result of greater spending on advertising and on hospital utilisation review (Evans, 1987; Quam, 1989). Evans (1990a) has described the effect of such activities as follows:

> A large and growing share of the American total is spent, not on doctors and nurses, but on accountants, management consultants, and public relations specialists. Their contribution to the health of the American public is difficult to discern (unless one is trained in neoclassical economics and is able to see with the eye of faith).

Note here recent experiences with the internal market in the UK NHS, which led to substantial increases in management costs (Maynard and Bloor, 1996).

Moral hazard

In insurance-based health care systems the problem of potential 'excess' demand exists because of what has become known as 'moral hazard'. The levels of demand and, therefore, provision are greater than would be the case in a perfect market with fully informed consumers. Excess demand results in the benefits from resources used in health care provision being exceeded by the benefits forgone (or opportunity cost)[3] from the use of these resources in an alternative which is not currently funded. Moral hazard is basically a change in the attitudes of consumers and providers of health care which results from becoming insured against the full costs of such care.

Moral hazard can be divided into 'consumer moral hazard' and 'provider moral hazard'. Each has two aspects. Consumer moral hazard arises on the one hand because the very fact of being insured reduces the (financial) costs of treatment at the point of consumption and hence makes being ill a less undesired state; a state less energetically to be avoided. Consequently, the incentive to adopt healthier lifestyles is diminished and the probability of requiring care rises. This is likely to be more significant in certain other spheres (e.g. car insurance) but it also applies to health. The other aspect of consumer moral hazard is the effect being insured has when sickness occurs and services are demanded: a zero or reduced price at the point of use encourages a higher rate of use than would otherwise be considered efficient; there is a wedge driven between paying for the cost of what is provided and the value of, or willingness to pay for, what is provided. Thus, the market fails to transmit efficient price signals to consumers.

Consumer moral hazard is the form in which moral hazard is most often characterised (Pauly, 1968). The phenomenon can also be explained diagrammatically. According to Figure 3.1, and from our previous discussion of demand theory in Chapter 2, it can be seen that a zero price of health care at the point of delivery would result in the overconsumption of health care relative to what would occur under normal market mechanisms. At what would otherwise be a prevailing market price of P_e, the amount of overconsumption is represented by the amount OQ_1-OQ_e. This overconsumption results in a welfare loss to society represented by the area ABQ_1 as a result of the benefits, to patients, of health care consumed being less than the cost of such care. For instance, the benefit of care

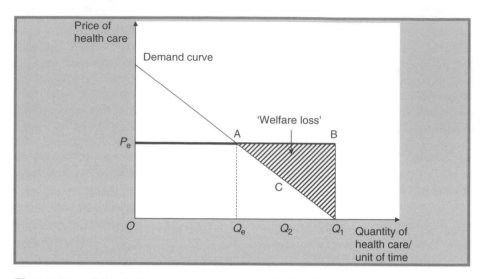

Figure 3.1   Effect of insurance on demand for health care

consumed at Q_2 is represented by the distance between Q_2 and point C whilst the cost of such care is P_e. More benefit (or welfare) to society could be obtained by shifting the resources used up by these excess demands out of the activities covered by health insurance and into some other health-inducing activity or even out of health care altogether.

It should be noted here that the characterisation of moral hazard as described is very neoclassical. In particular, the implication is that the demand curve in Figure 3.1 is that of a fully informed and rational consumer. However, we have already questioned this assumption and do so again in the section below on licensure and asymmetry of information. It will be argued in that section that the doctor (or supplier of care) can have considerable influence over demand for care. Thus, the traditional neoclassical view of the independence of supply and demand is broken. As it is not known where the demand curve of a fully informed consumer would lie, it is difficult to see how the welfare loss associated with excess demand can be measured. The relevance of the demand curve of a less-than-fully-informed consumer influenced by advice from suppliers is difficult to judge.

Provider moral hazard can result from a simple lack of awareness of costs or from the use of fee-for-service (FFS) remuneration methods for doctors in which fees depart from 'market prices'. In systems that use FFS methods of remuneration, doctors are paid a fee for items of service provided to patients. For example, a surgeon may receive a fee for a particular operation carried out, a radiologist for reading a mammogram, and general practitioners for a consultation or for providing a more specific item of service like a vaccination.

The conventional wisdom is that, in such systems, doctors have a financial incentive to provide care in excess of that which would be arrived at by trading with fully informed consumers. This phenomenon is also known in the literature as 'supplier-induced demand' (Evans, 1974; Rice, 1983; Cromwell and Mitchell, 1986) and will be more fully explored in the section below on asymmetry and licensure and particularly in Chapter 7. However, the important point is that in FFS systems problems of how much care is provided arise only when fees depart from the 'true competitive prices' which the doctor would have received. Thus, in accordance with the conventional wisdom, if the fee is greater than the true competitive price there will be an incentive to overprovide. But, contrary to conventional wisdom, if the fee is below the true competitive price, there will be an incentive to underprovide care.

These phenomena cannot be tempered by consumers as, first, they often do not have the knowledge to be able to judge what is appropriate and what is not and, second, it can be seen from the discussion above that consumers also have no financial incentive to moderate such behaviour anyway as a third party, the insurance company, will be paying for the costs of care. Traditionally, in the US, it is commonly thought that a further 'wedge' is driven between the cost of providing care and the value derived by consumers because it is often the employer who negotiates and pays insurance premiums. Thus, there are two 'third parties' to whom health care costs can be passed by both consumers and providers; insurance companies and employers. The effect that moral hazard (of all kinds) has on rising premiums which are ultimately borne by the consumer is thus accentuated by being partially disguised to the consumers themselves.

Similarly, in publicly orientated systems, such as the UK and Scandinavia, health care providers do not incur the full opportunity cost of provision of many aspects of care (e.g. diagnostic tests), thus rendering them prone to provider moral hazard arising from a lack of awareness of costs but not from payment by FFS. In many cases doctors are either not interested in or are not given information on the costs of items of resource use consequent upon their actions. In this case, it is the health authority (or, in England, primary care trust), and ultimately the taxpayer, who pays for care. Once again, therefore, the effects of moral hazard on health care costs in a centrally funded system are partially disguised to consumers. The market fails both to transmit information on costs to, and to impose responsibility for costs on, the supplier of health care.

It is worth noting that the danger of 'over-utilisation' due to moral hazard can be exaggerated. There are powerful grounds for supposing that the rate of utilisation chosen at prices reflecting the full cost of care would be too low anyway (see Culyer and Simpson, 1980, for a review). This arises because of the external benefits of health care in the form of the reduction in the probability of infection from communicable diseases for the rest of the community. Presumably, too, many people care sufficiently about others for them to experience a vicarious benefit from the knowledge that their health needs are better cared for than would otherwise be the case (Culyer, 1986). This issue is covered in detail below in the section on externalities.

Moral hazard is the aspect of insurance markets which has received most attention from economists. This is reflected in the fact that Chapters 6–8 of this book are

devoted to an examination of the evidence on different policy responses to this phenomenon. Policy responses to moral hazard do not have to be financial. Traditional
organisational responses to preventing overuse of expensive hospital services in
many developed countries have involved the use of primary care doctors as the
'gateway' to such services. Likewise, in lower income countries a similar policy was
to use 'barefoot doctors', such as in Papua New Guinea and, of course, China. Such
organisational considerations are, unfortunately, beyond the scope of this book.

Financially, consumer moral hazard has typically been countered in the following ways: use of co-payments (or user charges), whereby the insured person pays
some fraction or absolute amount of the supplier's charge; use of co-payments to
raise revenue for the system as well as to deter demand (such as in lower income
countries); medical savings accounts (MSAs); fixed periodic per capita prepayment by consumers directly to the provider of comprehensive health care, such as
a health maintenance organisation (HMO); provision of incentives for consumers
to demand care from selected providers, offering low cost packages of care, as in
the case of Preferred Provider Organisations (PPOs); and non-price rationing by
doctors according to judgements of clinical need usually resulting in consumers
incurring waiting costs for elective treatment.

The first five of these have been implemented mainly in private insurance-based
systems, such as the US, although versions of these are common in publicly
funded systems too. The sixth is more characteristic of publicly provided and
financed health care, such as in the UK National Health Service. The principles
underlying HMOs and PPOs are outlined in more detail in the following chapter.
Given our comments above on the relevance of the neoclassical approach to moral
hazard, some of these 'solutions' can be questioned in principle – particularly user
charges. So-called 'solutions' may simply bring along another set of problems.
This also highlights the importance of evidence on the effects of all of the above on
costs and health outcomes. This evidence is presented in Chapter 6.

Provider moral hazard has been typically countered by four main methods:
first, non-pecuniary incentives resulting mainly from the pressure of peer review,
which can also be bolstered by financial reward for 'good practice'; second, use of
a salaried service in order to cap payments to providers of care; third, financial
limitations imposed at a 'global' level by clinical or institutional budgets, at a case-
by-case level by prospective reimbursement for patients within diagnosis related
groups (DRGs), or by fixed periodic prepayments to HMOs or primary care doctors (e.g. general practitioner fundholders) for provision of their own care or even
for the purchase of hospital care on behalf of their patients; fourth, direct government regulation as a means of controlling providers, such as the limited list for
pharmaceutical prescribing by general practitioners in Norway, with financial
penalties imposed on those who unjustifiably prescribe outwith the list.

Each of these methods of controlling provider moral hazard is reviewed in
Chapters 7 and 8. In Chapter 7, evidence is presented on how different methods of
payment affect doctor behaviour, whilst in Chapter 8 the effect of different
reimbursement mechanisms on hospital behaviour is reviewed.

Adverse selection

Adverse selection results from asymmetry of information in the insurance market: that is, buyers of insurance tend to have more of an idea of their risk status than sellers of health care insurance. Initially, in a competitive market, if the insurance companies have no idea of individual risk status, a premium could be set reflecting the general health risks of the insured population. Thus, the premium paid by everyone who takes out insurance would be the same, reflecting the 'average' risk level of the insured population. This is what is called 'community rating'.

For some members of the insured population who perceive their own risk level to be lower than average, this community rating premium will be too high. They would then elect not to take out health care insurance and will not be covered in the event that the unexpected happens. The effect of this decision, however, means that the average risk level of those remaining insured will rise, because it is people of lower-than-average risk who have dropped out of insurance. Thus, to cover the projected health care costs of this population, premiums must rise. Once again, the result of this is that those perceiving their risk status to be lower than the average of those remaining insured will drop out of insurance, and the process will carry on. This process, whereby the best risks are selected out of the insured group, is called 'adverse selection'.

In a competitive system other phenomena would be expected to follow from adverse selection. The presence of a low-risk uninsured group of people sends a signal to insurance companies that there is potential to tailor premiums to levels of individual, rather than population, risk. This is 'experience rating'. If fine distinctions can be made, a premium will reflect assumed future risk level based perhaps on some idea of past history of personal and family health as a predictor for the future. As a result of this process, higher risk groups (typically the lower paid, elderly people and chronically sick people) will be required to pay higher experience-rated premiums to maintain coverage, premiums which they may not now be able to afford. The process by which low-risk individuals are drawn into low-premium plans is often referred to as 'skimming' or 'creaming off'.

How, then, does adverse selection constitute market failure? Two groups of people may be left uninsured as a result of adverse selection: those of low risk who start off the vicious circle by pulling out of insurance at community rates; and those in high-risk groups who cannot afford experience-rated premiums. Adverse selection constitutes market failure for the former group but (perhaps, surprisingly) not, on its own, for the latter. For the former group, the market fails because both insurer and customer would be willing to enter into a contract, but the necessary information required for such a transaction to be entered into is not transmitted from one party to the other via the market. The transaction is prevented by asymmetry of information about risk status. Low-premium insurance policies could be offered, but, because of asymmetry, insurance companies would have no a priori information on potential customers which would not allow them to prevent some high-risk people taking up such policies. Therefore, such policies will not be offered. Despite this failure of the market, society may not wish to respond anyway as it mainly affects a small and privileged group.

For the high-risk group, the market does not fail. Quite simply, their financial resources cannot cover the cost of insurance. As Evans (1984) points out, these people 'cannot afford Mercedes Benz's either, but that is no failure of automobile markets'. Despite this, it is this aspect of adverse selection which presents the more serious social problem.

Recently the US Employee Benefits Research Institute (1997) has estimated that the proportion of the non-elderly population in the US without insurance (private or public) has increased from 14.8 per cent in 1987 to 17.7 per cent in 1996 and Schroeder (2001) reported a steady increase from 31.8 million non-elderly people in 1987 to 42.1 million in 1999. These figures confirm the results of the large and growing literature on uninsurance and underinsurance in the US (Farley, 1985; Wilensky, 1988). This has been shown to lead to greater risks of poverty and restricted access to care, even for children (Wyszewianski, 1986; Hayward *et al.*, 1988; Newacheck, 1988; Quam, 1989).

The same problems have arisen in other countries, such as Australia, before the introduction of universal coverage through the state. In Australia, it was estimated that about 15 per cent of the population had no private or public insurance cover prior to the introduction of the first compulsory public insurance scheme there in the early 1970s (Deeble, 1982). This was despite the fact that elderly people received automatic cover as a designated priority group. The uninsured group was made up largely of Southern European migrants and those in low-income groups. The same was also true before the introduction of the second Australian public insurance scheme in 1984 (Palmer and Short, 1989).[4] In Canada, the financing of pharmaceuticals out of hospital provides an interesting microcosm of the US system. In Canada, about two-thirds of total drug costs is privately funded. The public sector pays 45 per cent of prescription drug costs. No province has first dollar coverage for all residents (most provide this for seniors). Public plans cover about 44 per cent of Canadians, private plans cover another 44 per cent and 12 per cent have no cover. Given that private insurance coverage is correlated with income, it is, of course, likely that those with no cover will also have lower incomes (National Forum on Health, 1997). It is interesting that the uninsured figures from Australia and Canada (of 15 and 12 per cent respectively) are close to the uninsured figure from the US.

These experiences indicate that, even in health care systems based on private health insurance but in which some attempt is made to provide coverage for those in special groups (such as elderly people in Australia and low-income people in the US Medicaid schemes), a substantial degree of adverse selection still exists. As we have said above, however, this does not, on its own, represent market failure for this group. The market has not failed in its transmission of information between suppliers and demanders of health care insurance. Whether this social problem is defined as market failure depends on externalities: that is, how much members of society care about the exclusion of others from access to needed health care. To continue Evans' analogy, members of society are less likely to care about the access of less-well-off people to Mercedes Benz cars than about access for these people to needed health care! Thus it is adverse selection and externalities acting in conjunction which determines society's response to this problem.[5] Therefore, it is the issue of externalities to which we now turn in order to identify whether anything should be done about the effects of adverse selection on high-risk groups and, if so, what the possible policy responses might be.

EXTERNALITIES

Externalities are spillovers from other people's production or consumption of commodities which affect an individual in either a negative or a positive way but which are out of the individual's locus of control. The costs and benefits of such spillovers are not relevant in market transactions because, when such transactions take place, consumers and suppliers consider only costs and benefits to themselves. However, there are clearly situations where external effects ought to be taken into account, so recognising a difference between private and social costs and benefits. As said in Chapter 2, if producers of commodities leading to negative externalities do not have to bear the costs of such externalities, too much of these commodities will be produced. If the cost of a negative externality were to be added to the other costs of producing a commodity, the price is likely to rise. It then follows that less of that commodity would be demanded. An example of this might be goods produced by manufacturers who pollute the environment. Forcing them to pay the cost of preventing or cleaning up this pollution will increase their costs and lead them to produce less of their good. Depending on the size of the negative externality, it can be seen that unregulated market forces may lead society away from its optimal provision of various goods and services.

In health care, there may be certain positive externalities whereby people benefit from other people's consumption of the commodity. Benefit may arise from knowing that others can consume a public health intervention, such as vaccination or health education message, which has direct effects on risks to one's own health (a 'selfish' externality).[6] An altruistic type of benefit may also arise from knowing that someone is receiving needed health care which does not necessarily impact on one's own health status (a 'caring' externality). This caring externality is often characterised by the concern some benevolent, rich and healthy members of society may have for those who are poor and/or unhealthy, although clearly the poor can be similarly concerned. A statement from Smith (1759),[7] as quoted by Skinner (1986), demonstrates that, despite being held up as the champion of self-interest, all he did was to recognise this as a characteristic, not a virtue. Even Smith recognised the existence of externalities, though (as expected, given the historical context) not explicitly for health care:

> How selfishly soever man may be supposed, there are evidently some principles in his nature which interest him in the fortune of others, and render their happiness necessary to him, though he derives nothing from it except for the pleasure of seeing it.

Smith was of the view that governments should protect individuals by involvement in road building, public education, help for the destitute, provision of a system of justice and provision of 'cultural' activities for workers to offset the adverse effects of economic advance. The economic theory underlying caring externalities in health care was developed largely by Culyer (1971).

As unregulated markets do not account for individuals' willingness to pay for external benefits, such markets will lead to underproduction of health care. Once this willingness to pay, or demand, is added to that generated by private individuals accounting for only their own costs and benefits, it follows that more health care would be provided.[8]

The question then is how to affect the transfer from the caring to the needy, to allow the needy to purchase his or her required health care. The problem of leaving this to the market is that the amount of the transfer will be less than if contributing individuals made the transfer through some other means. For instance, relying on the goodwill of people to seek out those who are sick so as to contribute to the cost of their health care is impractical and too costly, in terms of time and effort, for those who would like to contribute. Likewise, charities suffer from a similar experience because people often do not 'get round to' making a contribution or 'fatigue' sets in.

Yet, if the exercise is rendered costless, apart from the actual contribution made, more individuals would be prepared to make that contribution. The most efficient way of achieving this is through some mechanism of public health insurance or taxation. In such cases, governments bear the administrative costs of the transfer and more people will be willing to make the transfer. A progressive taxation system of premium collection has the added advantage of not only transferring wealth from those who are healthy to those who are not but also from those who are rich (which is frequently associated with better health) to those who are poor (which is frequently associated with poorer health) (Cooper and Culyer, 1971; Evans, 1984). Thus, a progressive taxation system may be a very efficient way of transferring monies to achieve health improvements from the consumption of health care and other commodities. One problem with universal public health care insurance and taxation is that it is compulsory to participate in the system of transferring monies. However, given that neither a free market nor a public system of financing care will satisfy everyone, it is a choice between two evils. Even in the privately orientated US, it would seem from survey results that the majority of the US population think either that the health care system there needs to be completely rebuilt or is in need of some fundamental changes to make it work better (Blendon *et al.*, 1997).[9]

Rather than responding to externalities through publicly financed health care systems, it could be argued that a possible policy response is simply to subsidise those deemed to be 'in need', regulate to some extent on the supply side and to 'leave the rest to the market', as in the case of foodstuffs. A cash subsidy for health care, however, has several problems associated with it. First, there is the problem of defining who is in need (and what that concept means) and estimating their treatment expenses in advance.[10] Second, there is the 'bleeding cheat' problem, as a result of which recipients of the subsidy may not spend it on what was intended (Archibald and Donaldson, 1976). In this case, the need for health care is so unpredictable that people may spend the money on something they perceive to be more urgent relative to health care insurance. Culyer (1991) has argued that a general subsidy is more likely to be appropriate for goods and services that are highly income elastic (i.e. highly responsive to changes in income) at low levels of household income. Such goods (e.g. food) are the most basic of necessities for which people, for the most part, will spend the subsidy in the intended way. This is unlikely to be so for health care. Vouchers could be used to tie consumption to health care, but such a system can be administratively cumbersome and difficult to apply in health care where people are not regular users of services, where there are problems of assessing quality, where services cannot be defined in discrete packages, where suppliers of care may not be sufficiently detached from those holding the vouchers and where too much information may be required to tailor the value of vouchers to the various levels of need which exist in the community (Saltman and von Otter, 1995).

Moreover, subsidising consumers of health care on the demand side ignores the influence of doctors on the supply side. A lack of perfect knowledge on the part of consumers results in asymmetry of information between the consumer and the provider of health care. Consequently, the former often seeks advice from the latter. This puts providers in a situation where they are not only a supplier but also a demander of care. Continually to subsidise consumers' costs of health care in such a situation, and particularly when providers are rewarded on an FFS basis, could result in a continual cycle of rising fees and further subsidies which would simply, and possibly substantially, increase the costs of health care to the community with little or no additional benefits to patients.

In addition, to maintain standards, licensure exists, whereby the only doctors who can practise are those who are appropriately qualified. This results in a situation of monopoly in which doctors (many, including the authors, would say rightly) are not subjected to competition from non-qualified practitioners (or 'quacks'). However, combining this with the problem of asymmetry of information between doctors and patients could result in doctors manipulating the health care market to their own ends and to the detriment of patients and the community, as in the case of escalating health care costs at little or no benefit to patients described in the previous paragraph.[11] If this problem did not exist then the problems of uncertainty and externalities alone would not justify the level of government intervention which exists in many countries. It is this problem of licensure and asymmetry of information to which we now turn in more detail.

LICENSURE AND ASYMMETRY OF INFORMATION

The need for a profession

There has never been, at least in modern times, a free market for doctors' services. Such a market could exist but it would involve no regulation on the supply side.

Thus, unqualified practitioners (or 'quacks') would be free to practice and consumers would make choices between all practitioners on the basis of their own assessments of quality and price. In health care, such a market would be problematical in that consumers have little knowledge of how health care will affect their health. Leaving consumers free to make choices in an unregulated market could result in mistakes being made (many of these being very serious). Such mistakes can be made by consumers in other markets, but mistakes in other markets are often less serious and amenable to remedy at small cost. This may not be the case with health care where mistakes can be serious and unredeemable (even fatal). Hence, societies tend to care more about such mistakes than those made when consuming other products (i.e. the externality effect is greater). Also, in many other markets, consumers use the market so much that they obtain the opportunity and thereby the ability to learn from mistakes, and, again, this is not possible in many areas of health care. Therefore, the need for standards and control over conduct in the health care market is universally accepted as consumers are unlikely to be informed enough to protect their own interests. This results in licensure whereby those permitted to practice must hold some minimum qualification. Inadvertently, however, this gives some degree of market power to those holding licenses to practice, in this case doctors. This degree of power may be enhanced when it is the profession itself which decides on numbers of entrants.

Thus, as Evans (1984) pointed out several years ago, any debate about free markets in health care is really based on rhetoric rather than the actual nature of things. The actual nature of things is such that the true question is one of who should have direct control over health care financing and provision, doctors or governments. Given patients' lack of knowledge and the nature of the doctor's role in advising patients, providing care and receiving recompense for that care, it is our contention that this role should be played by governments as representatives of the community and purchasers of much care on its behalf. Given their special position, doctors may have an incentive to overprovide care, the cost of which is not justified in terms of benefits to patients. Indeed, some of this care may be of no benefit whatsoever. It is the nature of the problem of asymmetry and the consequent 'special' position of doctors in the health care market which is discussed in more detail in the following sub-section.

The problem of asymmetry

In health care, ignorance on the consumer's part is not matched by ignorance on the part of the provider. Therefore, an asymmetry exists. In other production processes, like food production, some regulatory processes may be applied, such as in monitoring standards of products. But, in such cases, the consumer is still judged to be the best judge of his/her own welfare. This is not necessarily so in health care because of the technical relationship between health care and improvements in health. Basically, consumers desire improvements in or maintenance of health status. However, improvements in health status cannot be purchased in the market. The consumer is forced to purchase health care in order to achieve an improvement in health. Health care itself is normally of no value but is linked to health improvements via a 'technological' relationship about which doctors know more than consumers.

So, the market fails in its ability to inform the consumer of the contribution of health care to health status. In the words of Weisbrod (1978),

> What a buyer wants to know is the difference between his state of well-being with and without the commodity being considered. For ordinary goods, the buyer has little difficulty in evaluating the counter-factual – that is what the situation will be if the good is not obtained. Not so for the bulk of health care ... The noteworthy point is not simply that it is difficult for the consumer to judge quality before the purchase ... but that it is difficult even after ...

The debate about the need for government intervention, beyond subsidies, in the health care market follows from this aspect of market failure, in combination with externalities and problems of private health care insurance. This debate focuses on two issues: first, the need for licensure, which has been discussed above; and, second, whether doctors act as perfect agents, so eliminating the need for government intervention beyond subsidies and legislation permitting the introduction of licensure.

Are doctors perfect agents?

Given the lack of ability of consumers to judge what types, amounts and qualities of health care to consume, or even to judge when care is needed, the doctor is placed in a position of advising the patient on his/her consumption. That is the doctor acts as an 'agent' on the patient's behalf. This places the doctor in a unique position of influence in which s/he can act as both demander and supplier of health care. There are many other areas of the economy in which suppliers of care provide 'advice' to consumers, but they differ from health care in certain respects:

- advice from an expert third party may be brought in to protect the consumer from the supplier (e.g. when purchasing a car);
- one is often more sure of what the outcome should be after the purchase is made (e.g. the engine should start after the car has been fixed);
- the consequences of mistakes are less stark;
- other people tend to care less about mistakes made in other markets than about those made in health care (so, once again, the health care externality effects are different).

The question then is one of whether the doctor acts as a 'perfect agent' on the patient's behalf. As Williams (1988) eloquently points out, if the doctor is a perfect agent,

> The DOCTOR is there to give the PATIENT all the information the PATIENT needs in order that the PATIENT can make a decision, and the DOCTOR should then implement that decision once the PATIENT has made it.

The idea is that doctors objectively supply information to the patient who can then make a decision which maximises his/her utility. Thus, as Evans (1984) says,

> The perfect agent cannot at the same time be an economic principal – unless she is also a perfect schizophrenic. The provider has interests of her own – income, leisure, professional satisfaction, which are partially congruent and partly in conflict with those of the patient. The 'perfect agent' would need a split brain, one half advising the patient solely in the patient's interest, the other half reacting to the patient's resulting consumption choices in a self-interested, own-welfare maximising way. Economic analyses which assume self-interested, profit or income maximising providers must either implicitly assume such schizophrenia as well, or else assume away the asymmetry of information problem and the agency relationship entirely (thus removing any justification for regulation). Not surprisingly, such analyses rarely spell out their assumptions in detail.

Clearly the role of perfect agent places a great burden on doctors, so much so that Williams (1988) claims that the more recognisable form of his characterisation of the agency relationship is one of imperfect agent in which the words 'DOCTOR' and 'PATIENT' are reversed, and

> The PATIENT is there to give the DOCTOR all the information the DOCTOR needs in order that the DOCTOR can make a decision, and the PATIENT should then implement that decision once the DOCTOR has made it.

It seems then that doctors are not perfect agents. Indeed there is evidence that doctors do in fact possess the power to induce demand for their own services. The evidence is from systems based on FFS remuneration. Thus, the implication is that patients are encouraged to consume services of little or no benefit, on the recommendation of doctors, for which doctors then receive a fee. If this care is in fact of little or no value to patients in terms of health gains (or some more general measure of well-being), then such demand inducement constitutes an inefficient use of health care resources. Such resources could be used to greater benefit elsewhere in the health care sector or outwith health care altogether.

It is difficult to interpret much of the evidence on supplier-induced demand as it is not clear whether induced demand is for services whose benefits are greater than their costs. This is because of the great problem of measuring benefits in health care. Variations in treatment for the same condition within the same types of health care system are great. It is still not known what is the best level of provision and it is, therefore, difficult to determine what is excessive (Loft and Mooney, 1989; Andersen and Mooney, 1990; Senior *et al.*, 2003).

The evidence on supplier-induced demand has been reviewed in more detail on many occasions in the past (Donaldson and Gerard, 1989b and Rice and Labelle, 1990), and is based on international comparisons, population studies and quasi-experiments. Internationally, countries whose payment systems for doctors are based on FFS tend to experience higher rates of utilisation of services, even after controlling for differences in age, sex and population (Vayda, 1973; McPherson *et al.*, 1981; Vayda *et al.*, 1982, McPherson *et al.*, 1982; Vayda *et al.*, 1984). Population studies have noted the correlation between increased doctor to population ratios in specified geographical areas and increases in service use, and even in fees (Cromwell and Mitchell, 1986). Quasi-experimental work has demonstrated similar results on changes in utilisation in response to changes in fees (Rice, 1983). Whether all of this evidence constitutes evidence of the existence of supplier-induced demand is difficult to say unequivocally, as 'uninduced' demand, which is the baseline against which induced demand should be assessed, is difficult to measure (Phelps, 1985b; Mooney, 1994). This evidence is reviewed in more detail in Chapter 7 along with other means of remunerating doctors which may be of use in controlling such provider 'moral hazard'.

RELEVANCE OF ECONOMICS TO GOVERNMENT INTERVENTION

Collectively, the above arguments present a compelling case for government intervention in health care beyond provision of subsidies. Benefits to the community will be greater than could be achieved by an unregulated market. However, what is less clear is the extent to which such arguments have formed the basis of policy making regarding the introduction of publicly oriented health care systems around the world. As pointed out earlier in this chapter, many systems were already in place by the time such arguments were well formulated, mainly by Culyer (1971) and Evans (1984). New systems are also likely to emerge in the future, and, therefore, it is important to understand some fundamental arguments in order to avoid major pitfalls.

Also, ideological considerations have not been discussed, the debate in this chapter focusing more on purely economic justifications of government intervention. It has been argued, for instance, that, in most Western countries, two major factors which have led to the introduction of publicly financed health care systems providing universal coverage are the coexistence of a strong labour movement and a socialist (or labour or social democratic) government (Navarro, 1989). Indeed ideological considerations could be incorporated into the economic calculus, in that people place various degrees of value on the pursuit of justice and equality. Such considerations, however, would take us further into the field of political economy than we have the space to deal with here. Also, such considerations are much less the preserve of economics than the arguments presented above. What can be said, though, is that basic values and the way policy is formulated differs from country to country and, therefore, a health care system which suits Canadians may not suit Americans and a system which suits the British may not suit Australians. What people want from their doctors and from their health services will also vary from country to country. Such ideological and cultural factors should obviously have weight alongside economic considerations when deciding on the optimal health care system for any country.

Despite this, it does seem evident that the above arguments on market failure have been taken into account in previous policy formation, although not explicitly in the form expressed in this chapter, for example, the establishment of the UK NHS (Foot, 1973). The introduction of the UK National Health Service (NHS) was based on the principle that

> ... everybody in the country ... should have an equal opportunity to benefit from ... medical and allied services. (A National Health Service, 1944)

This was later revised to the desire to have

> ... equal opportunity of access to health care for people at equal risk. (Department of Health and Social Security, 1976)

The occurrence of adverse selection[12] and caring externalities could easily underlie such principles and this has certainly been the case in Australia, where 15 per cent of the population were not covered by public or private insurers prior to the introduction of the second Australian universal public insurance system, Medicare (Palmer and Short, 1989):

> The introduction of Medicare in February 1984 was designed to ensure that all Australians have access to medical and hospital services on the basis of need. (Blewett, 1988)

The same is true in Canada, where the reaction to the inability of private insurers to cover the high risk and/or poor, where the health needs were greatest, was

> ... to set up universal public systems in each province which would, through cross-subsidisation, be able to include these groups. (Evans, 1987)

Likewise the importance of government involvement in regulating fee structures has also been recognised in Australia and in Canada (Deeble, 1982; Evans, 1984). For private or public insurers to guarantee payment of medical fees which are set by the medical profession itself would simply result in a climate of continual fee increases being met by private and public payers. This could increase health care costs, perhaps substantially, at little or no benefit to patients.

The response of these countries to this phenomenon has been slightly different. In Australia, the Government sets its own fee schedule and reimburses only a fixed percentage of the fee (85 per cent for general practitioner care and 75 per cent for hospital care, whilst for the latter the 'gap' between 75 and 100 per cent can be privately insured against). In general practice, doctors can accept the 85 per cent Government coverage as full payment, thus waiving the patient's obligation to make up the other 15 per cent of the fee. Doctors are also free to charge above the government fee level, but this extra amount cannot be privately insured against. Consequently, fees tend to be driven down to the levels funded by the Government, thus giving the Government effective control over their level. In Canada the approach is more direct. Each Province produces a schedule of fees to which doctors must adhere. Both systems lead to much conflict between the medical profession and government. Another problem is that although such regulation gives each government control over fee levels, they do not have direct control over the volume of services provided. Presumably, institutional constraints, such as hospital capacity and the number of hours in a day, help to check the volume of services provided, particularly if governments have a large element of control over investment in such institutions (as is the case in Australia and Canada). However, continual negotiation between the medical profession (as suppliers of care) and governmental bodies (as negotiators of price on patients' behalf) seems to be successful in preventing cost escalation.

Despite subtle differences, it is the similarities between health care systems such as those in Australia and Canada and that in the UK which are most striking. Like the UK, the greatest proportion of health care funding in Australia and Canada comes from taxation and, as in Australia and Canada, in the UK, it is the government who acts on behalf of the community to negotiate rates of pay with the medical profession and to control investment in infrastructure and services.

The messages from the chapter so far are (1) for good reasons (such as maintenance of quality within the medical profession and achievement of economies of scale within hospitals) there is an absence of a market with several competing suppliers of care, (2) instead, there exists a united and powerful body on the supply side of the health care market, and (3) therefore, what is required is countervailing power on the demand side, best achieved by 'collective purchasing agencies to bargain with providers on behalf of individuals' (Evans, 1987).

The only way to maintain such countervailing power whilst achieving economies of scale and universal coverage of the population is through public monopoly of payment, that is, an NHS or social insurance system (Donaldson and Mooney, 1997). White (1995) recently outlined the health care system characteristics which have evolved as common to several countries:

- universal coverage through compulsory participation;
- comprehensiveness of principal benefits;
- contributions based on income;
- cost control through administrative mechanisms, including binding fee schedules, global budgets, and limits on the capacity of the system.

Obviously, the details across systems will be different and cost control will always be incomplete, as powerful interest groups will always favour expansion. But,

> ... in all developed countries, Wildavsky's (1977) law of medical money ('costs will increase to the level of available funds ... that level must be limited to keep costs down') has been understood and acted upon through the development of countervailing public authority. (Evans, 1997)

CONCLUSIONS

Hopefully, in this chapter it has been demonstrated that as well as strong social and ideological arguments in favour of extensive government intervention in health care, there are powerful economic grounds for such intervention.

Health policy makers in governments have to consider many questions when deciding whether to intervene in this market and on the form of the intervention. However, paramount among the questions to be asked are:

(1) Can the nation afford to spend a large proportion of its resources on the diseconomies and potential excesses of a private health care (insurance) system?
(2) Is it acceptable that, whilst such excesses exist, large groups in society have no cover and, in many cases, no access to care?
(3) Who should protect such groups?

Governments in most, if not all, developed nations have responded positively to such questions, necessarily going beyond simplistic subsidy-based 'solutions'. The extent to which government intervention in health care has taken place in OECD countries is demonstrated by the data presented in Table 3.1. Even in what Evans (1990) has called 'the rhetorically "free-enterprise" USA' it can be seen that, between 1990 and 1998, the percentage of health care which is publicly funded has risen, from 40 to 45 per cent. The percentage of care which is publicly financed is obviously higher in almost all other countries.

It can be seen, however, that, out of the 26 OECD countries for which complete data exist, 16 have reduced the share of total health care spending which comes from public sources between 1990 and 1998, with private insurance or user fees having grown in proportionate terms. Some of these changes have been substantial; for example, in Canada. In others, such as Australia, the UK, France and Germany, the increase in the share taken up by private financing has been much smaller. In none of these five countries has there been an explicit policy decision to increase private financing, the changes likely arising out of fiscal pressures in the early-mid 1990s. Of the seven countries experiencing a greater increase than Canada in the share coming from private sources, three are Nordic countries (Finland, Norway and Sweden) where explicit policy decisions were made to

Table 3.1 Total health expenditure, percentage of total which is public and ranking in terms of proportion of total which is public in OECD countries (1990 and 1998)

Country	1990 total health exp US$PPP	% public	Rank	1998 total health exp US$PPP	% public	Rank	Absolute % increase
Australia	1318	67	20	2085	70	18=	+3
Austria	1205	74	18	1894	72	14=	−2
Canada	1678	75	17	2360	70	18=	−5
Czech Rep	576	96	1=	937	92	1=	−4
Denmark	1453	83	7=	2132	82	6	−1
Finland	1292	81	10	1510	74	14=	−7
France	1520	78	12−	2043	77	8=	−1
Germany	1602	76	16	2361	76	11=	0
Greece	707	63	22	1198	56	23	−7
Iceland	1376	87	5	2113	84	3=	−3
Ireland	796	72	10	1534	77	8=	+5
Italy	1321	78	12=	1824	67	20=	−11
Japan	1082	78	12=	1795	78	6	0
Korea	371	37	25	740	46	25	+9
Luxembourg	1486	93	3	2246	92	1=	−1
Mexico	260	41	24	419	48	24	+7
Netherlands	1403	78	12=	2150	69	19	+1
N Zealand	937	82	9	1440	77	8=	−5
Norway	1363	83	7=	2452	76	11=	−7
Poland	258	96	1=	524	65	21	−31
Portugal	614	65	21	1203	67	20=	+2
Spain	815	79	11	1194	76	11=	−3
Sweden	1492	90	4	1732	84	3=	−6
Switzerland	1782	68	19	2853	74	14=	+6
Turkey	171	61	23	316	72	14=	+11
UK	968	84	6	1510	83	5	−1
US	2738	40	26	4165	45	26	+5

Source: OECD Health Data 2001.

introduce more private financing (Elofsson *et al.*, 1998), and whose level of private financing still remains significantly below that of Canada, Australia, France and Germany, but not the UK. New Zealand, too, has made an explicit policy decision to increase the share of private funding (Hopkins and Cumming, 2001), but still remains below Australia, for example, in this statistic. There are three others who have increased the share of private funding, one of which (Poland) is a former Soviet bloc country.

Four of the countries ahead of Canada (US, Korea, Mexico and Greece) have public shares of 56 per cent or less. However, the first three of these have moved to increase this share by 5–9 percentage points, whilst there is a high level of dissatisfaction with the public system in Greece (Liaropolous and Tragakes, 1998).

Thus public financing remains the dominant source of health care funding, with slight moves towards more private funding in some countries. We have already implied that not every country would want an NHS. In addition, some forms of financing, like charging patients for care, exist in all systems, although to differing degrees. The next question, then, is, given we accept the need for the Visible Hand in health care, what form should it take. More specifically, what kinds of basic systems exist for raising finance and what mechanisms exist within these systems to meet the basic challenges presented by moral hazard (on the part of consumers and providers) and adverse selection? This is the subject matter of Chapter 4.

PART II

HEALTH CARE SYSTEMS AND THEIR OBJECTIVES

METHODS OF FUNDING
HEALTH CARE

INTRODUCTION

Having established, we believe, that some level of government intervention is inevitable and unavoidable in health care, it then becomes important to consider the extent and form of that intervention. Therefore, although a major question may have been answered (that of whether governments should intervene in health care 'markets'), this leaves a set of complex questions still to be addressed, these being:

- How will funds be raised?
- What financial intermediary stands between the consumer and the service provider?
- What form does the 'insurance premium' take and according to what principles is it set?
- What payments out-of-pocket are made by the consumer at the point of use? Can other forms of reliance on consumer preferences be used?
- How are professional providers to be paid?
- How are institutions to be reimbursed?
- How will the 'market' be organised and to what degree will competition and equity be used within this?

Several plausible answers can be given to each of these questions. The main aim of this chapter is to outline the principal pros and cons associated with three basic methods of raising funds, which also covers the second question listed above. The third question is essentially about the objectives of the health care system which is addressed in Chapter 5. There is an abundance of empirical evidence with a bearing on the remaining questions, and this forms the basis of more detailed reviews in Chapters 6–9 respectively.

By way of further introduction, three points are worth noting. First, most Western countries operate a system of government approval for grants for proposed capital investments such as hospital buildings. Traditionally, for the most part, hospital management (or local health authorities) have paid no charges once the grant is allocated. In countries such as the UK this process is highly centralised, operating through the National Health Service (NHS). In others (Finland, France and Germany) the process involves regional and national governments. In Canada (at provincial level) and Sweden (at local government level) the process is more explicitly localised. More recently, systems of capital charges, including private finance initiatives (PFIs), have been used in many of these countries. PFIs involve the private sector in providing some or all of the capital funds which are paid back through the charges for services which hospitals recoup from public and (to a lesser extent) private purchasers. In many countries, public purchasers now have the costs of meeting such capital charges included in their operating budgets. Hospital managers may also be given a target rate of return on capital assets that they have to meet. Although still highly regulated, with applications for capital funding (whether through PFI or not) still approved by some arm of government, the aim of such schemes is to ensure that capital projects are more realistically costed and that the capital stock is more efficiently managed. There is much controversy, however, as to whether such objectives have been met (Gaffney *et al.*, 1999; Price, 2000).

In the US, hospital managers have more freedom to decide how much capital they need, with the public hospital system being subject to more regulation, in the form of guidelines for bidding arrangements and some kind of approval mechanism (US Congress, Office of Technology Assessment, 1995). Initial financing would normally be in the form of loans, donations or through hospitals' own funds. Increasingly, capital costs are incorporated in payment rates (including DRGs), although government does provide subsidies through tax exemptions (OECD, 1987). Although the subject of optimal methods of capital funding in the health care sector is receiving increasing attention, we deal with this issue no further than beyond this point.

Second, it should also be noted that two alternatives for basic funding systems have already been discussed: perfect markets and unregulated private health insurance. The former will not be described in this chapter. However, it is possible to modify private health insurance systems in attempting to control for moral hazard and adverse selection without necessarily involving governments. Therefore, possible modifications to private health care insurance will be outlined.

Third, in the absence of adequate empirical evidence, no single financing system is necessarily the correct one. Once the inevitability of government intervention is accepted, this can take many forms. In Canada and Australia, for instance, it was natural to move from the well-established systems of private insurance to systems based on public insurance; or at least to give the image of being based on public insurance.[1] In Australia, a private health care insurance system still exists to provide top-up cover over and above the universal public insurance scheme. In many Northern and Eastern European countries, on the other hand, systems funded largely from direct taxation have developed, as well-established private insurance markets did not exist when initial steps towards extensive government intervention were taken. As we have seen in Chapter 1, there is now more variation in Eastern Europe, with some countries moving towards social insurance and, in

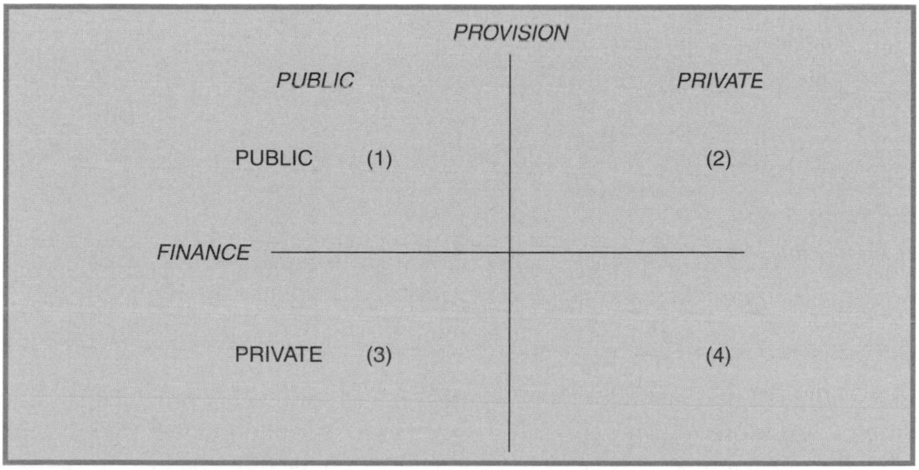

Figure 4.1 Public/private mix in health care financing and provision

Notes: (1) Public finance and public provision; (2) Public finance and private provision; (3) Private finance and public provision; (4) Private finance and private provision.

most, an increasing role for private financing. All of these experiences reflect why a system which has been developed, and is working well, in one country may not be acceptable to the population of another country and that there may be strong political reasons for any major changes that have been made.

Describing each alternative financing system is made easier by outlining two key issues in advance; these are common to all systems. First, we try to simplify the complicated nature of the public/private mix in finance and provision which may arise in different systems (see Figure 4.1 above), and, second, different methods of paying providers (doctors and hospitals) are briefly reviewed. The systems which are then outlined are: private health care insurance (including modifications, such as health maintenance organisations (HMOs) and preferred provider organisations (PPOs)); direct taxation; public health care insurance; and other sources of finance. Some other possible, but largely untried, methods of financing are then outlined. Each method is described in terms of three characteristics: principal sources of finance; methods of paying doctors; and methods of paying other providers, mainly hospitals. We conclude this chapter with a summary of how each method counters the problems of moral hazard and adverse selection.

PUBLIC/PRIVATE MIX IN FINANCE AND PROVISION

The organisation of financial intermediaries may be on a monopolistic, oligopolistic or competitive basis. In a monopolistic system, the financial intermediary is usually a public agency such as a government, a quango or a health corporation. In an oligopolistic system (i.e. one in which there are a small number of large inter-mediaries) finance can be controlled by public agencies or private agencies, such as insurance companies, or a combination of these. In a competitive system, a large number of small private intermediaries would exist. An example of this latter system is one based on the HMO (see section below for an explanation of HMOs) which provides a package of primary and tertiary care in return for a prepaid premium.

The provision of services, however, does not necessarily have to match the financial organisation. For instance, hospital care in many European countries represents a large vertically-integrated health system, in which finance and provision, are combined within one organisation. Thus, both finance and provision are public as in the case of quadrant (1) in Figure 4.1. In many countries, general practice would fall into quadrant (2) of Figure 4.1, such care being provided by self-employed doctors who, nevertheless, happen to receive almost all of their income from the public purse. A system based on HMOs, on the other hand, represents a similarly integrated (but privately funded) system which could fit into quadrants (3) and (4) buying in care from private or public providers. Also, it is important to recognise that systems do not have to be vertically integrated in these ways: a third party private payer, such as an insurance company, could also fit into segments (3) and (4). The basic point is that public finance does not have to match public provision, nor private finance private provision. Public provision could be financed by private arrangements (private insurance, direct charges, etc.) and private provision by public finance (e.g. prospective payments made by government agencies directly to private hospitals).

The arguments presented in the previous chapter provide a stronger case for government intervention in financing rather than in providing health care. Control of financial arrangements permits governmental bodies more direction of the health care system in the pursuit of societal objectives: as the collective purchaser of care on the community's behalf, a public body can negotiate terms of provision with more equal power to both public and private providers (Evans, 1987). Simply providing public services does not guarantee use by those groups for whom they are intended as less ill, rich or privately insured patients may be more 'attractive customers' for such hospitals than those more in need of care.

REWARDING THE PROVIDERS

When discussing the ways in which professionals may be rewarded, we will refer to the doctor as the principal health care professional. However, we recognise that in more recent times especially greater roles have been given to other health care professionals, such as nurses, and incentives concerning them are also important. It is partly for convenience and partly because of the focus on empirical evidence that we concentrate only on doctors. The incentives that affect doctors are not, of course, only financial. Personal pride in a professional job well done and the pressure of peer review (and the information on good practice that it can provide) are among the other features of the professional environment that can reward or penalise professional behaviour in non-pecuniary ways.

Of the financial incentives, fee-for-service (FFS) rewards according to the volume of service provided. As mentioned previously, FFS remuneration can lead to 'induced' and unnecessary demand by patients (for fee-yielding services) on the recommendation of their doctors, and also to cost inflation. Whether or not it does depends on whether fees are set above or below what they would have been in a truly competitive environment.

Capitation (usually found in the context of general practice) pays according to the number of patients registered with an individual doctor. This can provide a financial incentive to increase list sizes which could lead to utilisation or consultation levels with which the doctor cannot cope efficiently. Doctors may also have an incentive to refer patients on to hospitals or specialists for which they do not have to pay from the capitation fee. On the other hand, it provides no financial distortion of the purely professional role, given the list size and the available facilities: the doctor simply exercises professional judgements as best s/he can about patients' needs and how best they are to be met.

Salaried systems are similar in effect, save that they afford no incentive to increase list size. They also, however, carry the association of 'employee' that in many countries has usually been an anathema to doctors, particularly to general practitioners, though not to hospital doctors. Salaried systems, depending on their structure, may also lead to discontinuity of care as doctors move around in order to gain promotion.

These methods of paying doctors do not, of course, have to be seen as mutually incompatible. It is possible to combine salary, capitation and FFS in a single remuneration system.

Reimbursement of institutions like hospitals can be done in a variety of ways under either public or private insurance. Retrospective reimbursement involves the insuring agency in paying the provider for all 'reasonable' expenditures incurred on behalf of an insured person or group over the previous period. It notoriously encourages cost inflation and, possibly, unnecessary provision, particularly if coupled with FFS. This is because a hospital will have little incentive to curb expenditure if it is known that all such expenditure will be met by the funding body.

Prospective reimbursement is in principle better able to contain costs and lends itself much better to forward financial planning by both the institutions to be reimbursed and the financing agencies. Prospective reimbursement can be based on population-based formulae, as in the UK, where the health care 'purchaser' receives a share of the total funds allocated to the health system based on the size and characteristics (e.g. age, sex and morbidity) of the population covered, or according to planned workload with appropriate cost schedules for a variety of case-types. In systems, such as the UK model, in which the overall budget is global, there will be no incentives to allocate resources to those areas which are most productive, although 'internal market' mechanism have been devised to overcome this.

The prospective payment system widely used in the US public sector, is based on costings of diagnosis-related groups (DRGs). Funding is not global, but is based on individual cases. The cost units require careful estimation and continual updating. If used only partially, or if inaccurately done, they can lead to 'patient-shifting' whereby cases which are costlier than the estimate, or costlier than the average embodied in the estimate, are shifted into a less controlled part of the system (e.g. from inpatient to outpatient) or simply not treated at all. Likewise, 'cost-shifting' can take place whereby costs of care are shifted on to patients (e.g. private patients) not covered by the DRG reimbursement system.

PRIVATE HEALTH CARE INSURANCE

The uncertainty surrounding the incidence of ill-health, the efficiency of treatment and the cost of treatment means that health care is an appropriate case for insurance. Insurance can help individuals and groups (consumers and professionals alike) to adjust in preferred ways to these uncertainties. As has been seen, insurance may be achieved by government intervention, providing comprehensive public insurance, or a combination of government and private finance or a comprehensive range of private finance. For a given premium a set of health care risks may be insured against. In the case of pure private insurance, the insurance company covers specified risks of ill-health to the consumer and incurs the consequential expense of (hopefully effective) health care. Private insurance companies usually operate in a market with a small number of large companies (an oligopolistic structure). Although such a structure may achieve economies of scale, there is an incentive for companies to act together to strengthen their power in the market and in doing so keep premiums high and in line with each other.

In a situation of pure insurance (i.e. insurance without extra charges) the consumer pays a premium which might cover the use of all approved health care should the consumer fall ill. This premium is paid either in full by the consumer or shared by his/her employer (or perhaps by social security in the case of unemployed people). Premiums may also be tax-deductible. Having taken out insurance, the price facing the consumer at the point of using health care will often be zero.

As was explained in Chapter 3, community-rating is likely to yield, under private insurance, to experience-rating (unless prohibited) because other agencies will offer cover at lower premiums to the uninsured good risks. The poor, the medically indigent and the chronic sick will in any case not usually be covered by such agencies and will, in an entirely private system, be dependent on charity care. Governmental response for some at-risk groups (poor people, elderly people) then becomes almost inevitable (e.g. Medicare and Medicaid in the US).

Moral hazard also exists in private insurance-based health care systems. With a third party (i.e. the insurance company) paying health care bills on a full reimbursement basis and employers contributing heavily to premiums, neither the consumer nor the provider has an incentive to be cost-conscious (see Chapter 3 for definitions of consumer and provider moral hazard). The consumer faced with free or low cost health care at the point of consumption has little or no financial incentive to restrain demands on the service. Likewise, doctors have no financial incentive to moderate such demands. Indeed if rewarded on an FFS basis, as is often the case, they may have an incentive to generate demand for their services (the phenomenon of supplier-induced demand). If insurance is accompanied by retrospective cost reimbursement of providers (such as hospitals) by insurance companies, as used to be common in the US, moral hazard will be further exacerbated. Such a method gives no incentive to be cost-conscious.

To combat the problem of moral hazard, cost-sharing or co-payment schemes have been introduced by many intermediaries in private systems. Essentially the aim of these schemes is to place some financial burden on the consumer to eliminate or at least reduce 'unnecessary' use of health care. Individual schemes differ according to the nature of the financial arrangement but take four main forms: a flat rate charge for each unit of service; co-insurance (the insured individual has to pay a certain proportion of each unit of health care consumed); a deductible akin to the 'excess' in some motor vehicle insurance policies (the individual pays one hundred per cent of all bills in a given period up to some maximum amount beyond which insurance benefits are paid in full); or a combination of the last two.

Depending on the level of charges for health care, people in low-income groups or high-utilisation groups may be excluded from consumption as a result of lack of ability to pay. Thus, further government intervention may be required. There is also likely to be some anxiety about the effect on individuals' health if they are deterred from 'non-trivial' utilisation.

Another, more recent, method of combating consumer moral hazard has been the introduction of medical savings accounts (MSAs) (Gardner, 1995). These have two essential features: first, an individual- (or household-) specific account with balances earmarked for health care expenses; and, second, a high-deductible, catastrophic insurance plan to cover expenses above the deductible. Advocates would claim that these accounts, through encouraging greater personal responsibility on the part of consumers, enhance system efficiency. However, they are likely to suffer from many of the challenges faced by cost-sharing.

Cost-sharing need not, however, reduce the overall impact of supplier-induced demand. Doctors may, for example, switch their demand-inducing abilities from lower-income groups to those more able to pay. With the presence of supplier-induced demand, cost-containment does not seem so obviously achievable through cost-sharing. Even worse, serious health problems may be left untreated as more minor (but able-to-pay) cases replace more serious (not-able-to-pay) cases. The end result could be that the same amount is spent on health care but to less effect in terms of improvement or maintenance of the community's health.

Of course, some advocates of charges claim that doctors could discriminate between groups on the basis of ability to pay so that everyone would be able to afford the charge. However, this argument does not make sense. If everyone can afford the charge, there will still be much strain on the health care system. Again, the incentive for doctors, in such a situation, would be to concentrate on those more able to pay. Service use would remain the same, but more would be spent on health care because charges would be higher, and care would be going to those less in need.

In addition, and similar to the arguments on diseconomies of scale presented in Chapter 3, billing of patients and collection of payments under cost-sharing schemes, checking against fraud and so on, are likely to be administratively expensive.

To combat moral hazard in the hospital sector, DRGs are now used (or are being considered for use) in many countries as a means of controlling costs. For instance, since October 1984, US Federal Government payments for hospitalised patients over the age of 65 in the Medicare programme have been changed to fixed amounts of money by type of case which are set prospectively, rather than all 'reasonable' expenses being reimbursed retrospectively. This has changed the incentives for non-government hospitals, to which they have responded. Hospitals are experiencing some decline in utilisation. However, patients may have increased their use of other services not covered by the DRG system, for example, ambulatory visits to doctors' surgeries (see Chapter 8). Government-financed programmes in a primarily private market can also realise some of the gains from 'countervailing power' obtainable in more thoroughly collectivist systems, particularly by 'squeezing' doctors and hospitals in the way the US DRG system has done.

Consumers in a private insurance system are given a central role in choosing the nature and extent of their own health care coverage. They are able to purchase additional health care insurance according to their own preferences and, of course, ability to pay. The provision of high quality 'hotel' and other peripheral services is typically greater than in governmental systems.

Managed care: HMOs and PPOs

As indicated in Chapter 1, the greatest change in the US health care market in recent decades has been the increased move to 'managed care', as embodied in the proliferation of HMOs and PPOs. Health maintenance organisations are a product of private insurance systems. They represent one of the most prominent health care reforms and have had an influence in publicly funded systems beyond the US. HMOs provide (or arrange and pay for) comprehensive health care for a fixed periodic per capita payment (or 'premium') which is paid by the consumer (usually with a subsidy from employers or social security). Consumers do not usually pay charges at the point of use. The premium is set in advance and is independent of the volume of services provided to the individual during the period. Providers can be salaried or paid by FFS.

Adverse selection and experience-rating will inevitably arise if, as is likely, competition develops. Doctor demand inducement is not likely to be very prevalent, as not only must doctors compete for custom, usually on an annual basis, but also the annual HMO budget is fixed in advance. Doctors, therefore, will be cost-conscious with the residual between the budget and expenditure accruing to the HMO and, thereby, to the doctors. High spending doctors will then be financially penalised.

Organisationally, HMOs can be of one of four types: a staff model, in which all doctors are employed and/or contracted directly by the HMO; a group model, in which the HMO contracts with an independent group practice to provide services: a network model, in which more than one independent group is contracted to provide services; and an independent practice association (IPA) in which the HMO contracts several doctors in independent practice (Hillman *et al.*, 1989). Thus, there are many financial and organisational variations on the basic HMO model.

Consumers select the health care plan of their choice on an annual basis. Therefore more choice is thought to exist. Because consumers usually receive only a fixed subsidy towards payment (or a fixed percentage of the premium) they too have an incentive to be cost-conscious. Additionally, some HMOs do have user charges, particularly for drugs (Harris *et al.*, 1990).

As mentioned in Chapter 1, an important innovation in the Russian Federation, was the experiment which took place in St Petersburg, Samara and Kemerovo (Siberia) (Hakansson *et al.*, 1988) whereby hospital budgets for a number of specialties were transferred to polyclinics on the basis of average cost per case. Polyclinics were the main providers of primary care and were also involved in some specialised outpatient investigation, treatment and rehabilitation, their staff being salaried. Previously, with hospitals run on a separate budget, there was an incentive for polyclinics to refer patients on to hospital. This HMO-style experiment was aimed at improving the appropriateness of such referrals (Hakansson *et al.*, 1988). Subsequent to wider economic reforms the experiment collapsed but important lessons were learnt (see Chapter 8).

This vertical integration of financing for primary and tertiary care is also the aim of the UK and Dutch internal market reforms outlined earlier. The Russian and UK reforms are more supply-side orientated, however, as consumers cannot choose their health authority or polyclinic; they are covered as a result of being resident in a particular catchment area.

One recent major reform in private health care insurance markets in the US has led to the growth of PPOs. They have arisen in the US as a result of attempts by insurance companies to enter into competition with HMOs. Premiums are paid either by employers or are shared between employer and employee. Price at the point of use of services is zero. Insurers contract selectively with providers (e.g. primary care doctors and hospitals who provide care below a certain cost per case). The contract is on the basis of both a negotiated fee schedule which the preferred providers accept as payment in full and acceptance of utilisation review. User charges and deductibles tend to be lower in PPOs than under previous private insurance arrangements (Zwanziger and Auerbach, 1991).

Once more, adverse selection and experience-rating will almost inevitably develop within a care system based on PPOs, leaving the more costly groups without cover for health care unless they are subsidised. There is also no financial risk to primary care providers with respect to the volume of services provided. With

FFS as the basis for payment the doctor can, to some extent, still manipulate utilisation. However, this has a limit for, if cost per case rises above a certain limit, the doctor may not be selected as preferred provider at the next review. The incentive for hospitals to keep costs down arises because a set of prices has been agreed in advance.

Patients can choose between a limited set of providers or choose another provider on less favourable terms, so incentives also exist on the demand side. One specific advantage of PPOs is that they have enabled employers in the US to move quickly to control health care costs for employees who are already under FFS schemes. Companies either organise schemes themselves or persuade insurance companies to do it. Insurance companies cooperate as this provides a means of competing with HMOs.

DIRECT TAX SYSTEM

Health care finance may be provided by a public monopoly, as in the UK National Health Service. Under such a system, finance is raised by taxation, either in the form of general taxation, hypothecated taxation (i.e. earmarked taxes specifically for health services) or a general public insurance system (i.e. covering more benefits than only health care and with contributions that are not experience-rated). The Australian health care system provides a good example of an income-related hypothecated tax in the form of the Medicare levy. However, it has never been the intention that this levy should cover all of the public sector's health care costs, the majority being met from direct taxation.

The consumer's contribution to the financial intermediary (i.e. their 'premium') under the direct taxation system is, therefore, part of their total tax payment. But there may also be out-of-pocket contributions depending on the service in question and the individual's circumstances. The UK NHS principle seems to be that the tax payment covers all basic health care finance so that the consumer is able to use the health service at zero price. Where charges are levied the usual view seems to have been that they are nominal (i e. small enough not to impose financial hardship and also such as to have no significant effect on a person's health by deterring the consumption of effective health care). In the UK NHS, the role of waiting lists, waiting times and general practitioner consultations are important rationing devices for controlling the moral hazard that is inherent in any system having zero (or near zero) prices at the point of use. In publicly financed systems in low-income countries charges may not be nominal, but have an important revenue-raising role because the lack of infrastructure in such countries renders tax collection difficult.

A system of direct taxation removes the problem of adverse selection because of the absence of competition between financial intermediaries. By detaching premiums from expected risk levels and making them compulsory, a tax system redistributes wealth from those with low *ex ante* expectations of illness to those at high risk. Individuals are effectively charged one form of community rate; one which is dependent on ability-to-pay but not on previous experience of ill-health. A tax-financed system redistributes according to two indicators of individual well-being, health status and income. It can thus be more efficient than any form of redistribution based on income alone. That it *can* be does not of course guarantee that it *will*, especially as taxation systems become less and less progressive. It also provides the means of effectively capping total expenditure, provided that there is the political will to contain expenditure. It is also virtually free from 'loading' problems, representing probably the most efficient way of collecting monies to finance the health care system (often referred to as 'piggybacking' on to the existing system of tax collection).

The use of nominal charges may be seen to provide an incentive to the consumer to restrain some demand, particularly so-called 'unnecessary' ('frivolous' or 'trivial') demand. If that is all that is deterred then nominal charges can be seen as a mechanism which does not deter seeking care for genuine need and therefore does not adversely affect a person's health. Such charges do however raise a number of specific issues: how nominal is 'nominal'? What is frivolous and who defines it? How costly is it to operate a system of 'nominal' charges? What effect on the character of the patient–professional relationship do charges have? How best can one protect the poor, for whom even 'nominal' charges may deter utilisation, without also introducing a cumbersome, stigmatic and expensive bureaucracy?

Collective financing of health care may or may not be linked to public ownership of health services. In the UK NHS, almost all hospitals are publicly owned and hospital doctors are employed in such institutions on a salaried basis (although they are subject to regulation, in part by their Medical Association). Primary care services on the other hand are less formally organised and general practitioners (GPs) are private providers remunerated with a combination of FFS, capitation and other methods.

Within the public sector, however, there is no systematic financial signalling system of the sort a well-ordered market would provide. This would inform participants about intersectoral costs, such as GP versus hospital outpatient care, and internal hospital costs which could form the basis of clinical budgets or prepayments per case. Thus, in NHS-type systems, decisions about the optimal balance of services have traditionally been taken either in the face of considerable ignorance about likely cost and likely benefit or only after study in depth. The *system* does not generate a pricing mechanism for routine 'managerial' choices. Nor does it provide a continuing environment of penalties or rewards for inefficient or efficient behaviour. Those who commit resources (the doctors typically) usually do so in ignorance both of the financial cost of each clinical decision and of the true opportunity cost in terms of the health services that have *not* been provided to others. The budgeting systems that constrain doctors are also typically constructed in extreme ignorance about both costs and benefits. This ignorance can simultaneously lead to claims amongst some that the total health service 'financial cake' is not effectively used and amongst others that the service is underfunded. Moreover, it is impossible decisively to refute or support either of these claims – at least not with current levels of knowledge about costs and benefits. Publicly funded systems have wrestled with these issues for decades. Substantial investment has, therefore, been made in improving costing systems and many countries are now moving towards financial accounting, if not necessarily remuneration on a case-basis, using systems similar to DRGs.

Likewise, many countries have experimented with internal markets, partly in the hope that market discipline would provide incentives to improve information systems. Experience of markets in more private health care systems, does not encourage one to be confident that they handle things significantly better. One can, however, have a market in health care finance without a market in health care provision, and a market in provision without one in finance. To suppose that one must necessarily accompany the other is just not so, and the effects of each may be quite different, as pointed out above.

In Chapter 3, it was argued that a market in finance could not work according to societal objectives. However, reforms in various countries (most notably the UK, Sweden and New Zealand) over the past decade or more resulted in an attempt to implement markets for health care provision in those countries, particularly in hospital care (Secretaries of State, 1989; Hopkins and Cumming, 2001; European Observatory on Health Care Systems, 2002). In the UK, district health authorities, armed with revenue from central taxation, played the role of financing, or purchasing, care on behalf of their local community. They were permitted to purchase such care from independent NHS hospital trusts or the private sector, either within or outside the district. The aim was for these different types of hospital to compete for funds from district health authorities on the basis of cost and quality. As a monopsony buyer of services, a district health authority should, in theory, have a considerable amount of influence over setting standards of care required.[2] Such a system, in which provider markets operate within a single but largely universal system of finance, is known as an internal market.

In the UK, and partly based on the HMO-model of care, some general practices were given budgets for the purchase of certain forms of hospital outpatient care and elective surgery on behalf of their patients. The aim was to prevent inappropriate referrals, with general practitioners making judgements based on the cost and quality of hospital care. The UK system has now moved on to a system of more (and smaller) primary care trusts (at least in England) performing the purchasing role, with health authorities and fundholding having been abolished. Competition under this new system has been less actively encouraged by Government until recent proposals for the introduction of Foundation Hospitals, which will be given greater freedoms to raise capital for service developments and to compete for funding. The 'Dekker' reforms of the Dutch health care system also include proposals for an internal market whereby insurers will purchase services from suppliers of health and social care on the basis of cost and quality (van de Ven, 1989). The evidence on such internal markets will be examined in more detail in Chapter 8.

Additional features can be added into NHS-type systems, such as the strengthening of community representation on decision-making and 'watchdog' bodies and perhaps, the use of charges for 'hotel' services. Whether these are seen as 'enough' is a moot point, as is whether it is possible to introduce more market-orientated policies without losing the main advantages of public finance and without introducing stigma, dual standards of medical care, and other features that – in many European countries – seem to be disturbing to the bulk of the population. Of course, the great irony is that in all such countries, people are free to supplement their contributions to the public system with their own private insurance policy. Despite the attractions of such insurance (e.g. in providing faster access to treatment), it has not caught the imagination of the public in most European countries, although rising shares of total costs coming from private sources (see Table 3.1) do indicate some growth in uptake.

PUBLIC HEALTH CARE INSURANCE

A public insurance system can be administered by a monopolistic agent such as a quango, a regional government or a national government. Some of the most well-known systems of public health insurance exist in Canada, Australia, France and Germany. In such systems, premiums can be related to income in the form of a payroll tax; usually, everyone above a certain level of income pays a fixed percentage of their income to the insurance fund. This kind of system is often known as social insurance. It exists in Germany and is common in Latin America.

In some countries (e.g. Italy) substantial proportions of health care funding come from both social insurance (about 51 per cent in Italy) and from the central taxation fund (also about 46 per cent in Italy) (Taroni *et al.*, 1998). The same is actually true in Canada and Australia, where, despite the appearance of an 'insurance' system (through labelling it as such and through collection of small amounts known as 'premiums' or 'levies') the vast majority of funding is from general taxation.

In Canada, private insurance is not permitted for services covered by the public system. However, approximately 30 per cent of total health care costs are still privately funded as the public system covers mainly hospital care and physician visits only (see Table 3.1). Children, elderly people and poor people receive different levels of subsidy for pharmaceuticals and dental care in different provinces. In other countries, such as Australia, private insurance is permitted as a top-up to the basic system, so expanding choice over date and location of treatment for a limited group in society.

Except in the cases of exempt groups, wealth is transferred only from low to high risks and not necessarily directly from those of high incomes to those of low incomes, although risk and income tend to be negatively correlated. However, premiums can either be indexed to income or, as is possible with private insurance, be made tax-deductible. Premiums can be deducted directly, paid by employers or, for the unemployed, through social security. Payroll taxes, unless related proportionately to pay, can have the effect of raising the cost to employers of low-paid (typically less skilled) workers relative to higher paid workers. The resulting fall in demand for the less skilled leads to still lower wages for the already low paid and/or more unemployment. Moreover, arrangements would have to be made to ensure cover for the unemployed (voluntary or involuntary), the retired, and those not in the labour force, including dependents of those who are.

One difficulty with payroll taxes, like national insurance, relates to the incidence of the part paid by employers: is it a cost to employers (as superficially seems the case) or, if it is shifted, does it fall mainly on consumers via higher prices (forward shifting) or on workers in the form of lower wages (backward shifting)? The general belief amongst economists who have examined this question is that a generally imposed payroll tax falls on labour, regardless of who pays it (employee or employer). Ultimately, of course, both lower wages and higher prices imply that the burden falls on the general public, but it would impinge differently according to consumption patterns and employment status. It is also worth pointing out that a lump sum payroll tax whose final incidence is on employers is effectively a further tax on capital and corporate income and would tend to be progressive; if it were to fall on either employees or consumers it would tend to be regressive (taking a higher proportion of income as income falls).

Care would normally be provided free at the point of use of services under public health care insurance, although it would be possible to introduce co-payments and charges for 'hotel' services. GPs could be paid on the basis of salary, capitation or FFS (or some combination). There is the possibility of tight government control over fee schedules. Hospitals could be reimbursed in a variety of ways: retrospectively, prospectively, by size of the population served, item by item, globally, with or without peer review and with or without monitoring of outcome and the quality of care. Some hospital income may also come from FFS, nominal charges to patients, and for charges for 'hotel' and other on-site and peripheral services.

Competition *can* take place in a public health insurance system, for it is possible to envisage the presence of public and private service providers but with the private sector being subject to the same system of payment as the public sector (e.g. internal markets). The crucial aspect of a public health insurance system, is monopoly of finance. Generally, lack of competition between financial intermediaries prevents adverse selection and experience-rating. It may still be possible to introduce competition between such intermediaries, however, by having governments provide risk-adjusted subsidies to such intermediaries, similar to the Dekker proposals in the Netherlands.

In public insurance systems, there may also be economies of scale and the avoidance of the recording, billing, collection and enforcement costs (e.g. checking for fraud) of private insurance systems. Once again, advantages may be gained from competition amongst providers of care as the public insurance agency (as in Canada, a provincial government, or, more recently in most provinces, a health region/authority/district) acts as the collective purchaser of services on the community's behalf (Evans, 1987). This is similar to the internal market system in the UK NHS.

OTHER FINANCING MECHANISMS

Vouchers for health care are often voiced as an alternative method of financing although very little is documented about them. Vouchers are a system of tied subsidy, entitling the holder to trade the voucher in return for a service. They may be graduated according to the means of the holder, they may be able to be supplemented out of the holder's own pocket, and they may vary according to the services (and the period of time to which they relate) to which they entitle the holder.

The principal advantages of a voucher system in theory are that it serves consumer choice (the voucher holder may shop around for the insurance agency of choice, including financially integrated service organisations like HMOs, of choice) and controls adverse selection (by supplementing ability to pay).

In practice, given any likely public requirement about the comprehensiveness of the benefits of insurance cover, the 'standard' voucher is likely to be set at the equivalent of a community-rated premium with out-of-pocket 'topping up' restricted to the 'hotel' type facilities that may be insurable but are unlikely candidates for public subsidy. In the absence of private insurance, such a scheme seems to require a universal system of HMOs as the counterpart on the provider side.

It is possible to conceive of a voucher for family practitioner services only (general medical practitioners in particular), in which case it is directly equivalent to the capitation system (with similar differentiation possible according to, say, age of the consumer). But the GP's income would be channelled indirectly via the consumers rather than paid via a public agency. Consumers could remain as free (or as restricted) as they currently are to select the practitioner of their choice – and the general practitioners as free to accept patients. Practitioners could receive the voucher either when the patient presented or when the patient 'registers' with the practitioner of choice. The patient would necessarily, however, be tied to the doctor of choice for the period of validity of the voucher.

If vouchers covered pharmaceuticals, diagnostic tests not performed in the general practice and other such condition-specific services, the risks of moral hazard and adverse selection could become important and general practitioners would have an incentive not to accept patients whose costliness was expected to exceed the value of the voucher – unless topping up or extra-billing were permitted (which would in practice discriminate against the poorer risks who tend typically also to be the worst off in terms of income).

Since the advantages of vouchers can be achieved in other ways, it seems that they are not an attractive alternative to other methods of channelling resources to medical care, which may also be administratively less cumbersome. Setting and updating the value of vouchers is an enormous task. There is, however, no practical experience of vouchers for health care insurance on which to draw, so this conclusion is necessarily conjectural.

The various other means that have been proposed for finance (lotteries, on-site services, charitable donations) can be seen only as supplementary. They are inappropriate both in scale and predictability to the major funding problem, and may be administratively costlier than the alternatives discussed above. None has received the systematic analysis, either theoretical or practical, of the insurance methods. Each may have a useful minor role, especially when harnessing local goodwill and voluntary effort. They can also, however, distort health care planning: for example there may be sponsorship of capital projects that have neither been incorporated into the integrated planning of services nor fully taken into account as regards their longer term revenue consequences (i.e. once a machine has been bought from charitable donations, the money has to be found to staff and operate it). Such methods need to be employed selectively and can hardly be seen as more than marginal for either the public or private provision of health care.

Other methods, such as the issue of debt, and equity finance, are already available in the private sector and could become significant if there were a major shift from public towards private provision – especially for-profit provision.

CONCLUSIONS

Several plausible answers can be given to each of the questions posed at the beginning of this chapter, and we have identified the principal pros and cons associated with each. A final decision on which type of system to have cannot (or should not) be made solely by weighing up these purely qualitative issues. There is empirical evidence with a bearing on a number of them and this is the subject of more detailed review in Chapters 6–10.

Table 4.1 characterises the main options for raising finance and, within each, some principal variants regarding control of moral hazard by consumers, doctors and institutions and for dealing with adverse selection. HMOs and PPOs are really a product of private insurance systems and are aimed at controlling both consumer and provider moral hazard. Variants of these, such as general practitioner fund-holding have been used in publicly funded systems. Other methods, such as charges, can be used in all types of system. The options under public insurance and direct taxation systems are identical except that public insurance systems can include compulsory community-rated premiums plus an experience-rated subsidy.

As the most researched area in the field of health care financing, the issue of different methods of controlling moral hazard on the part of consumers and providers is covered in Chapters 6–8. Thus, the evidence on different methods of paying providers (specifically doctors and hospitals) and that on roles for pricing mechanisms are reviewed in those chapters. Modifications to voluntary insurance, free care at the point of delivery, and HMOs are also compared throughout these chapters. How different systems cope with the problem of adverse selection and equity in health and health care is the subject matter for Chapter 9. In Chapter 10, the issue of how we might use economics to address questions such as how much should be spent on health care and how health care priorities should be set is addressed.

Table 4.1 Options arising from funding arrangements for health services: controlling moral hazard and adverse selection

	Basic system for raising finance		
	Private insurance	*Public insurance*	*Direct taxation*
Controlling consumer moral hazard	Charges MSAs HMOs PPOs Fixed indemnity (i.e. cover for approved packages only)	Charges MSAs Non-price rationing	Charges MSAs Non-price rationing
Controlling provider moral hazard	Doctors: Fee for service Capitation Salary Competition (through HMOs etc.) Hospitals: Retrospective budgets Prospective budgets Payment by case (DRG) Payment by day Competition (through HMOs etc.)	Doctors: Fee for service Capitation Salary Payments for good practice Budgets Hospitals: Retrospective budgets Prospective budgets Payment by day Internal markets	Doctors: Fee for service Capitation Salary Payments for good practice Budgets Hospitals: Retrospective budgets Prospective budgets Payment by day Internal markets
Controlling adverse selection	Compulsory community-rated insurance plus experience-rated subsidy Vouchers Charges plus catastrophic insurance Special schemes for poor, elderly and disabled people	Integral part of the system (100% coverage of population) Can involve compulsory community-rated insurance plus an experience-rated subsidy	Integral part of system (100% coverage of population)

Before all of this, however, if governments are to intervene in health care funding, it is wise to consider what the objectives of such intervention might be. The act of government intervention in itself cannot solve the problems of markets raised in Chapter 3. Government intervention can take many forms, as we have seen in this chapter. To determine the success of different schemes, it is necessary to know what it is they are trying to achieve. This is the subject matter of the following chapter, Chapter 5.

5 ECONOMIC OBJECTIVES OF HEALTH CARE

INTRODUCTION

In this chapter the economic objectives of health care systems are explored in some detail. The point of doing this is to come up with some operational definitions that can be systematically used to judge performance. The key economic objectives relate to efficiency and equity. Defining the term efficiency is somewhat more straightforward than defining the term equity so this chapter is deliberately devoted more to the equity debate than the efficiency one. This imbalance is further justified by the fact that, up to now, we have given more space (in Chapters 2 and 3) to the notions of efficiency than to notions of equity.

Once equipped with some reasonable definitions, it is possible to conduct an empirical review of the performance of some health care systems. Subsequent review chapters therefore concentrate on efficient consumer behaviour (Chapter 6), efficient provider behaviour (Chapter 7 on doctors, Chapter 8 on hospitals) and equity (Chapter 9).

This chapter is divided into three parts. The first part is a brief introduction to efficiency criteria. The remainder provides a more extensive discussion about equity. After defining efficiency objectives, the confusion surrounding equity is addressed. Evidence on the existence of this confusion is demonstrated by highlighting equity criteria that emerge from policy statements. Economic and philosophical definitions of equity are briefly reviewed before we finally settle on some objectives. In the penultimate part of the chapter, we consider the extent of interaction between efficiency and equity objectives. In concluding, we list the efficiency and equity objectives to be used in reviewing empirical evidence on methods of health care financing.

EFFICIENCY

In Chapter 2 it was demonstrated that the automatic outcome of perfect markets is efficient behaviour – consumer satisfaction maximised at least cost to society. This is obviously a highly desirable outcome. The question that follows is, given the imperfections of the health care market, can social efficiency be achieved within a given health care system? The short answer is probably no, and the question then becomes how close can systems get to this outcome. In principle, social efficiency is an uncontentious objective of any health care system as the objective seeks the greatest improvements in well-being from available resources. This is synonymous with what economists term minimising 'opportunity cost' that is, minimising the cost to society of achieving these benefits.

Minimising opportunity cost is derived from the notion of scarcity and the need to make choices between competing claims on resources. In economic terms, the decision to commit resources to tackling a health problem denies society the opportunity of using these resources to tackle other health problems. Therefore, some opportunities for improving health remain unfunded. The gains forgone are called opportunity costs. It follows that costs are inextricably linked with benefits. The optimum, social goal in any health care market – a regulated market – can be defined as: maximise benefits and minimise costs. To have resources deployed inefficiently would mean that these resources could be re-allocated to increase output and thereby social welfare.

Achieving efficiency is therefore about comparing the costs (or resources spent) and benefits (or well-being produced) of competing health care interventions and ensuring that resources are allocated in such a way as to maximise gains to society.

There are two levels of efficiency: 'operational' efficiency and 'allocative' efficiency. Each of these is based on 'effectiveness'. These two types of efficiency and effectiveness represent different breadths of perspective – effectiveness being the narrowest and allocative efficiency the broadest. It is easier to talk about these levels as they apply to health care provision, but it should be noted that, in the context of this book, they are important for evaluating changes in financing arrangements.

Effectiveness

Effective health care does not necessarily imply efficiency. It simply means that production or consumption of something will yield satisfaction (or utility). Thus, at its narrowest, effective health care is about improving health status. Both operational and allocative efficiency, however, are necessarily conditional upon effectiveness. An example of effectiveness would be a drug with proven beneficial impact on a health condition. The focus is limited to the production of health gains.

Operational efficiency

Operational efficiency asks the question, 'given that some activity is worthwhile doing, what is the best way of providing it?' This perspective brings costs into the calculus alongside effectiveness. Operational efficiency involves the selection between alternative means of achieving the same ends and may, therefore, be interpreted as the pursuit of maximum output for a given level of resources or minimum cost for a given level of output.

An example of operational efficiency would be if there were a choice between an effective drug therapy and a surgical operation to treat a given condition. Assessment of the costs and effectiveness of each option determines which is the more operationally efficient. If drug therapy is both less costly and more effective then it is clearly to be preferred. The difficult judgement is if one treatment modality is less costly and less effective than the other (or more effective and more costly). In such a situation, the cost-effectiveness ratios of the alternatives determine which is most efficient, the lower ratio indicates greater operational efficiency.

The 'rules' for achieving operational efficiency are thus:

- if one means of achieving a given end is less (more) costly and produces the same amount of output then this option should (not) be preferred;
- if one means of achieving a given end is less costly and produces more output then this should be preferred; and
- if one means of achieving a given end is less expensive and produces less output then cost-effectiveness ratios should be computed, the lower ratio indicating the option with greater efficiency as its implementation will allow more 'health' to be produced from the given budget.

These rules are pursued through the techniques known as cost-effectiveness analysis (CEA) and cost-utility analysis (CUA). The former technique is more limited as the measure of output used is a uni-dimensional measure of health (e.g. lives saved, life years gained or reduction in disability days). Comparisons therefore have to be between alternatives with a similar single output. CUA enables a wider comparison of more disparate health care activities as the measure of output used is a unit known as the quality adjusted life year (QALY) (or some other variant such as disability adjusted life years). This can capture aspects of both quantity and quality of life in a single index. Therefore, health care programmes which save lives, improve quality of life and those which do both may all be compared. CUA is still limited to the comparison of health-producing alternatives because costs and benefits are not measured in the same unit of account. The question of whether the activity should be pursued in the first place cannot be addressed by either technique.

Allocative efficiency

Allocative efficiency judges whether an activity is worthwhile doing and, given that much health policy is about the scale at which programmes should operate, allocative efficiency may also address the question of scale, or as economists term it, marginal analysis. Just as operational efficiency infers effective health care, so allocative efficiency infers operational efficiency. If something is deemed worthwhile doing then it must be carried out in a way which ensures the optimum use of scarce resources. The social perspective is fundamental to allocative efficiency.

Table 5.1 Operational definitions of efficiency

Allocative efficiency	Pursuing health care programmes that are worthwhile (benefits exceed costs)
Operational efficiency	For worthwhile programmes, ensure that the best use is made of scarce resources to meet the programme's objective

Note: Following these criteria will automatically eliminate ineffective health care programmes.

This perspective ensures that due account is taken of all costs and benefits of interventions regardless of whether they fall within or outside the health care sector (e.g. on families and patients or the productive capacity of the economy).

The appropriate 'rules' to follow are those of the cost–benefit technique and are:

• to undertake activities where benefits outweigh the costs;
• to stop doing activities where the costs outweigh the benefits; and
• in deciding to alter the size of a programme, apply the above rules to the change being considered.

As cost–benefit analysis (CBA) is often characterised as using the same unit to measure costs and benefits (usually monetary units) this means that comparison can be made of any alternatives however disparate (e.g. comparing an increase on spending on health care with a similar increase on education) or indeed evaluation of a single programme can be made (e.g. Donaldson *et al.*, 1996). However, even when everything cannot be measured on monetary terms, CBA still provides a useful decision-making aid, whereby the trade-offs involved in a decision whether or not to fund an intervention are made explicit. Table 5.1 sets out the rules for pursuing efficient behaviour.

The rules of allocative efficiency capture the utilitarian ethic, the maximisation of satisfaction for the greatest number of individuals who collectively form society. It is important, however, to recognise the harm that over-zealous pursuit of allocative efficiency may lead to. It may create a pattern of resource and benefit distribution which discriminates against certain members of society; maximising health, or utility, from health care resources may not be conducive with a 'fair' distribution of health. It is to notions of 'fairness', or 'equity', to which we now turn.

EQUITY

Within most societies there exists, in some form or another, a concern that health care resources and benefits should be distributed in some fair or just way. McLachlan and Maynard (1982) have gone as far as to suggest this concern is of utmost importance, 'the vast majority [of people] … would elect for equity to be a prime consideration (of a health service)'.

The guiding principles underlying each health care system give an indication of the relative concern for equity. There are two basic types of health care system, libertarian and egalitarian (Culyer *et al.*, 1981). The former values consumer sovereignty and market forces whilst the latter is committed to the pursuit of community health.

However, it is more often the case that a health care system is a mix of libertarian and egalitarian values and hence, depending upon the balance of this mix, the importance of equity will vary between health care systems. Even the US health care system recognises the shortcomings of a total reliance upon market forces. Their main form of government regulation is in the form of the insurance schemes for elderly people (Medicare) and indigent people (Medicaid).

Usually, the concern for equity is interpreted generally as providing a basic level of health services to all. Unfortunately, this succinct definition is insufficient to stand up to careful scrutiny (Pereira, 1989). Searching for more specific interpretations requires that a number of sources of confusion surrounding the term equity be confronted.

By working through these issues we should be better placed to judge whether it is feasible to get a grip on some usable equity criteria. The remaining aims of this chapter are therefore fourfold: to highlight where the confusion surrounding equity exists; to demonstrate how policy pronouncements add to, rather than clear up, this confusion; to introduce some philosophical and economic theories on equity; and to bring all this together by producing some operational equity objectives for health care.

CONFRONTING THE CONFUSION: WHAT DO WE MEAN BY EQUITY?

Equity and externalities

First, an important distinction needs to be made between the caring externality and equity. The latter brings us into territory which is much more extensive than that covered by externalities. In Chapter 3, the caring externality was described as the spillover effect individuals get from others' production or consumption of a commodity. Thus, individuals care about seeing or knowing that others within their society receive timely, needed health care. This, however, is an individually based concern. Conventionally, the concern is expressed by richer members of society, as they are more likely to be the ones with resources to give in backing up their preferences. Because these members care and are able and willing to pay for some of the poor's health care consumption, a sub-optimal consumption pattern can be mitigated; rich people feel better than they would if they could not contribute to other people's consumption of health care. Hence, the caring externality, and other positive externalities relate to the notion of efficiency and are based upon underlying distributions of income, health and preferences for altruism within a society.

Equity is a broader concept, capturing the notion of fairness as an independent, external view. Reliance is not placed on the benevolence felt by the rich towards the poor but on the democratic process. Indeed, it is possible that the poor members of society, representing the majority view, might vote in favour of an equity objective discriminating against rich members' access to health care (e.g. cosmetic surgery not to be routinely offered as part of the public system). This would have to be accepted as fair.

Equity or equality?

The second, and simplest, point to clear up is that the terms 'equity' and 'equality' are not always interchangeable. Consider some dictionary definitions: equity is 'a system of justice based on conscience and fairness'; equality is 'the state of being equal' (Longman New Universal Dictionary, 1982). Equality is, thus, a particular interpretation of equity. It is concerned only with equal shares. Equity, however, is about fairness, and it may be judged fair to be unequal. In health care it may be judged equitable to have unequal access to services; groups more likely to be ill should perhaps be given greater access.

Equity of health care or health?

Does equity set out to achieve fair health or fair health care? At a cursory glance both ideas seem reasonable. In practice, however, most health care systems are not expected to set about the enormous task of achieving a fair distribution of health. This is in part at least because there are many other influences on health as well as health care.

More realistically health care systems are in the business of pursuing a fair distribution of health care as this reflects their locus of control. However, equality of health within the sphere of health care activities is often still upheld as the 'gold standard'. In our view, it is misleading to set such an unobtainable standard for four (to us) compelling reasons:

- equality of health is not a viable choice for an equity goal for a health service because it cannot be guaranteed as a basic human right. Genetically inherited conditions or natural deterioration in health over time inevitably conflict with this objective;
- it is still not known exactly what is meant by the term 'good' health;
- attempting to achieve good health may be seen as élitist in the sense that informed individuals are prevented from choosing their own level of health which may be somewhere below 'good' health (e.g. a person may choose not to give up smoking). Such a goal would necessarily impose the level of quality of life on a community. The objective should be provision of opportunity,[1] which is about health care rather than health; and

- Mooney (1987a) argues that the pursuit of equality of health will inevitably lead to equal health at a level which is less than current best health.[2] It would not be possible to raise society's health towards the higher level as this would prove too costly so pursuit of health would inevitably mean reducing the health of some groups in society.

Some may argue that credence can be given to a more limited interpretation of reduced health inequality; 'equality of outcome given the uptake of services by individuals in equal need'. This objective seeks to ensure that once individuals with similar conditions present to the health service they are treated with the same effective health care (i.e. two individuals diagnosed with breast cancer should be given the same treatment. This will ensure that their survival chances are similar). However, similar outcomes for individuals infers there may be no differences in preferences either for compliance or for other commodities which may influence health and thereby generate actual differences in final health status. So, once again, this form of expression can be criticised for its élitist perspective, once more leading towards the conclusion that objectives should be focussed on health care rather than health.

Horizontal equity

Table 5.2 summarises possible dimensions of health care equity in terms of either horizontal or vertical equity. Horizontal equity is concerned with equal treatment of equals. To make sense of the term we follow the advice of Mooney (1987b). Equal treatment for equals is about equal treatment for equal need. The term could not mean equality of treatment regardless of need because those in good health would not want to be treated the same as those with an ill-health condition, however mild! It was also argued in Chapter 3 that 'need' is the appropriate concept to focus on as the denominator variable. Horizontal equity can be expressed at any stage of health care production; input, process or output (Cullis and West, 1979; West, 1981). As shown in Table 5.2 the usual expressions are equality of expenditure (or resources), of utilisation, of access and of health, the last of which has already been rejected as a realistic objective of health care financing.

Equality of expenditure (or resources) says something about provision of health care resources but little about the services received or how that care affects health. Thus, equity defined in this way is quite limited. The main advantage, and reason for its prolific use, is the relative ease with which inputs can be measured and monitored.

There is an important distinction to be made between utilisation and access. 'Equal utilisation for equal need' requires both standardising medical practices for given conditions and equal compliance (e.g. two individuals living in different areas of the country receive the same treatment regime for their hip operations and both comply equally with post-operative physiotherapy). 'Equal access for equal need' provides individuals simply with the opportunity to use needed health

Table 5.2   Operational definitions of equity

Horizontal-equity criteria

   (1) Equal expenditure for equal need, for example, equal nurse cost per bed ratios in all acute hospitals.
   (2) Equal utilization for equal need, for example, equal length of stay per health condition.
   (3) Equal access for equal need, for example, equal waiting time for treatment for patients with similar conditions.
   (4) Equal health/reduced inequalities in health, for example, equal age- and sex-adjusted standardised mortality ratios across health regions.

Vertical-equity criteria

   (5) Unequal treatment for unequal need, for example, unequal treatment of those with treatable, trivial versus serious conditions.
   (6) Progressive financing based on ability to pay, for example, progressive income tax rates and mainly income-tax financed.

services. This term may legitimately lead to different patterns of utilisation for equal need as individuals may choose to comply with treatment to different extents. It does not rely on any element of coercion as equal utilisation might and therefore, is not élitist. As a result, we would argue that equality of access is the superior form of expression. In addition, equality of expenditure and of utilisation implies that medical practice is standardised for each type of need. The literature on medical practice variations shows this not to be the case (Andersen and Mooney, 1990; Senior *et al.*, 2003).

Equality of access becomes problematical if a price has to be paid for an equity–efficiency trade-off. For example, pursuit of equal geographical access to health services could mean that resource-intensive coronary care units should be provided equally in both sparsely and densely populated areas; clearly not an efficient strategy. The price of equity can be measured in terms of the loss of life and quality of life that could otherwise be achieved if resources were spent on their most productive uses. However, this is also a problem of the other concepts of horizontal equity in Table 5.2 and not just of equal access for equal need.

Equality of access cannot be measured in absolute terms but can be compared and assessed in relative terms (i.e. whether or not access in one area is more or less equitable than in another). This is because it is 'extremely difficult to state what equity is in any positive sense, but barriers to equity are readily identifiable' (Hall, 1991). For two communities to face equality of access of health care the following barriers need to be the same: geographical factors, for example, travel distances to health care facilities; availability of transportation resources and communication services; waiting times for appointments and treatments; and equally informed patients (i.e. about ill-health and the effectiveness of health care treatments). Some of these barriers have natural units of measurement and are, therefore, relatively straightforward to measure and monitor; for example, operating waiting times and appointments to see GPs or specialists. However, measuring and monitoring the extent to which patients have 'full information' (however that is defined) is more complex and open to differing interpretation. Indirect measurement is possible (e.g. schedules analysing patient knowledge) but will usually fall short of capturing the concept comprehensively.

In addition, Mooney *et al.* (2002) have highlighted the importance of cultural barriers to health services particularly in the context of providing health services to culturally distinct populations such as the Australian Aborigines and Torres Strait Islanders. Some of these barriers include language, attitudes of service providers towards race and the social alienation experienced by sections of such communities. They argue that the measurement of access in this context would require consideration not simply of the height of various barriers but rather how they are perceived by the individuals and communities.

In general, measurement difficulties inevitably mean that equality of access can often only be partially or inadequately measured or at best approximated. For instance, as will be seen in Chapter 9 it is common to find equality of utilisation being used as a proxy measure.

Vertical equity

Vertical equity addresses the question of the extent to which individuals who are unequal in society should be treated differently. In principle, unequal treatment of unequals is a sensible concept in the context of health care delivery. It may seem too obvious to be worth mentioning, but is, however, difficult to put into operation (Wagstaff *et al.*, 1989; Mooney, 1996). For example, the treatment needs for short-sightedness and obstetric care are clearly different. The harder question is assessing how unequally these conditions should be treated in pursuit of equity. Should one condition enjoy a higher standard of care because it is judged to be more important? If so, how much higher should it be?

The objective of financial equity is usually concerned with establishing a payment system based on ability to pay. McClelland (1991) explains the rationale for this concern. First, because ill-health can be unpredictable and uncertain, the impact of health care costs can be adverse, especially for poorer members of society. Protection against financial hardship owing to catastrophic illness is therefore desirable. Second, the consumption of goods and services which have an impact on health is regarded as important because health is regarded as being so important. Thus removal of financial barriers which impede consumption is, again, desirable. The concept of financial equity thus needs to be considered in two stages. The first is this broad achievement of vertical equity (payment based on ability to pay), the second that within groups of equal financial status (or however else vertical equity is to be defined) there is actual payment on fair terms, that is, regard is paid also to horizontal equity.

The horizontal perspective has been defined by Wagstaff *et al.* (1989) as 'the extent to which those of equal ability to pay actually end up making equal payments, regardless of, for example gender, marital status ...'. They suggest that it is conceivable that, in the UK NHS for example, anomalies in the personal income tax system may create a situation of inequity as some individuals with the same income may contribute different amounts to health care. This, unfortunately, is an area of equity that has been left relatively unattended in the literature, although this is touched upon in van Doorslaer *et al*. (1999a) and Wagstaff *et al*. (2000) and will be discussed briefly in Chapter 9.

The broader question of the pursuit of vertical equity in health care finance raises the following questions:

- How should ability to pay be defined?
- What should the relationship be between ability to pay and payments?

There is obviously an implicit regard for financial equity in those health care systems that have a large element of public finance and one which has been given some attention in the recent literature. Nevertheless, although we recognise the importance of vertical financial equity as a plausible health care objective, there are, at present, large gaps in knowledge as to how best this can be achieved.

The most comprehensive analysis has been described by Gottschalk *et al*. (1989). They describe four simultaneous goals of health care: to induce a socially efficient level of health care utilisation; to spread risk across people; to spread risk across a person's life; and to distribute resources according to need, where need reflects both income and health status. There are, obviously, efficiency/equity trade-offs to be made between these goals. For example, a society could be interested in achieving the first and third goals. If this were the case, then a possible financing strategy would be to use market prices at the point of consumption but allowing for long payback periods. On the other hand, if the latter three goals were to be pursued at the expense of the first, then general tax revenue could be used to finance health care and the extent of redistribution would be determined by the progressivity of the underlying income tax system.

In practice, in devising a scheme of fair contributions it is necessary to take account of the different forms of payment that can be made (i.e. out-of-pocket expenses, insurance premiums and tax revenues). A progressive system is usually most effectively achieved through taxation. Appropriate tax allowances, increasing tax-incidence with increasing income and exemption categories for certain groups, enable the pursuit of vertical equity.

There are, however, a variety of taxes (e.g. general income tax, local income taxes, pay-roll taxes, indirect taxes) and some will be more progressive than others. It is important, therefore, to establish not only the contribution of taxation to health care financing but also the source of taxation. Wagstaff *et al*. (1999b), for example, have shown that income-conditioned taxation is the most progressive.

A tax-financed health care system or a social insurance system would normally be expected to achieve some degree of vertical equity. Those health care systems that rely heavily on large out-of-pocket payments for finance are more likely to require additional regulation (e.g. means testing) to protect low-income and high-user groups satisfactorily.

Procedural justice

More recently an additional consideration has become more widely accepted. That is the notion that equity in health care has a procedural as well as a distributional dimension (Mooney, 1996; Sen, 2002; Mooney *et al.*, 2002). One interpretation is that it is involvement in the decision-making process rather than necessarily the outcomes that is seen as important from an equity standpoint. Mooney *et al.* (2002) highlight for instance the relevance of this form of procedural justice in the context of achieving equity in Aboriginal health. At one level, it may be related to the level of involvement of the general community in determining the level of funding to Aboriginal health and at another, whether Aborigines are able to exercise autonomy in determining how resources are spent.

Sen (2002) provides another interpretation of procedural justice based on the example of gender–related inequalities in health and the tendency for females to have better health and longevity. He argues that the cause of equity would *not* be advanced by policies that involve females receiving worse health care in order to achieve an equalisation of these dimensions of health. In effect procedural justice demands that 'no group – in this case women – be discriminated against in this way'.

Muddying the waters: equity policies and pronouncements

Confronting some of the confusion over operational definitions of equity may be best served by examining policy statements and pronouncements made by the World Health Organisation (WHO), along with those from some selected health systems.

Perhaps one of the more controversial attempts made recently to identify health care objectives was made by WHO in the 2000 World Health Report. It set five health system goals (health status; health equality; responsiveness; distribution of responsiveness and fair financing) and attempted to rank all its member states on the basis of how well their health systems contribute to the attainment of such goals (WHO, 2000). Performance was measured for each of these objectives on the basis of data drawn from national accounts and, given problems of data quality and availability, varying degrees of inference. A composite score for each country was then determined by an arbitrary weighting applied to each of these objectives. This system of ranking has been criticised for its implication that such objectives can be imposed uniformly across different societies (Williams, 2001). The difficulties in making broad international comparisons of objectives such as equity, justice or fairness are that such concepts are inherently dependent on the values of those espousing them. It seems inconsistent that these concepts can be imposed from outside by an agency such as WHO.

The objective of reduced inequalities in health, often stated along with others such as equality of access, is a popular objective of governments. There is little doubt as to its strong rhetorical appeal. For instance it is alluded to in major health policy statements in Finland (Ministry of Social Affairs and Health (Finland),

2001), New Zealand (New Zealand Ministry of Health, 2000), Sweden (Ministry of Health and Social Affairs (Sweden), 2001), Denmark (Kamper-Jorgensen, 2001), South Africa (Bradshaw, 1998) as well as in the World Health Report 2000. Furthermore, elements of the United Nations Millennium Development Goals (UNMDG) include objectives that entail narrowing the health differentials and incidence of diseases between the rich and the poor (United Nations General Assembly, 2000). Importantly, however, the UNMDGs are articulated within the context of broader economic and social development rather than as simply objectives for the health sector. This is an important distinction given that the social determinants of health generally extend to factors beyond the health care and that reducing health differentials is likely to involve substantial engagement of other sectors. This is a sentiment also reflected in the Acheson Report in the UK where only three of its 39 main recommendations for reducing health inequalities in the UK were directed at the NHS (Acheson, 1998; Exwothy, 2003).

Many countries have expressed support for equality of access regardless of ability to pay. The International Forum on Common Access to Health Care Services (2003) involving the Ministers of Health for Chile, Germany, Greece, New Zealand, Slovenia, Sweden and UK identified 'common access as a core principle – meaning universal health care according to need, not wealth'. Part of their joint statement was: 'We represent a group of countries with different political, organizational and financing structures, united by the value that health systems shall ensure all citizens universal and equitable access to health care.' Similarly the European Commission (2001) states 'access to health care is a right enshrined in the European Union's Charter of Fundamental Rights and an essential element of human dignity. It must therefore be guaranteed for all. This is all the more important when new products and treatments are marketed which bring improvements in care at a higher cost.'

Clearly the foundations of the US Medicare and Medicaid schemes rest on concern over incomplete private insurance coverage and unfair access to health care. The US Department of Health and Human Services (2003) specifies a strategic goal for 2003–2008 that emphasises the importance of extending access: 'Increase the percentage of the Nation's children and adults who have access to health care services, and expand consumer choices.'

Another dimension of access is waiting times which seems, in many countries, particularly those with social health insurance where services are more likely to be rationed in this way than through user charges, to have major political significance. Mossialos and Thomson (2003) highlight a number of European member states such as Denmark, Sweden and the United Kingdom which during the 1990s initiated, with mixed success, major programmes to reduce waiting lists.

The UK NHS (DHSS, 1976; UK Department of Health, 2003), Australia (NSW Department of Health, 1990, 1999), Sweden (Diderichsen *et al.*, 1997) and South Africa (McIntyre *et al.*, 2002) are examples of countries which have also been concerned with geographical access through the use of resource allocation formula, that is, ensuring that where one lives within a country does not affect access to health services by allocating funds to regions according to population numbers and some measure of need (although in South Africa, McIntyre *et al.* (2002) argue that the existing formula tends to reinforce existing inequities).

Concern for equality of utilisation was one of the factors influencing the change to a public insurance system in Canada as it was felt that health care utilisation was becoming too dependent upon income (Evans, 1987). The Romanow Commission established by the Canadian Government to examine the future of health care, in its statement on equity, re-emphasises utilisation as an important dimension of its objective 'equity means that citizens get the care they need, without consideration of their social status or other personal characteristics such as age, gender, ethnicity or place of residence' (Romanow, 2002). Carrin and Vereecke (1992) suggests that equity objectives in sub-Saharan Africa relate to equality of utilisation with improvements achieved by re-distribution of public health resources from urban to rural areas.

From this brief glance at how systems define their equity objectives, we find them to be widely varying. Indeed, as we have documented, health care systems may strive for both equality of health and of access without addressing the potential for conflict and how any such conflict should be resolved. The lack of clarity that can surround the notion of equity can be summarised by a statement written by an adviser to the Pan American Health Organisation many years earlier but that we believe still holds true today: 'The fundamental idea of equity is that of equal treatment for all the population ... the crucial notion is that whatever the level of access, it should be the same for all. Inequity results from the differences in the ability to obtain health care. ... Treatment and resources should go where they are most needed' (Musgrove, 1986).

This statement gives rise to three potentially conflicting health care equity objectives; equal treatment for all the population; equal access for all; and allocation on the basis of greatest need. Equal treatment for all is, as argued earlier, simply untenable. It should be equal treatment for equal need. However, equal treatment for equal need does not necessarily coincide with equal access for equal need, particularly if patients' preferences to comply with treatment differ. Resources allocated on the basis of greatest need may also be incompatible with equal access, particularly if access is defined in terms of geographical access.

So, although the discussion so far has attempted to confront some of the confusion surrounding the term equity, there are clearly issues that remain to be resolved. A logical next step is to ask the question 'can anything useful be gleaned from economic and philosophic theories or concepts?'

THE ECONOMICS AND PHILOSOPHY INTERFACE – THEORIES OF EQUITY

Fairness and justice are phenomena deeply embodied within philosophy and economics. In economics these phenomena form part of the area known as normative

Table 5.3 Some economists' concepts of equity

Economist/Theory	Concept
Musgrave (1959) Merit Good Theory	Individuals will choose to consume less health care than they 'should'. Government intervention aims to ensure appropriate consumption by increasing availability, and is thus concerned with equality of consumption.
Lees (1962)	The crux of the UK NHS was the provision of free health care at the point of use to ensure equal consumption of health care.
Titmuss (1970)	Social duty meant the UK NHS was concerned with providing the *opportunity* to promote health and altruism; thus the closest interpretation is equal opportunity to use health services (i.e. access) because this enables the promotion of both health and altruism.
Sen (1977)	Individuals are committed to the idea that others' opportunity to consume health care may be just as, if not more, important than their own; thus the appropriate definition is equal access for equal need.
Margolis (1982)	Individuals are interested in doing their fair share for the community, which leads them to want to contribute to making services available; thus the appropriate definition is equal access for equal need.

economics. A range of concepts have been offered by economists to explain these phenomena. Where these concepts directly relate to health care, the theories stem largely from the experience of the UK NHS. Table 5.3 briefly sets out some of these concepts. In the main, it appears that economists converge on the notion of equal access for equal need.

The philosophy debate is less helpful for explanations of health care equity. Table 5.4 outlines some of the main theories of justice. Both theories of entitlement and utilitarianism are too limited for the sort of concern that stems from an imperfect health care market. Rawlsian theory (Rawls, 1971) appears promising. However, the crucial question about what should be the prime concern, primary social goods (these are things like basic freedoms and liberties) or primary institutions (which include health services), remains unclear. So it seems that egalitarianism provides the most promising theory of health care justice. Although at its grandest, egalitarianism is about the concern for social, political and economic equality, in the context of health care it may be taken to mean equality of health or health care. Bearing in mind earlier arguments, the notion of equal access for equal need is to be preferred.

TOWARDS SOME OPERATIONAL EQUITY GOALS

In summary, it is clear that there is no one universal equity measure. Each health care system has to decide upon its own equity objective(s), decide how to

Table 5.4 Some philosophers' concepts of equity

Philosopher/Theory	Concept
Nozick (1974) Entitlement Theory	Limited theory of justice. Market mechanism is considered fair.
Utilitarianism	Misplaced theory of justice. Maximising greatest happiness for the greatest number, but ignores distributional aspects.
Rawls (1971)	A basic set of primary social Rawlsian theory goods are distributed (behind a 'veil of ignorance') so that the position of the least well off in society is maximised. Health care is not one of these goods but may be seen as a primary institution to achieve fair distribution of basic liberties and so on (Daniels, 1981). Even so, it is not clear if equity is about maximising consumption of primary social goods or health care. Therefore, it is possible that equality of utilization is desirable.
Egalitarianism	Equal shares of a distribution of a commodity. Could be taken to mean equality of health or equality of health care.

operationalise the objective(s), confront and resolve any potential conflict between equity objectives and then proceed to monitor performance accordingly. Despite an array of operational definitions, support for 'equality of access' seems very common. Another common equity objective, implicit within the organisation of health care systems, is the desire that financial contributions be based on ability to pay. Ideally, therefore, we advocate these definitions. Given practical problems associated with measuring 'access' it seems that operational definitions will inevitably focus more narrowly on the notions of equality of utilisation and of inputs. It is important, therefore, to bear their shortcomings in mind when attempting to assess performance of health care systems or changes to financial arrangements.

It has been argued that 'equality of health' is inherently wrong as a health care equity objective. As a constrained interpretation of 'reducing health inequalities', however, the goal of achieving 'equal outcome given the uptake of effective services by those in equal need' may be considered desirable although it is our view that equity objectives should be focused on health care rather than health.

INTERACTION BETWEEN EQUITY AND EFFICIENCY

It is inevitable that the ideal level of equity can not be achieved. Some will have to be forgone to achieve efficiency. Likewise, ideal efficiency will not be achieved. This trade-off is inevitable because of the notion of scarcity. If scarcity did not exist, there would be no need to consider equity (who gets and who pays what and how much) or efficiency (what are the costs and benefits of different arrangements). Equity must therefore come at a price. To redistribute an efficient allocation of health care resources according to some just criteria means that the pursuit of health care equity may result in an unnecessary loss of life or of quality of life. This is a strong argument for seeking to make equity objectives as explicit as can be. By so doing, the trade-off between efficiency and equity can be measured and societies placed in a position to judge for themselves whether such trade-offs are acceptable or not.

CONCLUSIONS

In setting the economic objectives of health care systems both efficiency and equity notions must be taken into account. Efficiency is easy and undisputed. It is sought at two levels; allocative efficiency determines the 'worthwhileness' of programmes and operational efficiency the best ways of producing worthwhile programmes. Within operational efficiency, one would also be concerned with cost containment, although, on its own this requires careful interpretation.

Equity is a less straightforward notion because it is about who receives costs and benefits rather than simply their magnitude. But, as we have argued in this chapter, there are two important dimensions; financial equity and equity of opportunity to use health care resources. Financial equity is assessed by the burden of financial contributions extracted from different socio-economic groups within society to pay for health care. It is deemed fair that payment is based on ability to pay.

The opportunity to use resources is a more difficult notion to measure and monitor as 'access' is a relative term. Therefore, equal access for equal need is the most desirable horizontal equity objective but in light of practical difficulties we recognise that proxy measures are sometimes inevitable, particularly equal utilisation for equal need. Finally, despite having argued against the notion of equal health as a health care objective, it is important to consider a slightly different notion; whether health care reforms lead to increased health inequalities. The second part of this book will judge the performance of some health care systems in relation to these economic objectives.

A REVIEW OF EMPIRICAL FINDINGS

CHAPTER 6

COUNTERING CONSUMER
MORAL HAZARD

INTRODUCTION

The problem of moral hazard, and possible solutions to it, is one of the most researched areas in the economics of health care, as witnessed by the content of the following three chapters. The concept of moral hazard was introduced in Chapter 3. Recall that it relates to inefficiency in health care use because insurance-based systems, in common with tax-financed systems, face the problem of potential excess utilisation: that is, use in excess of what it is felt the system ought to provide as a result of the benefits of this excess use being exceeded by benefits forgone (or opportunity cost). The reasons for the existence and persistence of such excess use are twofold: the absence (or the lowering) of a financial barrier to care on the side of demand; and, on the side of supply, the presence of financial arrangements which enable (even encourage) providers to supply wasteful amounts. Supply-side effects are often exacerbated by a legal environment that encourages what has become known as 'defensive' medicine, a style of practice that minimises the probability of legal action for malpractice – but often only at considerable cost. The problem of changing attitudes of consumers and suppliers of care in response to such 'perverse' financial arrangements has become known in the literature as the problem of 'moral hazard', and it is moral hazard which leads to potential excess utilisation of health care.

Remember, from Chapter 3, that the above concept of moral hazard is very neoclassical. We have already questioned whether excess demand can be measured as a result of consumers not being fully informed and, because of externalities, over-provision on the supply side is also difficult to measure. Despite these, policy-makers and economists have come up with many 'solutions' to moral hazard on the parts of consumers and suppliers.

Initiatives aimed at countering moral hazard on the part of doctors and hospitals are reviewed in the following two chapters. The aim of this chapter is to review the evidence from research on the effect of different methods of dealing with consumer moral hazard that have arisen in both publicly and privately financed health care systems. In keeping with the objectives of health care outlined in Chapter 5, the effect of these methods is examined in terms of three criteria: patient utilisation of health care in general and thus, impact on costs; utilisation by different groups of patients; and health status of individuals or groups (the latter to assess, in part, whether inequalities are increased).

In the following section, a number of possible counters to consumer moral hazard is introduced. The evidence of the effect of these counters on moral hazard on the part of the consumer is then reviewed. Finally, some conclusions are offered on whether the evidence demonstrates that some funding mechanisms reviewed are more likely than others to achieve broad health service objectives.

Since there have been so many analyses of insurance-based systems and of the ways they have struggled with the problem of moral hazard, much evidence is cited on insured consumers' reactions to charges. It should be noted, however, that this evidence is also relevant to health care systems which are currently publicly financed, as some insurance plans provide care 'free' (in the financial sense) at the point of delivery as is often the case in such publicly financed systems.

POLICY RESPONSES TO CONSUMER MORAL HAZARD

Policy responses to moral hazard do not have to be financial. Traditional organisational responses to preventing overuse of expensive hospital services in many high-income countries have involved the use of primary-care doctors as the 'gateway' to such services. Likewise, in lower income countries a similar policy was to use 'barefoot doctors, such as in countries like Papua New Guinea and China. Such organisational considerations are, unfortunately, beyond the scope of this book.

In Chapter 3, a list of possible financial counters to consumer moral hazard was provided. Repeating this list, it can be seen that consumer moral hazard has typically been countered in the following ways:

- Use of co-payments, whereby the insured person pays some fraction of the supplier's charge;
- Use of co-payments to raise revenue for the system as well as to deter demand, such as in lower income countries;
- Medical savings accounts (MSAs), whereby a fixed sum is deposited into an account for a consumer to spend on non-catastrophic services, with services over a certain monetary amount covered through an insurance-based system;
- Fixed periodic per capita pre-payment by consumers directly to the provider of comprehensive health care, such as a health maintenance organisation (HMO);
- Provision of incentives for consumers to demand care from selected providers, offering low cost packages of care, as in the case of Preferred Provider Organisations (PPOs);
- Non-price rationing by doctors according to judgements of need usually resulting in consumers incurring waiting 'costs' for elective treatment.

The first two reflect different uses of user charges, one explicitly aimed at countering moral hazard, as in many private-insurance systems, whilst the other counters moral hazard but also acts as a revenue-raising device. The third method has been proposed for use in the US and has been used in more publicly oriented systems, such as China. The fourth and fifth methods have been implemented mainly in private insurance-based systems, such as the US, more recently under the auspices of 'managed care', with the sixth being characteristic of publicly provided and financed health care, such as the UK NHS.

EVIDENCE ON COUNTERING CONSUMER MORAL HAZARD

Co-payments

Co-payments have been introduced in a number of countries to put some financial burden on the consumer to discourage 'unnecessary' use of health care or doctors' time. Individual schemes differ according to the nature of the financial arrangement but take four main forms: a flat rate charge for each unit of service; co-insurance (the insured individual has to pay a certain proportion of each unit of health care consumed); a deductible akin to the 'excess' in some motor vehicle insurance policies (the individual pays 100 per cent of all bills in a given period up to some maximum amount beyond which insurance benefits are paid in full); or a combination of the latter two.

Most evidence on the effect of co-payments on the demand for medical care has come from the famous Health Insurance Experiment (HIE) conducted by the RAND Corporation (Newhouse, 1974). Little work since has been as rigorous, although some other important studies will be referred to. Families participating in the experiment were randomly assigned to one of 14 different fee-for-service (FFS) insurance plans or to a prepaid group practice. The FFS plans had different levels of cost-sharing which varied in two dimensions: first, the co-insurance rates were zero (viz. free care), 25, 50 or 95 per cent; and second, each plan had a Maximum Dollar Expenditure limit (or MDE) on annual out-of-pocket expenses of 5, 10, or 15 per cent of family income, up to a maximum of $1000, beyond which the insurance plan reimbursed all covered expenses in full. Covered expenses included most medical services. In one additional plan, the families had free access to inpatient services but faced a 95 per cent co-insurance rate for outpatient services, subject to an annual limit of $150 out-of-pocket expenses per person ($450 per family). This, for practical purposes, is equivalent to a $150 individual deductible for outpatient care. Those randomised to the prepaid group practice were given a plan of benefits identical to the zero cost-sharing insurance plan (the 'free plan'). In all, 5809 persons were involved in the free plan and cost-sharing part of the experiment, and 1982 in the prepaid group practice part of the experiment.

The most detailed set of results from the HIE were reported by Manning *et al.* (1987), although most of the work was gathered together in a volume by

Newhouse *et al.* (1993). The results clearly showed that utilisation responds to amounts paid out-of-pocket. Per capita total expenses on the free plan were 45 per cent higher than those on the plan with a 95 per cent co-insurance rate. Spending rates on the other plans lay between these two extremes. Outpatient expenses in the free plan were 67 per cent higher than those on the 95 per cent co-insurance plan, while outpatient visit rates were 63 per cent higher. The largest, and statistically significant, decrease in use of outpatient services occurred between the free and 25 per cent co-insurance plans with outpatient expenses 37 per cent higher in the free plan. There were no statistically significant differences between plans for inpatient expenses because of the $1000 MDE. The outpatient deductible plan resulted in a reduction in outpatient expenses similar to that from the 50 to 95 per cent plans and also showed no significant differences in terms of inpatient expenses compared to the other plans. Generally, these results did not differ from the previously published analysis of the HIE data (Newhouse *et al.*, 1981).

Manning *et al.* (1987) showed that price elasticities for all health care are in the -0.1 to -0.2 range, that is, a 10 per cent increase in user price will cause demand to fall by 1 to 2 per cent. These values were consistent with those elsewhere in the literature (Davis and Russell, 1972; Newhouse and Phelps, 1974; Phelps and Newhouse, 1974). Analysis of the RAND data by individual episodes of care, rather than by plan, lend further support to the previous RAND results, reporting a price elasticity of -0.2 (Keeler and Rolph, 1988). Effects observed by Keeler and Rolph were limited to presentation for each episode of care rather than the amount of treatment carried out per episode. This highlights, unsurprisingly, the effect of co-payments on patients' initial demands for treatment rather than the content of treatment for each episode. Content of treatment is an area over which doctors can have more influence, indicating that charging for care does not necessarily cope with the problem of provider moral hazard.

Therefore, it is possible that one result of implementing charges would be that doctors would then concentrate more of their demand-inducing abilities on those who can afford to pay. The same amount would be spent on health care, but probably to less effect, as those more in need would have less access to services. This is a problem of the conventional neoclassical approach taken by the RAND study. Because of the influence of doctors, the response of aggregate utilization to charges was likely to be less than suggested by the RAND results. It may be that, in aggregate, those less in need but more able to pay for care simply replace those more in need but less able to pay. The 'influence of doctors' on utilization is assumed away in the design of RAND. Anecdotal evidence, that the US has the health care system where user charges are most widespread, and also the system with the greatest problems of cost control, would seem to support this (Evans, 1990a; Wordsworth *et al.*, 1996). Stronger evidence comes from the study by Fahs (1992) of physician behaviour following the introduction of user charges in the United Mine Workers Health and Retirement Fund (UMHRF). Fahs examined utilization by patients in a multispecialty group practice with whom not only UMHRF patients were registered but also patients covered by the United Steelworkers' health benefit plans.

The impact of cost-sharing on the former group was counterbalanced by increased servicing of the latter group, showing that 'compensatory actions will be taken by physicians following the reduction in benefits by a large insurance carrier' (Fahs, 1992). A similar result, whereby the system responds to user-charge susceptibility but maintains total costs as before, has been shown in Ireland (Nolan, 1993). There, less-well-off groups, with full coverage for publicly provided care, tend to use primary care services more, whilst better-off groups, who are more likely to carry private insurance, experience more (and longer) hospital stays. These results arose after controlling for important factors, such as health status.

The next questions to ask are whether the response of demand for health care to changes in its price is different for different groups in society and whether reductions in demand are for care which would otherwise have made no difference to people's health status. Lohr *et al.* (1986) compared those HIE families on all cost-sharing insurance plans (i.e. 25, 50 and 95 per cent co-insurance) with those families on the free care plan in terms of the probability of occurrence of episodes of care for specific diseases. They found that the effect of cost-sharing was often greater among low-income than higher-income persons. Low-income persons were defined as those whose family incomes were in the lower third of the income distribution (i.e. below $20 200 per annum with a mean of $11 000 per annum). The probability that a low-income adult would obtain care for acute pharyngitis if he or she were on the cost-sharing plan was 54 per cent of the probability for low-income adults having free care. For non-poor adults there was little difference between these probabilities. Differences were even greater amongst children (i.e. people under 14 years of age). For the eight acute conditions examined, probabilities of use of services for poor children on cost-sharing plans were between 33 and 68 per cent of those for poor children on the free plan. For non-poor children, probabilities of use of services on the cost-sharing plans were 65–219 per cent of those on the free plan. The figure of 219 per cent is an outlier which, according to Lohr *et al.* (1986), may be explained by a lack of precision in the estimate because the particular diagnosis concerned (trauma from acute sprains and strains) occurs less frequently in higher-income groups, hence yielding a small sample.

The results of the HIE for differential effects of charges on poor and non-poor confirm the results from previous studies of the effect of co-payments. Beck (1974) analysed the introduction of charges of $1.50 (Canadian) per office visit and $2.00 per house visit and for use of emergency or hospital outpatient services in Saskatchewan in 1968. He estimated the consequent reduction in use of these services to be from 6 to 7 per cent for the whole population but 18 per cent for the poor. Helms *et al.* (1978) assessed the impact of the introduction of a small payment (one dollar each for the first two consultations and 50 cents for the first two prescriptions per month) for (previously free) out-of-hospital services for some Medicaid beneficiaries in California. This group was compared to another group of Medicaid beneficiaries in California who were exempt from the charge. The result was that the co-payment reduced doctor visit demand by 8 per cent but increased hospital demand by 17 per cent, thus increasing overall programme cost. Since the HIE, differential use of general practitioner services by income group has been reported in Stockholm County, Sweden, where, between 1970 and 1995, charges have increased by more than three times the consumer price index (Elofsson *et al.*, 1998). Using data from the Swedish Survey of Living Standards, which contains three questions about health care use, as well as data on socio-demographic characteristics and a need indicator, it has been shown that an inverse income gradient, not apparent in 1988–89, appeared in 1996–97; relative to the highest income quintile the odds ratios for having needed-but-not-sought medical care were significantly higher in the lower income quintiles, and highest in the two lowest quintiles (Burstrom, 2002). Despite these results, it has been argued that, in Sweden more generally, the existence of user fees is not a very contentious issue, largely because, before health care was socialized, in 1970, patients paid out-of-pocket for a large proportion of services (Hjertqvist, 2002). In Taiwan, where universal health insurance was introduced in 1995, user charges to the previously uninsured dropped by two-thirds on average whilst those for the previously insured increased by 75 per cent, a much larger absolute change for the former. As intended by this policy, use of physician services increased in the former group, rising to the levels experienced by the latter, whose use, for the most part, remained unchanged (Cheng and Chiang, 1997). Reuveni *et al.* (2002) have also shown that, of those patients prescribed antibiotics in the Israeli health care system, those who do not take up, or only partially take up, their prescription are likely to be less well off and to cite 'cost' as a reason for this.

Lohr *et al.* (1986) also examined whether reductions in utilisation were for inappropriate or unnecessary medical use. They found significant differences between poor and non-poor children. For example, the probability of at least one episode of highly effective (as judged by several doctors at the RAND Corporation) ambulatory care for poor children in cost-sharing plans was 56 per cent of the level for those with free care compared to a figure of 85 per cent for non-poor children. Also, from the RAND study, Foxman *et al.* (1987) demonstrated that cost-sharing reduced appropriate as well as inappropriate antibiotic use to similar degrees.

Probably the most comprehensive piece of work carried out on this issue since RAND, was the evaluation of the impact of the introduction of prescription drug cost-sharing for elderly persons and welfare recipients by the Quebec Government in 1996 (Tamblyn *et al.*, 2001). The cost-sharing scheme involved a replacement of a Can\$2 fee per prescription for seniors and free medication for welfare recipients with a combination of coinsurance (25 per cent per prescription, with an income-based maximum) and a deductible (of Can\$25 every three months). An interrupted time series of data 32 months before and 17 months after introduction of the policy was analysed. The results show that use of essential drugs decreased by 9.12 per cent amongst elderly and by 14.41 per cent amongst welfare recipients. Corresponding decreases in use of less-essential drugs were 15.14 and 22.39 per cent respectively. (Lists of drugs classified as essential and less-essential are provided in the paper.) However, because essential drugs were used twice as often as less-essential, the absolute reduction was greater for essential drugs for both groups. It does seem that, although consumers will respond to charges, their decisions may not be optimal, especially if reductions in 'appropriate' use result in the need for more costly treatment later on. Solanki *et al.* (2000) have also shown that user charges for preventive services, such as Pap smears and mammography, have resulted in reductions of 1–9 per cent in the use of such services within recommended screening intervals.

Despite these results, the HIE studies of health outcomes showed negligible effects of cost-sharing on general measures of health for both adults and children (Brook *et al.*, 1983; Valdez, 1986). The conflict between these findings and those of Lohr *et al.* (1986) and Foxman *et al.* (1987) could be due to one or more of at least three effects. First, although some people on the free plan received benefits (in improved health status) from care for which medicine has effective interventions to offer, others in the same group may have suffered compensating adverse effects from their care (Lohr *et al.*, 1986). Such adverse effects may result either from more consumption by free care enrollees of treatments for conditions for which medical care has relatively little effectiveness (thus prompting 'sick role' behaviour such as staying home from school or work which might not otherwise have happened), or from iatrogenic exposure to antibiotics or minor tranquillisers or other psychotropic agents, leading to adverse effects not experienced by those on cost-sharing plans.

Second, the measures of health used were very limited. The actual indicators were general health, health habits, psychological health, and risk of dying from any cause related to measured risk-factors such as high blood pressure. The number of deaths in the experimental groups was too small to permit any meaningful analysis of survival. Most of the observations were made on a population of healthy adults under the age of 65. This population is less likely to require or benefit from health care than other groups, like elderly people, who were excluded from the study. Some condition-specific measures were used. For instance, it was demonstrated that the free-care plan was associated with improved visual activity (for those with poor vision) (Brook *et al.*, 1983). Also, the free-care plan resulted in improved control of blood pressure, particularly amongst high-risk groups. The cause of the difference, it has been claimed, was additional contact with doctors in the free-care group, resulting in better detection and treatment (Keeler *et al.*, 1985). Similarly, adverse effects of cost-sharing on health status have been found for oral health, particularly in younger age groups (under 35 years of age) (Baillit *et al.*, 1985). Also, in the US, but not part of the HIE, a cohort study, taking account of insurance status, socio-demographic factors and health status, and using the 1987 Medical Expenditure Survey, showed that increased risk for out-of-pocket costs is associated with higher subsequent mortality amongst elderly people with supplemental health insurance (Doescher *et al.*, 2000).

The third possible explanation for the lack of a general health effect in the HIE could be that the total duration of observations (three years for 10 per cent of enrollees and five years for the rest) was too short to reveal possible long-term cumulative effects of reduced consumption of medical services (Relman, 1983).

The measures excluded potential benefits from medical consultations in the form of reassurance and information, and so have a bias towards underestimation of the welfare losses brought about by cost-sharing.

In the UK, charges have been levied on non-exempt groups for prescriptions and dental care. Groups who are exempt from such charges include children under 16 years of age, retired pensioners, pregnant and nursing mothers and those on low incomes. Birch (1986) has shown that real increases in prescription charges for non-exempt people has led them to reduce their per capita consumption of prescriptions by 7.5 per cent over the period 1979 to 1982 compared to a per capita increase in consumption by the exempt group of 1 per cent over the same period. It has also been demonstrated that elderly consumers of dental care who are not exempt from payment of charges are four times more likely to receive emergency care only than elderly people who are exempt from such charges. The former group is also 340 times more likely to receive a check-up only and, when receiving treatment, receive 40 per cent less treatment than exempt patients (Birch, 1989). Such effects could be due not only to charges but also to differences in health status between groups compared which can justify the differences in consumption, or, in the latter example, to greater abilities of dentists to induce demand for services to exempt groups.

More rigorous control over such factors was exerted in the Quebec study, where separate pre- and post-policy cohort studies were conducted to examine the effect of cost-sharing on adverse events (Tamblyn *et al.*, 2001). It was found that the rate (per 10 000 person months) of serious adverse events associated with reductions in use of essential drugs increased from 5.8 in the pre-policy group to 12.6 in the post-policy group for older people and from 14.7 to 27.6 in the welfare-recipient group. In the older group, emergency department visit rates increased from 32.9 to 47.1 (per 10 000 person months) and, in the welfare-recipients group, from 69.6 to 123.8. Statistically, it was shown that these increases were primarily associated with reductions in the use of essential drugs, whilst reductions in uses of non-essential drugs were not associated with increased risks of adverse events or emergency department visits.

User fees in low- and middle-income countries

For many countries the financing of health care exclusively by revenue from general taxation has become unsustainable due to constrained economic circumstances and low or stagnant growth of the health sector. In most low-income countries, third party financing covers only the health care costs of a small proportion of the population. Many governments have attempted to raise additional funds for the health sector by introducing, or in some cases reintroducing, user charges.

For example, many of the 29 African countries that have some kind of national system of user fees participate in the Bamako Initiative. This is a cost sharing scheme launched by the African Ministers of Health in 1987. A key principle of the initiative is that everyone in a community is expected to pay something towards health care (World Bank, 1996). Therefore the rationale for a user fee system is typically couched in terms of the potential efficiency (and possibly equity) gains and improvements in health service sustainability to be achieved through partial or full cost recovery (McPake, 1993; Gilson *et al.*, 1995). With the enactment of such initiatives, it is widely argued that the debate in low-income countries has shifted from whether or not to introduce user fees to *when* and *how* they should be implemented (Dor and van der Gaag, 1988; Gilson and Mills, 1995). There is a growing literature on the effects of user fees in developing countries (Mwabu and Mwangi, 1986; Creese, 1991; Griffin, 1992; McPake, 1993; Thomason *et al.*, 1994; Gilson *et al.*, 1995; Mwabu *et al.*, 1995; World Bank, 1996; Thomas *et al.*, 1998; Audibert and Mathonnat, 2000; Chawla and Ellis, 2000).

Such fees generally have two roles. The first is that they generate revenue and therefore enable health programmes to be partially or fully self-sustaining. The extent to which this can be achieved however is dependent on both the price elasticity of demand (it is possible that the introduction of a fee or an increase in an existing charge can choke off demand) and the transactions costs of collecting such fees. The other role of user fees is that of a device for rationing health services since the imposition of a charge on services will divert away potential patients who can not or choose not to pay.

Looking at user fees as a revenue-raising device, some studies show that visits to health services do diminish with the introduction of user fees (Benyoussef and Wessen, 1974; de Bethune, 1989; Waddington and Enyimayew, 1990). In a study of the effect of a price increase in health facilities in Zaire, de Bethune and colleagues found a decrease in utilisation after a sudden increase in prices. In addition, marked differences have been noted in the health care utilisation patterns of those living in urban and rural areas. In Ghana, Waddington and Enyimayew (1990) reported that three years after the introduction of user fees, a substantial drop in utilisation had not been reversed. In terms of the types of services most likely to be affected by the introduction of charges, a strong positive relationship between income and number of prenatal visits has been reported (Heller, 1982). This is said to be indicative of a strong income-preventive care relationship more generally (McPake, 1993).

In contrast, other studies have revealed that the attendance of public services increases with cost recovery when accompanied by an improvement in the availability of drugs (Reddy and Vandermoortele, 1986; Gilson, 1997; Audibert and Mathonnat, 2000; Geest *et al.*, 2000) and other measures to improve the quality of health services such as better motivated and skilled staff (Litvack and Bodart, 1993; Audibert and Mathonnat, 2000). The process whereby governments re-invest revenue from user fees into the health care system to promote quality is less than clear (McPake, 1993). There is surprisingly little evidence on the mechanisms for re-investing funds or on the factors influencing these mechanisms.

Examining user fees as a rationing device, another theoretical benefit of financial participation by users is that a more efficient health system can be developed by communicating to patients price signals and various incentives that lead to more 'rational' use of the public and private resources given over to health. However, the regressive implications of such a policy have been widely debated

(Creese and Bennett, 1997; Gilson, 1997; Audibert and Mathonnat, 2000). One of the key issues involves the demand for health care by the poor who are reported to be more price-elastic than the rich (McPake, 1993; Audibert and Mathonnat, 2000).

The evidence on the distributional consequences of user fees is mixed. In a number of countries it has been suggested that cost recovery through the introduction of drug fees, has had no seriously detrimental effects on the poor (Diop *et al.*, 1995; Nolan and Turbat, 1995; Audibert and Mathonnat, 2000). For example, the initial effects of cost recovery through user fees in Mauritania has been reported as largely positive regarding the improvement in quality of health care and the overall level of utilisation of basic health facilities (Audibert and Mathonnat, 2000). It has been suggested that this is a result of service users being 'globally' willing to pay when the quality of health care improves. It is further argued that cost recovery, where accompanied by a 'fair' supply of essential drugs and by better motivated staff, can promote the efficiency of a health system.

Similarly, in Niger an optimistic picture of cost-sharing has been described (Chawla and Ellis, 2000). There was no evidence of serious reductions in access or increase in cost. Interestingly, while the introduction of user fees in government health facilities did not dampen demand, it did reduce the probability of seeking treatment by informal providers. Individuals reporting an illness were more likely to visit formal providers and less likely to be treated only at home or by healers and other informal providers. Again, the authors claim that this is largely attributable to improvements in the quality of services but acknowledge that little is known about the exact nature of the interactions between the formal and informal sectors. However, even when demand for services is not greatly reduced by fees, the income effect on the poor can be significant and can contribute to the further impoverishment of the most needy sections of the community.

In contrast, other studies reveal that the introduction of user fees has in fact lead to a substantial reduction in the demand for health services by the poor (Thomason *et al.*, 1994; Nolan and Turbat, 1995). For example, a study of the demand effects of user charges in a district health care system in Kenya revealed that during the period of cost-sharing in public clinics, attendance dropped by about 50 per cent (Mwabu *et al.*, 1995). This drop prompted the government to suspend user fees. Over the next 7 months attendance at government clinics increased by 41 per cent. In addition, the suspension caused a significant number of patients to move from private providers to government health facilities.

In China, which has seen recent changes in its health care system towards more of a free market, hospital sustainability now depends more on revenue from user charges. This is exacerbated by systems of bonus payments to hospital workers for raising revenue. In examination of the impact of such charges on care for stroke patients, Tu *et al.* (2002) found that insured groups (representing those on higher incomes) receive more care, experience longer stays and lower charges relative to the uninsured. Judgements about which group is closer to optimal care are difficult, but, quite clearly, care is influenced by charging, even for serious conditions.

One response to the potentially regressive implications of user fees has been the use of exemption policies. Proponents of user fees have argued that efficiency and equity goals can be simultaneously promoted through the use of exemptions for low-income groups and improvements in the services offered to these groups (Griffin, 1992; Willis, 1993). This typically involves a policy of price discrimination by facility, geographical area or service (McPake, 1993). From the few attempts that have been made to assess the effectiveness of exemption schemes in protecting equity, results indicate problems with reaching the target groups, costs of administration, failure to monitor and adjust schemes over time and the inappropriate use of revenue collected (Waddington and Enyimayew, 1990; Hecht *et al.*, 1993; Nolan and Turbot, 1993; Gilson *et al.*, 1995). Concerns have also been expressed about the risks, at a political level, of favouring certain geographic areas or groups (Devereux, 1999).

Finally, there is relatively little discussion in the user fees literature of the role of communities in health service financing. Some have argued that sustainability of a user fees system may be enhanced through widespread community participation in the process (Thomason *et al.*, 1994; Mwabu *et al.*, 1995). The implication is that 'grass root' participation in discussion about the need for cost-sharing and its mode of implementation can promote greater national consensus on user fees. Parker and Knoppenberg (1991) described the accountability of the health services to the population as 'a central feature of community cost sharing'. This also appeared to be the case in Papua New Guinea, where it was noted that fee collection was more profitable in those health facilities with an active community health board and where there tended to be other revenue generating ventures underway (Thomason *et al.*, 1994). On the other hand, the introduction of user fees in Zambia has been reported as having led the community to feel 'disowned' and excluded from having a voice in service direction (van Der Geest *et al.*, 2000). Some have identified the tension that exists between 'neo-liberal conceptions of a consumer' central to many recent market-orientated reforms, and the 'communitarian values associated with participatory democracy', implying that it is often the latter approach which will lead to greater community involvement (Mosquera *et al.*, 2001).

Four key messages, at least, can be drawn from the literature on user fees in lower income countries. First, quality considerations are a critical factor in ensuring the long-term success of cost-sharing. The imposition of user charges is likely to be reversed or neglected if the charges are not adequate to allow for a noticeable improvement in service quality, or if the revenue from fees cannot be properly used because of highly centralised expenditure control procedures. Limited administrative and management capacity may also hinder the implementation of a financing system based on user fees (Thomason *et al.*, 1994). Health workers, for example, require training in the management of fees including methods of cash collection, protection and accounting.

Second, in many cases health care demand has been noticeably reduced following the introduction of user fees. Even where improvements in service quality have been demonstrated, it is unlikely to be sustained if it results in large inequalities in service utilisation. User charges have been revoked because they have been perceived to be inequitable (Mwabu *et al.*, 1995). A workable system of exempting the poor from fees is a crucial element of a sustainable user fee system.

Third, models estimating the welfare effects of the introduction of user fees[1] have shown that the losses associated with an introduction of charges could in fact be counter balanced by improvements in the quality of government health care facilities (Mwabu and Mwangi, 1986; Gertler and van der Gaag, 1990). Ignoring for the moment the practical difficulties of re-investing revenue to achieve the desired welfare effects, there remains the problem of the regressive effect of user fees. For example, Gertler and van der Gaag (1990) found user fees to be highly regressive with the poorest group of consumers suffering an overall welfare loss equivalent to up to 10 per cent of their income.

Fourth, the effectiveness of different exemption strategies is generally not well understood. There is growing evidence however that there are considerable transactions costs associated with the development and implementation of effective targeting mechanisms. These derive from a lack of quality and up-to-date information on the socio-economic status of population groups through to problems of training staff in the management of fees. The degree of community participation in, and control over, user fees schemes is also likely to influence their sustainability.

In summary, the strongest message to come from the literature is that user fees in low-income countries have been easier to impose than to enforce or sustain. The evaluation of user fees has been patchy and, in particular, the relationship between quality and utilisation has been relatively neglected. However, assuming that overall social welfare can be maximised by improving implementation efficiency and through improvements in service quality, the distributional consequences of user fees continue to mar the success of many health financing policies relying on user fees. In his review of user charges for health care, Creese (1991) argued that 'any change in the allocative principles of the health sector has both costs and benefits' (p. 309). Some of the evidence suggests that a more market-based approach may contribute to better care by encouraging quality-based competition among providers. Other studies have indicated that this may be at the risk of excluding the neediest.

Medical savings accounts

In essence, MSAs aim to put more control of health care spending into the hands of individual patients, by enabling them to 'purchase' health services directly through funds held in their account (Gardner, 1995). Types of account are variable. In the US, it has been proposed that individuals take out high-deductible insurance, and place the savings in premiums from such insurance into MSAs, the money from which can then be used to pay for minor medical expenses (Bond *et al.*, 1996). Costs of catastrophic care would be met from the insurance component (Grimaldi, 1996). Participation is voluntary. In Singapore, where participation is compulsory, contributions range from 6 to 8 per cent of income, depending on age. Contributions are tax free and are shared equally with employers. Self-employed people pay in full, and an endowment fund offers charity-style relief for the poor (Barr, 2001). Catastrophic expenses are covered in part by a voluntary insurance scheme, with the remainder of costs to be paid out of pocket up to a maximum amount once the MSA balance is spent (Gratzer, 1999). It is unclear how such a scheme would operate in a more traditional publicly funded health care system, one option being for government to assign an amount to be paid into a person's or family's MSA, with restrictions being placed on what could be purchased and on how unspent balances could be used.

By having individual consumers take account of the financial consequences of their actions, the idea is that costs are controlled and services are more likely to be provided in line with consumer preferences (Gramm, 1994; Gratzer, 1999). Further to this, it may be the case that if consumers are required to pay for services at the point of consumption, they may invest more in knowledge about their health. This investment would support the aim of more appropriate care received, as well as potentially more efficient use of resources. What is not clear is whether, in fact, members of the general public can comprehend many of the medical complexities, or if a more hands on role is even sought. Clearly, if MSAs were to be introduced in health care systems more widely, such fundamental questions, through survey work and limited piloting, should occur at the outset.

Another potential advantage of MSAs is that services not traditionally covered, such as alternative medicine, could be purchased with money in the account, thereby prompting individuals to take a broader 'wellness' perspective on their health. As such, the concept of MSAs, at least in theory, allows an individual more control over minor medical expenses (e.g. GP visits) while at the same time not exposing them to risks of catastrophic costs should accidents or more serious illnesses arise.

While MSAs are a relatively new concept in health service financing, there have actually been a fair number of published papers, primarily from the US and Singapore, discussing their impact on the health care system. Unfortunately, no studies were identified which explicitly examined the potential costs (to the system and the patient) and health outcomes (to the patient), and simulation studies and descriptive pieces do not provide adequate evidence about what would happen in actual practice. The majority of studies from the US relate more to employer and health system costs than patient outcomes.

Keeler *et al.* (1996) examined the impact of MSAs on 23 157 sampled households through the RAND Health Expenditures Simulation Model. In this model, a number of options were explored, including the level of the catastrophic deductible and variations in who funds the account. Taking into account the fact that not all Americans would choose a MSA approach, the analysis found that health spending would change by +1 per cent to −2 per cent. Thus, this modelling study suggests that implementation of MSAs would have little impact on overall health care costs in the US. However, without information on patient outcomes, it is not possible to determine if, despite the lack of cost savings, such an approach would lead to more efficient service provision.

In a cross-sectional study of non-elderly adults, comparison between comprehensive insurance and a combination of MSAs with catastrophic insurance was made (Ozanne, 1996). Findings suggested that medical spending would be reduced by between 2 and 8 per cent with the MSA/catastrophic insurance option. However, as Grimaldi (1996) points out, such an approach would likely appeal to only a small segment of the US Medicare population, thus reducing overall health care savings. Indeed, Sheils (1995) points out a fundamental flaw in the voluntary approach to MSAs taken in the US; that is, rational consumers would choose between an MSA and traditional insurance scheme on the basis of whichever would be financially more beneficial to them. Therefore, such a scheme can only raise programme costs. At the time of writing, MSAs have not captured the imagination of the US public, employers or insurers, with low rates of uptake. One country, however, where MSAs have been touted as having achieved a great deal of success is South Africa (Matisonn, 2000). Here, MSAs have been taken up by about half of the 20 per cent of the population which carries private insurance. However, it is this segment of the population, given the economic situation in that country, to whom policy-makers would have been looking to make substantial savings in health care costs anyway.

Limited evidence from other countries does not clear up the unresolved issues from the US literature. While Singapore has integrated MSAs into their health system, reports differ with respect to the effectiveness of this reform (Hurley, 2000). For example, Hsiao (1995) and Barr (2001) report that hospitals did not compete on price, and the per capita cost of health care rose faster after the introduction of the new health care model which included MSAs. However, another study stated that costs were controlled following the introduction of this reform (Massaro and Wong, 1995). One of the most meaningful comments from this literature was a recommendation to pilot MSAs at local or regional levels before fully implementing this reform (Massaro and Wong, 1995).

In addition, China has also started to use MSAs, to a more limited degree. However, again actual assessment remains elusive (Hurley, 2000). One paper stated that while MSAs hold promise as a viable model of health care finance, there is the potential for risk selection, cost-shifting and reduction in equity. Further, in recommendations for other countries, these authors state that if such a reform was to be implemented, supply-side reforms would also be required (Yip and Hsiao, 1997). As well, as with the US literature, none of these papers on Singapore and China assessed the impact on potential health outcomes; it is not possible to judge whether a reform would lead to improved efficiency without information on both costs and outcomes.

A recent review article by Hurley (2000) states that while unambiguous evidence does not exist, it is possible to draw on empirical evidence for other demand-side incentives such as user charges. Most notably, it is argued that MSAs are unlikely to control expenditures, and in fact implementation could actually lead to increased overall spending. The basis of this point is that individual purchasing is less influential than that of large-scale insurers, and that, consequently, less fiscal control can be exerted over the 'everyday' health care expenses covered by the accounts whilst catastrophic problems continue to be funded through conventional means.

One further argument put forth is that equity would likely be compromised with this approach, particularly if unused portions of the account can be rolled over for use in other non-health sectors. In this case, individuals could conceivably face a choice between health care and other goods; for those who can afford the other goods, there is no problem, but for the poor, health might (legitimately, from the point of view of the individual) be sacrificed in order to purchase food or hous-ing. Even if poorer people choose to spend on health care, it is likely that they will reach their limit sooner, thus entering the point whereby they are responsible for full costs of (non-catastrophic) care. Indeed, there is evidence that the elderly and poor in Singapore still have difficulty meeting the costs of health care (Barr, 2001), a point reinforced by WHO's ranking of Singapore as 101 out of 191 countries in terms of fair financing of health care (WHO, 2000). It seems that there is substantial potential for transferring of income from poor to rich as a result of an MSA model of health care financing. Equity in access, too, is a problem in Singapore. Many treatments, which would be regarded as standard in many other countries are not covered by the MSA or insurance schemes, making access to treatment problem-atic for the very poor and even low- and middle-income earners (Barr, 2001).

Health may also be adversely affected. If results from the user charges literature can be extended to MSAs, where consumers are also taking responsibility for deciding on when they should use health care, it would seem that the same poten-tial exists for reducing use of both essential and less-essential care. One further important point is that the ability and willingness to take on the role of 'consumer of health care' would likely vary across socio-economic and age groups, which raises further equity issues (Donaldson *et al.*, 1991; Lupton *et al.*, 1991).

Many questions about the administrative details of MSAs necessarily arise. For example, where would the money for the accounts come from? Most likely in many countries, at least at present, governments would collect the current amount of tax, but then deposit a portion of the tax bill directly into individuals' accounts. There are likely to be significant administrative costs associated with this. Another question would be what to do with leftover funds in the account? One model might be for the individual to have the option to roll over any unused portion of the account to the next year, or withdraw the unused amount for personal spend-ing. If the former approach was taken, money could be invested in the form of a retirement fund. This would also enable people to save for future medical expenses which may arise in old age. One further question would be around how withdrawals would be administered. It is feasible to go as far as using debit cards, whereby authorised medical providers would have a type of bank machine to process automatic payments.

If a more 'consumerist' model were accepted for health care, further important issues would have to be addressed. With governments simply allocating the same amounts to health care, but ending up giving the money to consumers instead of health authorities, the total spend on health care will not have changed. However, consumer expectations will likely change. Without altering the total spend, waiting lists are unlikely to be reduced, as even with consumer oriented changes at the margin, without systematic marginal analysis from the supply-side, having no more resources in total is unlikely to have the desired effects. Yet the nature of the contract between consumer and provider may have altered in that consumers would likely expect quicker access once diagnosed with a condition requiring treatment. The legal and consequent implications of this may be quite different compared with many current systems.

Fixed periodic per capita payment

The fourth way of countering consumer moral hazard is the use of fixed periodic per capita pre-payments paid by consumers directly to a provider of comprehensive health care, such as an HMO. Consumers receive a fixed subsidy towards payment, or a fixed percentage of the premium, from employers or government agencies, and so have an incentive to be cost-conscious. Several years ago, Enthoven (1980) suggested that 60 per cent of a family's actuarial premium be deducted from the family's taxable income, giving them an incentive to 'shop around'.

With the continued growth of managed care through the 1990s, the literature on HMOs has grown too. While it would seem that HMO plans do decrease hospitalizations, it is unclear if total costs are lowered (Sullivan, 2001), and evidence that is available does not provide a clear answer on quality of care between HMO and non-HMO plans (Miller and Luft, 1997; Miller and Luft, 2002). Ultimately, as Kemper *et al.* (1999) argue, it may be that HMO plans will appeal to some individuals but not others, noting that those in HMOs may receive more primary care and face lower out-of-pocket costs, but at the same time face increased barriers to accessing providers, receive less specialist care and overall report less satisfaction of care. The debate is further complicated by apparently differing results for HMO and non-HMO plans depending on an individuals' health state and income level (Ware *et al.*, 1996; Dellana and Glascoff, 2001).

Results from the RAND HIE demonstrate that outpatient visit rates from HMO enrollees were similar to those for people on the free care insurance plan. However, expenditures per person in the HMO group were 72 per cent of those on the free care FFS plan. This difference is a result of a markedly less hospital-intensive style of care in the HMO plan (Manning *et al.*, 1984, 1987). An additional result, from Dowd *et al.* (1986), demonstrates that HMO cover also led to reduced lengths of hospital stays as well as reduced admissions. For the seven diagnosis related groups (DRGs) Dowd and his colleagues studied, patients in pre-paid group practices exhibited significantly shorter lengths of stay than similar patients in FFS plans. This result was obtained after controlling for the effects of patients' age, sex, medical condition and severity of illness. Although lengths of stay were analysed, effects on outpatient treatment (which may have been greater in pre-paid group practice) were not.

Since the RAND study, a myriad of literature has arisen comparing HMO and FFS plans on utilization rates and health outcomes for specific disease groups. While it would appear that utilization rates are lower with HMO plans (Miller and Luft, 1994; Sullivan, 2001), there is not a clear pattern for hospital and physician resource use by plan type and there have been mixed results in terms of outcomes (Miller and Luft, 1997, 2002).

For example, a study in the late 1980s demonstrated that Californian legislation allowing public and private third party payers to negotiate contractual agreements with individual hospitals led to a significant reduction in total hospital costs (Zwanziger and Melnick, 1988). Further, a recent study comparing group and staff HMO elderly hip fracture patients to FFS patients found HMO enrollees to have improved functioning and ambulation while utilizing less physician services (Coleman *et al.*, 2000). Of note, others have found similar inpatient management levels but improved survival rates for HMO patients, as was the case for elderly patients with syncope (Getchell *et al.*, 2000).

In contrast, Yelin *et al.* (1996) compared utilization and outcomes for rheumatoid arthritis patients in pre-paid group practice and FFS settings over an 11 year follow-up period and found no difference in quantity of services used and no differences on outcomes including symptoms, functional status and work disability. Baseline data, however, did show the pre-paid group to be more educated than the FFS group, thus introducing a bias likely to favour the HMO plan, at least in terms of outcomes (given similar educational levels, the pre-paid group practice population may have fared worse than the FFS population). Even so, others have also found similar survival patterns between HMO and FFS plans, at least in the case of stroke patients (Retchin *et al.*, 1997).

While much of the data on managed care comes from the US, the experience of Switzerland is also relevant to this discussion. One study found that individuals in Geneva who switched from an indemnity plan to managed care had increased satisfaction with the insurance coverage, but decreased satisfaction with health care, while health status remained stable (Perneger *et al.*, 1996). Utilization and costs were not studied. On balance, the evidence both from the US and elsewhere would appear to suggest that service utilization is decreased with HMO plans, but that health outcomes and quality of care results are equivocal. More negative experience comes from the Netherlands, where several attempts have been made over the past 15 years to introduce managed competition, through having sickness funds compete for enrollees, who would pay a community-rated premium (which would come with a risk-adjusted payment from the Government). This reform remains far from being realised due to rigidly defined entitlements in insurance legislation, price regulation, and lack of information, all of which hamper abilities to adequately risk adjust premiums, to contract effectively with providers and to vertically integrate with other providers (van Doorslaer and Schut, 2000). Greß *et al.* (2002) have shown that greater competition between sickness funds in Germany has led to considerable switching between such funds by consumers. However, much of the success of the German reforms (i.e. in achieving switching behaviour) is based on risk selection, with better off clients moving into low-cost plans. Greß *et al.* (2002) state that, without a more advanced risk-adjustment mechanism, such reforms threaten the stability of the health care system.

Returning to the US, further complicating factors appear to be health status and income levels, as well as the related issue of age. Ware *et al.* (1996) found that elderly and poor chronically ill sub-groups in HMO plans had worse physical outcomes than in FFS systems, but that this difference was not observed for the average patient. Yet another study, which perhaps supports these results, found that HMO hospital re-admission in the frail elderly was greater than that for patients in FFS plans (Experton *et al.*, 1999). In addition, a recent study found that those who are unhealthy are more likely to have greater satisfaction with FFS plans, while healthy individuals are more likely to report a higher level of satisfaction with HMO plans (Dellana and Glascoff, 2001). In essence, the interpretation here is that those who need less services tend to favour HMO plans, which does fit with the evidence of lower utilization rates in HMOs. Referring back to Kemper *et al.* (1999), it would indeed appear that HMOs will appeal to some individuals and not others.

Earlier evidence, also relating to this issue of sub-groups within the general population, is provided by part of the RAND HIE. Here, 1673 individuals were randomly assigned to one HMO or to an FFS plan in which care was provided free at the point of delivery (Ware *et al.*, 1986). On average, those people assigned to the HMO suffered no adverse effects when compared with those in the 'free' FFS plan. However, health outcomes in the two systems of care differed for those individuals in both high- and low-income groups who began the experiment with health problems. For those in the high-income group who were initially sick, the HMO produced significant improvements in cholesterol levels and in general health ratings by comparison with the free FFS plan. For those in the low-income group (i.e. those in the lower fifth of the income distribution) who were initially sick, HMO care resulted in significantly more bed-days per year due to poor health, more serious symptoms and a greater risk of dying compared with free FFS care. However, this evidence was disputed by Wagner and Bledsoe (1990) who claim that such differences may be due to chance as analyses of results by income group were based on small sample sizes and large standard deviations.

The suggestion from this evidence is that HMOs may have to select risks in order to achieve cost savings without adversely affecting health. This confirms results from other work on risk selection in HMOs (Berki *et al.*, 1977; Juba *et al.*, 1980; Buchanan and Cretin, 1986; Moser, 1987; Porell and Turner, 1990), although such results have been recently contradicted in the study by Schaefer and Reschovsky (2002) showing the main attraction of HMOs to be that of being lower cost regardless of risk status. Whether HMOs select good risks or good risks select HMOs is not clear. Potentially sicker people may prefer to stay in an FFS system. It should be noted, however, that such selection (or 'cream skimming') is consistent with what one would expect in competitive environments (see section in Chapter 3 above).

One suggested way of overcoming such problems is a 'community rated' voucher system which would give poor risks more purchasing power than good risks (Goldsmith, 1988). It has been asserted in public discussion of this strategy that the administration of such a system may be very costly relative to many existing systems and, if consumers were free to 'top up' their contributions, access to better quality care may be restricted to higher income groups, thus resulting in a two-tier system. It has also been argued that, for certain groups, such as older people, a voucher system would do little to alleviate their lack of ability to cope with the complexities of the medical care market (Oberlander, 1998). We do not know of any evidence, however, on any of these points.

Finally, different models of HMO plan type may effect utilization and quality of care. Group and staff models have rosters of patients and display similar characteristics to the 'gatekeeping' model used in general practice in the UK NHS. Independent practice associations (IPAs) use FFS-remuneration, and practitioners see only some HMO patients. The latter are less restrictive and, in some plans, patients can even self-refer to specialists. A study in the early 1990s compared a random sample of 42 staff, group and IPA model HMOs and found that group and staff model HMOs scored more favourably than IPA models on level of services provided, preventive care and various quality of care outcomes (Burns, 1991). Interestingly, however, IPA models were found to result in better patient satisfaction and access. The lesson here, of course, is that not all HMO plans are alike, and thus caution must be asserted in making sweeping claims, in terms of service utilization and quality, between HMO and FFS systems. Of note, a recent study by Reschovsky *et al.* (2000) made the similar point, in their more detailed investigation of managed care, as they delineated between FFS, PPOs, open model HMOs and closed model HMOs.

So, where does all of this evidence leave us, specifically in terms of the countering effect of HMOs on consumer moral hazard? The first point to highlight, as was likely observed in reading this sub-section, is that HMOs also rely on providers of care to change their behaviour, as a response to being faced with a fixed budget per annum. Thus, HMOs act simultaneously on consumer and provider moral hazard. As HMOs vertically integrate financial arrangements, making the HMO financially responsible for primary and hospital care, they affect both primary and hospital doctors, which are topics for consideration in the following two chapters. The second take home message from the studies reported here is that the evidence is not completely clear. Reasons for the difficulty in deciphering clear effects of HMOs on utilization and outcomes are that, overall, there have been relatively few studies which have explicitly examined these issues, and those that have often used different methods and have varying scope (Miller and Luft, 1997, 2002). Coupled with the different types of HMO plans, the ability to make an overall assessment is limited. At issue, and the third key message on this topic, is whether HMOs can lower total resource consumption while improving quality (Miller and Luft, 1997). While the evidence, on balance, may suggest that utilization rates with HMO plans are reduced, it is simply not clear whether total health care costs are also lower (Sullivan, 2001).

If anything, it seems that the market is simply segmenting in a natural way, with consumers choosing the plans which suit them best. Indeed, Kwon (1997) has shown theoretically and empirically that consumers will trade-off quality and premium level to select the combination desired, resulting in FFS plans being associated with both higher income (and, thus, willingness to pay) and higher severity of illness amongst enrollees. Indeed, other analyses have shown that the market is responding to such a situation with increasing enrollment in more-traditional Blue Cross and Blue Shield plans since the mid-1990s and, to compete with this, managed care plans are now offering less restrictive and higher cost packages (Cunningham and Sherlock, 2002; Draper *et al.*, 2002). This may be a good thing, but does counter any evidence that HMOs reduce costs overall. Evidence of this has been shown recently by Altman and Levitt (2002), demonstrating, in a simple chart, that, over the years, no major reform of the US system, including managed care, has abated cost increases. Lee and Tollen (2002) claim that health care premiums in the US rose by 11 per cent in 2001 and were forecast to increase by 12.7 per cent in 2002. In short, reducing premiums for good risks will not reduce overall system costs. What is needed, thus, is more research to assess fully the extent to which HMOs affect consumer behaviour in health care, and the related impact on both services used and health outcomes obtained.

Preferred Provider Organisations

Despite having been around for almost two decades, the literature pertaining to PPOs is limited, particularly with respect to evidence on cost and quality. PPOs contract with lower cost doctors and hospitals and offer themselves to company employees at a lower cost than competing alternatives. Consumers may choose between the contractors and remain free to use other providers of care, but on less favourable terms.

The most interesting evidence on PPOs comes from the US Government's Civilian Health and Medical Program of the Uniformed Services (CHAMPUS) Reform Initiative, which began in 1988. A private contractor was paid on a capitated basis to provide service for all beneficiaries residing in the demonstration areas. For such beneficiaries, there was a choice between maintaining current coverage or registering with an open-enrollment HMO or a PPO. Physicians were reimbursed through FFS. In the PPO option, co-payment was reduced by 5 per cent from the standard rate but non-network providers could be used at the standard rate. In contrast, those in the HMO plan were limited to network providers but received better preventive care coverage and faced lower out-of-pocket costs. For both plan types, cost control was attempted through utilization review and fee discounts.

A study by Goldman (1995) found that both HMOs and PPOs have lower costs through deterring inpatient admissions rather than lower length of stay, and that HMOs have higher use of ambulatory care relative to PPO and FFS models. This author goes on to state that evidence found in this initiative supports the finding from the HIE that beneficiaries respond to the level of coverage provided. Further work on the CHAMPUS Reform Initiative found that managed care models reduced utilization but maintained patient access and satisfaction, in comparison to matched control sites (Zwanziger *et al.*, 2000). Interestingly, because of its lower out-of-pocket costs and minimal control mechanisms, the HMO plan was attractive to many patients. However, as a result, the HMO option increased costs to government as a result of higher utilization and administration expenses (Zwanziger *et al.*, 2000). The point made here is that HMO plans generally keep costs down with control mechanisms such as capitation and gatekeeping which offset pressure resulting from low co-payments, but such control mechanisms were not in place in this initiative. This conclusion is supported by findings in which the HMO and PPO affects on government costs were disaggregated, with the observed increase due to HMO enrollees (Goldman *et al.*, 1995). Unfortunately, none of the reported findings on this unique initiative explicitly state the potential effects of the PPO plans on activity and costs independent of the HMO results. As such, we now turn to several other studies which have examined PPOs.

Attempting to control for case mix in comparing PPO and non-PPO users with one of seven primary care diagnoses in a Californian health care plan, Wouters (1990) found that outpatient expenditures were likely to increase as a result of PPO use. This may be consistent with less inpatient use. Drug costs were also higher, whilst diagnostic costs were lower for PPO users. Again attempting to control for case mix, Garrick *et al.* (1990) analysed non-PPO and PPO claims data by episode of care for patients. For PPO patients, charges per doctor were lower but charges per episode of care were higher. The authors concluded that the increased frequency of visits may have been doctor induced, to offset discounts, or patient generated, since there were no co-payments in the PPO. However, it is the doctor who is likely to have more of an influence on the content of the episode once the patient has made initial contact. Zwanziger and Auerbach (1991) found that PPO enrollees incurred increased expenditures as a result of expanded outpatient use and ineffective utilization management which swamped the effects of reductions in inpatient use and discounted fees.

Further evidence comes from a study which examined 1996–97 data from 27 257 non-elderly individuals covered by private insurance. Individuals were grouped into one of four insurance types and measures included utilization and patient satisfaction (Reschovsky *et al.*, 2000). Key findings were that the use of primary care increases and the use of specialists is reduced in moving from FFS to PPO to open model HMOs and to closed model HMOs. The study also found similar rates of preventive care, hospital use and surgeries between groups, and that patient satisfaction was lower with closed model HMOs. One final point of importance in relation to consumer moral hazard is the finding that the likelihood of having unmet or delayed care did not vary between plan type. Behind this finding is that those in less managed care plans are less likely to cite problems with provider access and convenience and more likely to cite financial barriers to care. As with the CHAMPUS studies, this would seem to imply the need to examine issues of demand and supply factors in tandem in attempting to counter moral hazard.

As Smith (1997) points out, after presenting results from data collected in the late 1980s that PPO plans appear to be cost saving in comparison to traditional plans, issues of access, quality, consumer satisfaction and provider satisfaction all require greater attention as research in this area continues. One California-based study which has addressed satisfaction, at least with respect to preventive services, found that PPO enrollees were less satisfied with preventive care than HMO enrollees (Schauffler and McMenamin, 2001). On the other hand, another measure of satisfaction is the growing importance of PPOs, as consumers in the US are turning to them as well as to the more-traditional 'Blues', offering more limited coverage for a broader range of services *vis-à-vis* comprehensive coverage for a limited range of services, which is the traditional managed-care approach. As noted in the previous section, this is adding to health-care cost growth in the US and, thus, is being combined with a return to greater use of user charges and MSAs in attempts to combat the premium growth also referred to above (Robinson, 2002), with the consequent possible effects described earlier in this chapter. Noting the exponential growth of PPOs since their inception (Verrilli and Zuckerman, 1996), clearly more work in this area is warranted before firm conclusions can be drawn.

Non-price rationing

There is also little evidence about the effect of waiting time on use of services for which there is no monetary cost. The main point with non-price rationing, such as waiting time, is that in largely publicly funded health systems, waiting time can be used to limit demand where patients would otherwise incur zero cost at point of care (Cullis *et al.*, 2000). As such, waiting time becomes another mechanism to counter consumer moral hazard. Waiting for health services is commonly employed in Canada, Britain, Australia, New Zealand and the Nordic countries (Cullis *et al.*, 2000).

At issue is whether health outcomes are adversely effected due to the imposed waiting for services (Naylor, 1991). In comparing wait time and outcomes for knee replacement surgery between Canada and the US Coyte *et al.* (1994) found that although Canadian patients do wait longer for surgery, overall satisfaction levels between the two groups were similar. In fact, a series of recent studies based on Canadian, US and UK data on surgery for hip fractures have consistently found that wait time is not a determinant of post-surgical mortality (Hamilton *et al.*, 1996; Hamilton and Bramley-Harker, 1999; Ho *et al.*, 2000). However, two studies have found that pre-surgical delay is associated with post-surgical hospital length of stay (Hamilton *et al.*, 2000; Ho *et al.*, 2000). Another interesting finding from this body of work is that higher income individuals had slightly shorter waits for surgery, but that income has no effect on post-surgical outcomes (Hamilton *et al.*, 1996).

Further evidence on waiting time for general practitioner care has been cited by Potter and Porter (1989). Using data from the RAND HIE and the University of Minnesota Centre for Health Services Research (1987) and from Bloom and Fendrick (1987), they estimated that mean waiting times in the UK and the US were one day and three days respectively. They also concluded that outpatient waiting times were about the same for both countries, but that access to specialists in the US was, in general, greater. Despite this latter result, the longest waits for specialists in the UK were for elective procedures (e.g. 80 days for plastic surgery) with those treatments requiring more urgent attention receiving such attention (e.g. pulmonology). However, US–Canada comparisons have revealed that the population in the latter country wait 3–4 times longer for radiation therapy for various types of cancer (Mackillop *et al.*, 1995), although this study was not set up to examine delays in diagnosis in the US which are caused by financial barriers to access (Cella *et al.*, 1991; Mandeblatt *et al.*, 1991), or impacts of such delays on outcomes. To date, most of the work in this area has focused on length of stay and mortality data, but of course, health outcome can also be measured in terms of quality of life, and it is here that more research is required (Naylor, 1991). Further, if it is found there is greater morbidity due to waiting in various specialty areas, decision-makers must also recognize that there is an opportunity cost associated with decreasing the wait time (Naylor, 1991). That is, as the resources required to decrease waiting time could be used elsewhere in the health system, the benefits lost from those alternative uses of the resources must be weighed against the benefit gained through having people waiting for a shorter period of time. Such analyses will not be easy, but are necessary to assess the full impact of wait time on health outcomes, and ultimately how best to use the limited resources available in the health system. One recent study, using administrative data, has shown that longer waits for surgery for five common surgical procedures are not associated with increased primary care costs pre- or post-operatively and that shorter waits are associated with longer stays in hospital (Quan *et al.*, 2002). This indicates that surgeons are setting priorities appropriately.

In summary, while the evidence to date does not indicate that waiting time has an adverse effect on outcomes, further work is required to make a more complete assessment. Based on the data that is available, it is plausible to conclude that non-price rationing through wait time does appear to be a valid option in curbing demand for services and thus is a potentially sound mechanism for countering consumer moral hazard. Naylor *et al.* (1993) reinforce this point by stating that such rationing, by clinical urgency, has inherent advantages in terms of meeting need than does rationing by price or insurance. It should be pointed out, however, that the analogy between a price and waiting is not exact (Lindsay, 1980). There is a 'cost' of waiting imposed on patients, but in the NHS, it is not one that is avoided by not joining a waiting list, unless one moves into the private sector (Culyer and Cullis, 1976; Cullis and Jones, 1985). As a means of rationing resources within publicly funded health systems, therefore, waiting time provides no 'deterrent effect' on the demand for care (unless one dies while waiting). It is important to distinguish between the sort of time-cost that does operate like a price (e.g. travel time, waiting in a surgery), which is avoidable by not demanding care, and waiting for an appointment or for admission, the 'costs' of which are not avoided by not being put on a waiting list, except by incurring further expense (through private insurance or direct out-of-pocket payment) in 'going private'.

CONCLUSIONS

Not surprisingly, the evidence suggests that, at the individual level, introducing cost-sharing results in reduced utilization of health care relative to free care at the point of delivery. Further, there is evidence to show that most of this reduction in utilization is by people in lower income groups and even children. The evidence additionally suggests that it is effective treatments for which demand is reduced as well as trivial or placebo care. On top of these equity implications, the irony is that, at the level of the health care system, charging patients for care in high-income countries is unlikely to save health care costs if doctors still remain free to concentrate their demand-inducing abilities on those who can afford to pay. The result would be that the same amount of money is spent on health care but to less effect on the health of the community, as those more in need of care would have less access to it. Thus, naive neoclassical solutions to consumer moral hazard may have serious unintended consequences which will not be picked up by neoclassical analysis of their implementation. Charging (small amounts) for care in lower income countries, however, should not be dismissed to the same extent, largely because there simply may be no other alternative method of raising funds for the system. However, the claims that charges have equity-inducing effects should be treated with great caution; vulnerable groups can be adversely affected.

In response to proponents of charges (who he sees as medical associations and private insurance companies in Canada), Evans (1990a) has summed up the evidence as follows:

> There is an occasional nod in the direction of the conventional rhetoric of economics, that charging 'consumers' of health care will result in reduced utilization and costs, but it is quite obvious that no one really believes this. If medical associations thought that there was any risk of a reduction in their members' workloads and incomes, they would not be such staunch advocates of charging patients. In fact, however, medical associations are quite familiar with the American experience, showing that utilization rates continue to climb even at very high rates of direct patient payment.

MSAs are likely to have similar effects to user charges, combining a lack of cost savings for the system overall with undesirable equity effects. This may be why, to date, they have not caught the imagination of policy-makers or health care consumers.

Through less hospital use, HMOs result in less costly modes of care compared to insurance plans with effectively free care at the point of delivery although, once again, this seems to be at the expense of people in low-income groups. It remains unclear the extent to which such 'savings' are built on the back of risk selection too. Surprisingly, there has been much less research on the impacts of PPOs. Once again, however, for the system overall, it seems that such managed care innovations have failed to contain health care costs. This is likely because the basis of much of the US system is still one which allows a greater degree of consumer choice than in other countries. In such circumstances, consumers can, and now do, elect to go into higher cost plans. Good risks can elect themselves into lower cost plans, but saving costs for them will not save costs for the whole system.

Little is known about the effect of non-price rationing, such as using waiting time. Some studies have shown that longer waits are not detrimental in terms of health effects, whilst others have shown that such waits are associated with longer post-surgical lengths of stay. Access to primary care does not seem to be a problem in more publicly orientated systems relative to the US, although access to more specialist services is less (in the sense of taking longer) in such public systems. However, as pointed out by Naylor (1991), the basis of such public systems (i.e. allocation according to clinical urgency rather than ability to pay) does have some inherent advantages in allowing the system to meet more need. This would make such a system more likely to meet the equity objectives outlined in Chapter 5. Given the lack of ability of the above interventions to control costs, it is likely that the public system is more efficient too.

Keeler *et al.* (1985) noted that, although free care resulted in better control of hypertension than charging, effects in both charged and free-care groups were greater in those who had an initial screening examination after which personal doctors were notified of patients' hypertension status. Once again, as with HMO results reported above and suggestions that charges do not deal adequately with provider moral hazard, such results highlight the importance of influencing providers of care as well as, and perhaps to a greater extent than, consumers. This is where the emphasis in public systems, such as in the UK and Canada, is placed, and it is this side of the market to which we now turn.

COUNTERING DOCTOR MORAL HAZARD

INTRODUCTION

Provider moral hazard can take one of two forms: specifically, that which occurs within identifiable actors in the health care system, for the most part doctors; and, more generally, that which occurs within institutions, without being narrowed down to the behaviour of identifiable individuals or groups of people. In this chapter, we are concerned with the former of these. In the next chapter, the latter issue will be addressed within the context of different financial arrangements for payment of hospitals for the care they provide.

Moral hazard on the part of doctors occurs for two related reasons. First, on the supply side, a third party (such as an insurance company or a government agency) often pays for care which is provided by doctors. With this third party bearing the costs of care, doctors will have few incentives to moderate the amount of care they supply. They do not have to bear the full costs of their decision-making and are often not even aware of the costs they have incurred. Second, on the demand side, there is asymmetry of information between patients and doctors regarding the technological relationship between health care and its effects on health. In such situations, the patient seeks advice on what services to demand from the very person who is supplying these services, the doctor. Thus, the doctor is placed in the unusual position of being both a demander and a supplier of a service for which s/he bears little, if any, financial burden. Such a situation will almost inevitably lead to overutilisation of services. This latter type of doctor moral hazard is most often associated with systems of payment based on fee-for-service (FFS) in which the doctor receives a fee for each item of work performed (e.g. an operation or a consultation). More work done leads to more income for the doctor. It is often claimed that much of this work results in 'overuse'; that is, for services which are of little or no therapeutic value *vis-à-vis* the cost of providing them. In a perfect market, with fully knowledgeable consumers, provision would be less. But it should be remembered that such markets still fail to account for certain factors, such as externalities. Thus, some 'overuse' of services may be warranted, implying that some doctor moral hazard is efficient. So, certain types of doctor behaviour, such as supplier induced demand, should not be seen as all 'bad'.

Thus, an important part of the health care funding debate relates to the method of payment of doctors; different payment systems have different financial incentives for doctors which in turn have different implications for the cost and quality of care provided. For example, some methods of payment may restrict costs but have more adverse effects than other methods on the use of services by the population as a whole, on the use of services by different groups within the population and on the population's health status. It is the aim of this chapter to summarise the available evidence (mostly from the US) on the effect of different methods of paying doctors in terms of these three criteria. Once again, the importance of this evidence depends on health service objectives. Therefore, the chapter will conclude by considering the results in the light of some of these objectives.

METHODS OF PAYING DOCTORS

In two comprehensive reviews of methods of remunerating doctors, Maynard *et al.* (1986) and Donaldson and Gerard (1989a) outlined six main ways of paying doctors: (i) FFS remuneration; (ii) salaries; (iii) reorganisation of allowances in order to permit payment for 'good practice', assessment being based on standards, which may be set by professionals themselves; (iv) capitation payments for primary care, or to cover all costs of care, as in the case of health maintenance organisations (HMOs) in the US and general practitioner fundholding in the UK (Secretaries of State, 1989), although, in most cases, fundholding covered only a limited range of maternity, diagnostic and elective hospital services; (v) charges to patients for a part or the full cost of care; and (vi) private practice, allowing market forces to determine both quality and rewards. Another form of influence on doctors' activities, though not strictly financial, is direct government regulation of what they can and cannot do. This can have a financial element in that if doctors do not behave accordingly, they could be subjected to financial penalties. Governments in, for example, Australia, Norway and the UK have used this type of control to limit the range of drugs which general practitioners can prescribe. Another recent attempt to control drug costs has been reference-based pricing, whereby a regulator (usually a government) classifies drugs according to ingredients and funds in full the least cost drug in the class, with the extra costs of other drugs being met by the patient or some other funder, depending on the scheme.

The first three and the last (i.e. direct regulation) of the above forms of payment/control mainly affect doctor behaviour as does the fourth as usually defined. However, capitation payments within HMOs aim to give both doctor and patient incentives to provide, and look for, low cost care of acceptable quality. Therefore, it is important to examine evidence on the effect of HMOs on doctor behaviour when reviewing methods of remuneration. The fifth method, charges, is clearly aimed at patients rather than doctors and has been discussed in detail in the previous chapter. Charges to patients will not be discussed any further in this chapter, but, as we have pointed out in Chapter 6, it would be naive to assume that they will affect only patient behaviour. Charges may reduce (or control) use of services by some groups of patients, but, if this is the case, doctors remain free to switch their demand-inducing abilities to those willing and able to pay for care.

The sixth method of payment, through market forces, is not reviewed here because, in its present form, it would open up the market to non-qualified practitioners which could affect the quality of service unacceptably. Not since the commencement of registration for doctors allowing the exclusion of non-qualified practitioners (in the early twentieth century in countries such as Australia and the UK) has such a situation existed (Peterson, 1978; Allen, 1982).[1] Thus, market forces beyond the elements of competition which exist in the six other alternatives are unlikely to appear on the shortlist of options in a review of the payment of doctors.

FFS remains an important form of remuneration and has probably been researched more than other methods, usually within the context of trying to detect whether supplier-induced demand exists or not. Therefore, we start with discussion of the evidence on FFS, what it implies for the existence of supplier-induced demand and the extent to which this matters for health policy.

FEE FOR SERVICE: DOES SUPPLIER INDUCEMENT REALLY EXIST?

Supplier-induced demand: evidence and explanations

Remunerating doctors by fees for each item of service provided rewards doctors according to the amount of work carried out. The conventional wisdom is that this encourages the use of services by patients on the recommendation of their doctors, thus inflating health care costs with possibly little or no effect on health itself. This power of doctors to recommend, or induce, demand for their services is known as 'supplier-induced demand'. In line with our definition of provider moral hazard, supplier-induced demand is the amount of demand, induced by doctors, which exists beyond what would have occurred in a market in which consumers are fully informed.

The phenomenon is thought to be more likely to exist in systems of remuneration based on FFS rather than under alternative reimbursement mechanisms. However, despite the many indications from empirical work as to the existence of supplier inducement in FFS environments, neoclassical (and other) economists remain convinced that observed increases in health care utilisation which can be 'explained' by the inducement hypothesis can also be 'explained' by the straightforward market forces outlined in Chapter 2. This point is explored in more detail below.

Another dilemma in this field is that 'true competitive prices' for doctors' services are not known. In FFS systems, problems of how much care is provided only arise if fees actually depart from these true competitive prices. Thus, in accordance with the conventional wisdom of the supplier-induced-demand school, if the fee is greater than its true competitive price, there will be an incentive to overprovide.

But contrary to this conventional wisdom, if the fee is below its true competitive price, there will be an incentive to underprovide care. Therefore, although supplier inducement may be shown to exist for some types of care, this may not be the case across the board. This argument is further complicated, however, by the hypothesis that doctors have in mind some 'target income' which they seek to achieve (Evans, 1974). In such a case, general underpricing of fee levels may lead to greater provision of services than if fees were, in general, higher. By providing more services, doctors maintain their target income.

Adding to this the argument that some utilisation above the truly competitive level may be justified anyway (because of externalities), one is left to judge how much of each type of care provided is appropriate. So-called 'overutilisation' may be appropriate in that it is still allocatively efficient. We have already seen, in Chapter 6, how charges for care lead to reductions in utilisation by certain groups for some well proven therapies. The basic problem, noted by Loft and Mooney (1989) and still relevant today, is that, despite the proliferation of evidence-based medicine, so little is known about what represents best medical practice in the sense of being either effective or efficient.

Therefore, much of the evidence cited in the remainder of this sub-section may appear ambiguous, depending on which way one looks at it. This evidence is of three types: cross-country comparisons of health care utilisation and doctor payment; tests of the effects of changes in doctor to population ratios on utilisation and on doctors' fees; and quasi-experimental.

Early research in this area resulted in a considerable body of evidence from cross-country comparisons showing that (after controlling for differences in age, sex and population) higher rates of common surgical procedures in Canada and the US compared with those in the UK are due to factors such as lack of agreement about indications for surgery, variations in use of technology, national priorities and values, and payment of a fee for service in Canada and the US, and not to differences in the incidence or prevalence of disorders. The different rates appear to have little effect on outcome; although the latter have been measured only crudely (Vayda, 1973; McPherson *et al.*, 1981; Vayda *et al.*, 1982; McPherson *et al.*, 1982; Vayda *et al.*, 1984).

Some studies have examined the effect of increases in doctor-to-population ratios within specified geographical areas in health care systems based on FFS remuneration. For example, in response to an increase in the supply of doctors, doctors may encourage patients to use more services in order to maintain their income. This is supposed to explain the noted correlation between increased numbers of doctors within a geographical area and increased use of services (Fuchs, 1978; Cromwell and Mitchell, 1986; Phelps, 1986).

However, there are other possible explanations. The neoclassical interpretation would be that greater numbers of doctors increase their availability to patients, other access costs are reduced or the increase in use as supply increases may simply be meeting previously unmet needs. With supply increasing, fees and non-monetary costs (related to waiting time and access) go down and, naturally, the amount of care demanded by patients will increase (i.e. there is a movement along the demand curve as 'price' falls). Increased utilisation is compatible with both hypotheses and can be interpreted as either a demand shift initiated by doctors or as a normal market response by consumers to lower costs to them.

Thus, it seems that studies employing doctor-to-population ratios as an independent variable provide ambiguous results. However, as Reinhardt (1978) has argued there is still one unambiguous test of supplier inducement using such ratios: that is, a test of the effect of doctor supply on doctors' fees. Neoclassical theory predicts a negative effect on fees with an increase in supply (i.e. if supply goes up, price, or fees, should go down). Fees could also fall in an inducement world, but only in an inducement world could fees rise or be maintained at the level they were previous to the increase in supply. With fees as the dependent variable in an econometric model, then, assuming other variables are adequately controlled for, a zero or positive coefficient for the doctor–population ratio independent variable is not compatible with neoclassical theory; supplier-induced demand exists.

Despite being the definitive test when using doctor to population ratios, there is little evidence regarding the effects of such ratios on doctor fees. Wilensky and Rossiter (1983) found the effect of such ratios to be insignificant in each of five model specifications, a finding which Rice and Labelle (1989) consider to be 'most readily consistent with the demand-inducement model'. Cromwell and Mitchell (1986) found a strong, positive influence of surgeon density on surgeon fees.

Despite the argument in favour of effects on fees being the unambiguous test, it is possible that non-financial demand-side factors (such as access and waiting costs) are reduced by an increase in the supply of doctors to a level whereby so much demand is forthcoming that fees are pushed up beyond their previous levels. So, once again the evidence is ambiguous.

One Irish study of general practitioners used doctor-to-population ratios as an independent variable, but with more detailed survey data which discriminated between patient- and doctor-initiated return visits (Tussing and Wojtowycz, 1986). They found a positive relationship between doctor-to-population ratios and the proportion of return visits arranged by the doctor.

Using a quasi-experimental before-and-after type design, an examination of the effect of increasing reimbursement rates for some services and decreasing the rates for others in Colorado's Medicare system found that a 1 per cent decrease in the reimbursement rate for medical services resulted in a 0.61 per cent increase in medical service intensity (measured by numbers of standard units of quantity provided) and that a 1 per cent decrease in the reimbursement rate for surgical services resulted in a 0.15 per cent increase in the intensity of the surgical services provided (Rice, 1983). Similar results were shown for auxiliary services, such as laboratory tests. Changes in practice and doctor characteristics over time were controlled for and these results appear to be consistent with doctors adjusting patient use so as to maintain a target income (Evans, 1974).

Two subsequent analyses lent some further support to the 'target income' hypothesis. The first was of US and Canadian data on doctor services per capita and doctor fees (Fuchs and Hahn, 1990). Using 1985 data, fees for procedures were about three times higher in the US than in Canada, whilst those for evaluation and management were about 80 per cent higher. However, per capita use of services is higher in Canada, the authors suggesting that this may result from universal insurance and 'from encouragement of use by the larger number of doctors who are paid lower fees'.

The second study, in Copenhagen, investigated the effects of changing general practitioners' remuneration from a capitation-based system to a mixed FFS and capitation system (Krasnik *et al.*, 1990). The behaviour of practitioners in Copenhagen City, where the change took place, was compared with that of practitioners in Copenhagen County, where remuneration remained the same; the latter group was already on the mixed remuneration system. Patient contacts did not increase significantly, despite payment of a fee for service. However, rates of examinations and treatments that attracted specific additional remuneration rose significantly. Referral rates to secondary care and hospital fell, a result confirmed by a less-rigorous subsequent study in Germany (Kinder, 2001).

Does all of the above evidence support the existence of supplier-inducement? Not necessarily. Mooney (1994) in a re-interpretation of the Copenhagen study, states that rates of examination and other treatments attracting fees increased precisely because a fee was paid for them, whereas this had not been the case before. A neoclassical argument, therefore, would say that a change in price (from zero to some fee level) caused a movement along the supply curve in a positive direction. More recent work from Norway, in which it was possible to compare physicians remunerated by FFS (who, it could be argued, would respond to greater competition by increasing activity) with those remunerated by salary (who would not be motivated to respond in such a way), showed that neither group increased output in response to changes in physician density (Grytten and Sorensen, 2001). This result is consistent with those of other studies (Stano, 1985; Grytten *et al.*, 2001).

Thus, as Phelps (1986) points out, the empirical work seems to have reached the limit of its ability to inform us on this issue; some studies have not been able to detect supplier-induced demand, whilst others, but not all, it seems, can be reinterpreted using a non-inducement argument. There remains the question of what level of supplier-induced demand is optimal. The Copenhagen study suggested that it is possible to encourage GPs to carry out some procedures on an FFS basis, thereby resulting in more of these procedures being conducted in general practice and less in hospital. Whether this is more efficient is not answered in the study – or in any other that we know. The existence of externalities also suggests that some level of supplier-induced demand (rather than none) is optimal. Thus, in line with Mooney's reinterpretation of the Copenhagen study, it may not really matter whether supplier-inducement exists. Rather, we know doctors respond to incentives, and we can design incentive systems, therefore, to encourage 'optimal inducement'.

Finally, much of the research on FFS has begged the question if this form of remuneration is so bad, why do several countries stick with it. One reason, identified by Emery *et al.* (1999) amongst others, is that a FFS system involves less financial risk for physicians. Passing on financial risk to doctors, through a capitation system, for example, which sets an explicit limit on available resources, means that budgets have to be set accurately. If this cannot be done, governments will then have to think about how to deal with the likely overspends which would follow, which is especially problematic for a highly politicised good like health care. Robinson (2001), in outlining four key features of clinical practice (for more on this, see below) argues that FFS wins out over capitation on two of these; physician productivity and patient service (where we want long hours, many procedures and attentiveness to the needs of individual patients) and risk acceptance (as discussed above). These arguments are supported by the Copenhagen study, but also by an earlier empirical study which showed that moving from FFS to salary can lead to inappropriately low levels of home visiting by GPs (Kristiansen and Holtedahl, 1993). Thus, it seems that the choice is not a dichotomous one (i.e. FFS versus some other payment system), but that FFS has a place within any remuneration system, being used to meet some health care objectives to which other remuneration methods are less suited.

Intervening to set fees

If it is thought necessary to control the powers of doctors to manipulate demand and fee setting, health policy-makers would appear to have two options as regards remuneration:

(1) Intervene heavily in fee setting, as many governments (Canada and Australia) and other third party payers (as in Germany) have done; or
(2) Move to a different form of payment altogether.

The latter course of action is discussed in the following section, whilst examples of the former course are the subject matter of the remainder of this sub section.

In Chapter 3, we discussed the roles of the Australian and Canadian Governments in fee setting. The reason for such intervention is that it is recognised that for public or private insurers to guarantee full payment of medical fees which are set by the medical profession itself would simply result in a climate of continual fee increases being met by private and public payers. This would substantially increase health care costs at possibly little or no benefit to patients.

What the experience of these countries demonstrates is that the responses of governments to such a problem could vary. In Australia, the Government sets its own fee schedule and reimburses only a fixed percentage of the fee (85 per cent for GP care and 75 per cent for hospital care, whilst for the latter the 'gap' between 75 and 100 per cent can be privately insured against). In general practice, doctors can accept the 85 per cent coverage as full payment, thus waiving the patient's obligation to make up the other 15 per cent of the fee. Doctors are free to charge at a rate above the Government's set fee, but the amount above the Government's fee cannot be privately insured against. Thus, there is a tendency for doctors to compete for patients by minimising patients' out-of-pocket contributions by directly billing the public funder (Medicare). The proportion of consultations directly billed has risen from 52 per cent in 1984–85, when Medicare was introduced, to 78 per cent in 1994–95 (Hall, 1999). Although there is the appearance of doctors being given 'freedom' to charge what they want, this competition drives fees down to the amounts funded by Government, thus giving the Government effective control over fee levels.

In Canada, the approach is more direct. Each Province produces a schedule of fees to which doctors must adhere. Attempts to control overall costs of physician billing have been introduced, however, through the use of physician expenditure caps in Alberta and Nova Scotia. These were introduced in 1992; in Alberta the total cap increased by 5.5 per cent in the first year, but was followed by reductions of 10 and 5 per cent in the two years after that, whilst, in Nova Scotia, there was no increase for the first two years and 3 per cent after that. Such an innovation raises interesting incentive issues. For government, the costs of 'policing' utilisation are reduced as they are less interested in what happens within the total spend. Physicians face a common property problem, whereby one physician's call on the budget reduces what is available for others. Therefore, Nova Scotia placed limits on each individual's spend, but Alberta did not. Yet, the latter controlled costs bet-ter, with increases in utilisation of just over 2 per cent in 1994–95 compared with 7 per cent in Nova Scotia. Hurley *et al.* (1997) have shown that Alberta's relative success is likely due to several other factors. First, the initial increased budget in Alberta likely affected physician's abilities to absorb the changes. Second, these abilities were likely enhanced by the higher fee levels and lower density of doctors in Alberta. Third, other factors were more likely the less personalised relationship between government and medical association in Alberta and the ways in which the membership of each association was consulted, a more inclusive approach having been taken in Alberta, giving individuals more of say in policy despite the cutbacks. In addition, the Alberta Government had a lot of popular support, mak-ing implementation less politically threatening to them.

Germany has had a bit more success with setting global budgets for physician expenditures, where, in 1987, caps were set to expand at the rate of growth in income per sickness fund member (Henke *et al.*, 1994). A conversion factor for lev-els of fees was retrospectively calculated each quarter; thus, during 1987, whilst billing grew by 9 per cent, physicians' incomes grew by only 0.5 per cent. This pro-gram has been modified since, with varying degrees of success. Some provinces in Canada have used a similar scheme of basing the subsequent year's fee increases (or clawbacks) on previous year's expenditure levels, but without an explicit cap (Ferrall *et al.*, 1998).

Even in the US, fees have been manipulated by regulators in order to achieve more efficient outcomes. This has been done by altering relative fee *levels*. Examples of this are: reductions in fees for surgical interventions (e.g. caesarian sections) in maternity care relative those for natural births, which successfully increased the rate of the latter and decreased the rate of the former (Gruber *et al.*, 1999); and raising Medicare fees for prenatal services relative to fees derived from other funders, which appears to have improved access and birth outcomes

(Currie *et al.*, 1995; Gray, 2001). Both Australian and Canadian systems lead to much conflict between the medical profession and government. However, a positive way of looking at this conflict is simply as a situation in which a strong supplier of services (the medical profession) meets a strong demander of services on the community's behalf (government). The result is some kind of compromise in fee levels which works in the interest of the greater good, similar to the invisible hand of Adam Smith in Chapter 2 when fragmented suppliers were faced with fragmented demanders. The worse scenario would be one in which one side or the other was fragmented whilst the other was united.

Another problem is that although regulation of fees gives governments control over fee levels, they do not have direct control over the volume of services provided. Indeed there was evidence from Canada that services per capita had continually risen since the introduction of public insurance (Barer *et al.*, 1988), leading some provinces to use global expenditure caps of the sort referred to above. However, the growth has been at no greater a rate than in the US despite maintenance of lower fees in Canada over the same period. In addition, presumably institutional constraints, such as hospital capacity, help to check the volume of services provided, particularly if governments have a large element of control over investment in such institutions (as is the case in Canada or Australia). It does seem that continual negotiation between the medical profession (as suppliers of care) and governmental bodies (as negotiators of price on patients' behalf) can be successful in preventing cost escalation.

Finally, a modification to fees, either as a supplement or as a substitute has been the use of target payments. In one study, by Kouides *et al.* (1998), the intervention was a target payment of an additional 10 per cent (US$0.80) or 20 per cent (US$1.60) payment on top of the standard fee of US$8 for each influenza immunisation made over the target rates of 70 and 85 per cent respectively of the eligible population registered with each primary care provider. In another, by Ritchie *et al.* (1992) FFS was replaced by a target payment whereby GPs received a lump sum if they immunised at least 70 per cent of the population and a higher such payment if they reached 90 per cent. These studies were the only two included in a systematic review of target payments by Giuffrida *et al.* (2002). The first randomly allocated 54 practices to receive the intervention or not, whilst the latter was an interrupted time series in 95 practices, with six observation points before and after the introduction of target payments. The Kouides *et al.* study showed increases in immunisation rates in the target payment group relative to the control group, but the differences were not statistically significant. The Ritchie *et al.* study could not show that the overall linear trend in primary and pre-school immunisation rates had changed. Less rigorous studies, ultimately not included in the systematic review, have each shown that target payments did have significant effects on the uptake of cervical smears and immunisations (Hughes and Yule, 1992; Fairbrother *et al.*, 1999). Giuffrida *et al.* (2002), however, conclude that there is insufficient evidence to conclude whether target payments are an effective method of improving quality of care. Despite this the intuitive logic of target payments has been taken up by the

UK Government in its new (as of 2003) GP contract, the core of which is FFS remuneration based on ten quality targets. However, concern has been expressed that pharmaceutical and other costs are likely to rise by focusing on such targets (e.g. for reducing cholesterol levels), the opportunity cost of which has not been assessed (Maynard, 2003).

Returning to an earlier argument, it also seems that, although tight control may be required when using fees as part of a remuneration package, they may still represent a useful form of payment for certain services. There could be areas to which a degree of importance is attached and for which targets have to be reached. For instance, the target may be 100 per cent coverage for vaccination rates; an obvious financial incentive being to offer a fee for each vaccination. In certain circumstances, FFS may result in improved effectiveness and less overall cost, and, thus be an important part of a blended payment system (Kristiansen and Holtedahl, 1993; Robinson, 2001).

ALTERNATIVES TO FEE FOR SERVICE

Salaries

Maynard *et al.* (1986) claimed that the advantages of a salaried system are that it would make health care planning easier, as doctors' salaries would be known in advance, and that promotion could be related to performance. They also noted some disadvantages. General practitioners and hospitals would have little incentive to compete for patients. Indeed, they may have an incentive to please superiors rather than meet the health care needs of patients. Continuity of care may suffer as primary care doctors, without a financial stake in their practice would be more likely to move away from their original locality. There may also be problems in motivating doctors who have reached the top of the promotion ladder. Non-financial considerations (such as ethics and caring) – which of course may be powerful – aside, why should a doctor, with a guaranteed salary, and no prospect of it increasing, do their best for the patient in front of them? The incentive may be for doctors to refer patients inappropriately to other departments or to other doctors in order to minimise time spent with them. Merit awards, if related to some index of performance, could be used to overcome this problem – current (i.e. 2002) UK National Health Service merit awards for consultants vary from £2360 per annum (a basic discretionary increment, of which there can be five awarded in total) to £56 090 per annum (roughly a doubling of salary earned from the NHS for a senior physician). However, the system of awards is not related to performance and tends to suffer from lack of fairness, openness and considerations of service contributions (Riordan, 2001). Although some have defended the UK system (Tobias, 1994), it is currently under review (Department of Health, 2001).

One US study of doctors serving as residents in a single clinic compared utilisation patterns under salaried and FFS payment regimes (Hickson *et al.*, 1987). Doctors were randomly assigned to receive a salary or FFS reimbursement: the latter group scheduled more visits per patient. No results were reported on diagnostic testing or on health status. Since this study, many others have made similar comparisons and have come up with similar results, as confirmed in two recent systematic reviews (Gosden *et al.*, 1999, 2002). Of course, for many of these subsequent studies the results are less rigorous, despite controlling for physician and patient characteristics, as it may be the case that lower users of resources self-selected into salaried remuneration schemes. A subsequent study from the Netherlands, still suffering from problems of selection bias, showed that salaried paediatricians spend longer with their patients than those remunerated by FFS (van Dulmen, 2000), and that this time was spent collecting clinically relevant data. It is acknowledged, however, that to treat the same number of patients, more paediatricians would have to be recruited under the salaried system. Hutchinson and Foley (1999) have also shown, in their Canadian study, that rates of antibiotic use are higher in FFS relative to salaried physicians, and, again, show that care in the salaried group is likely more appropriate. The explanation offered for such results is that FFS physicians have to cope with larger volumes of patients, who are also free to visit a competing physician, and so the patients are offered a prescription to prevent the latter occurring.

Finally, Chaix-Coutourier *et al.* (2000), in their systematic review, suggest that, where salaried remuneration has been forced upon physicians, they tend to trade income for leisure, a result reinforced by studies by Kristiansen and Holtedahl (1993) and Ferrall *et al.* (1998). It seems that there are no studies which have examined service use by different groups or impacts on health status.

Special payments for good practice

Under this method of payment, GPs would receive a combination of capitation fees, fees for items of service and some allowances, and hospital doctors would receive a basic salary with additional merit awards, as in the existing situation in the UK. The difference would be that allowances and merit awards would be based on 'good practice'.

Although there are significant challenges in measuring this on a routine basis (Hern, 1994), attempts have been made, although these have rarely been tied to a financial incentive scheme. There is evidence that doctors will respond to incentives to earn 'bonuses'. Health Stop, a major chain of for-profit ambulatory care centres in the US, paid its doctors a flat hourly wage until mid-1985, after which a system of bonuses was introduced whereby the doctor's bonus depended on the gross income individually generated (Hemenway *et al.*, 1990). Not surprisingly, in one year from the period under the waged system to that under the bonus scheme, the number of laboratory tests and x-rays performed per visit rose by 23 and 16 per cent respectively. Real revenue from charges grew by 20 per cent, mostly as a result of a 12 per cent increase in the average number of patient visits per month.

Of course, such changes may not be desirable, but, again, do demonstrate that doctors will respond to performance incentives placed in front of them. It is obviously important to tailor allowances and merit wards to the achievement of 'good practice' rather than simply doing more for patients. This would encourage more standard setting and review. Despite the challenges in defining 'good practice' mentioned above, a study analysing the costs and effects of standard setting in general practice for five common conditions of childhood in the North of England has shown that standards for common conditions of childhood can be compiled by small groups of physicians, and, in a controlled before and after study demonstrated for one condition, recurrent wheezy chest:

- Reduced prescribing of antibiotics but increased prescribing of therapeutic drugs (mainly bronchodilators and oral steroids), an overall small cost increase;
- Increased follow-up and better compliance with drugs;
- Substantially improved outcome relative to cost (outcome measured by the reduced numbers of days spent wheezing, breathless, coughing or awake at night) (North of England Study, 1990).

Thus, addressing standards can result in improvements in both process and outcome, and may result in a more efficient, if more costly, health service. For the four other conditions no outcome effects were detected. Drug costs were reduced for bedwetting, increased for acute vomiting and itchy rash, whilst antibiotic costs for acute cough fell along with an increase in the cost of bronchodilators. Experience in France has been rather different. Despite the implementation of regulatory practice guidelines there in 1993, awareness of guidelines amongst GPs is low (Durieux *et al.*, 2000) and has resulted in few changes in practice, even although it is possible for physicians to be fined (Durieux *et al.*, 2000). Although the impact of medical culture is difficult to measure, this is likely to explain some of the differences between the UK and France as well as the lack of incentives (or incentive enforcement) in the latter country (Durieux *et al.*, 2000; Shortell *et al.*, 2001).

Reviews of studies in which clinical guidelines have been evaluated by use of rigorous controlled comparisons have shown that virtually all led to improvements in the process of care, with a similar result for the smaller number of studies in which impacts on health outcomes were assessed (Grimshaw and Russell, 1993; Thomas *et al.*, 1998). Some impacts on health outcomes have been small, however, which raises questions about whether the benefits outweigh the costs. Current research is focusing on different ways of implementing guidelines and changing clinical practice, as, to date, many methods for doing this have produced disappointing results (Davis and Taylor-Vaisey, 1997; Wensing *et al.*, 1998; Heffner, 2001).

There is also limited evidence of the effect of peer review on the use of specific services, although peer review is common activity within HMOs and PPOs. Two studies have shown that providing clinicians with information on their own use of laboratory tests as well as that of their colleagues had no effect on laboratory use (Grivell *et al.*, 1981). Recent reviews of implementation of guidelines have shown that the effects on behavioural change are stronger when accompanied by reminder systems and interactive educational programmes (Grimshaw *et al.*, 2003).

127

The introduction of formulae for antibiotics in general medical practice has been shown to reduce antibiotic costs without increasing the number of patient consultations, home visits or referrals to hospital (Needham *et al.*, 1988). In addition to this, it has been demonstrated that examinations of general medical practitioners by trained assessors resulted in their prescribing fewer drugs than before examination whilst a control group prescribed more (Grol *et al.*, 1988). A subsequent review of formularies showed that those developed by consensus along with continuing education and feedback on drug usage saved costs. It was also shown that more appropriate drug use resulted, although the effects of such changes in practice on health status, however, have not been examined (Pearce and Begg, 1992). More recently, a before and after study in China showed substantial reductions in drug usage (from 67 per cent of medical costs in 1992 to 51 per cent in 1996) as a result of the introduction of a drug list policy and hospital expenditure capping (Hu *et al.*, 2001). However, the separate impacts of the policies could not be disentangled and, again, health impacts were not assessed.

Capitation

Capitation is often used as a method of payment in primary care. Doctors receive an annual payment in advance to care for each individual who elects to join their list. The main advantage claimed for this method is that it motivates doctors in the primary care sector to practice in a way that encourages patients to join their lists; although it would be to the doctor's advantage to attract only low-cost people. The early 1990s in the UK saw policy changes, whereby capitation rates increased from accounting for approximately 47 per cent of general practitioners' income to 60 per cent so as to give general practitioners more encouragement to compete to attract patients (Secretaries of State, 1989). Thus, practices which, according to patients, are more 'attractive', would be financially rewarded. The problem with this proposal is that very little is known about what patients take into account when assessing their general practitioner or, indeed, whether this is something which patients actively wish to do. Over the years, studies have shown a distinct lack of behaviour of the sort one would expect from the fully-informed consumer described in Chapter 2 in the way people choose their doctor (Leavy *et al.*, 1989; Salisbury, 1989; Donaldson *et al.*, 1991; Lupton *et al.*, 1991; Lupton, 1997; Meerabeau, 1998; Pector, 2000; Almond, 2001; Calnan and Gabe, 2001). Others are less negative, showing that many consumers do change GP due to dissatisfaction (Billinghurst and Whitfield, 1993), also by assessing aspects of quality (Bornstein *et al.*, 2000) and that US consumers do perceive differences in waiting times and access to specialists but less so with respect to provider quality (Harris *et al.*, 2002).

Another advantage of such per capita payments is that they sever the link between amount of service provided and financial reward and hence involve minimal distortion of purely professional medical judgement. Relative to FFS payment, capitation may encourage more preventive activities as the doctor's future income does not depend on further consultations resulting when the patient is ill.

However, guaranteed payment may encourage some GPs to cut their financial and personal costs by curtailing consultation time, by prescribing more, or by increased referral to hospitals. At the beginning of the 1990s, there was very little evidence on the effects of capitation, especially on health outcomes and quality of care. However, this literature has grown substantially over the past 10 years, especially in the US. Therefore, the remainder of this sub-section is divided further, to deal with capitation as it is usually thought about in non-US publicly funded systems and then with studies of managed care, most often in the form of HMOs, mostly in the US. Evidence on GP fundholding, which had been used in the UK NHS throughout most of the 1990s, will be presented in the first of these sub-sections, as it was a natural extension of the more-limited form of capitation.

Evidence on capitation in publicly funded systems

Although it is known that in European countries, other than the UK, GPs are more likely to refer public insurance patients (for whom they receive capitation) to hospital than privately insured patients (who pay on a FFS basis), it is not clear whether such differences in referral rates are due to the payment systems or the different health status of people in the public and private systems (Donaldson and Gerard, 1989a).

Other comparative evidence of specific changes towards capitated systems of payment is conflicting. A study of capitation against FFS and full capitation (through an HMO) in New York showed that capitated practices potentially would save Medicaid 38 per cent compared with matched groups of patients in the FFS system (Rosenthal *et al.*, 1996). However, this study was unable to control for physician selection (i.e. capitated practices may have been lower referrers already) or patient selection (i.e. lower cost patients may have selected capitated practices). In Norway, some municipalities elected to pay all GPs, in part, by capitation, with the proportion of income derived from FFS being reduced. Between 1993 and 1996, referrals by GPs involved in the experiment increased by 42 per cent (Iversen and Luras, 2000). This result is consistent with that from the Copenhagen experiment referred to in an earlier section of this chapter, which showed that a movement from capitation to part capitation/part FFS led to less referrals (Krasnik *et al.*, 1990) because, in the latter case, GPs were being paid fees to deal with cases in their own surgeries.

Another well-known experiment in the use of capitation rather than FFS took place in Ontario, Canada, with the introduction and expansion of Health Services Organisations (HSOs) there since the early 1970s. Contrary to expectations, Hutchison *et al.* (1996) found that capitation did not reduce hospitalisations, using a control group of general practitioners who remained in the FFS system as a basis of comparison. There are a number of explanations for such a result, as outlined in an excellent contextual paper on the history of this experiment by Gillett *et al.* (2001). First, there was no clear policy guidance from the Ontario Ministry of Health as to what was expected of HSOs. Second, the scheme was voluntary, and, therefore, populated by people who already agreed with the philosophy of capitation (i.e. they were already low referrers and, thus, unlikely to become even lower referrers as a result of the change in remuneration). Third, this situation was exacerbated by calculation of the capitation fees according to provincial average FFS payments. Practices participating in the HSO experiment, therefore, got more money than their already low-cost practice style warranted, and, given a lack of guidance from government, did not necessarily use the money in the ways expected; rather than providing more clinics and so on, some money was used to improve facilities and was even taken as income. Furthermore, assuming that the FFS practices continued to provide care in the ways they previously had done, overall costs to the system would rise, as those who are already low-cost providers (i.e. the ones who elected to become HSOs) would be receiving capitation payments based on the provincial average costs incurred in the FFS part of the sector. The experience related by Gillett *et al.* (2001) covers other reasons why this experiment did not appear to work and provides good contextual evidence on how *not* to set up such schemes, and, therefore, valuable information for any such future innovations.

The UK Government, in 1991, attempted to mitigate some of the problems of capitation by implementing a system of budgets for GPs from which payments could be made for diagnostic tests, surgery and maternity care provided in hospitals. This innovation was known as GP fundholding and ran under that name until the election of a Labour Government in 1997.[2] The current scheme is similar, and, it could be argued, has extended the range of hospital services which can be bought to virtually all such services. The fundholding practices were given a budget (which came out of the local health authority's funding allocation) from which to purchase care for their patients, including a limited range of hospital services, specialist services and drugs. It was believed that GPs would be more effective purchasers for their patients than a health authority manager. The GP was closer to the patients and thus presumably could act more effectively in meeting their needs and the GP was more able to negotiate with local hospitals. The mechanisms of having to keep within budget combined with the freedom of patients to change doctor were aimed at achieving greater fiscal responsibility and improvements in quality.

Entry into the fundholding scheme was voluntary, and initially open only to practices with 11 000 or more patients. Later, smaller practices with patient lists as low as 5000 were allowed to join the scheme as well. By 1997, half the population was covered by fundholding practices, which controlled over 10 per cent of hospital and community health service spending. The form of fundholding evolved further with 'community' or 'total' fundholding, extending the range of services which were purchased by the fundholder, and consortia of fundholders or more formal pooling of multi-fundholders (Goodwin *et al.*, 1998).

Another key innovation of fundholding was that there was a financial incentive for those who joined the scheme to be more efficient: they were able to keep any savings from their budget and invest them into improvements in patient care and certain aspects of practice improvement. The cash-limited budget of the fundholder allowed for the possibility of moving funds between components of the budget, so the fundholder had the power to allocate the resources as they saw fit. Not only was there an incentive to improve efficiency in the surplus retention, but also there was a threat of loss of fundholding status if repeated failure to meet the budget was observed. On the other hand, there was also a limit to the financial liability of the fundholding practice from the risk of patient selection: if expenditure on a given patient exceeded a certain amount (£5000) then the local health authority was responsible for the excess spending.

The budgets were set on the basis of historical costs initially. This was criticised for rewarding inefficient practices (Baines *et al.*, 1997a). It was intended that, eventually, a form of weighted capitation would be used and in fact, in 1993–94, simple versions of a weighted capitation method were employed which accounted for age. Later on, more complex weighting schemes were employed which accounted for age, gender and the number of temporary residents in a region (Baines *et al.*, 1997a).

Among the UK's 1991 'internal market' reforms, general practice fundholding was one of the most studied. However, like the other reforms, evaluation of this aspect suffered from the lack of a planned and rigorous overall evaluation. Further, the existing evidence is plagued by a series of problems which adversely affect the ability to draw firm conclusions. First of all, as has been pointed out, there were a series of changes in the NHS which were all introduced around the same time. This confounds the ability to attribute any observed changes to fundholding alone. Second, the feature that practices voluntarily self-selected into the fundholding scheme confounds the evaluation via observational techniques: fundholders tended to be better resourced and in more affluent areas than non-fundholders so they are not a random sample (Petchey, 1995) and there is documented evidence which shows that the practices which entered the fundholding scheme in the first wave were measurably different from those who entered later (Bains and Whynes, 1996; Baines *et al.*, 1997b; Whynes *et al.*, 1997a). Thus the differences between fundholders and non-fundholders may not be attributable to fundholding status *per se* but to other (unmeasured) differences in these practices. Third, there was suggestion that potential fundholders might have an incentive to engage in strategic behaviour: since budgets were set on a historical basis initially, potential fundholders have an incentive to inflate their budgets in the year prior to becoming fundholders to enable them to reap definite savings in their first fundholding year (Baines *et al.*, 1997a). However, there is no empirical evidence to support this in prescribing (Whynes *et al.*, 1997a,b). These limitations affect the interpretation of the empirical evidence, and must be kept in mind.

There are no studies which directly assess the technical or allocative efficiency of fundholding, but there is a body of empirical literature which assesses various specific issues which are related to efficiency. This body of literature on fundholding has recently been comprehensively reviewed by Goodwin *et al.* (1998) including evidence related to efficiency and equity. (For a complete list of references evaluating fundholding, see the reference list contained within this comprehensive review.)

One of the most studied aspects of fundholding was the impact on GPs' prescribing. In the UK, most drug consumption is paid for from the NHS budget with non-exempt patients paying a small fixed fee, with the usual exemptions of children, older people, pregnant or new mothers, and recipients of social security. Reducing the drug budget was one of the key objectives of the scheme. There is some consensus in the literature that fundholders were able to curb the rise in prescription costs compared with non-fundholders at least initially (Wilson *et al.*, 1995). This reduction was achieved largely via a lower cost per item of prescribing, through measures like increased use of generic alternatives, although there is some evidence of reduced volumes too (Wilson *et al.*, 1995). After the first few years of entry into fundholding, continued cost reductions, as one would expect, were observed to level off as savings were more difficult to achieve given both shrinking budgets following surpluses and given that the obvious cost reducing measures would have been already implemented.

Another aspect of fundholding which received some attention in the literature was the impact on rate of referrals to specialists and emergency care. It was hoped that by having GPs bear the financial responsibility for their referral decisions to specialists, inappropriate referrals would be reduced, thus freeing resources for more appropriate use. On the other hand, there was also a concern that fundholders might have an incentive to shift costs to the health authority, that is, by referring patients to emergency care which came out of the health authority budget and not that of the fundholders. Until recently, the small body of literature on these issues was inconclusive; it appeared that, in England, referral rates did not alter after the introduction of fundholding, whilst, in Scotland the introduction of the scheme did lead to reduced rates of referral for certain groups (Coulter and Bradlow, 1993; Howie *et al.*, 1994). However, more sophisticated statistical analysis, composing fundholding and non-fundholding practices, and accounting for the fact that fundholding was voluntary, showed that fundholding status reduced waiting times of fundholders by 5–8 per cent (Dusheiko *et al.*, 2003).

Other results on fundholding relate to impacts on prices charged to fundholders, the location of care, administrative costs, and the investment of any surpluses. Propper *et al.* (1998) have shown, through rigorous regression analyses, that, market forces, measured by variables such as numbers of NHS providers in a given area and market share counted for by a provider, have had an impact in reducing prices charged to fundholders across eight common procedures. There also appears to be more services provided by fundholding practices after they became fundholders, such as more outreach clinics by hospital clinicians resulting in a shift in the location of secondary care, although it is not clear that this is attributable to fundholding *per se*. Further, whether this represents an efficiency improvement is not demonstrated. The administrative costs of fundholding are high, with some estimates suggesting that they are not outweighed by the cost savings. A further issue is whether the savings achieved by fundholders, and the practice-based investments made by the fundholders with these savings, represent an efficiency improvement. There is much debate but little evidence on this question.

With respect to equity, there were two issues which arose regarding the impact of fundholding. First of all, the potential for 'cream skimming' was a concern whereby fundholders would have the incentive to select only healthy patients since ill patients would jeopardize the fundholders' abilities to make savings on their budget. However, there is no evidence that this was an issue. This is likely due to the provision which limited the per patient liability of the fundholder to £5000 per annum. The second issue was that patients of fundholders would receive preferential access to care, because of their improved ability to negotiate favourable terms with hospitals. There is some evidence that this did in fact occur and that it represented a two-tierism in access to care which was not acceptable. This arose, though, because fundholding did not cover all practices. In 1997, in England, the new Labour Government replaced fundholding with primary care groups (now trusts) which are responsible for the purchase of most hospital, community and primary care for their populations. These primary care trusts cover all practices, and cooperation rather than competition is encouraged between purchasers and providers (Le Grand, 2002). The encouragement of cooperation and the less-direct involvement of GPs in purchasing do, to some extent, dilute the incentive effects on the primary care trusts, especially when combined with central government initiatives, such as national service frameworks and national treatment guidelines to which trusts are expected to adhere. Although difficult to interpret in terms of attribution to these reforms, increases in hospital activity have not been as great as during the 1989–90 to 1996–97 period, with the total number of GP consultations falling between 1996–97 and 1998–99 (Le Grand, 2002). A more sophisticated case-weighted activity index, measuring units of resources used per unit of activity, showed improvements in efficiency during the period of the internal market and has fallen since (Le Grand, 2002). Waiting lists did, however, decline, from 1.16 million in 1997 to 1.04 million in 2001 (Le Grand, 2002), although it has been suggested that 'success' on waiting lists has resulted merely because, amongst the plethora of performance criteria introduced since the 'abolition' of the UK internal market post-1997, those related to wasting time are most easily measured (Goddard *et al.*, 2000; Scott and Farrar, 2003). Despite the apparent success on waiting lists, Le Grand (2002) attributes the lack of success on other indicators at least in part to a lack of the incentives that would be induced by competitive pressures.

In summary, the evidence is, once again, not clear cut. However, it could be argued that fundholding, by giving greater financial responsibility to GPs and allowing patients to change doctor, displayed the greatest potential within the UK set of reforms to improve efficiency in health care provision.

Such reforms have also taken place in other countries. Sheiman (1995) outlines the experiments in some parts of Russia (e.g. St Petersburg), which included giving polyclinics budgets from which to purchase all hospital care. There seems to be no doubt that hospital use decreased. However, concerns about quality of care remain, as formal quality control mechanisms were not in place. Even in the US, HMOs have taken different forms, with group and staff models having rosters of patients and displaying similar characteristics to the 'gatekeeping' model used in general practice in the UK NHS, as opposed to independent practice associations (IPAs) where FFS-remunerated practitioners see only some HMO patients.

The latter are less restrictive and, in some plans, patients can even self-refer to specialists. Evidence comparing these types of plans is conflicting. The gatekeeping plans have been shown to do better in terms of level of services provided, preventive care and some aspects of quality of care, whilst IPAs seem to do better on measures of satisfaction and access, and there is little difference between the two in terms of cost (Burns, 1991; Escarce *et al.*, 2001). It is to the area of managed care more generally to which we now turn.

Evidence from studies of managed care

Another way of avoiding inappropriate referrals is to extend the UK Government proposals and integrate totally payment for primary and hospital care, as in HMOs. The more recent UK and Russian reforms are thought to be based in part on this model. As outlined above, there are many variants of this model, but, generally, under this system, the providers (e.g. a group of primary care doctors) receive an annual per capita payment in advance and have to provide comprehensive health care in return, buying in hospital care when needed. Thus the temptation to refer on or prescribe inefficiently is reduced (Peebles, 1992; Bischof and Nash, 1996).

HMOs (and other health care intermediaries in the USA) have an annual 'open season' during which they compete to retain existing customers and to attract new customers. This gives the organisation the incentive to provide comprehensive care at minimum cost, otherwise patients will look for another health care plan as they receive only a fixed subsidy from employers towards payment of the premium.

As long ago as the 1980s, strong evidence on HMOs came from the RAND health insurance experiment in the US, much of which was cited in the previous chapter. Results from the managed care part of this experiment demonstrated that use of outpatient services, including GPs, was similar among HMO patients and people on the 'free' care insurance plan. However, expenditure in the HMO group was 72 per cent of that in free care insurance group, the difference being a result of a markedly less hospital-intensive style of care in the HMO (Manning *et al.*, 1984, 1987).

Since RAND, there has been a proliferation of US studies on the impact of managed care (mainly HMOs) on cost, quality of care and health outcomes. However, only two of these are randomised trials. Leibowitz *et al.* (1992) examined the use of services of Medicaid patients randomised to enrolment in an HMO or to remain in FFS care. Participation in the HMO was voluntary, however, so patients could disenrol. Use by those remaining in the HMO was lower. However, use amongst those refusing enrolment in the HMO was higher than the FFS group. The authors concluded that the voluntary enrolment of Medicaid patients into an HMO led to higher costs due to favourable selection. This conclusion on selection is supported in a review of the evidence by Hellinger (1995).

Three papers arose from another Medicaid randomised trial in Minnesota (Lurie *et al.*, 1992; Lurie *et al.*, 1994; Coffey *et al.*, 1995). The first of these showed that longer term outcomes (measured through the Global Deterioration Scale) were worse in the HMO group. The second study detected few differences between prepaid and FFS groups in terms of process of care for elderly hypertensives and diabetics. The last study showed a similar result for non-insitutionalised older people. One study, in which physicians in the same practice changed from FFS to capitation, showed that, after the change, there were less hospital admissions, but longer lengths of stay and more ambulatory visits (Stearns *et al.*, 1992). The longer lengths of stay likely resulted because the capitation payments covered only primary care whilst specialists were paid according to a reduced fee schedule.

These results have been confirmed by other studies of Medicaid populations (Badgett and Rabalais, 1997), of more general populations (Kralewski *et al.*, 2000) or of several conditions (Dowd *et al.*, 1986), with capitation being associated with lower rates of prescribing, hospital admissions and days, and lower patient care costs than similar patients in FFS plans.

There are several studies which now exist in various areas of clinical practice. Studies of preventive practice, covering immunisation, various physical examinations for screening, blood pressure measurement and prevention of workplace injuries show either no difference between managed care plans and FFS or greater provision of such services under managed care (Carey *et al.*, 1990; Retchin and Brown, 1990; Udvarhelyi *et al.*, 1991; Arnold and Schlenker, 1992; McGrail *et al.*, 1995; Schoenman *et al.*, 1997). Of course, these differences can lead to managed care being more costly (Schoenman *et al.*, 1997). One study of hypertensive patients in primary care showed that patients under capitation had less tests ordered, lower overall charges but were equivalent to FFS patients in terms of blood pressure control at one year (Murray *et al.*, 1992). A similar result has been shown for ambulatory sensitive conditions (such as asthma), with less hospital admissions amongst HMO enrolees (Josephson and Karcz, 1997). Breast and colorectal screening studies show little difference between FFS and managed care plans in terms of stage of cancer at presentation and outcomes (Vernon *et al.*, 1990; Vernon *et al*, 1995; Lee-Feldstein *et al.*, 2001). Prostate screening has been shown to be higher amongst FFS physicians, although the guidelines for this screening procedure are unclear (Edlefsen *et al.*, 1999). In the area of childbirth, capitation has been shown to lead to less low-birthweight babies whilst providing equivalent prenatal care (Klinkman *et al.*, 1997). It seems that for areas like prevention, which requires co-ordination and is probably not that well rewarded under FFS, managed care does relatively well.

Moving to care of more vulnerable groups, managed care does not perform so well. In studies of home care provision for Medicare beneficiaries, either little difference has been found relative to FFS (Adams *et al.*, 1995) or FFS leads to more costs but also better outcomes in terms of physical and mental functioning (Shaughnessy *et al.*, 1994; Schlenker *et al.*, 1995). The latter set of results has also been shown for stroke (Kramer *et al.*, 2000). In care of people with mental illnesses, the result reported by Lurie *et al.* (1992) is supported by those from the study of Utah's Medicaid prepaid mental health plan (Popkin *et al.*, 1998; Manning *et al.*, 1999) in which less care with traditional providers occurred, but with worse outcomes in the prepaid group. Disenrollment of more severely ill patients has been shown to occur under capitation in Los Angeles (Kapur *et al.*, 1999). Although results for youth in juvenile justice and child welfare systems seem to be better, with the prepaid plan leading to less inpatient stays and shorter lengths of stay, some cost-shifting to facilities not covered by the managed care scheme was shown to occur (Cuellar *et al.*, 2001). Experience in Colorado seems to be more positive, where quality of life improved and admissions to hospital were less in subjects studies after the introduction of capitation relative to those interviewed before (Warner and Huxley, 1998). Also in Colorado, a controlled before-and-after study showed that capitation led to lower costs of mental health care for children (Catalano *et al.*, 2000). Colorado's success may be to do with the facts that more non-hospital alternatives were likely available and the mental health agency moved to capitation without employing a managed care intermediary. Otherwise, it seems that managed care struggles with these areas, for which there seems to be a strong volume–outcome relationship.

One study of care for angina showed little difference between FFS and managed care groups in terms of characteristics, process of care or outcomes (Every *et al.*, 1998) whilst another, despite showing that overall rates of anginal medical therapy were low, also showed that such rates were higher in HMOs (Samuels *et al.*, 2000). HMO referral systems have been shown to lead to less emergencies, redo bypass operations, catheterisation complications (which yields a lower operative mortality) and more appropriate rates of revascularisation compared with FFS care (Langa and Sussman, 1993; Starr *et al.*, 2002). Studies of the chronic condition rheumatoid arthritis, however, have shown no difference in services used or in outcome measures (functional status, work disability and systems) when comparing similar groups receiving HMO and FFS care (Yelin *et al.*, 1986; Ward *et al.*, 1998). Using hospital discharge data for two self-contained geographic areas within California, Haile and Stein (2002) have shown that managed care is associated with more inpatient complications, and that such complications occur in hospitals with higher amounts of managed care penetration (i.e. patients within any given hospital tend to be treated similarly).

The problems with most of the studies reported in the last three paragraphs is that most of them suffer from selection effects. HMOs achieve some, or all, of their cost savings either by selection of good risks (or by being selected by good risks) or, as has been shown in some randomised trials, to the detriment of the health of ill people in lower income groups (Buchanan and Cretin, 1986; Ware *et al.*, 1986; Moser, 1987; Wagner and Bledsoe, 1990; Leibowtitz *et al.*, 1992).

Despite the methodological weaknesses of many of the above studies, two important reviews, of 37 peer-reviewed studies by Miller and Luft (1997) and of 79 such studies (Miller and Luft, 2002), concur with the overall conclusions that managed care produces better, the same or worse care depending on the particular organisation and particular disease group. More vulnerable groups tend to do worse under managed care. Useful papers on the impact of organisational factors are by Debrock and Arnould (1992) and Flood *et al.* (1998), showing the importance for service use of factors such as which types of physician the patient sees first, types of compensation for physicians within the organisation and whether or not it is a for-profit organisation.

Hospital clinicians as budget holders

In addition to the evidence on GPs as budget holders, there is limited evidence on the effects of budgeting in the hospital sector.

In proposing to make clinicians budget holders, the UK experiment with clinical budgeting in the 1970s and 1980s attempted to increase the awareness of and provide incentives for clinicians to be more efficient. Information on costs and clinical activity was provided to each budget holder (e.g. a group of clinicians working in a particular specialty). Planning agreements with clinical teams (PACTs), based on previous workloads, prospectively determined activity levels and the declared nature of the incentive structure for participants, that is, some fixed percentage of any savings made could be given back to budget holders and spent on improving patient care. The results demonstrated that PACTs led to little or no change in resource use in five categories of revenue expenditure which were analysed (Wickings *et al.*, 1985). The five categories were drugs, x-ray films, x-ray chemicals and equipment, equipment for medical and surgical purposes and laboratory instruments. However, these results were not surprising because the extent to which clinicians could determine how the budget was allocated and choose between different factor mixes in determining their production function was very limited. Also, it is difficult to separate the possible effects of PACTs from others, such as the introduction at around the same time of performance indicators and of general management, since the experiment was not controlled.

It is encouraging, however, that a (also uncontrolled) before-and-after study has demonstrated that, in response to information produced by clinical budgeting, it was possible to reduce drug costs on long-stay wards for elderly people by 34 per cent with no adverse effects on patients' physical and mental states (Gibbins *et al.*, 1988). A small controlled before-and-after study led to similar results, with 15–27 per cent reductions in clinical chemistry and haematology tests after feedback of laboratory use and cost data, within a general hospital in England (Gama *et al.*, 1991). More recently, schemes employing incentives, such as the ability to retain at least some savings, and assessed in before-and-after studies have proved more successful in achieving cost savings. However, these schemes were accompanied by strategies such as education and active feedback (Kerr *et al.*, 1996) and support of major clinical leaders (Hopkins, 1999).

Government regulation

Direct government regulation of health care providers is not necessarily solely through financial control. But it can be in the sense that if such providers do not comply with the regulation, they can be subjected to financial penalties. There is some evidence on the effect of government regulation to control providers.

Irwin *et al*. (1986) examined the effect on prescribing of the limited list in a computerised UK general practice of 3000 patients. Such a list indicates those drugs which cannot be prescribed for a patient to obtain free of charge or at preferential rates in the UK NHS. For drugs 'on the list' Irwin *et al*. found significant decreases in the amounts of cough and cold remedies, vitamins and antacids prescribed, whereas no change occurred in prescribing laxatives, benzodiazipines or analgesics. Much of the decrease was for prescriptions issued for 'non essential' reasons (especially vitamins). However, the prescribing of irons and penicillins (which were not on the list) increased, the former probably being a result of substitution for decreased vitamin prescriptions.

Yule *et al*. (1988) analysed prescribing habits of 17 doctors in the north-east of Scotland after the introduction of a limited list, asking them what they would have prescribed in each situation had the list not existed. For the drugs listed, NHS expenditure was reduced, but not by as much as expected. In many cases, costs to patients increased as a result of more private prescribing and over-the-counter purchases.

Many other countries operate a 'limited list' of sorts (Smith, 1985) and some impressionistic evidence is available on their cost-effectiveness. At first sight, the Norwegian system appears to be quite strict; before any drug is registered for use, manufacturers must produce evidence on its quality, safety, efficacy, cost and need. However, despite this, there is a special licensing clause whereby a doctor can prescribe a drug which is not currently available. Such licences are commonly issued. One study compared anti-inflammatory use in the Netherlands, where 22 products were available, with that in Norway, where only 7 were on the market (Dukes and Lunde, 1981). The average Dutch rheumatologist prescribed 12–13 of the 22 drugs, using only 7 regularly. In Norway, the average rheumatologist used four to six of the seven drugs available. But, 40 per cent made use of the licensing system to prescribe drugs not on the national list. No outcome effects were tested.

In a review of experiences with limited lists in various countries and contexts, Pearce and Begg (1992), showed that limited lists can save costs and improve outcomes through promoting more rational prescribing. However, lists tended to be more effective if based on provider consensus and with continuing education and feedback on drug use. National-level lists tended to be less effective. A review of 22 studies of the use of 'restrictive formularies' at US state or national levels showed that many such studies employ weak methods to assess impact, but that it is unclear whether costs are saved, due to substitution of other products not on the list and the passing of costs onto consumers, and that overall costs may increase (Lexchin, 2002). Limited lists have been employed more recently in countries such as China. In Shanghai, where a list was employed along with a budget cap, drug costs were reduced dramatically, from 67 to 51 per cent of total health care expenditures, between 1992 and 1996 (Hu *et al*., 2001).

A more recent direct regulatory policy on pharmaceuticals, and, to some degree, an extension of the limited list, has been reference-based pricing. Generally, this policy involves the reimbursement of a group of comparable or interchangeable drugs at a common rate, sometimes the lowest price drug in that class or some average or negotiated rate. This policy still needs to be rigorously evaluated (Grootendorst and Holbrook, 1999). In theory, it should reduce drug costs, as was shown in the eight classes of drugs to which it was applied in British Columbia, Canada in 1995 (Narine *et al.*, 1999). However, the policy may have knock-on effects by increasing costs for other forms of related care not included in the scheme (Grootendorst and Holbrook, 1999). Indeed this is what happened as a result of the reference-based pricing policy introduced in Germany in 1993 (Giuliani *et al.*, 1998), leading to conclusions that other measures (such as some form of global budgeting) is required to go along with it. Schneeweiss *et al.* (2002) examined the impact of reference-based pricing on the cost of Angiotensin Converting Enzyme (ACE) inhibitors in British Columbia for two years before and one year after implementation. Use of ACE inhibitors fell by 11 per cent, but use of anti-hypertensives overall remained unchanged. The policy did save Can$6.7 million in the first 12 months. However, patients with low-income staus were more likely to discontinue anti-hypertensive therapy altogether, reflecting a general trend which existed before reference-based pricing.

In Australia, a two-stage regulatory procedure exists. A company wishing to introduce a new drug to Australia submits it first to the Drug Evaluation Committee, which decides on safety. Quality and cost are then considered by the Pharmaceutical Benefits Advisory Committee. The scheme is strongly supported by doctors and patients and has kept prescribing costs below those in Britain (Smith, 1985) and appears to be consistent, tending to reject applications showing a relatively high cost per life year gained (George *et al.*, 2001).

In countries like Norway and Australia, the only disenchanted party seems to be the pharmaceutical industry; it tends not to locate manufacturing plant in these and other highly regulated countries, Canada being another example (Sketris and Hill, 1998). All of these countries are sparsely populated which may be another factor; demand is not sufficient to warrant a manufacturing presence there. Presumably communities lose out from such absences, though this has never been quantified.

The results of all of these studies do demonstrate, however, that regulation can change behaviour. More regulation to encourage generic prescribing and local formularies could lead to more efficient changes in prescribing habits from the point of view of health services, although the effects on the costs and benefits to the community at large are not known.

Getting the best of all worlds: blended payment systems

Until recently, studies and debates on physician remuneration have tended to be dichotomous, discussing the merits of one payment system relative to another as though they are substitutes. However, this is clearly not the case. The use of 'blended' payment systems, through which policy-makers presumably try to take advantage of the best of each type of reward mechanism, is quite common. One of the longest standing blended systems is that in the UK, where, priori to 1990, GPs received about 46 per cent of their income through capitation (to try and encourage prevention), 42 per cent from allowances (to try, amongst other things, to encourage practitioners to form group practices) and 13 per cent from FFS (to try and encourage good immunisation rates). To some extent, this blend of incentives worked. The second was so successful that it was deemed unnecessary (and, therefore, abolished) by 1990, and the blend was changed to 60 per cent captitation (also to encourage practitioners to compete more for patients), 19 per cent from allowances, 11 per cent FFS, and the remaining 11 per cent aimed at encouraging prevention and health promotion through new forms of payment, such as target payments (Hughes, 1993).

Robinson (2001) states that experiments with competition in the US over the past 20 years have inevitably led to different forms of remuneration. Thus, although, in the US, methods of payment do still tend be 100 per cent one or other, with FFS still dominating, in 1994, amongst primary care providers rewarded by FFS, 37.5 per cent did not have this as their sole form of remuneration (Conrad *et al.*, 1996).

Robinson (2001) provides a clear statement of why we might want to mix payment systems. He defines, four 'key features' of clinical practice and compares FFS and capitation with respect to these features. The features are:

- *Physician productivity and patient service*: whereby we might want to encourage long hours, many procedures and attentiveness to patients' needs. FFS performs well here, whereas capitation does not.
- *Risk acceptance*: whereby physicians should be rewarded for treating the sickest patients, rather than skimming off the healthy and avoid ill patients. Again, FFS performs relatively well on this dimension, whilst capitation performs poorly to the extent that it is poorly adjusted for patients' needs.
- *Efficiency and appropriate scope of practice*: whereby physicians should be rewarded for neither over- nor under-treating patients. Now FFS begins to have limitations, and capitation begins to look advantageous, as the former may be unnecessarily inflationary, with the latter thought to do well in combating supplier-induced demand.
- *Cooperation and evidence-based medicine*: whereby physicians are encouraged to cooperate with each other and to adopt best practices and narrow variations in care, as shown by the evidence. Here, again, FFS is likely to be counterproductive, with capitation, being more population-based, offering the potential to gear care towards patterns of need, and being supported by protocols based on evidence.

Robinson (2001) also discusses salaries, stating that the paucity of their use (presumably in the US context) should be understood in the light of the organisational structures that employment and salary presuppose. To some extent, this argument carries over to more publicly funded systems. However, salaries still have a role in encouraging recruitment in underserved areas, and have been shown to be effective in doing so (Sorensen and Grytten, 2000; Williams *et al.*, 2001).

CONCLUSIONS

Much research has been produced about the effect of different methods of payment on doctors' performance. But, still, some important gaps remain. One of the best-documented areas concerns the effect of payment by FFS on supplier-induced demand. Despite doubts about the adequacy of the data and thus the evidence, many support the view that FFS remuneration leads to induced demands for fee-yielding services by patients on the recommendation of their doctors. Such a view is accepted almost unquestioned by many health economists. Many studies have been published which have failed to show such a result, however. The effects of supplier-induced demand on service use by different groups and on health status are not known. A major question, of course, is whether all this matters. Having shown, in many instances that physicians respond to this method of remuneration, we know we have an important tool for policy implementation. Thus, it does seem that fees can be used as part of a remuneration package, although tight control of fee schedules is required, and fees must be targeted in line with priorities in order to maintain effectiveness at least cost.

Salaried payments probably lead to less utilisation relative to FFS. But apart from this result, from a small number of studies, little more is known about effects of salary on utilisation or outcome. Again, however, it likely has a place in an over-all remuneration system, having been shown to meet objectives in areas (such as recruitment of physicians in rural areas) where other forms of payment do not seem to have worked. Problems with motivation mean that salaries may be better accompanied by some kind of performance-based merit awards. This raises issues of measurement and the need to set standards, on which substantial progress has been made over the last 10 years. However, no scheme has yet linked such standard setting to financial reward.

The effect of receiving a fixed per capita payment in advance, such as in HMOs in the US, is now one of the most researched areas in health care financing. The results show that HMOs seem to lead to a less hospital-intensive style of care. Despite this, lower income groups fare worse in this system than in an insurance system with free care at the point of delivery. HMOs seem to do well on primary care/prevention and less well on issues of caring for vulnerable groups, such as the mentally ill. Results for other areas of care are mixed. HMO-style innovations in public systems, such as GP fundholding, have proven difficult to evaluate. However, the evidence does indicate that this innovation showed potential to lead to efficient changes in health care delivery. The UK Government has now moved to a different system, but one in which GPs are not as central in directing and paying for health care delivery. Thus, early results on this are not promising, in part due to the related dilution of market-type incentives.

Evidence on another type of payment which can be fixed prospectively, budgets, is equivocal, though, again, its potential has been demonstrated. The same can be said for more direct forms of regulation, such as formularies.

The importance of such results depends on the objectives of health care provision. Once again, it seems that charges and HMOs can be ruled out in terms of achievement of these objectives when compared with free care at the point of delivery. Although more evidence is required, it does seem that there will be no one system which dominates all others on all relevant criteria. Hence, the advantages of blended payment systems, which have existed for some years in some countries, such as the UK. The evolution of many systems towards this 'horses for courses' approach would seem to make sense in terms of permitting the maximum range of health and health care objectives to be met through the remuneration system. However, despite reaching a positive conclusion in the sense of mixed systems as a good solution, no doubt policy-makers will continue to experiment with new forms of payment. The way forward here is pointed by Scott and Farrar (2003) who raise many issues (such as the social contexts of incentives, rewarding teams and experimentation with salary structures, amongst others) which could be profitably investigated in the future.

8

COUNTERING MORAL HAZARD IN THE HOSPITAL SECTOR

INTRODUCTION

Financial incentives operate on institutions as well as on individual actors within any health system. Therefore, it is important to review the effect of different methods of financing on hospital behaviour. This is not only because there is a large, though incomplete, volume of literature on the subject of hospital financing but also because hospitals are the single most identifiable group of users of health care resources in any economy. For instance, in 1982, the hospital sector accounted for approximately 42 per cent of health care expenditures in the US and Australia, 41 per cent in Canada and 62 per cent in the UK (OECD, 1987). In 1999, these corresponding figures were 40.5 per cent, 43.3 per cent, 42.3 per cent for the US, Australia and Canada (with no estimate for the UK) (Rheinhardt *et al.*, 2002). Obviously, then, the nature of reimbursement of the hospital sector will play an important role in determining not only the level and nature of hospital activity itself but also the extent of control over total health service costs.

Variations in methods of hospital funding exist both within and between public and private health care systems. Over the last two decades, several countries introduced or proposed new methods of hospital reimbursement. Well-known innovations in the US are the Medicare Prospective Payment System (PPS) based on diagnosis-related groups (DRGs) and the introduction of more competition in the health care market as reflected in the California selective contracting system and the growth of health maintenance organisations (HMOs). Both HMOs and DRG-type systems have also been discussed in the context of the Australian health care system, and many European countries (e.g. Denmark, Hungary and Norway) have introduced DRG or DRG-like systems as well. Still other innovations such as performance-based contracts (PBCs) gained some notoriety through the 1990s in the US. The UK has employed a range of contract types since the internal market reforms introduced there in the early 1990s. These include purchasers contracting with hospitals on bases of open-ended (or 'block') funding, funding for a specified number of cases, or even funding additional referrals on a cost-per-case basis. Canada has maintained a stable method of hospital reimbursement, global budgeting, throughout the 1980s and 1990s. It is important, therefore, to reflect on the evidence which now exists on the effects of different methods of payment on hospital efficiency and to highlight areas for further research. These are the aims of this chapter. Some of the above types of reimbursement can be mixed; for example, many hospitals operating within an internal market might use DRG-type costing systems as a basis for information.

One problem in devising optimal financial incentive mechanisms for hospitals has been the lack of development of theoretical models of hospital behaviour. This problem is discussed in more detail in the following section. Thereafter, three main methods of hospital reimbursement are introduced and their possible effects on the price and quantity of hospital care are discussed. In the fourth section, evidence of the effect of each payment system on hospital costs, throughput and patient outcome is summarised. The effects of hospital ownership on efficiency are briefly examined in a separate section as it is often assumed that private ownership represents greater competition and is, therefore, positively associated with efficiency. This last issue is not strictly one of finance, but is related to financing and is of importance given the 'public versus private' debate which often takes place in political circles. Before concluding, we summarise the evidence to date and propose a possible solution to the problem of hospital funding.

THEORETICAL PERSPECTIVES

Problems of traditional economic models of hospital behaviour have been reviewed in Evans (1984), McGuire *et al.* (1988) and Donaldson and Gerard (1991, 1993). The lack of a satisfactory theory (economic or otherwise) of hospital behaviour makes it difficult to predict how hospitals are expected to react to different methods of hospital reimbursement and to determine performance criteria for assessing these reimbursement methods.

Regarding prediction, it is difficult to derive hypotheses from traditional competitive market models. In the classic model of economic behaviour, hospitals would act as profit-maximising 'firms', responding to the preferences of fully informed and knowledgeable consumers. In this model, each 'firm' is regarded as being so small, and one of so many, that it cannot exercise control over any aspect of market behaviour, except its own cost structure. Without the possibility for collusion, 'firms' are forced to compete on the basis of price, as fully knowledgeable consumers will seek out those 'firms' with the lowest prices. 'Firms', therefore, have an incentive to operate at minimum cost in order to enable prices to be set low enough to attract as many consumers as possible. Those not operating at least cost would have this reflected in higher prices, to which consumers would respond by switching their consumption to other 'firms' within the health care industry or in other industries.

As described in Chapter 2, but concentrating more specifically on the hospital sector, consumers' preferences would play a crucial role in deciding on the amount of resources to be allocated to hospital care in general and, more specifically, to each type of hospital care. The result would be an efficient allocation of resources to hospital care (allocative efficiency). At the same time, hospitals, being profit maximisers, would seek to produce consumers' most highly valued types of hospital care at least cost, so acting in a technically efficient manner. This combination of allocative and technical efficiency ensures that consumers' utility is maximised at least cost to society.

However, because of market failure, described in Chapter 3, the hospital market does not operate like this. Consumers' preferences do not have much of a role in the allocation of resources to hospital care because of the existence of externalities and consumer ignorance in a market where the principal adviser on the consumer's behalf is also a supplier of care (Evans, 1984).

On the supply side, hospitals are not profit maximisers, simply responding to the well-informed demands of consumers. Given their size, and lack of competition, hospitals will inevitably exert a degree of discretion over their activities, even if consumers were well-informed. In addition, ownership and management are separated in hospitals, as in many large companies. Management objectives are unlikely to be as profit-driven as those of owners, thus relaxing the incentive to produce the most highly valued care at least cost. Analyses of hospital behaviour are further complicated by yet another division of responsibilities: those of the doctor and the administrator. In many countries, doctors are not even employed by the hospitals in which they work: without responsibility to administrators, doctors make decisions regarding admission and treatment of patients. Doctors, taking on a role of advocacy, and administrators, with more of a global view of hospital activity and costs, may even respond differently to the same method of hospital reimbursement. Such complicated structures make it difficult to determine exactly who, if anyone in particular, within the hospital reacts to the financial incentives associated with different reimbursement schemes.

All of these factors contribute to the difficulty of generalising about hospital conduct. Who reacts to incentives, how they react, and whether different people within the same hospital react independently or together, will depend on physical structures, power structures and relationships within the hospital and wider health care environment. The following quotation from the classic paper by Harris (1977) sums this up nicely:

> ... the hospital must solve this capacity problem with a wide variety of non-price related decision rules. There are loosely enforced standards, rules of thumb, side bargains, cajoling, negotiations, special contingency plans and in some cases literally shouting and screaming.

Such factors are better analysed using sociological and behavioural techniques. Through the use of such techniques, it may be possible to build up a more general model of hospital behaviour at a later date. But until then, the role of more general predictive economic models of hospital behaviour will be severely limited.

One area of economic theory, however, which offers much potential for application in the area of health care is principal–agent theory. This applies well in situations where a purchaser (or 'principal') does not have the same information as a provider (or 'agent'). One could characterise some kind of insurer or health authority as a principal and a hospital as an agent. Given asymmetry of information, the aim of the principal is to devise a contract inducing more effort from the agent and which minimises costs. Of course, for this to work, both the principal has to be satisfied that aims are achieved at acceptable cost and the agent has to be satisfied with the returns (Laffont and Tirole, 1993). In many respects, the reimbursement mechanisms reviewed later in the chapter are examples of attempts to induce greater efficiency in the health care system in a situation of information asymmetry. The incentive scheme most explicitly related to principal–agent theory is that of PBC. Here, the most basic form of a contract will define a base level of compensation and allow for additional compensation based on measures of quality and treatment outcomes. A public purchaser, for example, might choose to reward a good-performing substance abuse treatment provider with extra funding in the next contract year (Commons and McGuire, 1997). As well as more common funding reforms, evidence on the more recent innovation of PBC as applied to health care is reviewed later in the chapter.

Despite such progress, the current lack of theory highlights the need to learn from experience with different reimbursement mechanisms. It is reasonable to conclude that hospitals will respond differently to different funding mechanisms. Some attempt at predicting such responses will be made in the next section, although the relationship of the predictions to some prior economic theory is not always entirely clear.

On performance criteria, the diminished role of the consumer leads to decisions affecting both allocative efficiency (i.e. what types of health care to provide) and technical efficiency (i.e. how best to provide each type of health care) resting largely with suppliers of care operating in a regulated system: policy decisions are made at various levels (national, regional and local) and tend to blur the notions of allocative and technical efficiency. In addition to the diminished role of the consumer, much health care remains unevaluated. This makes it difficult to determine what, and how much, health care should be provided by hospitals. Suppliers do not seem to be able to get this right, as witnessed by classic articles on variations in surgical rates within countries and by evidence on inappropriateness of care (Lowry, 1978; Morgan *et al.*, 1987; Greenspan *et al.*, 1988; Vayda *et al.*, 1982; McPherson *et al.*, 1982; Winslow *et al.*, 1988a,b). Such variations persist for a range of serious conditions (Bijker *et al.*, 2001; Feasby *et al.*, 2001; Huskins *et al.*, 2001). Thus, the allocative question, 'whether hospitals should be doing what they are doing and to the extent that they are doing', for the most part, remains largely unaddressed.

In the hospital sector it is easier to focus on technical efficiency in answering 'how well are hospitals doing what they are doing?'. It is mainly the question of technical efficiency which is to be addressed in presenting evidence on different methods of hospital reimbursement (e.g. whether hospitals behave in a technically efficient manner), although questions relating to allocative efficiency will be raised (e.g. if hospitals cut costs at the expense of health outcomes, is this desirable?).

For the most part, alternative funding mechanisms will be compared in terms of cost per day, cost per case (mainly as reflected in length of stay) and effects on total hospital costs (mainly as reflected in hospital throughput) and less often (because of lack of data) in terms of effects on outcome, equity of outcome and equity of access. Once these later pieces of data are introduced, questions relating to allocative efficiency can be asked (but not necessarily answered).

METHODS OF REIMBURSING HOSPITALS: A CASE OF MINDING OUR *P*s AND *Q*s?

Hospitals supply care to patients and are reimbursed by the patients directly or, more likely, by a private insurance company or government agency. In a simple model, the total amount expended by these payers on any hospital during any time period could be said to be made up of the price of each medical/surgical treatment offered by the hospital multiplied by the number (or quantity) of times each treatment is carried out, summed over all treatments. More formally, for any hospital,

$$TE = \sum_{i=1}^{n} P_i Q_i \tag{1}$$

where TE is total expenditure on hospital care, P_i is the price of treatment i and Q_i is the quantity of treatment i carried out by the hospital. The number of treatments available in the hospital is n. Therefore, in attempting to control total expenditure on hospital care, reimbursement schemes can act on the variable P_i, the variable Q_i or on a combination of the two ($P_i Q_i$). This can be done at the level of different treatments (setting different fixed prices for different treatments, so constraining P_i), setting clinical budgets at departmental levels (so constraining $P_i Q_i$) or at the level of the whole hospital (setting a global hospital budget without regard to individual departments, so constraining $\sum P_i Q_i$).

The amount of operating surplus (or profit) per unit of treatment offered by a hospital will depend on the cost of inputs to treatment relative to price, and total surplus for the period will further depend on the number of treatments carried out. Thus,

$$\Pi = \sum_{i=1}^{n} P_i Q_i - \sum_{i=1}^{n} C_i Q_i \tag{2}$$

where C_i represents the cost of inputs to treatment i and Π represents operating surplus. The quality of care provided by any hospital will be reflected in C_i which can be varied up to, but not beyond, the level of P_i. According to this simple model, a hospital will break even where $\sum P_i = \sum C_i$.

A more generalised form of $\sum C_i Q_i$ is

$$TC = CQ \tag{3}$$

where C is equal to the average cost per admission to a hospital, Q is the number of admissions and TC is the total cost of hospital care. It is necessary to specify this latter form of the total cost equation because, although different reimbursement schemes focus on prices and quantities as expressed in equation (1), results of studies of their effects are often reported in the form of the variables in equation (3); reporting effects on average hospital costs per admission or discharge and numbers of cases admitted to or discharged from hospitals. For the remainder of this section, reimbursement schemes will be described in terms of equation (1), although many of the results reported in the following section are reported in the more general form of equation (3).

Given the inevitability of government intervention, there are three main methods by which hospitals may be reimbursed: retrospective reimbursement at full cost; prospective reimbursement per type of case or level of workload; and competition (regulating on the supply side to allow market mechanisms to decide on level of payment and amounts of care provided). Each method has important implications for hospital activity through the inherent incentives they offer to hospital budget holders and hospital doctors. How each of these systems impacts on P_i, Q_i and P_iQ_i is discussed in the remainder of this section.

Retrospective reimbursement at full cost (minding neither P_i nor Q_i)

Under a system of retrospective reimbursement at full cost, a hospital receives payment in full from financial intermediaries for all 'reasonable' expenditure incurred during the previous year. Such a system encourages hospital budget holders to maximise hospital income by encouraging either as much work as possible or long lengths of hospital stay with patients being subjected to many (perhaps excessive) diagnostic tests and procedures as well as being provided with care of possibly unproven value. As well as a lack of incentive to control the quantity of care delivered, this system offers no obvious incentive to control the price of such care. Since retrospective reimbursement is usually linked with paying hospital doctors by fee-for-service (FFS), the two mutually reinforce one another. Such a payment system provides no incentive for hospital budget holders to be cost-conscious, indeed full cost retrospective payment encourages the escalation of costs through its inherent inflationary bias.

Prospective reimbursement (minding P_i, $P_i Q_i$ or ΣP_iQ_i)

Under a prospective reimbursement system, hospitals contract with financial intermediaries to work within a predefined budget. This may be very tight, based on general population or utilisation criteria usually integrated into a system of hospitals and services, as in Canada, the UK, Denmark and the Australian public hospital sector, or much less tight but also direct in the linking of the hospital to the reimbursing agency, as in the US and the Australian private hospital sector.

Under the former, hospital workload is usually estimated by funding agencies from historical hospital activity data. This estimated workload is then given a fixed price per type of case and combined with estimates of levels of workload to determine a hospital's budget for the forthcoming financial year. Budgets can be administered at the global level of the whole hospital or at a departmental level with teams of clinicians (sometimes known as clinical budgeting). Control is exercised over P_iQ_i or ΣP_iQ_i, thus permitting control over the cost and quantity of care as long as the department or hospital remains within the overall budget. Incentives can be offered whereby the hospital or department is permitted to retain at least a part of budget surpluses on the condition that such surpluses are spent on patient care.

One PPS makes particular use of DRG information to categorise hospital inpatient activity and set prices per case. DRGs group inpatients according to diagnosis and resource use, and the reimbursement rate per case is set prospectively for each DRG category according to the average cost for that DRG. Thus price per case is constrained by the funding body and the hospital is free to decide on quality and quantity, in terms of length of stay, procedures administered or number of cases admitted.

The introduction of a PPS based on DRGs, initially in the US Medicare programme, was seen as a means of controlling hospital costs. A budget holder under this system is encouraged to minimise hospital costs per case in order to maximise hospital net income. It may be expected, therefore, that PPS encourages hospital efficiency by keeping costs as close as possible to, or below, average costs. In particular, costs per admission and per case may be expected to fall. Minimising costs could, however, be achieved through one of several routes: shorter hospital stays, substitution of less expensive inputs for costlier ones, reduction in the quality of hospital care or a combination of all three. It is important to know exactly what factors have contributed to reduced costs if claims that hospital efficiency improves with a PPS are to be substantiated. Indeed, efficiency may be sacrificed if cost-savings are achieved at the expense of quality of care and hence the health status of patients. In developing a theory of doctor behaviour under prospective reimbursement, Ellis and McGuire (1986) predict this response if (as is likely) hospital doctors do not act as perfect agents when treating patients.[1] Moreover, the effect may be, through lowering inpatient stays, to lower costs per case while at the same time raising overall costs through a knock-on effect on throughput, similar to the effect of FFS payment to doctors on supplier-induced demand as described in Chapters 3 and 7.[2]

Further effects of a PPS of this nature are known as 'cost-shifting', 'patient shifting' and 'DRG creep'. This was worse when the US Medicare PPS applied only to Medicare inpatient services. However, since the Balanced Budget Act of 1997, post-acute services, special nursing facilities and home health care are now included (Newhouse, 2002).These changes also involved reductions in payments for patients in some DRGs who were discharged after a short stay to a post-acute facility. Hospital costs can thus be reduced by shifting costs and/or patients into other sectors of the health care system not under the jurisdiction of PPS. Other patients may include private patients and other sectors may include outpatient departments, day hospitals, long-term care facilities or primary care. 'DRG creep' results from deliberate or inadvertent mis-classification of cases into DRGs which make cases appear more complicated than they actually are, thereby attracting a higher prospective payment than if 'correctly' classified.[3] To date, evidence on this has been ambiguous.

As well as price per case, price per day could also be constrained. Under this mechanism of reimbursement, one would expect to observe much the same effects as under a price-per-case system except – and it is an important exception – that there is no incentive to moderate length of stay.

Competition (minding P_i, Q_i or P_i and Q_i together)

Hospital care in the US in the past has been dominated by large institutions, principally of three types: privately owned for-profit; voluntary not-for-profit; or publicly owned. More recently, however, competition in the US health care market has grown rapidly with the introduction of HMOs, as it has in some European countries. As outlined in Chapter 4, HMOs are competitive organisations that must attract customers who enrol each year for a fixed fee in return for a guaranteed health care package. The 'health care package' includes both primary and secondary care to be provided by the HMO or other suppliers who are paid by the HMO.

Advocates claim that HMOs are efficient organisations for two reasons: first, they are paid a fixed capitation sum and the doctors in them have their pay linked to the performance of the HMO in generating (net) income, so there is no incentive for HMOs to 'overtreat' patients; and second, HMOs must compete for their per capita payments, with no automatic residual component to income being received unless HMOs can attract customers, thus leading to claims that quality is maintained at least cost. Thus, one can expect P_i or Q_i to be moderated under such competitive systems.

Owing to the absence of market mechanisms in health care systems which are provided and/or financed by government monopolies, such as the UK National Health Service (NHS), there exists no natural pricing mechanism through which the supply of health care resources can be efficiently matched to demands. In theory, this may be overcome by introducing 'quasi-markets' or 'internal markets'. Such artificial markets may be created through rules and regulations. According to the nature of these rules and regulations, incentive structures may be set up to reward producers and/or consumers for efficient behaviour.

For example, the basic content of the reforms of the UK NHS were published in the White paper on 'working for patients' (Secretaries of State, 1989). District Health Authorities (DHAs) were responsible for purchasing comprehensive care on behalf of their catchment populations. Major acute hospitals became self-governing, offering services to DHAs in return for block funding, funding for a specified number of cases, with additional cases funded on a cost per case basis. The boards of directors of such hospitals were ultimately responsible to the Secretary of State and, subject to some restrictions, could acquire and dispose of assets, raise funds, retain operating surpluses and build up reserves, employ whatever staff they consider necessary and determine pay and conditions of staff.

In this way, responsibility for finance and provision of services was separated, a DHA being faced with its own hospitals, self-governing hospitals and the private sector competing for contracts and cases. The DHA, it is claimed, would choose between providers on the basis of cost, outcome, availability, convenience and so on. It was responsible for ensuring provision of core services (such as accident and emergency departments) which must be provided locally and for monitoring quality of services (e.g. through patient surveys). Funding for training, research and specialised services were provided centrally for whatever hospitals happen to provide such services.

An additional proposal was that some general practices (those responsible for the care of more than 11 000 people subsequently reduced to 9000 people), if they so wish, be given more responsibility (through holding a budget) for the purchase of elective inpatient services, outpatient services and diagnostic tests on behalf of their patients, similar to HMO arrangements in the US. Later, some practices took responsibility for the budget for all such services. The aim was that GPs too would choose care for patients on the basis of both cost and quality. Patients remained free to change practice, budget allocations being suitably adjusted. In DHAs where general practices opted for budgets, the DHA had its budget reduced by the amount allocated to these general practices for 'buying in' hospital services.

This represents only a brief description of the UK Government reforms, but it is hoped that the general principles have been conveyed. Further reforms have taken place in the UK since, but it is the ones described which have been evaluated and the more recent reforms, introduced since a change of government in 1997, do contain important remnants of the internal market, as discussed in Chapter 7 (also, see below). The 'Dekker' reforms for the Dutch health care system also include proposals for an 'internal market' whereby insurers will purchase services from suppliers of health and social services on the bases of cost and quality (van de Ven, 1989). Internal markets of the sort canvassed by the UK Government are largely a priori in nature and, even after a decade or more, limited evidence exists concerning their impact. Again, as is probably now clear, one would expect this impact to be on both P_i and Q_i.

One system which has parallels to those in the UK and the Netherlands Governments' reforms is the selective contracting scheme in California. Introduced in July 1982, this scheme permits Medicaid and private insurers to contract selectively with hospitals and other providers of care, the aim being to stimulate price competition among these providers. Both Medicaid and private insurers can negotiate terms and conditions with each specific provider whom they will reimburse for services to their subscribers. Previously, this could not be done because of the threat of antitrust prosecution of funders by providers. The California State Medicaid programme has used the system to negotiate discounts with hospitals, as have private payers (Melnick and Zwanziger, 1988). Likewise, the Leningrad (subsequently St Petersburg) experiment, mentioned earlier in Chapter 1, was a forerunner of the UK proposals. In this experiment, polyclinics, the main provider of primary care, were given budgets to purchase hospital care for 37 conditions (Hakansson *et al.*, 1988).

EMPIRICAL EVIDENCE ON REIMBURSING HOSPITALS

The early empirical evidence on reimbursing hospitals relates largely to comparisons between prospective and retrospective reimbursement systems in the US, although more recent evidence has also come forth from Europe and Australia. Some empirical evidence is also available on clinical and global budgeting. Regarding competition, much recent evidence has emerged from the advent of HMOs, and this has already been reviewed in Chapters 6 and 7. More evidence from publicly orientated systems, such as those in the UK and Sweden, has emerged in recent years, and, although limited, allows some conclusions to be drawn. Evidence on the Californian 'experiment' with competition contributes further to conclusions which can be drawn based on experience to date.

Retrospective versus prospective reimbursement

The studies referred to in reviewing comparisons of retrospective and prospective payment systems both in the US and elsewhere are listed in Tables 8.1 and 8.2. These examine the effect of regulatory controls on the price (P_i) of care only, hospitals being free to decide on quality and quantity.

Studies of effects on length of stay and cost are listed in Table 8.1. The introduction of a DRG based financing system in Italy in 1995, with the aim of controlling growth in hospital costs, led to a decreased average length of stay for most of nine common conditions examined (Louis *et al.*, 1999). This study also identified an increase in day hospital admissions in comparing data before and after the reforms, but found little or no change in readmission rates. In contrast, Giammanco (1999) found that readmissions did increase in both public and private hospitals in Sicily post-reforms (although more so in public hospitals), but, as with Louis *et al.* (1999), significant reductions in average length of stay were observed.

In Australia, Xiao *et al.* (2000) examined the impact of casemix funding for five public hospitals in the Northern Territory. Similar to the Louis *et al.* (1999) study, this work found a decline in average length of stay, as well as an increase in the number of casemix-weighted discharges and no change in readmission rates. In contrast, studies in Norway (Magnussen and Solstad, 1994) and Portugal (Dismuke and Sena, 1999) found little effect of the change in hospital financing, and mixed results dependant on the technology under examination.

Earlier evidence from the US on the effect of DRGs on hospital costs is also conflicting. Guterman and Dobson (1986) presented results showing that length of stay had fallen by 9 per cent, which was more than in any previous year since Medicare's inception, but that admissions had also fallen by 3.5 per cent. The

Table 8.1 Retrospective versus prospective reimbursement: effects on length of stay

Authors	Description of study	Results
Louis *et al.* (1999)	Comparison of pre- and post-1995 reform data (DRG based hospital financing system) for nine common conditions in Italian hospitals	Decrease in average length of stay; increase in day hospital admissions; little or no change in readmission rates
Giammanco (1999)	Comparison of pre- and post-1995 reform data for public and private hospitals in Sicily	Decrease in average length of stay for both public and private hospitals; readmissions increased in both hospital types, but more so in public hospitals
Xiao *et al.* (2000)	Impact of casemix funding on five public hospitals in the Northern Territory of Australia	Decline in average length of stay, increase in number of casemix-weighted discharges and no change in readmission rates
Magnussen and Solstad (1994)	Pilot of four hospitals introducing case-based financing in Norway, compared to reference hospitals	No substantial impact on hospital efficiency
Dismuke and Sena (1999)	Experience of a phased implementation of a DRG system in hospitals over the course of the 1990s in Portugal	Mixed results in technical efficiency depending on the technology being considered
Guterman and Dobson (1986)	Before-and-after study of Medicare claims data including only hospitals subjected to Medicare PPS (which commenced in 1983)	Length of stay fell by 9% from 1981 to 1984
Sloan *et al.* (1988)	Before-and-after study of US national cohort of hospitals, using 34 hospitals in non-PPS states and non-Medicare patients as controls	Post PPS: Length of stay in ICUs constant; CAT scanning increased at slower rate; use of non-surgical techniques declined; use of routine tests declined
Newhouse and Byrne (1988)	Before-and-after study of all Medicare patients including all hospitals so as to control for patient shifting	1981–84: Length of stay increased by 9% 1981–85: Length of stay fell slightly (by 3%)

authors emphasised that this counter-intuitive result should be treated with caution since other factors were not controlled for, the possibility being that hospitals could still react to the increase in empty beds by raising admission rates. Interestingly, total expenditure on inpatients still increased, due partly to an ageing population and partly also to 'DRG creep'. In a controlled before and after study aimed at assessing the effect of Medicare prospective payment on the use of

Table 8.2 Retrospective versus prospective reimbursement: effects on outcome/quality of care

Authors	Description of study	Results
Louis *et al.* (1999)	Comparison of pre- and post-1995 reform data for nine common conditions in Italian hospitals	Severity of illness for hospitalised patients increased for most conditions; differences in adjusted mortality rates small
Wells *et al.* (1993)	Examined impact of PPS for depressed elderly patients in US acute care hospitals	Higher percentage of clinically appropriate admissions and improvement in quality of medication management; no difference in one year post-discharge mortality
Draper *et al.* (1990); Kahn *et al.* (1990a); Kahn *et al.* (1990b); Kosecoff *et al.* (1990); Rubenstein *et al.* (1990)	Uncontrolled before-and-after study comparing multiple time points pre-Medicare PPS (in 1981–82) in five US states. Various factors, such as hospital size and casemix, were controlled for. Five conditions were examined (congestive heart failure, myocardial infarction, pneumonia,cerebrovascular accident and hip fracture)	Implicit review judged improvements in quality of care: reduction from 25% to 12% receiving 'very poor care'; increase from 4% to 7% in patients discharged early and in unstable condition Measures of stability showed increase from 10% to 15% in patients discharged unstable Mortality: in hospital fell 3.5%; 30-day mortality fell 1.1%; 180-day mortality unchanged

medical technologies in hospitals, Sloan *et al.* (1988) found that length of stay within intensive care units did not change as a result of introducing prospective payment, whilst the use of many non-surgical procedures either continued to increase at a slower rate (e.g. CAT scans) or actually decreased (e.g. occupational and physical therapy). In this study, results for the non-Medicare control population mirrored those of the Medicare population, the most plausible explanation for this being that PPS influenced treatment patterns of the former group in addition to the latter for which it was intended. Effects on use of outpatient services and patient outcome were not estimated.

Newhouse and Byrne (1988) suggest that a fall in length of stay as a result of the Medicare PPS is simply an artefact of limiting analysis to only hospitals included in the PPS. When looking at all Medicare patients in all hospitals in 46 US states, Newhouse and Byrne found average length of stay rose slightly between 1981 and

1984 before falling, in 1985, to just below the 1981 average. One contributing factor to the doubt about PPS leading to reduced lengths of stay is reckoned to be patient shifting to modes of care not included in the PPS, a factor partly controlled for by analysing changes in length of stay in all hospitals.

Finally, the RAND study of the effects of the US Medicare PPS (see below) demonstrated a 24 per cent fall in length of stay for Medicare patients over the period 1981–82 to 1985–86 (Kahn *et al.*, 1990a). Despite its complexity, this study was uncontrolled and did not account for the criticisms of Newhouse and Byrne (1988).

Studies of the effect of such innovations on quality of care and outcome are surprisingly limited. Again, referring to the Italian study by Louis *et al.* (1999), post-1995 reforms found that severity of illness for hospitalised patients on most of the nine conditions under study did increase, while differences in adjusted mortality rates pre- to post-1995 were small. Further, in a US based before and after study, Wells *et al.* (1993) found that following PPS implementation, depressed elderly patients in acute care hospitals had improved quality in medication management and a higher percent of clinically appropriate admissions, but no change in one year post-discharge mortality. These results indicate that more appropriate uses of resources have been encouraged by such reimbursement schemes.

The RAND Corporation published several papers from its nationally representative study in a single issue of the Journal of the American Medical Association (Draper *et al.*, 1990; Kahn *et al.*, 1990a,b; Kosecoff *et al.*, 1990; Rubenstein *et al.*, 1990). Results from these papers demonstrated reductions in inpatient and 30-day mortality over the study period whilst 180-day mortality remained unchanged. Implicit review judged improvements in quality of care. However, there were substantial increases in numbers of patients discharged in an unstable condition. The main problem with these results is that it is not clear what would have happened to such measures in the absence of the PPS over the same period of time.

So, what is one to conclude on the effects of PPS on length of stay, cost and outcome? The old adage that 'more research is required' would seem to be appropriate here. Menke *et al.* (1998) state that despite broader adoption of Medicare's DRG system in the US, little is known about case-based payment in the general population. While one may conclude, as others who have reviewed the literature (e.g. Coulam and Gaumer 1991), that PPS has lead to a decrease in average length of stay, it is likely that outpatient visits have also increased, although this may be appropriate. While this issue of cost-shifting is discussed in more detail below, of greater significance here is the lack of meaningful quality and outcome data to inform whether further proliferation of prospective systems based on DRG-like methods is warranted. Interestingly, results from European and Australian settings are conflicting in terms of length of stay and cost, and importantly, strides to gauge the impact of PPS on the quality and outcome side have not been made. Clearly, in order to determine the best use of limited resources, in the context of hospital payment systems, more research on the effect of quality and outcomes is required (Zwanziger *et al.* 1994a; Braithwaite *et al.*, 1998).

Cost- and patient-shifting

Evidence on cost-shifting from inpatients to outpatients is also contradictory (see Table 8.3). The national survey in the US by Guterman and Dobson (1986) found outpatient expenditure to be increasing, but no more than past trends would have suggested, whilst Russell and Manning (1989), after examining Medicare expenditure projections to 1990 as estimated in 10 successive years, concluded that the PPS was having a major impact on Medicare's hospital expenses and that the savings were only partly offset by an increase in outpatient expenditures. Evidence on the changing distributions of doctor charges under Medicare found, on the other hand, large shifts from inpatients to outpatients (Fisher, 1987). Between 1982 and 1985 the proportion of doctor charges for inpatient activities fell from just over three-fifths to just under a half, mostly offset by increases in the share of services in outpatients.

Evidence of shifting costs from patient groups subjected to prospective payment to groups not subjected to such payments (i.e. private paying patients) has also

Table 8.3   Effects of prospective payments on cost-shifting

Authors	Description of study	Results
Guterman and Dobson (1986)	Before-and-after study of Medicare claims data	Outpatient expenditures post-PPS increased but no more than past trends would imply
Fisher (1987)	Before-and-after study of distribution of allowed physician charges under Medicare, comparing pre-PPS (1982) with post-PPS (1985)	1982: 61% of charges for inpatient services; 5% of charges related to outpatient services; 30% of charges related to office visits 1985: 50% of charges related to inpatient services; 12% of charges related to outpatient services; 32% of charges related to office visits
Dranove (1988)	Changes in prices charged to private patients regressed with profits from government-funded (Medicaid) patients in 79 hospitals in Illinois while accounting for case mix and occupancy	Hospitals responded to reductions in Medicaid payments by increasing prices to private patients
Russell and Manning (1989)	Compared hospital and outpatient expenditure projections for Medicare beneficiaries made before Medicare PPS with those made after, adjusted for inflation and admission rates	Hospital expenditure in 1990 US$18 billion less (in 1980 dollars) than expected before PPS went into effect. Little effect on outpatient expenditure projections
Clement (1997)	Examination of California hospital data from the 1980s and early 1990s	Cost shifting did occur but the ability of hospitals to cost shift decreased over time

been demonstrated. This was achieved by regressing changes in prices charged to private patients against profits from government-funded patients in 79 hospitals in Illinois after attempting to control for case mix and occupancy (Dranove, 1988). However, the key factor that Morrisey (1995) points out is that cost shifting *per se* only occurs when one group pays more *because* another group pays less. Thus, evidence of a different cost per inpatient day for private insurers and public insurers is not necessarily evidence of cost shifting. That said, Clement (1997) provides evidence based on California data from the 1980s and early 1990s that suggests that cost shifting did occur, but that the ability of hospitals to shift costs over time decreased. Again, with the contradictory evidence, Zwanziger *et al.* (2000a) have called for further analysis to better understand cost shifting and hospital behaviour.

Carroll and Erwin (1987) addressed the issue of patient shifting under competing reimbursement systems (see Table 8.4). This was a before-and-after study which investigated the impact of introducing prospective payments on the health state of inpatients upon discharge to long-term care facilities. Believing that prospective payments would induce shorter hospital stays, a significant increase in the disabilities and health problems of patients admitted to long-term care facilities upon hospital discharge was predicted. The data for 353 patients admitted to 10 long-term

Table 8.4 Effects of prospective payment on patient-shifting

Authors	Description of study	Results
Carroll and Erwin (1987)	Before-and-after study of impact of Medicare PPS on health state of patients on transfer to long-term care	Post-PPS, patients more likely to be incontinent of bladder, have naso-gastric tubes and be on dietary supplements. No more likely to be catheterised or less ambulant
Morrisey *et al.* (1988)	Before-and-after study of PPS on probability of transfer of Medicare beneficiaries from hospital to subacute care and on length of stay for five DRGs. Hospital and patient characteristics controlled for	Length of stay declined but not statistically significant at conventional levels. Probability of transfer increased, in particular for stroke, pneumonia and major joint and hip procedures
Sager *et al.* (1989)	Before-and-after study of Medicare PPS on location of elderly people at death using national mortality data specific for age and location of death. Controlled for overall mortality and changes in number of nursing home beds	1981–82 (pre-PPS): little change in proportion of deaths occurring in hospitals or nursing homes 1983–85 (post-PPS): progressive decline in proportion of deaths in hospital and increases in deaths in nursing homes

care facilities in Georgia were examined. The results showed significant statistical differences for three treatment and health status variables. Patients in the post-PPS group were more likely to be incontinent of bladder, to have naso-gastric tubes and to be on dietary supplements, suggesting a shift of the more dependent patients into long-term care facilities. However, catheterisation and ambulatory status did not show any significant differences between the groups. It was concluded, therefore, that minimal patient-shifting from hospital to long-term care facilities took place. However, only Medicare beneficiaries were considered, and no other forms of shifting than to long-term care facilities were explored. Moreover, the PPS occurred early in the transition period towards total implementation of the DRG system. As a result, only initial responses of hospitals and long-term care facilities to the PPS were measured. The study design thus had clear defects.

Further, more rigorous studies, however, do support the hypothesis that prospective payment has led to increased transfers to sub-acute care. Morrisey *et al.* (1988) found that the introduction of the Medicare PPS increased the likelihood of early discharge from hospital to sub-acute care and reduced length of stay for five common DRGs. Sager *et al.* (1989) examined changes in location of death of elderly people after the introduction of the Medicare PPS, the increase in nursing homes being greater than expected and accompanied by a decline in the percentage of deaths in hospitals. Resulting effects on quality of life for the clients concerned and, therefore, the efficiency of such transfers is not known. Finally, a review of the literature through the 1980s, cited earlier (Coulam and Gaumer 1991), also found an apparent increase in discharges to nursing homes under PPS. More recent studies on the impact of PPS on patient shifting were not identified in the literature. This is likely because of the changes in Medicare reimbursement described by Newhouse (2002). These changes led to reductions in spending on post-acute care, special nursing facilities and home health care of 17–45 per cent between 1997 and 1999. Of course, problems remain in attributing this reduction to the changes in financial incentives, and problems with such new incentive schemes still remain (e.g. it is more difficult to monitor the quality of such services). Once more, such changes could be appropriate, resulting from better matching of patient to provider, similar to the arguments in favour of PBC below (Lu *et al.*, 2002).

Clinical and global budgeting

As regards regulatory control over price times quantity, some work has also been carried out on clinical and global budgeting (see Table 8.5). In proposing to make clinicians budget holders, the UK experiment with clinical budgeting attempted to increase the awareness of, and provide incentives for, clinicians to be more efficient. The evidence on the effects of clinical budgeting on costs and outcomes has already been reviewed in Chapter 7, and, although found to be equivocal, some potential for positive results was displayed where adequate educational support was provided (Wickings *et al.*, 1985; Gibbens *et al.*, 1988; Gama *et al.*, 1991; Kerr *et al.*, 1996; Hopkins, 1999).

Table 8.5 Effects of budgeting on costs and outcomes

	Effects on cost	
Authors	*Description of study*	*Results*
Mushlin *et al.* (1988)	Uncontrolled before-and-after study of effect of prospective payment at hospital level on quality of care, availability and outcomes	More admissions for maternal problems associated with pregnancy and acute myocardial infarction
Redmon and Yakoboski (1995)	Examined global budgeting in France since its inception in 1984	Inpatient expenditure growth did slow through reductions in service volume, relative price of services remained unchanged

Many countries use global budgeting or expenditure caps to constrain growth in hospital and/or physician expenditures, but empirical assessment has been difficult as such budgeting is often utilised amidst other reforms (Wolfe and Moran, 1993). In essence, a global budget is simply an overall target or limit for spending that covers a defined set of services (Ashby and Greene, 1993). While global budgeting offers the potential for cost savings, it is thought that reductions in volume and increases in price are required to meet budget targets over time.

Evidence from France suggests that, since the introduction of global budgeting in 1984, inpatient expenditure growth was slowed, but this was done primarily through reductions in service volume, while relative price of services remained unchanged (Redmon and Yakoboski, 1995). Another experiment with global prospective hospital budgeting, in the US, resulted in appropriately reduced inpatient admissions for some conditions (e.g. less elective inpatient surgery for which more care was provided on an ambulatory basis) and stable community-wide outcomes along with increased admissions for apparently more serious problems associated with the management of maternal illness and acute myocardial infarction. The authors concluded that such results demonstrate that community-wide prospective payment can be financially and clinically successful (Mushlin *et al.*, 1988). Evidence, from Roos *et al.* (1990) and Globerman *et al.* (2002), comparing the Canadian and US systems is mixed, showing, in the main, few differences in survival rates for various hospital procedures.

It has also been claimed that annual global prospective hospital budgeting has resulted in a significantly less rapid rise in hospital expenditures in Canada than in the US (Evans *et al.*, 1989). Despite this, the system of hospital financing is similar in Sweden, which has one of the highest cost health services in the world. Therefore, it is not necessarily the ability to cap costs which counts, but actually

159

exercising that ability. In any case, further properly controlled studies are required to assess fully the impact of global budgeting on both the realisation of cost containment as well as patient outcomes.

Competition

Studies used to examine the effects of competition on costs and outcome are listed in Tables 8.6 and 8.7. In the US, a comprehensive review of work up to the mid-1990s

Table 8.6 Effects of competition on costs

Authors	Description of study	Results
Robinson (1996)	Impact of HMOs on hospital capacity, utilisation and expenditures from 1983 to 1993 in California	Expenditures grew less rapidly in markets with high HMO penetration
Gaskin and Hadley (1997)	National sample examining the impact of HMO penetration on hospital expenditure	High penetration HMO markets had a slower rate of growth in expenses then low penetration markets
Bamezai *et al.* (1999)	National data examining hospital expenditure in relation to HMO penetration and hospital competition for 1989 and 1994	HMO penetration is not enough; also need high level of hospital competition to restrain growth in hospital costs
Mukamel *et al.* (2001)	Examined the effect of HMO market penetration and HMO competition on mortality, for a large national sample	HMO market penetration and increased HMO competition associated with lower mortality
Propper and Soderlund (1998)	Examined the impact of UK NHS internal market reforms on expenditure	Found indication that competition resulted in lower prices being offered to smaller purchasers; significant but delayed effect on costs apparent
Tambour and Rehnbert (1997)	Examined productivity in Swedish health councils between 1990 and 1994	Productivity improved for internal market and budget county councils, with higher rate in internal market councils
Robinson and Luft (1988)	Controlled before-and-after study of California's selective contracting experiment. Other factors, such as case-mix, mix of payers, teaching roles, ownership status and numbers of local physicians were controlled for. Controlled comparison was with 43 states in the US.	1982–86: cost inflation down 10.1%, with effects concentrated in areas of high competition
Zwanziger *et al.* (2000)	Examined effects of selective contracting on a large set of hospitals in California from 1983 to 1997	Hospitals in more competitive areas had a lower rate of increase in both costs and revenues

Table 8.7 Effects of competition on outcomes

Authors	Description of study	Results
Cubellis (1997)	Examined surgical outcomes over a nine-year period in a set of California hospitals	Selective contracting was found to have a beneficial effect on open heart surgery outcomes
Ware *et al.* (1986)	Randomised controlled trial of prepaid group practice HMO versus FFS care	On average: no differences between HMO and FFS in terms of health habits, psychological health, risk of dying and general health Low income, initially sick: more bed days and more serious symptoms in HMO than in 'free' FFS Low income, high risk: greater risk of dying in HMO High income, initially sick: general health rating better in HMO than 'free' FFS High income, high risk: risk of dying less in HMO

found that HMO patients on average consume fewer hospital resources due to shorter lengths of stay, fewer ancillary resources being used and a lower rate of admission (Miller and Luft, 1994). More recent work has confirmed these findings and furthered the issue by examining not just the effect on hospitals of HMO versus non-HMO plans, but also in looking at the impact of the level of HMO penetration and the degree of competition between HMOs. For example, Robinson (1996) investigated the impact of HMOs in California from 1983 to 1993 and found that hospital expenditures grew at a less rapid rate in markets with high HMO penetration than those with low penetration. Giving further weight to this perspective, this finding was mirrored in a 1985 to 1993 national sample (Gaskin and Hadley, 1997). The containment in high over low penetration markets in the California study was due largely to reductions in volume and service mix, but also due to changes in bed intensity and bed capacity (Robinson, 1996). This has been confirmed in a later review by Miller and Luft (2002). As such, the assertion has been made that greater HMO penetration leads to moving hospitals to the periphery of health care, in lieu of non-hospital ambulatory services, with Miller and Luft (2002) showing that increased penetration leads to more preventive activities but reduced access to uncompensated care and high-cost technology (such as magnetic resonance imaging).

Taking this work a step further, Bamezai *et al.* (1999) examined national US data and found that expenditure growth in hospitals is related not only to HMO penetration but also the degree of competition in the hospital market. However,

Mukamel *et al.* (2001) argue that lower mortality is related not to competition between hospitals but rather to HMO market penetration and increased HMO competition. It is not clear, though, if these results are explained by the effect of penetration on practice or due to a selection bias, with HMOs being attracted to areas with better hospital care. In any case, taking this literature as a whole, it is clear that HMOs intensify price competition between hospitals (Dranove and White, 1994), which can significantly reduce hospital cost inflation (Robinson, 1991), so long as barriers to selective contracting are removed, as discussed below.

Evidence from Europe has also come to bear on internal markets throughout the 1990s. In the early to mid-1990s, economists were sceptical that competition was leading to improvements in resource allocation in the UK (Maynard, 1994). However, later that decade, evidence did arise to support the view that competition does lower prices, albeit partially (Propper, 1996). Further work also indicated that competition did have an effect, with lower prices being offered to smaller purchasers (Propper and Soderlund, 1998). Still, even if there was an apparent effect of competition on costs, such impact on an annual basis is small, and measuring changes in quality in a comprehensive manner is difficult. However, controlling for important characteristics (such as hospital size and teaching status) and exploiting the policy changes of the 1990s (whereby there was no competition until 1991, actively encouraged competition until 1995, less encouragement in 1996 and active discouragement post 1997), Propper *et al.* (2004) show that there was a negative relationship between mortality, post-treatment for heart attack and competition. Of course, a fall in quality may be expected to accompany a fall in costs and such a relationship, between competition and outcomes, may not exist for other services.

Ironically, however, although many elements of the internal market have been retained in the reforms of the Labour Government since 1997, there is less of an emphasis on competition. More 'top-down instruments of performance management' (Smith, 2002) have been introduced, such as centralised target setting for disease and health inequality reductions and treatment times, National Service Frameworks (setting standards for specific conditions or services), and the National Institute for Clinical Excellence (which issues detailed guidance on the use of technologies). Monitoring is undertaken through a Performance Assessment Framework (a set of about 60 performance indicators) and the Commission for Health Improvement (which inspects and reports publicly on every NHS organisation). The reception of these reforms has been mixed. Smith (2002) states that they represent a more sophisticated approach to performance management than has ever been used in the NHS. However, as mentioned in the previous chapter, early indications are that moving the emphasis away from competition has had a detrimental effect (Le Grand, 2002). The recent re-introduction of Foundation Hospitals in the England, may, in part, be a response to this problem; hospitals are ranked according to how well they perform and, if ranked in the lowest category, they are given a period of time to reach certain targets, and, if they fail to meet these, private management teams and those from other (say, neighbouring) hospitals can compete to take over the management of the 'failing' hospitals. This 'franchise' scheme remains unevaluated. However, reflecting a point raised by McGuire and Hughes (2003), in the context of internal markets more generally, it is unclear the extent to which (now smaller) purchasing units (i.e. Primary Care Trusts (PCTs)) will be able to exert any authority against (still) large 'three-star' Foundation Hospitals. This could be characterised as leading to less of a focus on population health as more resources are 'sucked' into acute services, which may or may not be efficient. To redress the balance on the English system, it may be necessary to have fundholding and/or health authority purchasing reappear, although, for political reasons, with a different name.

In Sweden, Tambour and Rehnberg (1997) found that productivity in health councils from 1991 to 1994, for both internal market and 'control' county councils, improved, with the rate of productivity being higher in internal market councils. However, they found that market mechanisms were only one factor in productivity gains, with the resource allocation system (e.g., performance based) and other health care reforms also having an impact. Further work from Sweden suggests that internal market reforms did aim to reduce costs but in the end did not generate much competition between hospitals (Harrison and Calltorp, 2000). This study also presents evidence that quality of health care was not adversely affected by the reforms.

This leads into a discussion on yet another innovation in health care, that of PBCs. The basic idea behind PBCs is simply to reward good performance. That is, a PBC sets a base compensation and then offers an opportunity for further compensation on the basis of improvements in quality of care or treatment outcomes (Lu *et al.*, 2002). The context is one where both a purchaser and provider exist, so that the provider can be rewarded by the purchaser for good performance through additional funding. A comprehensive review of the empirical evidence of PBCs by Lu and Donaldson (2000) highlighted the potential for this reform, although a key concern was found to be valid and reliable outcome measurement.

In addition, the PBC literature surveyed in this paper indicated that organisations must develop an information system to track outcomes, and that both positive and negative consequences, through 'unintended incentives', can arise. For example, if funding is based on good performance, providers have an incentive to treat selectively patients with a greater probability of having an improved outcome. In relation, though, more efficient matching between patients and providers may also arise due to the financial incentive resting on the performance of the provider. That is, the incentive exists for those 'mis-matched' patients to be referred on to more suitable providers, which in turn will aid in avoiding a poorer outcome and the accompanying financial penalty (Lu *et al.*, 2002). One further issue pertaining to PBCs is the potential for reporting better treatment outcomes than actually exist, leaving purchasers to discern enhanced performance due to a true effect and a gaming effect (Lu, 1999). In summary, noting these challenging issues, the limited practical evidence does suggest that PBCs do have the ability to improve both accountability and efficiency in health care.

As mentioned earlier, selective contracting appeared in California in the 1980s as a means of fostering price competition among health care providers by encouraging the use of a type of HMOs called preferred provider organisations (PPOs). An extensive review of the literature found selective contracting to have enabled managed care plans to obtain lower prices from hospitals, particularly when there is more competition in the hospital market (Morrisey, 2001). However, limited evidence exists on the effect of selective contracting on quality or health outcomes.

Early work by Robinson and Luft (1988) demonstrated that the Californian strategy reduced hospital cost inflation by 10 per cent over the period 1982 to 1986 compared with 43 control states, but that the effects were almost entirely confined to areas of high competition (i.e. local markets with more than ten competitors). These results were confirmed in a study which examined a large set of hospitals in California over a 14-year period (1983–97). Zwanziger *et al.* (2000b) found that hospitals in more competitive areas had a substantially lower rate of increase in both costs and revenues, which was attributed to the growth in selective contracting. However, it was unclear if the cost reductions were due to increased efficiency or reduced quality. In essence, with selective contracting, providers negotiate in advance with contractors to accept fixed payment rates. By excluding high cost providers, and with the introduction of price competition, third party payer's expenditures are reduced, the conclusion being that price competition, based on California's experience, can change provider behaviour (Zwanziger *et al.*, 1994b).

Despite these arguments in apparent favour of selective contracting, empirical evidence in California also suggests that costs escalated for over half the public hospitals through the 1980s as uncompensated burdens rose. As many counties were left without a public hospital by 1990, access to those hospitals by the poor diminished (Mobley 1998). Not to discount this concern, Cubellis (1997) did find that over a nine-year period (1984 to 1991), selective contracting in a set of California hospitals had a beneficial effect on surgical outcomes for open heart surgery. The key factors contributing to this effect were patient concentration (high volume resulting in high quality outcomes) and contractor monitoring of patients in network hospitals. Earlier work, also referred to in Chapter 7, is presented here in Table 8.7 (Ware *et al.*, 1986). In summary, empirical evidence from the US and Europe would seem to indicate that competition has served to reduce hospital expenditures. That said, as a whole, the impact of competition on quality and health outcomes has not adequately been assessed to date. More detailed work, examining the precise impact of competition on hospital costs is required, as is quite clearly the impact on outcomes. Finally, as pointed out in Chapters 6 and 7, although not an issue related to moral hazard in the hospital sector *per se*, the potential failure of HMOs due to patients selecting out of plans must be considered more broadly in weighing out what reforms should be accepted, and which should be left alone.

DOES OWNERSHIP MAKE A DIFFERENCE?

Given the extent of private ownership of hospitals in a number of countries it is useful in this context to address the question of whether hospital ownership makes any difference to efficiency. This can be done by examining, for like groups of patients, whether one type of hospital care costs less than another with no detrimental effects on patient outcome or, in studies where case mix is not controlled, whether there is evidence that the less costly type of care achieves this gain as a result of treating less complicated cases or, more accurately, through avoiding treating more complicated cases (i.e. 'cream skimming'). Such comparisons are important as it is often implicitly assumed that private ownership leads to greater efficiency.

Early studies in the US compared investor-owned chain hospitals with not-for-profit community hospitals (Lewin *et al.*, 1981; Pattison and Katz, 1983; Sloan and Vraciu, 1983; Becker and Sloan, 1985; Watt *et al.*, 1986). The former generated greater net income (revenue minus operating costs) but also higher operating costs per admission and per day in four out of the five studies reviewed (Table 8.8). Costs per admission ranged from being 4 per cent lower to 8 per cent higher in investor-owned hospitals. However, adjusting for occupancy still does not make up the cost difference (Institute of Medicine, 1986). The greater net income of the for-profit hospitals, despite their higher costs, was explained by their larger mark-up over costs and greater use of high profit activities such as laboratory tests (Lewin *et al.*, 1981; Pattison and Katz, 1983; Watt *et al.*, 1986). It has been suggested that, unless it is assumed that for-profit hospitals treat patients in greater need, or produce a higher outcome, then the greater use of high-profit tests and other procedures indicates the discretionary use of these services – a species of supplier-induced demand (Relman, 1983). Data on outcome show no consistent pattern of mortality rates across types of hospital ownership for Medicare patients who had undergone elective surgery between 1974 and 1981 (Gaumer, 1986).

Longitudinal data from 1985 to 1996 examined medical expenditures and health outcomes for non-rural Medicare beneficiaries hospitalised for heart attacks (Kessler and McClellan, 2000). This study found that areas with a presence of for-profit hospitals had a 2.4 per cent lower level of expenditure overall, with the same patient health outcomes. In contrast, Silverman *et al.* (1999) examined data from 1989, 1992 and 1995, and reported that spending was significantly higher for each year under study in for-profit as compared to not-for-profit areas for all categories studied (hospital services, physician services, home health care, and services at other facilities). However, this study did not consider outcomes, so conclusions about relative efficiency cannot be made.

Following the trend of ambiguity, Sloan (1998) compared cost and quality of care for 2700 Medicare patients in 1400 facilities in for-profit, not-for-profit and government hospitals. They found no significant differences between cost and patient outcomes between hospital type for hip fracture, coronary heart disease and congestive heart failure. However, in a study which examined quality of

165

Table 8.8   Studies of effect of ownership on costs

Authors	Description of study	Results
Sloan and Vraciu (1983)	Comparison of for-profit chain and not-for-profit hospitals under 400 beds in Florida	Cost per adjusted day: for-profit 3% lower Cost per adjusted admission: for-profit 4% lower
Pattison and Katz (1983)	Comparison of for-profit chain and not-for-profit private hospitals in California, excluding large teaching, Kaiser, rural, specialty and tertiary	Cost per patient-day: for-profit 6% higher Cost per admission: for-profit 2% higher
Becker and Sloan (1985)	Regression analysis of national - sample of for-profit chain and not-for-profit hospitals, adjusting for case-mix, teaching status, size, and area characteristics	Cost per adjusted patient day: for-profit 10% higher Cost per adjusted admission: for-profit 8% higher
Watt *et al.* (1986)	Comparison of national samples of 80 matched pairs of for-profit chain and not-for profit hospitals adjusted for case-mix differences	Cost per adjusted admission and per adjusted day: for-profit higher but not significantly different
Kessler and McClellan (2000)	Longitudinal data from 1985–96, examined medical expenditures and outcomes for Medicare beneficiaries hospitalised for heart attacks	Areas with presence of for profit hospitals had a 2.4% lower level of expenditure with the same outcomes
Silverman *et al.* (1999)	Data from 1989, 1992, 1995 to calculate spending in areas served by for-profit and not-for-profit hospitals	Significantly higher spending for each year under study in for-profit areas for all categories
Sloan *et al.* (1998)	Compared cost and quality data for 2700 Medicare patients hospitalised in for-profit, not-for-profit and government facilities	No significant differences identified for cost and outcomes
Thomas *et al.* (2000)	Quality of care examined by hospital ownership for Colorado and Utah patients in 1992	For-profit ownership had significantly higher preventable adverse outcomes than non-profit ownership

inpatient care by hospital type in Colorado and Utah in 1992, the findings were that for-profit ownership had significantly higher preventable adverse events than not-for-profit ownership (Thomas *et al.* 2000). In Bangladesh, one study compared private and public hospitals on a number of quality aspects including responsiveness and communication (Andaleeb, 2000). In this study, private hospitals were consistently rated higher by consumers.

Noting the confusion in the literature, a thorough review provides the following insights (Constance *et al.* 2000). First, the effect of the difference in ownership is minimised in a competitive market. Second, the association between ownership and patient outcomes varies depending on the dimension under consideration. For example, the evidence is mixed or inconclusive with respect to ownership and access to care, morbidity and mortality, while an association between for profit status and adverse events is consistently supported. A similarly ambiguous set of results was obtained in the review by Currie *et al.* (2003). Of 34 studies reviewed, most were indeterminate with respect to relative costs, quality of care or efficiency, a conclusion which is contrary to more selective reviews of the literature on this topic. Further assessment of content and context lead the authors to argue that much of the evidence on for-profit and not-for-profit comparisons is irrelevant to debates on contracting out in Canadian health care and, presumably, by extension, to other publicly funded health care systems:

> The main objective of for-profit hospitals, of course, is to make profits. This is achieved, in part, by selling services, the characteristics of which are not necessarily fully accounted for in empirical studies. In a market-orientated environment, such hospitals cannot be criticised for selling a service for which consumers are willing to pay. This is like criticising Rolls Royce or BMW as being inefficient because they sell expensive motor cars! The fact that many for-profits show higher margins of surplus than not-for-profits would seem to indicate that they are, in some sense, more efficient, even if more costly. (Currie *et al.*, 2003)

This reinforces the point made several years ago by Richardson (1987) that:

> private hospitals did achieve their main objective, namely an increase in profits. The hospitals responded to the incentives provided by the US health care market. It is not their concern that revenue to them is a cost to the remainder of society. It is possible that in another market with a different set of incentives a more favourable social result would be achieved.

Perhaps this is what the UK Government tried to achieve by incorporating private hospitals into an 'internal market' where finance and contractual arrangements remain publicly controlled (for the most part) and heavily regulated. This policy has been reinforced recently in Canada, Australia and the UK (Alberta Health and Wellness, 1999).

TOWARDS A SOLUTION: BACK TO BUDGETING?

The most depressing conclusion from this review is that despite much work, the relative efficiency of most reimbursement mechanisms has yet to be determined. This is mainly because of a dearth of data on patient outcomes. Competitive initiatives in the form of HMOs seem to achieve cost savings, mainly through reductions in the quantity (i.e. number of hospital admissions) rather than price of services used. However, such effects may be achieved at the possible expense of patient outcome. Internal markets seem to be able to reduce hospital cost inflation by affecting both price and quantity, but their effects on quality of care and patient outcome are still unknown. What is more, the effects of internal markets in

California were achieved only in local markets containing several competitors. There may be less potential for such competition in hospital markets in other countries, such as the UK, although some studies have shown that potential does exit. In addition, given previous research demonstrating that US citizens are two to three times more likely to be admitted for common hospital procedures than their UK counterparts (McPherson *et al.*, 1982; Coulter *et al.*, 1988; Francome and Savage, 1993; Cherkin *et al.*, 1994), the 40 per cent reductions in admissions achieved by the HMO in the RAND HIE would still leave US admission rates higher than in the UK. This suggests that the scope for such cost savings in health care systems like the UK NHS is, of course, less than in the US. This argument also highlights the danger of unthinkingly transferring results of valuable US studies of interesting US initiatives to non-US contexts.

Initiatives regulating solely on the price of hospital care have the fundamental weakness of a lack of control over quality and quantity of care provided. This has been demonstrated by the evidence highlighting the indeterminate effects of PPSs using DRGs. Indeed, the study by Newhouse and Byrne (1988) means that evidence on whether PPSs reduce the length of hospital inpatient stays at all, and hence reduce cost per case, must be treated as equivocal. As a means of controlling total expenditures PPS also remains vulnerable to any compensating increases in patient throughput. Although more research is necessary on this subject, there is limited evidence that achievement of short-term goals of shorter lengths of stay and fewer tests through the use of DRGs may have adverse long-term effects in terms of greater hospital admissions and worse medical outcomes. Current evidence is unclear about the extent of cost-shifting and patient-shifting under PPS. A safeguard in any one hospital is obviously for all beneficiaries to be contracted under the same payment system, but how this would affect other non-hospital sectors is not clear. It would prevent cost-shifting but not patient-shifting and would still leave the system vulnerable to knock-on effects on throughput. The question of whether patient-shifting and knock-on effects represent efficient practice would still need to be answered.

The usefulness of such results on PPSs for health care policy depends on the intended use of case-mix classification systems. Evidence points to the conclusion that DRGs are useful as a planning tool (e.g. to standardise care provided for particular conditions) within a system of global prospective budgeting rather than using DRGs themselves as the principal mechanism for financing care. However, even using DRGs as a standardisation tool can be called into question at this moment in time. The problem is that DRG standardisation cannot be useful as a planning tool until more is known about what represents efficient clinical practice. The current implication is that reducing variations around the prevailing average cost of treating people in any DRG will result in increased efficiency. However, small variation around the mean is not necessarily any better than large variation if we have no idea what efficient practice is (Donaldson and Magnussen, 1992). Instead, we need to focus on establishing efficient practice criteria before introducing the planning and incentive mechanisms to achieve it. In this process, DRGs should ideally be used as an end point and not a starting point. The literature referred to earlier in this chapter on variations in care, comprehensively reviewed by Andersen and Mooney (1990) further highlights the need to establish efficient practice criteria, especially when there has been little research done to date on the impact of such variations on health outcomes.

Obviously, reductions in length of stay could be accompanied by more admissions, thus putting more demands on hospital resources. However, this should not prevent consideration of appropriate resource use relative to patient outcomes in trying to achieve an optimal use of such resources. In this respect, the limited evidence presented in this chapter is supportive of this approach. Control of total costs (i.e. price times quantity) through clinical and global budgeting has been seen to be effective in cost control without being harmful to patients.

Therefore, we propose that the starting point for hospital funding (which has already been reached in the UK) should involve clinicians being given budgets based on historical costs. In working with such budgets, it would be possible to examine current uses of factor inputs as well as outcomes achieved. Once current uses and outcomes are known, it should be possible to examine whether clinicians can achieve either the same levels of outcome at less cost or improved outcome for the same cost. Then funding (possibly DRGs) could be based on efficient health care practice and standardisation would be according to efficiency rather than current average cost.

Of course, this is why the results of the clinical budgeting in the UK are so important. However, to use such results to standardise payments for care on the basis of average cost would inhibit the ability of an internal market to price spare capacity at marginal cost.[4] This is why DRGs do not have to be the end point – nor even, necessarily, an intermediate point.

CONCLUSIONS

One of the most striking messages to emerge from this review has been the indeterminate effects of attempts to control hospital costs by regulating prices only: more specifically, the US Medicare PPS using DRGs remains vulnerable to compensatory increases in patient throughput, despite cost per case and cost per admission being reduced. Cost-shifting and patient-shifting under any PPS are potential problems. HMOs have achieved cost savings which could be a result of selection or reductions in quality of care. Other competitive innovations, such as those in selective contracting in California, reduce costs, but only in areas with high concentrations of hospitals and with unclear effects on patient outcome. In publicly funded systems, competition does appear to have had a positive impact on productivity whilst reducing costs. Performance-based contracting has potential, although, as with all reforms, it is difficult to obtain reliable information on quality of care and outcomes. Private ownership does not necessarily result in more or less costly hospital care.

To date, many innovations in hospital funding have focussed too much on cost minimisation as an objective. What is important is the identification of cost reductions which can be achieved with little or no effect on patient outcome. In this respect, we propose that the most fruitful way forward in this area is to use clinical budgeting to monitor both costs and outcomes, thus establishing efficient modes of practice in hospitals. Based on the limited evidence on outcome to date, it is regulatory controls of total costs (or price times quantity), at global and clinical levels, which appear to offer the greatest potential for maintaining patient outcomes at lesser cost. It now seems that some element of regulated competition or performance-based contracting would enhance this potential.

ACHIEVING EQUITY

INTRODUCTION

Chapters 6, 7 and 8 have all been concerned with reviewing empirical evidence about different financial arrangements for health care and their effects on efficient consumer and producer behaviour. But, as indicated in Chapter 5, a system's health care objectives are not exclusively concerned with efficiency. Equity, too, is an important objective. The desire to achieve a fair allocation of health care resources prevails within any given society although its precise meaning and importance depends on cultural beliefs and social attitudes.

The overall aim of this chapter is to determine how successful different methods of financing health care are at achieving a fair allocation of health care resources. Sometimes international comparisons can be made but more often success will be judged according to a country's own equity objectives. Thus, where appropriate, the equity objectives selected in Chapter 5 (Table 5.2) will be scrutinized – financial contributions according to ability to pay; and equality of access. In Chapter 5 we outlined the problems of defining and measuring access. Therefore, it will be seen in this chapter that evidence on equality of access is often proxied by evidence on equality of expenditure and equality of utilisation.

In pursuing this aim a number of areas of enquiry are explored. Is there evidence to suggest that population coverage of and access to health care insurance are sizable problems? If so, do they seem to be getting larger? What policy recommendations and actions might countries use to mitigate such adverse effects? Do substantially publicly financed health care systems do better as regards coverage and access to health care than more privately financed systems?

In the following section the possible forms of government intervention in health care financing are discussed with respect to their impact on equity. This is followed by a review of the evidence on vertical equity; by examining the relationship between income and health care contributions and by examining the evidence on effects of patient charges and community financing on equity. Finally the evidence on equity as equality of access is reviewed. We do this by drawing some broad international comparisons and then by examining more detailed evidence from three countries; the US, Canada and the UK.

THE ROLE OF GOVERNMENT IN HEALTH CARE FINANCING

One aspect of health care equity may be considered by looking at how comprehensively health care systems cover their respective populations. However, comprehensive coverage is not a sufficient condition to guarantee the provision of adequate insurance protection. Protection must cover the risk of financial hardship and provide sufficient access (however defined) to health services.

As discussed in Chapters 3 and 4, the failure of voluntary health care insurance markets to provide comprehensive insurance cover gives government intervention legitimacy. Such intervention may be by helping the market to work or by taking greater control. There are potentially four ways that government intervention can ensure comprehensive cover: making subsidised insurance compulsory; using tax revenue to finance care that is mostly free at the point of use; using subsidies to offset experience-rated premiums; and requiring community-rating for catastrophic insurance. These options therefore represent a continuum of levels of government intervention.

Making health care insurance compulsory controls all effects of adverse selection. A publicly financed insurance system purchasing health insurance through an agency of the state can purchase or provide insurance cover for the whole community on a community-rated basis. A public intermediary can also embody redistributive policies into health care financing in a way which a private market cannot. The purchase of insurance for the whole population enables the financial intermediary to separate the value of insurance contributions from the expected risk levels of each individual (i.e. community-rating). Alternatively the government can provide the insurance and charge 'social insurance' premiums on a community basis. Compulsory participation may be by consumers, by employers or by both.

Providing free health care is similar in effect to compulsory public insurance in that competition between financial intermediaries is removed. The extent of progressivity of the taxation system used to extract contributions may provide the opportunity for payment according to community-rating or a more pro-poor and pro-ill formulation. It is prudent to recognise that unless community-rated systems are subsidised, community-rating itself may cause people to be uninsured since it raises prices for low risks above their expected value. However, compared to full experience-rating, community-rating probably causes more poor people to become insured but more good risks to become uninsured. How large these empirical effects are is not known.

Both these means of countering selection bias in the voluntary insurance market have been widely implemented in various forms. The remaining two methods require minimalist government intervention but, to date, there has been limited experience of how either solution might work in practice.

It is believed that experience-rated premiums with subsidies could check adverse selection in the voluntary health insurance market by introducing subsidies to individuals at high risk of needing health services. This would ensure access to health care by making higher premiums affordable. Subsidies could take many forms, either cash or in kind. One method could be to use health vouchers enabling individuals to purchase health insurance. A variation on this is the policy of 'lifetime community rating' which involves setting of premiums such that they take account of individuals' life time risks averaged over the lifetime of enrolment. Therefore those who first enrol at a young age enjoy lower premiums than someone who first joins at a later stage in life. This, along with a tax subsidy, has been employed recently in Australia as a means of stemming the flow of patients out of private health insurance – a manifestation of the adverse selection problem associated with mandatory community rating (Willcox, 2001).

The final possibility would be selective community rating which would divide the means of purchasing health care into health risks that impose 'large' financial losses and those that impose 'small' financial losses. Thus the first part would have a special regulated insurance market for catastrophic coverage and a second part for regular care. Alternatively the second part could be out-of-pocket payments. In this form the worst effects of adverse selection would be controlled, the lack of cover for major health care expenses. It may still be necessary to provide subsidies for low-income groups for whom the regular premiums or out-of-pocket expenses would take up too large a proportion of their income. Some theoretical foundation for this solution is given by Pauly (1986). The main benefit from insurance comes from cover against large financial losses, as occurs in the event of a catastrophic illness.

EVIDENCE ON VERTICAL EQUITY

Are health care systems successful in achieving an equitable basis for the financing of health care? Do richer members of society finance a disproportionately greater share of health care expenditure than poorer members and is there adequate protection from catastrophic expenditure? For many health care systems vertical equity in financing is an overt objective (e.g. UK and South Africa). For many others it is implied (e.g. Canada) and for yet others it is seen as desirable (e.g. most low-income countries). For the few health care systems which rely predominantly on private sources of finance (such as in the US) vertical equity is much harder to recognise as a transparent objective.

Income and health care contributions

A number of early studies have addressed the question of vertical equity. In these studies it has been usual to examine the distributions of health care finance in relation to post-tax (disposable) income distributions for each country. Gottschalk *et al.* (1989), for example, compared the financial arrangements of the US, UK and Dutch health care systems. The results showed the UK having the most progressive method of paying for health care with 90 per cent of health care finance from general taxation. The Dutch health care financial arrangements were proportional; for seven of the ten income deciles the proportion of medical care bill paid was similar to the proportion of income received. The US sources of health care finance on balance were extremely inequitable. The highest income decile was the only group which contributed less to health care financing. All other income deciles received smaller shares of post-tax income but greater shares of health care payments were extracted from them. Furthermore, this situation was greater the lower the income decile.

These studies were limited because the nature of the analyses was such that they compared distributions of disposable income with distributions of health care contributions. This means that while it was possible to determine whether or not each system was progressive, the relativities between health care systems could not be examined, that is, how much more progressive or regressive in its financing one health care system is compared to another. To do this a single measure of progressivity is required for each system. This question was, more recently, addressed by a European group of researchers working under the banner of ECuity. They measured the degree of progressivity of the various forms of payment for health care: public payments – direct taxes, indirect taxes, general taxes and social insurance – and private payments – private insurance and direct payments – using Kakwani indices for which a positive value represents progressivity and a negative value regressivity.[1] These were compared across a number of European countries and the US (see Table 9.1) and are based on a comparison of the distribution of income before and after payments for health care are made (Wagstaff *et al.*, 1999a).

There are, however, some important caveats to bear in mind when interpreting the Kakwani index (van Doorslaer *et al.*, 1999a). First, it does not provide a

Table 9.1 Progressivity (Kakwani) indices for health care expenditures

	*Total public**	*Total private***	*Total payments*
Denmark (1987)	0.0372	−0.2363	−0.0047
Finland (1990)	0.0604	−0.2419	0.0181
France (1989)	0.1112	−0.3054	0.0012
Germany (1989)	−0.0533	−0.0067	−0.0452
Italy (1991)	0.0712	−0.0612	0.0413
Netherlands (1987)	−0.1003	0.0434	−0.0703
Portugal (1990)	0.0723	−0.2287	−0.0445
Spain (1990)	0.0509	−0.1627	0.0004
Sweden (1990)	0.0100	−0.2402	−0.0158
Switzerland (1992)	0.1389	−0.2945	−0.1402
UK (1993)	0.0792	−0.0919	0.051
US (1987)	0.1060	−0.3168	−0.1303

Notes
* Total public comprise direct taxes, indirect taxes, general taxes and social insurance.
** Total private comprise private insurance and direct payments.

Source: Wagstaff *et al.* (1999a).

complete picture of the total redistributive effect of a system's health care financing as account must also be taken on any horizontal inequities in the financing system; that is individuals with the same income through various circumstances may pay different amounts for health care (e.g. through concessions available for different groups within the tax system or variations in eligibility to different social health insurance schemes determined by employment type). Another limitation is that health care payments may actually result in changes in the ranking of individuals in terms of income distribution. In other words, where individuals sit on the income ladder in terms of the amount of money they have available to spend may change as a result of paying for health care (this is referred to in the literature as 'reranking'). Because the Kakwani index measures only the before and after distributions, it would not be sensitive to cases where, for instance, income was directly redistributed from one individual to another so that there was simply a switch in rankings between the two. Wagstaff *et al.* (1999b) indicate that the overall redistributive impact of health care financing is ultimately relatively minor compared to that effected by personal income taxation.

Table 9.2 summarises the findings from a companion paper that examines the overall redistributive effect of health care financing in 12 OECD countries. It found that Finland, France, Italy, Spain and the UK were progressive overall. The countries that were regressive were Denmark, Germany, Netherlands, Portugal, Sweden, Switzerland and the US (van Doorslaer *et al.*, 1999).[2] Such findings, to a large extent, depend on the different sources of health care funding upon which each country draws and the balance between such sources. The evidence suggests that direct and general taxes are generally progressive; indirect taxes and direct payments are regressive; social insurance payments, with a few exceptions, tend to be

Table 9.2   Redistributive effect of health care expenditure

	Total public[*]	Total private[**]	Total payments
Denmark (1987)	0.0024	−0.0021	−0.0005
Finland (1990)	0.0055	−0.0039	na
France (1989)	na	na	0.0070
Germany (1988)	−0.0086	−0.0004	−0.0062
Italy (1991)	0.0070	−0.0021	0.0048
Netherlands (1992)	−0.0096	0.0005	−0.0086
Portugal (1990)	0.0030	−0.0110	−0.0090
Sweden (1990)	na	na	0.0040
Switzerland (1992)	0.0036	−0.0136	−0.0102
UK (1993)	0.0044	−0.0020	na
US (1987)	0.0063	−0.0223	−0.0173

Notes
[*] Total public comprise direct taxes, indirect taxes, general taxes and social insurance.
[**] Total private comprise private insurance and direct payments.
n.a not available.

Source: van Doorslaer *et al.* (1999).

progressive and; private insurance, also with some exceptions, tend to be regressive. Therefore countries that rely more heavily on direct taxes rather than indirect taxes can expect to be more progressive overall and vice versa.

In terms of specific issues of access and financial hardship, it appears that the US system has more documented problems than most countries. Poor individuals are more exposed to the risk of financial hardship than are richer individuals and there are a significant number of hospitals and physicians threatened with bad debt because individuals do not have adequate protection. Short and Banthin (1995) have estimated that 29 million people in the US under the age of 65 are underinsured to the extent that they lack cover for catastrophic illness.

Recently, in a study comparing findings based on large random surveys conducted in the US, Canada, Australia, New Zealand and Britain, it was found that a third of respondents in the US reported out-of-pocket payments exceeding $500 a year compared with 24 per cent in Australia reporting payments of over $500 per year, 14 per cent in New Zealand, 13 per cent in Canada and 2 per cent in Britain. Only 7 per cent of US respondents reported no such payments in contrast to Britain with 44 per cent, with the other countries falling somewhere between (Schoen *et al.*, 2000).

Evans (1993) looked at potentially catastrophic out-of-pocket charges associated with low levels of Medicare coverage for people requiring kidney transplants in the US. For instance, the Medicare reimbursement for such procedures in 1988 was $39 625 whilst the actual charge was on average, $87 700.

Xu *et al.* (2003) examined the incidence of catastrophic payments for health care by households across 59 countries based on existing household survey data. Their criterion for catastrophic payment was if the financial contribution by a household exceeds 40 per cent of income after subsistence needs are met. They found that the proportion of households facing catastrophic payments tended to be higher in those countries that rely more on out-of-pocket payments for health care, those with higher levels of poverty and where there is a higher share of GDP spent on health (see Table 9.3 for selected results). Most developed countries had fairly low rates of catastrophic expenditure except Portugal, Greece, Switzerland and the USA who each had more than 0.5 per cent of households facing such expenses. Amongst low and middle income countries, Namibia and Djibouti stand out as having less than 0.5 per cent of households falling into this category. Those countries with highest rates of household catastrophic spending tended to be located in so-called transitional economies (Azerbaijan, Ukraine, Vietnam and Cambodia) or in Latin America (Argentina, Brazil, Colombia, Paraguay and Peru).

Perhaps the most comprehensive available evidence to date on equity of health care finance can be found in the World Health Report 2000 which evaluated all member states on the basis of a number of criteria (WHO, 2000). In summary, the countries deemed to be the fairest included Colombia, Luxembourg, Belgium, Djibouti, Denmark, Ireland, Germany and Norway and the least fair were Sierra Leone, Myanmar, Brazil, China, Vietnam, Nepal and the Russian Federation. Rankings were based on an analysis of household expenditure on health as a proportion of income in each country. Although the report highlights from its findings

Table 9.3 Proportion of households with catastrophic health expenditures

Country	Proportion
Argentina	5.77
Azerbaijan	7.15
Brazil	10.27
Cambodia	5.02
Canada	0.09
Djibouti	0.32
Greece	2.17
Namibia	0.11
Paraguay	3.51
Peru	3.21
Portugal	2.71
UK	0.04
Ukraine	3.87
Vietnam	10.45

Source: Xu *et al.* (2003).

the importance of pre-payment and the reduced reliance on out-of-pocket payments as a means of more equitably financing health care, the study uncovered exceptions where out-of pocket payments were found to be progressive (India) and where pre-payment is regressive (India, Pakistan, Guyana, Kyrgyzstan, Nepal, Peru and the Russian Federation). As the methods used in these WHO rankings have been extensively criticised (see Williams (2001), Wagstaff (2002), Musgrave (2003) and Richardson *et al.* (2003)) the findings need to be interpreted cautiously.

Charges and community financing in low-income countries and transitional economies

Low-income countries especially, with their typically limited tax bases, need to look for sustainable alternatives (as opposed to say, donor contributions) as a means of financing their health services. Two important areas are user charges and community financing. According to recent data 60 per cent of all low-income countries (i.e. below $1000 per capita) use such charges. These form 40 per cent of the revenue that is collected for health services. In contrast, only 30 per cent middle- and high-income countries rely on user charges to the same extent (WHO, 2000).

User charges have been recommended for use in lower income countries, most notably by the World Bank (Akin, 1988; Shaw and Griffin, 1995). Part of the thinking is that improved health care access for the poor can be achieved by driving richer individuals into the private sector. The poorest individuals and those of high risk remain exempt from the public sector charges. The policy is targeted at the middle-income groups. Usually there is a perceived difference in quality of service between the private and public sectors, the private sector seen to be providing the higher quality. With the introduction of charges into the public sector those middle-income groups previously opting out of the paying private sector can expect to increase their demand as it now looks more attractive. In addition it has been argued that user fees provide an instrument by which policy-makers, through the setting of different fee schedules, encourage users away from expensive tertiary services into primary and preventive care (Shaw and Griffin, 1995). Other arguments for user charges are that they promote sustainability by mobilising resources in health and also enable improvements in quality of services. A number of critics have rejected this and high-lighted the inequities associated with such fees (Evans *et al.*, 1993; Creese, 1997). (See also Newbrander *et al.* (2001) which looks at both sides of the argument.) In many low-income countries, the issue is complicated by the presence of informal charges that exist over and above official user fees. Indeed, in such cases, the introduction of 'free' services can lead simply to the substitution of formal for informal charges.

In the former Socialist countries of Eastern Europe, the evidence suggests that out-of-pocket payments are increasingly playing a major role in the financing of health services – for instance, there have been reports of gradual increase in such payments throughout the 1990s in Estonia (European Observatory on Health Care Systems, 2000a), Czech Republic (European Observatory on Health Care Systems, 2000a), Albania (Nuiri and Tregakes, 2002), Hungary (European Observatory on Health Care Systems, 1999a), the Russian Federation (European Observatory on Health Care Systems, 1998) and Poland (European Observatory on Health Care Systems, 1999b). In Croatia, the burden of such payments as a proportion of income was found to be six times larger in a low-income group than that for a high-income group (Mastilica and Bozikov, 1999). Furthermore, although the evidence is by nature not always accurate, in a few countries such as the Russian Federation (European Observatory on Health Care Systems, 1998), Albania (Nuiri and Tregakes, 2002), Poland (European Observatory on Health Care Systems, 1999b; McMenamin and Timonen, 2002) and Kazakhstan (Ensor and Savelyva, 1998) informal payments are viewed as increasingly problematic. In the case of Poland in particular, where they are estimated at 40 per cent of Poland's health expenditure, it has been argued that at such a scale, the presence of these type of payments seriously jeopardise government reform initiatives (McMenamin and Timonen, 2002). Similar arguments have been put forward in Kazakhstan where it is estimated they comprise 30 per cent of the national health care expenditure (Ensor and Savelyva, 1998).

The empirical evidence cited below suggests that the user charges have been beset with various problems in implementation.

An early case study by Stanton and Clemens (1989) examined the likely impact of charges on public health services in Bangladesh. They found, first and foremost, that there was minimal ability to pay for health care. In 50 per cent of households surveyed food expenditure accounted for 72 per cent of income and 53 per cent of families spent less than 1 per cent of their income on health. Second, there were two especially vulnerable groups, women and the poor, who would be most affected if user fees were introduced into the public sector. Examination of utilisation data for government hospitals showed that while under utilised overall, they provided substantial health care to these vulnerable groups. So the conclusion reached was that raising additional finance from user charges in Bangladesh's public sector would be judged inequitable.

More recently, a number of studies in Bangladesh have explored in greater depth the circumstances where user fees may be considered feasible. Routh *et al.* (2000) finds evidence of a significant willingness and ability to pay for family planning services especially amongst middle-class clients. Similarly, Thomas *et al.* (1998) explored possibilities for charging wealthier patients for services using methods of self-selection (i.e. maintaining differences in some visible aspects of quality) in order to enable cross subsidisation of services to the poor.

A similar kind of question was addressed in Kenya by Mwabu and Mwangi (1986); could user charges imposed in the large government health care sector be used to raise finance to expand or improve health services in an equitable way? Mwabu and Mwangi answered this by simulating the effect using probabilistic demand schedules. The results indicated that under certain conditions user charges may improve equity. These conditions were that (a) fees were re-invested in government clinics and (b) fees were levied only on government clinic facilities and not across the board of public health services. Equity could improve because fees used to improve quality of care in government clinics would obviate the need to incur additional transportation expenses to seek quality treatment in the private sector. Overall, demand for government clinic services was forecast to increase. However, the richer individuals were more responsive to fee rises on this service as they curtailed demand by a greater amount as fees rose, preferring instead to seek their treatment privately. Thus, overall poor and sick individuals could become better off under the imposition of selective user charges. To enhance equity further, the authors suggested that a selective charging policy across health areas could be introduced depending on some index of a community's health status in different areas. The evidence as to the success of applying exemptions for user charges however is mixed (Newbrander *et al.*, 2001). Some of the reasons that have been identified for their failure have been the administrative problems they pose, poor information available regarding the eligibility of various groups, administrative costs, social and cultural constraints such as the stigma and effort involved in the process of applying for exemptions and the sometimes non-transparent nature by which they are granted (Gilson *et al.*, 1995). It has been found in Kenya that exemption and fee waiver schemes are fraught with implementation difficulties (Newbrander *et al.*, 2001).

Community financing relies on contributions (cash, in kind or labour) from the individual, family or community to support some of the cost of health services. The question of whether community financing can be used to improve equity remains, at least for now, unanswered. Clearly a necessary condition for the achievement of equity through such financing is that such schemes are sustainable. However achieving sustainability requires an adequate degree of risk pooling – not always achievable if the cost of insurance is to remain open to those in high risk and at the same time remain affordable to low-income individuals (Davies and Carrin, 2001). Some have asserted that community financing will be inequitable by its very nature (Abel-Smith and Dua, 1989; Carrin and Vereeck, 1992). It places undue reliance on contributions from the poor or sick themselves. Evidence from other countries is hard to come by although Abel-Smith (1986) suggests 'health insurance contributions levied as a proportion of earnings are much fairer than many other taxes imposed on developing countries'. In Vietnam, it was found that a voluntary health insurance scheme was effective in reducing out-of-pocket expenditures by around 200 per cent and that expenditures fell by more for poorer groups than the rich (Jowett *et al.*, 2003).

A community insurance scheme of self-employed women in Gujarat State, India provides evidence that such schemes aimed at the poor can be important in increasing access to services and furthermore improving social solidarity (Ranson, 2002). One important factor in ensuring the success of such schemes is that they are targeted at groups with strong pre-existing social ties. In Ethiopia it was found for instance that administrative costs and potential for adverse selection were minimised when community insurance programmes tapped into existing social arrangements known as eders (Mariam, 2003). However, because of the specific nature of the population targeted by these types of community schemes, their scope for risk pooling to enable comprehensive coverage for catastrophic risks remains limited (Kawabata *et al.*, 2002). It has been suggested that in response to this problem, reinsurance could be used a means of ensuring the solvency of such schemes (Dror, 2001).

EVIDENCE ON EQUITY AS ACCESS

Comprehensive coverage, either by public programmes or by a mix of private and public finance, does not guarantee appropriate access to services. A recent study examined the basic package of services covered in social health insurance schemes of France, Israel, Luxembourg, the Netherlands, Germany and Switzerland and found that there was 'considerable variation' across systems as to the type of services that were included (Polikowski and Santos-Eggimann, 2002). However it also identified a set of core services deemed to be 'uncontroversial' inasmuch as they were common to all the social health insurance schemes surveyed. These services were: medical care (hospital and outpatient care, medical psychotherapy, rehabilitation, selected preventive services, maternity services); outpatient physiotherapy; outpatient speech therapy; prescription drugs; laboratory tests and investigations; therapeutic aids and appliances; nursing home care; home care; transport; and services abroad. Importantly, the level of co-payment associated with coverage was often found to vary by service type and also across countries – pharmaceuticals and dental care in particular were two categories highlighted. Maternity services, on the other hand, were the only category in which treatment was free in all six countries. Overall it was concluded that high out-of-pocket payments are being used extensively as a tool to ration the use of services at the expense of equity of access to services.

Although it appears from this that there is some commonality as to the core services within a basic package, it masks the details of how well health care systems perform according to specific operational definitions of equity in the delivery of health care. For example, there is a wide variation in the services offered under the US Medicaid programme across different states (Thorpe *et al.*, 1989; Docteur, 2003).

How successful, therefore, are health care systems at meeting their horizontal equity objectives? The scope of such a question is very broad as each health care system may have a number of equity objectives.

One recent study attempted to examine this issue by assessing equal use for equal need in a cross country comparison of service use across income groups (van Doorslaer *et al.*, 2000). The study examined data from ten European countries and the US based on various national health surveys conducted between 1987 and 1996 in these countries. In general, those in lower income groups in all the countries tended to use more health services, but, once standardised for need, it was found that in five countries (Finland, East Germany, Netherlands, Sweden and the US) there tended to be a pro–rich bias in the use of physician services (due mainly to greater use of specialists amongst the rich). With regard to GP services, utilisation tended to accord with the level of need across all countries suggesting equity in the use of such services. The usage of inpatient hospital services also did not appear to differ across income groups any more than expected based on the level of need except in two countries, the UK (see later in this chapter) and Belgium, where, in both cases, there was evidence of a pro-poor bias. Overall, in terms of aggregate imputed health care expenditure, no strong evidence was derived of any significant difference in use across income groups once controlling for need (although there was some sensitivity in these results depending on how need was defined since five measures were used). It can be concluded from these findings that, in general, all the countries examined seemed to perform reasonably well in relation to the objective of equal use for equal need and equal expenditure for equal need.

However, such objectives do not necessarily match those set by the countries themselves. In Chapter 5 we tried to document some of them. The evidence presented in this section cannot be comprehensive as that would require a book in itself. What follows is a selection of some important empirical findings using the interpretations of performance set out in Table 5.2.

First, we present evidence from several countries on access in the pursuit of equity. There are few systems for which comprehensive data on equity exist. We have identified three (the US, Canada and the UK) and, therefore, feel a case study of each is important before going on to draw some conclusions.

Some brief international comparisons

As regards OECD countries, only the US stands apart from the rest as having a problem of comprehensively covering its population for the risk of ill-health

Table 9.4 Percentage of the population covered by government assured health insurance in the OECD 1960 and 1997

	1960	*1997*
Australia	100.0	100.0
Austria	78.0	99.0
Belgium	58.0	99.0
Canada	71.0	100.0
Czech Republic	100.0	100.0
Denmark	95.0	100.0
Finland	55.0	100.0
France	76.3	99.5
Germany	85.0	92.2
Greece	30.0	100.0
Hungary	100.0	99.0
Iceland	100.0	100.0
Ireland	85.0	100.0
Italy	87.0	100.0
Japan	88.0	100.0
Korea	na	100.0
Luxembourg	90.0	100.0
Mexico	na	72.0
Netherlands	71.0	72.0
New Zealand	100.0	100.0
Norway	100.0	100.0
Poland	100.0	100.0
Portugal	18.0	100.0
Spain	54.0	99.8
Sweden	100.0	100.0
Switzerland	74.0	100.0
Turkey	5.8	66.0
UK	100.0	100.0
US	6.9	33.3
OECD Median	85.0	100.0

Note: na not available.

Source: Anderson and Poullier (1999) with original source being OECD Health Data 1998: A comparative analysis of twenty-nine countries.

which requires health care. Table 9.4, reveals the extent of public coverage of health care in 1960 and 1997 (Anderson and Poullier, 1999). Government based coverage in the US (Medicaid, Medicare, Indian Health Service, civil service or coverage through the military) in 1997 was 33 per cent of the population – significantly lower than for any other country listed. The comparison provided in the table indicates also that all countries in the OECD without universal coverage in 1960 have increased significantly the level of coverage by 1997 (including the US). By 1997 only Mexico, Turkey and the US fell short of providing universal public coverage – Germany and the Netherlands, although with public coverage rates of less than 100 per cent, allow their wealthier households to opt out of public cover through private insurance.

The evidence from Australia, during periods in the 1970s and 1980s when no compulsory public insurance scheme was in place, provides further evidence of the shortcomings of predominantly privately financed health care. During these periods it was estimated that 15 per cent of the Australian population (usually Southern European migrants and those in low-income groups) had no insurance cover (Deeble, 1982; Palmer and Short, 1989).

Despite the introduction of a publicly funded universal health insurance system in Australia in 1983, evidence of inequities in access to services has continued to emerge. For instance, because services tend to be heavily concentrated in urban areas, residents in rural areas are faced with limited availability of services. Furthermore, because medical practitioners are given the discretion to charge above the rate at which the government reimburses for such services, patients in rural areas tend to be faced with higher co-payments due to less competition in such regions. In a study of GP services for women, Young and Dobson (2003) indeed found that out-of-pocket costs were significantly higher in rural areas. In addition, evidence exists that, after controlling for self-assessed health status, higher co-payments for rural residents is in turn associated with lower use of GP services (Young *et al.*, 2001).

Similar concerns about differences in access to services across geographical regions as a result of a growing reliance on user fees have occurred in Finland – another country where there is ostensibly universal coverage (Koivusalo, 1999).

In contrast, a study in Norway came up with some positive findings in relation to the achievement of equal use for equal need by finding no significant relationship between income and utilisation of primary care services. It was argued, however, that more could be done from a public policy perspective since this particular objective was limited insofar as it does not afford individuals the choice of purchasing a greater than average number of services or service of higher than average quality (Grytten *et al.*, 1995).

The World Health Report 1999 noted that rather than increasing coverage for basic health care, many countries have in recent years been engaged in a process of dismantling social protection – particularly those of the former socialist states:

> In the decades up to the 1980s, many socialist countries had established universally accessible health care systems. Although these may have been inefficient, bureaucratic and unresponsive to patients' needs, basic care and, in many cases, secondary and tertiary care as well, was effectively prepaid and available to almost the entire population for little or no payment at the time of need. Most people in these countries have found that they now have to pay more – officially or unofficially – for their health care, access to care is increasingly reflecting ability to pay. (WHO, 1999)

Although there is inadequate data from low-income countries most have substantial problems of ensuring universal and adequate health care insurance. A large part of the explanation is because of high population growth, and increasingly severe stringency placed on health care finance. It has been argued that low-income countries tend to lack institutional and organisational capacity in terms of taxation collection to enable publicly funded universal health insurance. This is reflected in the observation that in OECD countries, general taxation revenue represents over 40 per cent of GDP, whilst in low-income countries it is less than 20 per cent (WHO, 2000).

As a result of these major fiscal problems in achieving universal access – estimates of the cost of doing so globally range from $25 to $100 billion (Preker *et al.*, 2002).

Despite this, the example of Thailand illustrates that universal coverage is feasible within the context of, at least, some middle-income countries. It recently introduced a national programme providing universal coverage to be financed from general taxation. Prior to this scheme, around 30 per cent of the Thai population were uninsured. Under the new arrangements, provincial health authorities are reimbursed on a capitation basis and users are charged a co-payment of around $US0.70 (Streshthaputra and Indaratna, 2001). The programme covers primary and hospital care – including prevention and control activities (Tangcharoensathen *et al.*, 2002).

Other countries that have also recently established programmes of universal coverage are South Korea (Lee, 2003), Taiwan (Cheng, 2003) and the Philippines (Hindle *et al.*, 2001). McIntyre *et al.* (2003) observe that within low- and middle-income countries, attempts at introducing social health insurance have mainly been concentrated in Latin America and Asia as opposed to African nations.

In China, the opposite picture emerges. Prior to the economic and political reforms of the 1980s, a large part of the population was covered by the Rural Cooperative Medical Scheme (Liu *et al.*, 1995; WHO, 1999). Since then, the uninsured have increased in number to presently comprise four-fifths of the population (WHO, 1999). This has occurred alongside increasing levels of financial autonomy amongst public service providers and growing reliance by them on user fees and profits from the sales of medications as sources of revenue.

Recent evidence from China based on a comparison between 1993 and 1998 suggests, perhaps not surprisingly given the changes to the financing of health care, growing disparities in access to health care between rural and urban areas and rich and poor with those in lowest income quintiles and rural populations being most disadvantaged (Gao *et al.*, 2002).

In the remainder of the chapter we examine the evidence on horizontal equity in the US, Canada and the UK. In doing so, we also offer our own judgement of performance.

US: no explicit equity objective

What of horizontal equity within the US health care system? The US health care insurance market is extremely diversified. There are over 1000 private insurers offering fee-for-service (FFS) plans, preferred provider plans, health maintenance plans and more (OECD, 2001). Collection and compilation of information about population coverage and adequacy of plans is thus messy and difficult. It is difficult to determine the explicit definition of an equity objective in the US as it is clear that consumer choice (and its consequent market base) is regarded as an important objective which may conflict with any equity goal. Equal access for equal need may be a goal as highlighted in Chapter 5. Attempts by government-sponsored programmes consequently seem to be about helping the market work 'better'. Not only are Medicare and Medicaid publicly financed programmes but the large employer-sponsored insurance programmes are financed in part by pay-roll taxes.

The issue of access can be looked at in terms of several aspects: the extent of insurance coverage; its effect on access to services for those in equal need; geographical equity; and the effect of competitive innovations (like HMOs) on access.

Estimates of the numbers of Americans with no health insurance coverage have been reported extensively over the years. The general trend has been an increase in the proportion of non-elderly persons without insurance coverage, increasing steadily from 31.8 to 42.1 million between 1987 and 1999 (Shcroeder, 2001). The latest figure represents around 14 per cent of the working age population (Docteur *et al.*, 2003).

Many workers who may be eligible for insurance often are unable or choose not to purchase cover due to the prohibitive cost (Thorpe and Florence, 1999). It was found for instance that the average monthly premium for an employer-sponsored family policy was $529 in 2000 (Gabel *et al.*, 2000). The US Census Bureau estimated that in 2000, 32 per cent of the Hispanic population were uninsured compared with 12.9 per cent of the White population, 18 per cent of Asian and Pacific Islanders and 18.5 per cent of the Black population (Docteur *et al.*, 2003). Furthermore, the levels of uninsured do vary significantly by state. In Minnesota the number of uninsured is 6.7 per cent of the non-elderly population whereas in Texas it is 25 per cent with such differences also reflected across local communities (Shroeder, 2001).

A number of studies have been conducted over the years that have found that those without insurance cover have failed to receive needed medical care (Hayward *et al.*, 1988; Newacheck, 1988; Quam, 1989; American College of Physicians and American Society of Internal Medicine, 2000; Ayanian *et al.*, 2000; Baker *et al.*, 2000). Ayanian *et al.* (2000) found, based on random household telephone surveys of over 100 000 individuals aged between 18–64 in 1997 and in 1998, that the long- and short-term uninsured adults were less likely to see a needed physician due to reasons of cost than the insured. In addition, the long-term uninsured were less likely to have made a routine visit to a physician over the previous two years and were less likely to access services such as cancer screening, cardiovascular risk reduction and diabetes care.

Although Medicaid is seen as a safety net, its performance in providing health care insurance for the indigent comes under serious attack in a number of studies. Bovbjerg *et al.* (2002) estimated that 37.3 per cent of low-income workers were without any insurance coverage in 1999. This is despite a number of recent reforms that have been implemented as a means of extending Medicaid coverage including relaxation of various restrictions such as the 100 hours per month work limit, income and asset ownership limits. Furthermore there has been additional support aimed at children through the States Childrens Health Insurance Program (SCHIP).

According to early analysis by Trevino *et al.* (1991) the extent of Medicaid coverage was not adequate for eligible ethnic Americans. The Hispanic Health and Nutrition Examination Survey examined the characteristics of the uninsured. Despite a half of Mexican Americans, two-thirds of Cuban Americans and just under a half of Puerto Ricans being employed, large proportions (50 percent or more) of these populations lived below the poverty line and were uninsured. More recently, Carrasquillo *et al.* (1999) have noted substantial increases in the level of uninsured amongst Black and Hispanic populations between 1989 and 1996 and increases within not only poor but also middle-income families. It has been noted that even though Hispanics comprise only 13 per cent of the population, they nonetheless account for 25 per cent of uninsured (Schroeder, 2001).

Even when provided with Medicaid coverage, however, out-of-pocket charges are likely to remain a major problem for many. Such expenses may be due to, deductibles, co-insurance and the cost of private insurance for those services not covered. Gross *et al.* (1999) estimate that 60 per cent of Medicaid beneficiaries living below the poverty line spent 50 per cent of their incomes on such out-of-pocket health care costs.

The law in the US provides for a mandatory minimum level of emergency care and as a consequence, emergency departments of hospitals are required to assess and stabilise any individual presenting for treatment regardless of ability to pay and insurance status (Docteur *et al.*, 2003). From the provider perspective the problem of inadequate insurance protection may consequently lead to unpaid medical bills and accumulated bad debts although hospitals providing emergency care of this nature to uninsured patients are, in certain states, eligible for some reimbursement from a state-provided uncompensated care pool (Weissman *et al.*, 1999).

Perhaps surprisingly, a study has found that those who do not pay their hospital bills tended to be those in very low-income categories – individuals who would otherwise be eligible for Medicaid assistance or free care. This suggests that there are significant barriers to accessing Medicaid or free hospital-provided care even amongst those who may be entitled to such support (Weissman *et al.*, 1999).

An early multi-hospital study of patients' socio-economic status and use of hospital resources has demonstrated higher costs of treatment for poor people. They were found to have had 3–30 per cent longer hospital stays and 1–18 per cent higher hospital charges (Epstein *et al.*, 1990). Findings of this nature have equity implications insofar as achieving equal access would entail supplementary payments factored into the reimbursement of services for the poor. However, more recently a study of the costs of hospitalisations for Medicare patients has told a different story. It found that, after accounting for cost differences already built into Medicare reimbursement, the low-income groups had no difference in the cost of treatment despite, on average, 2.5 per cent longer length of stay (Kominski and Long, 1997).

There have been numerous studies that have examined the relationship between ownership status of hospitals and their propensity to provide uncompensated care (Pattison and Katz 1983; Herzlinger and Krasker, 1987; Lewin *et al.*, 1988; Frank *et al.*, 1990; Young *et al.*, 1997 and Needleman *et al.*, 1999).

Uncompensated care generally comprises of services provided to uninsured patients who are unable to pay their bills or services provided free of charge. With a trend towards the conversion of public hospitals to for-profit ownership, a concern has been the corresponding reduction in the levels of such uncompensated care (Needleman *et al.*, 1999). Reduction in the provision of these services is seen to be detrimental in terms of access for the poor – in Florida where such hospital conversions have been increasing, 60 per cent of the state's poor are not covered by Medicaid and almost half of the minority population have no insurance coverage (Needleman *et al.*, 1999). However, interestingly whilst change in the level of uncompensated care has been detected in public hospitals that converted into for-profit status, no such difference has been detected in the level of uncompensated care between non-profit and for-profit hospitals (Young *et al.*, 1997; Needleman *et al.*, 1999).

Access to health care across ethnic and racial groups has also been highlighted as a problem. Amongst Medicare beneficiaries Blacks tend to use significantly less services than Whites (Gornick *et al.*, 1996; Schneider *et al.*, 2002). For instance, it was found that after adjusting for age, sex, Medicaid insurance, income, education and rural/urban residence, the Black population were nonetheless less likely to receive eye examinations in cases of diabetes, beta-blockers after myocardial infarction and follow-up after hospitalisation for mental illness (Schneider *et al.*, 2002). Such racial disparities are also reflected within the uninsured population – 16 per cent uninsured Latino children compared with 7 per cent of uninsured White children have not been seen by a physician in the past two years (Flores *et al.*, 2002).

In a study examining access to care amongst immigrants it was found that non-citizens and their children had less access to regular ambulatory or emergency room care. Forty-one percent of non-citizen adults, 38 per cent of non-citizen children and 21 per cent of citizen children with non-citizen parents had no contact with emergency room or ambulatory care in the previous year. This compares with a corresponding figure of 21 per cent of native adults and 13 per cent of children of citizens (Ku and Matani, 2001).

In comparison to socio-economic and racial characteristics, rurality as a source of health service inequity has received relatively little attention. Indeed it has been argued that to a large extent the disadvantages faced by individuals in rural areas are related to the higher levels of poverty, chronic disease and uninsured individuals residing in these regions (van Dis, 2002). Indeed, Rosenthal and Fox (2000) suggest that the poorer health outcomes of the rural elderly in comparison with those living in urban areas is 'influenced more by social position, insurance status, clinician access, and economic access than by geography'.

However where disparities have been detected, these have largely been seen as a result of supply-side constraints and in particular, the shortage of physicians located in such areas (Rabinowitz *et al.*, 1999; Rabinowitz and Paynter, 2002;

van Dis *et al.*, 2002). Rural residents comprise 20 per cent of the US population but are serviced by only 9 per cent of the country's physicians. Furthermore this situation is likely to worsen as it has been reported that only around 3 per cent of recent medical graduates plan to do rural practice (Rabinowitz *et al.*, 1999; Rabinowitz and Paynter, 2002). This shortfall in physicians means reduced access to services as individuals become faced with higher travel costs (Meden *et al.*, 2002). Furthermore, rural residents are likely to also incur higher out-of-pocket costs associated with illness since difficulties in accessing services means a greater reliance on informal care (Rosenthal and Fox, 2000). Contributing to this problem are the lower rates of Medicare reimbursement for services in rural areas – 40 per cent less for hospital services and 30 per cent for physician services. Such differences in rates are typically due to lower wage costs, less extensive diagnostic workup which in turn is due to less readily available diagnostic services (Rosenthal and Fox, 2000).

Van Doorslaer *et al.* (2000) examined the performance of the US in terms of equal use for equal need in the study mentioned earlier as part of the ECuity project. They found that given the same level of need, those with high incomes tended to use physician services more than those with lower incomes – reinforcing the view that the poor lack access to such services. No such pattern was evident however in relation to inpatient days or overall imputed health expenditure.

The variety of health insurance plans that exist in the US system, with differing incentive structures for consumers and providers, allows tremendous scope for diverse health care access. As it is not possible here to review these plans comprehensively, we choose to concentrate on one major area, the impact of competition through health maintenance organisations (HMOs), on access for disadvantaged groups.

HMOs are a form of managed care offering comprehensive coverage for a predetermined premium. However, beyond that, they take a variety of forms (e.g. prepaid group practices, independent practice associations, staff models or networks) depending on the contractual arrangements between the HMO and doctor(s). Despite their popularity falling in recent years they appear to have been more effective at slowing health care cost escalation and excessive utilisation than traditional FFS insurance plans (see Chapters 6 and 7). Why? Is this control due to more cost-effective provision or the squeezing out of high health risk individuals? If it is the latter then cost control will flounder in the long term, as now appears to be the case according to very recent evidence.

It might be expected a priori that compared with regular FFS insurance plans, HMOs would be selected by individuals who perceived their health risks as high and who expect to make relatively high use of services as this makes sense from the consumer's point of view. Furthermore, since HMO plans cover dependents and encourage preventive practices, such HMOs might expect to attract young, expanding families.

However, HMO providers may wish to behave in a way which is not in line with these expectations. Providers may attempt to select low health risk individuals with low expected use of health services into HMO plans. In this way, providers are acting in a way which is consistent with profit-maximising behaviour under competitive pressure, even if the members are committed to community-rating. Thus, it is not clear, a priori, what, if any, contribution HMO care makes to the problem of adverse selection. Furthermore, as HMOs have evolved from within a system of FFS insurance plans there is likely to be some consumer loyalty towards FFS plans regardless of health risk.

If HMOs do skim off the best risks then one would expect to see better health risks enrolled in HMO plans compared with FFS plans. Early studies and reviews were mixed in their conclusions. Berki and Ashcraft (1980) were sceptical about the charge of skimming under HMO care. Blumberg (1980) rejected it. Eggers (1980) supported favourable selection in a study of Medicare beneficiaries as did studies reported by Buchanan and Cretin (1986), by Moser (1987) for non-elderly enrollees and by Porrell and Turner (1990) for Medicare beneficiaries.

More recently, Morgan *et al.* (1997) examined Medicare enrolment and inpatient data for Florida between 1990–93 and compared service use and other characteristics of beneficiaries in the Medicare FFS system with those enrolled in HMOs as well as those recently disenroled. The study found strong evidence of cream skimming involving both selection of individuals less likely to utilise services and the disenrolment of those who have higher levels of service use. It found that inpatient service use for HMO enrolees in the year prior to enrolment in a HMO was on average 66 per cent lower than the level found for FFS Medicare beneficiaries. For those disenroled from HMOs, the rate of service use was 180 per cent of that for the fee for service group immediately after disenrolment. The finding in relation to the selection of healthier individuals for HMOs was supported by Hamilton (1999) although the conclusion regarding disenrolment was not.

Another issue is whether, once enrolled, HMO beneficiaries have less access to services. The recent evidence is again mixed.

Miller and Luft (2002) provide a recent review of the literature examining the performance of HMOs. Relevant here were their findings of how such organisations fared in terms of providing access to care. This was measured on the basis of a variety of indicators such as difficulty in arranging an appointment, being able to contact usual provider, amount of travelling required, having an unmet need and having a usual provider. Of the ten studies that evaluated this aspect of service delivery, four had unfavourable findings in relation to HMOs, two were favourable and four found no difference. Two studies where there was evidence of poorer access to services derived such findings on the basis of surveys with enrolees regarding their satisfaction with services (Pina, 1998; Reschovsky *et al.*, 2000). Such levels of personal dissatisfaction however were not found to necessarily reflect greater levels of unmet health need (Reschovsky *et al.*, 2000).

Finally, another interesting finding in relation to the development of HMOs and other managed care organisations is the impact they have upon the level of charity care provided by physicians. Cunningham *et al.* (1999) found evidence of a tendency for doctors who earn a high proportion of their income from managed care (including HMOs) and those doctors who practice in regions where there is a high penetration of such organisations to provide less of such care. Such tendencies could be attributable to the cost pressures imposed by managed care arrangements.

Judgement: the evidence presented suggests that the US has substantial problems of ensuring universal and adequate health care insurance. This continues to be a growing problem, particularly for poor, ethnic Americans and those living in rural areas. This leads to great problems in achieving equal access for equal need, and competitive reforms, such as HMOs, have done nothing to ameliorate this situation.

Canada: objective – equality of utilisation

The evidence as to the success of the Canadian health system in achieving equality of utilisation is mixed. Dunlop *et al.* (2003) examined the relationship between socio-economic status and utilisation drawing on data from the 1994 National Population Health Survey. They found that utilisation of physician services, both primary and specialist care, was strongly related to self-perceived need. Furthermore, the likelihood of visiting a primary care physician was not related to income. However, in terms of specialist care, it was found that those in higher socio-economic groups tended to make greater use of services of specialists indicating inequities in access for such services. Such results are similar both in relation to GP and specialist services to those found by McIsaac *et al.* (1997) in Ontario based on the 1990 Ontario health survey.

An earlier study using data from the Canadian Health Survey were used by Broyles *et al.* (1983) to examine the extent to which the use of physicians by beneficiaries insured under the Canadian Medicare programmes was determined by medical needs rather than non-medical factors such as patients' financial status. They showed that medical needs, as measured by medical conditions, number of accidents, disability days and the use of prescription drugs, were the dominant determinants of both the decision to seek treatment and the volume of services consumed. An individual's ability to pay (as defined by economic status and occupational status) did not contribute to an explanation of this pattern of use. Another early study by Manga *et al.* (1987) confirmed the above finding, using a similar, but refined measure of need.

There have been a number of studies that have examined the link between income and service use for various specific health conditions. The findings here tend to paint a more negative picture of the health care system's ability to achieve equity in utilisation despite universal coverage.

Alter *et al.* (1999a) examined the relationship between income and access to specialised cardiac care after heart attack, and found that those in higher income categories tended to have higher levels of use as well as reduced waiting times. Furthermore, at one year post-treatment, low-income patients tended to have higher mortality (see also Alter, *et al.*, 2003).

Kapral *et al.* (2002) had similar findings in relation to stroke victims where those in low-income groups tended to have lower use of in-hospital physiotherapy, occupational therapy, speech pathology, had longer waiting times for carotid surgery and higher risk of death at both 30 days and 1 year post-treatment.

As reflected in recent studies, waiting for care in the Canadian system is an important indicator of equity. Shortt and Shaw (2003) examined whether waiting times varied by socio-economic status. They drew their data from medical records over 8 years in an academic health centre and compared the average waiting times for patients from regions classed as low and high socio-economic status. Out of twenty-two common medical procedures, for only one, in prostatectomy, was there found to be a statistically significant difference (on average 4.4 days shorter wait for the high socio-economic status region). The authors concluded that there was little evidence that residing in low socio-economic status regions meant higher waiting times.

Similarly, in an earlier study Morris *et al.* (1990) reported the success of cardio-vascular services in Manitoba to give highest priority to cases with greatest urgency. The study examined patient characteristics and indications for cardiac catheterisation on the elective care list with immediate care. It was found that immediate care patients were sicker than those put on the elective list according to various indicators. They were also more likely to enter hospital via the emergency room. Elective patients stayed in hospital for shorter periods. However, mortality among the two groups was similar. The study concluded that those patients needing immediate care and those who could wait with a low probability of a poor outcome were being successfully identified in Manitoba.

Alter (1999b) however found that although waiting times for angiography largely reflected clinical indications, there was some evidence of inequities in waiting times based on the affiliation of physicians. It was found that those patients whose doctor had some affiliation with a catherisation facility tended to have shorter waiting times.

Judgement: the evidence as to whether equal utilisation for equal need is achieved is mixed. It seems to be achieved in relation to primary care services but use of specialist procedures tends to be skewed in favour of the rich. However, it should be noted that equality of utilisation is not as sound an equity objective as equality of access. Thus the evidence can only be interpreted as providing tentative measures of equity.

UK: objective – equal access for equal need

The UK equity objective can be looked at in terms of both social class and geographical equity.

It might be expected that the absence of major financial barriers in the UK NHS would mean that access to health services is unlikely to be significantly inequitable across income groups. However, a number of early studies did indeed find evidence of unequal access and receipt of care (e.g. Cooper and Culyer, 1971; Maynard and Tingle, 1975; Le Grand, 1978; Black Report, 1980; Blaxter, 1984; Whitehead, 1988; Townsend *et al.*, 1987; Carstairs and Morris, 1989; Waller *et al.*, 1990 and Davey Smith *et al.*, 1990). More current research is more favourable due in part to developments in methodology (Collins and Klein, 1980; O'Donnell and Propper, 1989; and van Doorslaer *et al.*, 2000). The two former studies used the General Household Survey data to obtain information on self-reported morbidity ('not sick', 'acutely sick', 'chronic sick without restrictions' and 'chronic sick with restrictions') and use of health care services. Collins and Klein concentrated on primary health care use and found no consistent bias supporting the hypothesis that lower socioeconomic groups (SEGs) make lower use of services when standardised for self-reported morbidity. In fact, for two morbidity groups they found the reverse. For example, for men reporting acutely sick the utilisation rate for SEG 1 (professional class) was 40.9 per cent compared to 71.0 per cent for SEG 6 (unskilled, manual class). The remaining morbidity groups showed no class gradients.

The authors concluded that the NHS does better than its equity principle of equal access for equal need because, if anything, there was a slight pro-poor distribution. However, this conclusion is potentially misleading as utilisation, not access, has been measured.

The authors also commented on why other work cited above found pro-rich distributions of health care. The confounding factor in these studies was the inclusion of not sick people who use health care. They obviously used GP services for other purposes (e.g. health prevention and promotion) and as they constituted a large proportion of the primary care user group (39 per cent 'not sick' people used primary care services) this group can mask the effects of utilisation on other morbidity groups. Indeed, in Collins and Klein's analysis the 'not sick' group exhibited a slightly pro-rich distribution, as might be expected given that higher SEGs tend to be more highly motivated to use preventive and health promotion services.

O'Donnell and Propper extended Collins and Klein's analysis to cover all NHS services and also report a pro-poor distribution of utilisation within morbidity groups during 1985. They suggested that this distribution was consistent with (rather than better than) equal access for equal need as supplementary data indicate that, as health status in poorer income groups is, on average, lower, so need will be greater. Yet again their measures were of utilisation rather than of access making their conclusion, once more, potentially tentative.

The most recent analysis in this area by van Doorslaer *et al.* (2000) is largely consistent with these findings. It uncovered no real evidence that physician contact (either for GPs or medical specialists) differed according to income once differences in need were accounted for (although there was a small, statistically significant pro-poor bias found for GP use once need was defined by chronic illness). No statistically significant difference in outpatient visits was recorded across income groups but for inpatient care days, a greater amount of use was found amongst the poor even when controlling for all available measures of need. Overall, in terms of health expenditure, there was some evidence of pro-poor bias but such differences were found not to be statistically significant once need was determined on the basis of self-assessed health – although it was significant when chronic illness was used as the measure of need. Such findings are in a similar vein to Collins and Klein and O'Donnell and Propper, potentially limited because it involved the measurement of use rather than access.

In a recent review of the literature on equity of access to services in the UK, Goddard and Smith (2001) generally found some evidence of inequalities of access, mainly in relation to specific service types: preventive services and certain inpatient procedures. They indicate, however, that the existing evidence is 'patchy' – reinforcing the point that it is focused mainly on utilisation rather than access. Furthermore the studies tend to lack analysis of the underlying causes of potential inequalities.

Waiting for health services is another important indicator of access in the UK health care system. Equal access for equal need in this context means appropriate use of waiting times as a filter in the passage of a patient from family practitioner to hospital outpatient clinic and subsequently as inpatients waiting for admission. This issue of waiting times and waiting lists has gained much political importance recently particularly in the wake of the internal market reforms initiated in the early 1990s. Dixon and Glennerster (1995) hypothesised that these reforms, and in particular the development of GP fundholding, would lead to a two-tiered system of care where patients of fundholding GPs would receive preferential treatment in hospital because of the purchasing power associated with fundholder status. Such disparities could then be reflected in differences in waiting times.

Propper *et al.* (2004) examined the effect of GP fundholding on waiting times for patients. They found that waiting times for patients of GP fundholders were lower, on average by 8 per cent, only if the GP directly paid for the service. In situations where the fundholder selected hospitals for the patient but did not pay out of his or her budget, waiting times were no different than those for patients of non-fundholding GPs. Furthermore, the reductions in waiting times were only confined specifically to those services paid for by the GP with no spillover effect into other services areas. The finding suggests that hospitals do respond to the financial incentives and supports the hypothesis that a two-tiered system of care, at least in respect to waiting times, arose as a result of the reforms. The finding in this study was consistent with that of Dowling (1997) who examined the records of over 57 000 patients in the West Sussex region and found that fundholding practices had consistently shorter waiting times for hospital services than non-fundholding practices.

Tellingly, earlier studies undertaken prior to the NHS reforms generally showed no evidence of any significant inequities in waiting times for services. Bloom and Fendrick (1987), in their analysis of hospital waiting lists found that those who waited tended to be of relatively low medical priority. Potter and Porter (1989) in comparing waiting times between the US and the UK found that for GP services they were higher in the US; in terms of outpatient waiting times there was no difference between countries; and for specialists, waiting times were higher in the UK – although those requiring urgent care in the UK still received it.

One issue that had acquired greater importance with these reforms was cream skimming amongst fundholding GPs (Dixon and Glennerster, 1995). Such behaviour would be motivated by much the same incentive as present within HMOs in the US – as discussed earlier. The evidence in the wake of these reforms, however, does

193

not appear to support this hypothesis. Lynch (1998) in an analysis of 208 practices in Scotland found that the treatment strategies chosen, and type of patients enrolled by fundholding GPs was inconsistent with cream skimming behaviour. Likewise Propper *et al*. (2002) found no evidence of adverse selection with no change in the observed morbidity of patients after GPs changed to fundholder status.

With the election of the Labour Government in 1997, a number of changes have been instituted aimed at replacing the internal market in favour of a more primary care led health system (e.g. replacement of GP fundholder system with primary care trusts) (UK Department of Health, 1997). At present, not much is known about the impact of these latest changes in policy direction on access to services.

In addition to these factors, the UK NHS is concerned with equality of geographical access. Le Grand (1982) explained that supply factors such as the distribution of medical facilities and staff are crucial access determinants.

The original work of the Resource Allocation Working Party (RAWP) was based on this concern for geographical access. The RAWP terms of reference were to secure 'a pattern of distribution [of NHS resources except GP services] responsive objectively, equitably and efficiently to relative need' (DHSS, 1976). The RAWP budgetary formula for regional health areas (RHA) was derived from regional populations weighted to reflect the need for services (there were seven categories of service, excluding GP services) and adjustments made for cross boundary flows. Need was measured using age, sex and standardised mortality ratios (SMRs). The policy was implemented within the constraints of zero resource growth. This meant that, as a typical RHA budget was of the order of £1 billion, a 0.1 per cent shift in resources (about £1 million) would be a significant gain to one region and a significant loss to another. In the early years of the policy, resources were redistributed mainly from the South of England (particularly the London regions) to the North.

In 1991, revisions were made to the formula, resulting in different formulae being used in England, Scotland and Wales (Moss, 1998). The version used in England between 1991 and 1995 was heavily criticised because of its 'empirical' approach, based on regression analysis where need was modelled on the basis of hospital utilisation (Diderichsen *et al*., 1997). The flaw in this approach is that allocating on the basis of need defined in relation to existing utilisation is unlikely to address unmet need (Sheldon *et al*., 1993).

After 1995, the UK Department of Health used in England a modified version of a formula developed at the University of York based on small area ecological studies; the impact of which would have been to reallocate more funds to poorer inner city areas (Carr-Hill *et al*., 1994; Smith *et al*., 1994; Diderichsen *et al*., 1997). That formula, however, was subject to the same problem in terms of its characterisation of need being modelled on the basis of existing utilisation. Nonetheless as a result of the operation of this formula during 1993–94 and 1998–99 the range of distances between actual and targeted allocations fell appreciably across health authorities (Glennerster *et al*., 2000). Table 9.5 indicates that in 1993/94, the health authority with the allocation most over target received an allocation 21.13 per cent above target while the region most below target was below by 15.68 per cent – a range of

Table 9.5 Progress towards achievement of RAWP targets in UK NHS, 1993/94 to 1998/99

	Most over target HA	Most under target HA	Range
1993/94	21.13	−15.68	36.81
1994/95	15.50	−10.20	25.70
1995/96	14.60	−13.00	27.60
1996/97	13.08	−7.88	20.96
1997/98	8.16	−6.23	14.39
1998/99	8.64	−5.24	13.88

Source: Glennerster H. *et al.* (2000).

36.81 per cent. By 1998/99 this range had fallen to 13.88 per cent indicating that resources over this time were being allocated more in line with need as defined by the formula. This however followed a period from 1988 where allocations were allowed to diverge significantly away from RAWP targets and inequities between regions grew (Glennerster *et al.*, 2000).

The most recent version of the formula was announced in 2003 and set out the target shares of resources allocated across primary care trusts. The aim of this version was to reflect in particular the funding needs of a health service in which utilisation was seen to be primary care led (UK Department of Health, 2003).

Judgement: More recent and methodologically sophisticated evidence supports equal social class utilisation for equal need although the measurement of morbidity and social class remain problematic. The evidence does not relate to the objective of equal social class access for equal need. The NHS's performance on equal geographical access for equal need has improved over time although the evolution of the recent NHS reforms will determine whether this success continues.

CONCLUSIONS

In this chapter selected evidence has been presented to demonstrate the performance of various health care systems in relation to equity criteria. Although attempts have recently been made to compare health care delivery systems with one another (e.g. ECuity and WHO), such approaches are inherently limited as there is no universal and absolute measure of equity in health care delivery. In terms of international comparisons of equity in health care finance, some important findings have nonetheless emerged. As borne out in the findings presented earlier, the degree of progressivity/regressivity within a health care financing system depends on the mix of financing sources. Those systems that are based on social insurance and rely more on direct and general taxes tend to be more progressive and those that are based on private insurance and rely more on direct payments tend to be more regressive.

195

Therefore, regarding fairness with which health care systems are financed, largely publicly financed systems in developed countries, especially those predominantly tax-financed, are the most successful at meeting equity objectives. However, this does not mean that, political and public opinion willing, further improvements cannot be made. In the UK and Canada health care payments are extracted primarily on the basis of ability to pay (although a case could be made for making them still more progressive). Such progressivity is not present in US health care. Instead, we find US health care extremely inequitable with only the highest income decile contributing a smaller proportion to health care monies than is their proportionate share of income.

Although US society at large, and health professionals in particular, are concerned about the equity consequences of their health care system, it seems they are not prepared to pay for equity improvements by financing a change to some form of social insurance system. It has been tentatively argued that the recent growth in social insurance financed health care systems in middle-income countries such as in Thailand is the fairest way of financing these countries' health care costs.

Coverage of health care insurance (or access to health services in the case of publicly financed systems) is not at issue in developed countries except for the US where the problem is significant. Low-income countries are also likely to face problems with insurance coverage although examples of community-based health insurance schemes such as in India hold some promise. It also appears to be the case that many economies currently in transition such as former socialist economies are in the process of dismantling social protection. The US health care system clearly discriminates against ethnic minorities, the poor and those living in rural areas. Frequently they have no cover, or they remain inadequately protected, particularly against the expense of catastrophic illness. These problems seem to be growing rather than contracting in the wake of numerous financial developments and reforms, especially HMO arrangements and prospective payment systems.

Two of the three countries (Canada and UK) selected for in-depth analysis of horizontal equity achievements have, in our judgement, been cautiously encouraging. They both have largely publicly financed health care and the evidence about each generally seems to point to equal access at least in relation to primary care services. In both cases, however, there seems to be some evidence of unequal utilisation for certain specific services. In Canada, this is particularly the case with specialist treatment whilst in the UK, some evidence of unequal access to preventive and some inpatient services exists.

However, we argue that the equity objective of equality in use is somewhat misleading, it should be equality of access for equal need that is sought. At the same time, however, we recognise the inherent difficulties of measuring access compared with the relative ease with which utilisation may be assessed.

One fairly straightforward indicator (albeit partial) of access is waiting times. Some of the evidence that examined the NHS internal market reforms of the 1990s had indicated inequalities here. It suggested that waiting times could be adversely influenced by financial incentives created by fundholding status.

Currently, the most recent and methodologically sound evidence claims success with equality of access. However, careful scrutiny shows that the measures used are in fact, once again, measures of utilisation. Thus we feel the claims made by Collins and Klein, O'Donnell and Propper and van Doorslaer *et al.* need to be re-evaluated in terms of access.

The evidence provided in this chapter goes to prove that simply having a publicly financed health care system will not guarantee equity. However, compared with the US, these equity failings, particularly in developed countries, are less severe, as basic levels of provision (e.g. emergency care and primary care) are usually available to everyone.

For the US system, evidence of geographic disparities between rural and urban populations in access to services seems to compound problems it faces with equity. Furthermore, we find that an important organisational form that has evolved in the health care delivery market, HMOs, is selective in the type of individuals enrolled (i.e. low health-risks). This does not fare well for long-term equity let alone the short-term where, as indicated earlier, large proportions of the non-elderly population either have inadequate or no health insurance coverage.

Of the four possible solutions that can simultaneously counter the effects of adverse selection and support caring externalities, only two (providing free health care and making health care insurance compulsory) have been tested to date. It could, perhaps, be worth experimenting with the other two solutions (experienced rated premiums with subsidies and selective community-rating) in appropriate settings to see if greater equity can be achieved. For example, experienced-rated premiums with subsidies could be tried in the US setting, whilst selective community-rating could be tried in a system that favours a substantial private insurance market. The recent reforms in Australia mentioned earlier where community-rating has been replaced by 'life time community rating' and a 30 per cent personal tax rebate on insurance premiums provide an interesting example of a response to the problem of adverse selection and also of a policy measure aimed at bolstering the role of private insurance. However, given that private health insurance premiums tend to be regressive (with or without such a rebate), there are likely to be serious concerns about the equity implications of this form of private sector subsidy.

The main lessons from this chapter are that, first, predominantly private health care systems appear less equitable. Second, predominantly publicly financed systems do better. While public finance cannot ensure equity in principle and private finance does not preclude it, in the real world it is clear that publicly financed systems are likely to do better in the pursuit of equity. This may well be in large part because the reason that many systems are public is precisely because of the importance placed on equity objectives.

PART

IV

FUTURE CHALLENGES

FUTURE CONSIDERATIONS: SETTING THE HEALTH CARE BUDGET

INTRODUCTION

So far we have considered how best to finance health care at the level of both individual actors (such as consumers and doctors) and corporate actors (such as hospitals) within the health care sector. This leaves two questions unanswered: 'What should the size of the health care budget actually be?' and, in relation, 'How should the health care budget be set?' Despite the difficulties involved in answering these questions, it is our contention that in the future the best evidence relating to them will come from the application of economics to health care and other health-producing activities.

In an unregulated competitive health care market, it would be simple to answer the question of what the size of the health care budget should be: 'leave it to the market'. There would never be any reason even to address the question explicitly, as the 'appropriate' level of spending would be determined by the 'invisible hand' guiding transactions between fully informed patients and health care providers. As we have seen, however, most health care markets are (justifiably) heavily regulated. There is no automatic mechanism, like the market, to guide the system to the appropriate level of spending.

The aims of this chapter are fourfold: first, to examine evidence on the determinants of total health care spending; second, to show that there is no one correct level of spending, despite the fact that much analysis assumes that there is; third, noting the second aim, to demonstrate that no matter the size of the budget there are economic approaches which can contribute significantly to determining how best to spend the *given* budget; and, fourth, to be reminded of the role of broader social contributions to health beyond (just) health care.

It is important to examine the determinants of health care spending because it may be that the variables affecting the total spend are those about which little can be done directly. For instance, if gross domestic product (GDP) is *the* important determinant, little can be done by way of direct health care policy in setting the budget; governments should aim to increase GDP if they want to enhance the budget for health care. Cultural factors may also be difficult to manipulate in policy terms. Examining these determinants involves looking at health care spending and its determinants across countries at a very broad level, which presents a number of methodological challenges.

In moving beyond analysis of the determinants to look at appropriate levels of spending, and, more importantly, how best to spend the resources available, we are basically asking 'Where do we go from here?' In addressing this question, it is necessary to consider the benefits (i.e. enhanced well-being) which health services contribute to the community relative to the resources spent. It may be that more should be spent on health care but only if the benefits outweigh the costs. Likewise, it may be that less should be spent, but only if there are some treatments whose costs outweigh their benefits.

In responding to this, some studies attempt to use naive and problematical international comparisons of spending on health care and its broad outputs. Accepting that different countries have different starting points in terms of the size of the health care budget, there are still useful techniques which can take us a long way in helping to set the right level of health care budget within a country. In fact, the key is in adhering to the fundamental economic principles of opportunity cost and the margin; one means of operationalising these principles, as discussed, is through the application of programme budgeting and marginal analysis (PBMA).

Finally, as has been widely recognized over the last three decades, health care *per se* is but only one input into the 'production' of health. As such, while it is important to divide up health care resources in the best means possible, preferably through using approaches like PBMA, it is also important to recognise that improving the allocation of the health care budget will likely only result in relatively small improvements in population health. Thus, this chapter closes with an analysis of the social determinants of health. The implication of this discussion is that it may be that less should be spent on health care *per se* if more well-being would be produced by diverting those resources to other non-health care activities.

WHAT ARE THE DETERMINANTS OF TOTAL HEALTH CARE SPENDING?

There is enormous international variation in the size of health care expenditures per head, even when one has attempted to make the comparisons as consistent as possible and has used purchasing power parities to convert national currencies into dollars of (roughly) equal purchasing power. Table 10.1 shows the most recent results available for OECD countries. Such variation leads to the question of what the determinants of health care spending are. In examining this question, it is thought that an understanding of the determinants might yield insights into whether and how expenditure can be controlled, and the role health policy might play, particularly in those countries where spending is high (and rising fast) in relation to others.

The literature clearly indicates that the main determinant of the amount a country spends per head or as a share of GDP is income (Cichon *et al.*, 1999). The result

Table 10.1 Per capita health care expenditures, 1998

	Total expenditure on health as % GDP, 1998	Total expenditure on health exchange rate/ capita, US$, 1998	Total expenditure on health/capita, US$ PPP*, 1998	Total expenditure on health/ capita, NCU**95 GDP price, 1998
US	12.9	4 165	4 165	3 957
Germany	10.3	2 697	2 361	4 607
France	9.4	2 324	2 043	13 221
Netherlands	8.7	2 172	2 150	4 091
Norway	9.4	3 108	2 452	22 004
Denmark	8.3	2 730	2 132	17 206
Luxembourg	6	2 571	2 246	87 496
Canada	9.3	1 850	2 360	2 685
Belgium	8.6	2 112	2 050	73 589
Austria	8	2 100	1 894	25 164
Finland	6.9	1 737	1 510	8 842
Japan	7.4	2 242	1 795	2 95 991
Britain	6.8	1 636	1 510	896
Ireland	6.8	1 577	1 534	977
Italy	8.2	1 702	1 824	26 69 044
Spain	7	1 043	1 194	1 44 047
Greece	8.4	965	1 198	2 36 361
Portugal	7.7	859	1 203	1 40 031

Notes

* Purchasing power parities provide a measure of the command of one dollar over resources which is more consistent across countries than simple exchange rates.

** National Currency Units.

Source: OECD, 2001.

that health care is a luxury good[1] was originally found by Kleiman (1974) in an international cross-sectional study, but was most prominently researched by Newhouse (1975, 1977). In Newhouse's 1977 study, he examined determinants for health care expenditure in 13 countries, and found that national income explained 92 per cent of the variance in the level of expenditure between countries. Since that time, many studies have replicated these findings (Hitris and Posnett, 1992; Gerdtham *et al.*, 1988; Roberts, 2000). For a comprehensive international review, readers are referred to Di Matteo and Di Matteo (1998). There is also broad agreement that the income elasticity (i.e. percentage rise in spending divided by percentage rise in income) lies between +1.18 and +1.48. Results from a number of studies are displayed in Table 10.2. Only one, Parkin *et al.* (1987) casts some doubt on the general finding that health care is a luxury good.

More impressionistic evidence, presented in Table 10.3, also supports the basic finding that the level of health care spending is largely determined by national income. As can be seen, low-income countries (as proxied in the table by a lower human development index ranking) tend to spend smaller proportions of GDP on health care: the percentage of public expenditure on health care ranging from 0.7 to 1.3 per cent in lower income countries, 2.3 to 4.9 per cent in middle-income countries and 6.3 to 7.0 per cent in high-income countries.

Noting that the majority of expenditure is indeed determined by income, what about the other, approximately 10 per cent of expenditure seemingly not associated

Table 10.2 Studies of the association between national income and health care spending

Author	Method	Income elasticities
Newhouse (1977)	Single-variable regression analysis of per capita GDP on per capita medical care expenditure from 13 developed countries. Expenditure measured in US dollars at annual average exchange rates	+1.35
Parkin *et al.* (1987)	As above, but from 23 countries using exchange rate and from 18 countries using PPP*	+1.18 (exchange rate) +0.90 (PPP)
Culyer (1988)	As above, but from 20 countries	+1.35
Culyer (1989)	As above, but from 20 countries and using PPP instead of exchange rates	+1.35
Moore *et al.* (1992)	As above, but from 20 countries and using both PPP and exchange rates	+1.14 (exchange rate) +1.48 (PPP)

Notes
* Purchasing power parities provide a measure of the command of one dollar over resources which is more consistent across countries than simple exchange rates.

Table 10.3 Expenditure in health in low-, middle- and high-income countries

Country	HDI* ranking (out of 173)	Public health expenditure as % of GDP, 1998	Per capita health expenditure (public and private combined, PPP US$), 1998
Low income			
Pakistan	138	0.7	18
Togo	141	1.3	9
Nepal	142	1.3	11
Mozambique	170	0.7	8
Medium income			
Mexico	54	2.6	236
Belarus	56	4.6	85
Panama	57	4.9	246
Belize	58	2.3	82
High income			
Norway	1	7.0	3182
Sweden	2	6.6	2145
Canada	3	6.6	1939
Belgium	4	6.3	2137

Note
* Human Development Index.
Source: United Nations Development Program (2002).

with income? Over the last two decades, a number of additional explanatory factors have been found, including the use of primary care gatekeepers, the proportion of inpatient to ambulatory care beds, the total supply of doctors, an aging population, patient cost at point of delivery, and the mix of public/private financing (Leu, 1986; Gerdtham *et al.*, 1992; Hitiris and Posnett, 1992; O'Connell, 1996; Gerdtham *et al.*, 1998). However, still other studies have disputed many of these claims (Moore *et al.*, 1992; Barros,1998; Zweifel *et al.*, 1999; Roberts, 2000).

On balance, one factor which the evidence does seem to indicate to be a likely determinant of expenditure is the type and mix of financing (i.e. the degree of public versus private finance) (Cichon *et al.*, 1999). The divergence in trends in health care costs in Canada and the US since the introduction of compulsory public insurance around 1971 in the Canadian system illustrates the potential importance of the method of overall financing of the health system, as seen in Figure 10.1. But this may be only part of the story, as the amount of centralised control could also play an important role. For example, it has also been widely felt that, in the UK, stringent public expenditure controls have held costs down. In addition, Feldstein (1977) argued that the uncontrolled nature of hospital reimbursement by insurance companies in the US both stimulated technical progress towards more costly provision and weakened incentives for cost control. One potential anomaly

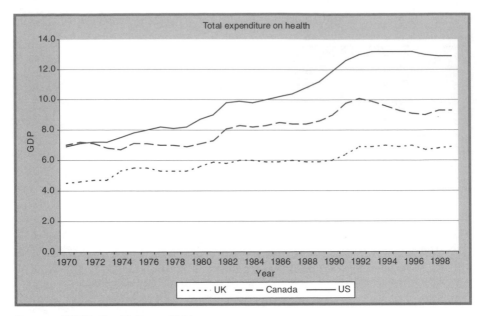

Source: OECD Health Data, 2001.

Figure 10.1 Health care expenditure as a percentage of GDP: US, Canada and UK, 1979–99.

(addressed further below) may be Sweden, which is often cited as a high-spending but publicly financed health care system.

The key point here is that cost containment is feasible (Culyer, 1988), and further that long term structural change can seemingly influence expenditure (Getzen, 2000). Leu (1986) tentatively concluded that the higher the public/private ratio in total funding, the higher the total spend; while the more centralised the health budgeting system, the lower the spend. This seems to be confirmed by Culyer's detailed study of Canada (Culyer, 1988) and by the work of Evans (1982, 1984 and 1986). Public finance enables the consumption of care that would not otherwise be taken up; centralisation enables the squeezing of fee schedules and tighter control on budgets. What this illustrates is that a highly regulated system *can* choose to spend more or not. Less regulation may give less freedom to make such a choice. How such choices are articulated from consumer to provider is difficult to characterise.

In Sweden, this is done through the localised democratic system; a local community can decide to spend more on health care and raise the money through increased taxation. Such 'choices' will reflect cultural expectations. Aaron and Schwartz (1984) have argued that, to some extent, Americans collectively 'choose' to spend more than Britons on certain treatments which are still beneficial to patients (e.g. coronary artery bypass grafts), whilst British planners and doctors 'choose' not to provide as much of other treatments whose benefits they see as not worth the costs incurred (e.g. intensive care). Continued study may shed further light on these issues.

Returning to the results from the aggregate studies, outlined above, it should be noted that inconsistency, to some degree, can be expected with the type of international analyses typically conducted in examining health care expenditure. Problems include discrepancies in expenditure compilation (Tokita *et al.*, 2000; Kanavos and Mossialos, 1999) and issues such as currency conversion (Hitiris and Posnett, 1992). Parkin *et al.* (1987) also point to problems of using highly aggregated data which do not account for differing patterns across countries in terms of spending on institutional/non-institutional care or the mix of personnel. As a result, Kanavos *et al.* (1999) state that more within-country work is required to determine key effects on health care expenditure in addition to GDP.

To this end, several important within-country studies can be found in the literature. One Canadian study (Di Matteo and Di Matteo, 1998) based on 1965–91 data, found the key determinants of provincial expenditure to be per capita income, proportion of the provincial population over age 65 and real provincial per capita federal transfer revenues. They also found that while health care expenditures had risen substantially since 1960, the overall share of provincial expenditure on health care has remained stable. Further, similar to Barer *et al.* (1987), the contribution of per capita expenditure due to aging was found to be statistically significant but in reality the contribution was quite small relative to other factors.

A Japanese study (Tokita *et al.*, 2000) found income to be a significant predictor across precincts, as well as the number of beds and doctors per capita and the use of medical technology. Taking a slightly different approach, Meerding *et al.* (1998) examined the demand on health care resources caused by different types of illnesses and demographic factors in the Netherlands. This study found the main determinants of health care use to be old age and disabling conditions. Similarly, in a large US study, Goetzel *et al.* (1998) examined modifiable risk behaviour and measured the impact on employee health expenditure. Not surprisingly, they found depression, very high or low body weight, high stress, high blood glucose levels, tobacco users and a sedentary lifestyle to be associated with increased health care expenditure. Overall, such within-country studies can provide additional insight, and further work may indeed shed greater insights.

In summary, national income is the major predictor of overall health care expenditure. A small predictive amount is left unaccounted for, and while many explanations have been put forth, supported to various degrees by international analyses, it is plausible that structural reform issues (e.g. the mix of private/public funding and degree of centralised control of the system) drive the remaining expenditure in a given country. This fits with the account of Getzen (2000) and matches empirical cost containment of overall expenditure by governments. We would thus support Cichon *et al.* (1999) that, 'It is important to understand that the level of health spending is a matter of policy and choice, although it is constrained by the wealth of the country and other priorities competing for use of the country's resources.' Income level is the key determinant of health care expenditure internationally, but there is also some scope for policy impact.

Importantly, though, as will be illustrated shortly, policy responses can also occur at a different level, for example, within regionalised health organisations, whereby less influence is exerted on overall expenditure but much more scope is available for re-allocation within the existing budget, in the hope of improving patient benefit and population health. This issue is examined following a more directed discussion about the appropriate level of spending, and the relationship between inputs and outputs of health care.

WHAT IS THE APPROPRIATE LEVEL OF SPENDING?

There is much controversy in deciding where societies are on an input–output curve like that in Figure 10.2. Are they at point (a) – as many doctors urge – where the pay-off to increased health care spending is high? Or are they at (b) – towards the point Enthoven (1980) has called 'flat of the curve' medicine, where the pay-off to higher spending is zero? Or are they at (c) – as Illich (1976) has argued – where the pay-off is negative and health services manufacture ill-health?

Unfortunately, this evidence is hard to assess. It consists on the one hand of very broad indicators of 'input' and 'output' whose correspondence with the true inputs and – especially – the true outputs is very approximate and whose causal connection is tenuous. On the other hand, there are more precise methods, as discussed in the next section, which do represent a way forward in that much more investment in these activities will take countries much closer to setting an optimum health care budget.

The 'broad' approach has been to examine mortality, morbidity and health care expenditure across (usually OECD) countries. An 'international comparisons

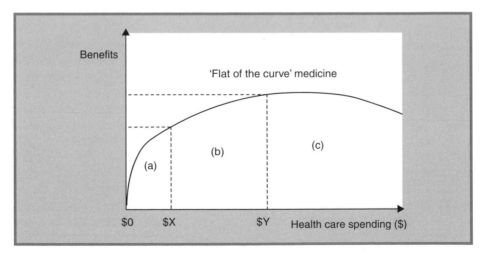

Figure 10.2 Diminishing marginal returns to health care

industry' has become established using such data not because it tells us what we want to know but rather 'because its there'. An underlying implication of this work is that there is a 'magic number' (a percentage of GDP spent on health care) to which all societies should be moving.

From the 29 OECD countries for which a comparison can be made (see Table 10.4), take the position of Australia. Some countries appear to spend less than Australia and achieve better health outcomes (e.g. Sweden and Japan). However, other countries spend more, but do not necessarily do better than Australia in terms of

Table 10.4 Health care expenditure per capita, male life expectancy and perinatal mortality (OECD countries)*

	1997 per capita expenditure, US$ PPP	*1997 life expectancy males at age 40 years*	*1997 perinatal mortality death/1000 total births*
Australia	1932	37.8	6.6
Austria	1820	36.2	6.5
Belgium	1972	36.6	6.8***
Canada	2180	37.7	6.6
Czech Republic	929	32.6	5.9
Denmark	2031	35.2	8**
Finland	1495	35.4	5.1
France	1977	36.7	7
Germany	2335	35.9	6.5
Greece	1181	37.5	9.5
Hungary	672	29	9.9
Iceland	1923	38	5.8
Ireland	1473	35***	10**
Italy	1735	37.3	6.9
Japan	1808	38.6	6.4
Korea	771	33.2	6**
Luxembourg	2134	n/a	6.9
Mexico	402	37.4	13.7
Netherlands	2009	36.2	7.9
New Zealand	1346	37.3	6.5
Norway	2149	37.2	6.1
Poland	448	31.3	10.5
Portugal	1149	34.7	7.2
Spain	1155	37.1	6.3
Sweden	1712	38.1	5.4
Switzerland	2697	38.2	6.9
UK	1407	36.4	8.3
Turkey	268	32.2	21.9
US	4015	36.2	7.3

Notes
* Slovakia was omitted due to a lack of data ; **1996 data; ***1995 data.
Source: OECD, 2001.

health outcomes (e.g. US and France). Can anything be inferred from these data about the allocation or misallocation of health care resources in Australia? Unfortunately not.

Although the mortality data of Table 10.4 may provide crude indications of the health-related quality of life, they are not measures of the potential product of health care. If health care productivity was to be measured in terms of mortality or morbidity, one could only do so by examining whether changes in mortality or morbidity arose – that is, by reducing the rate or by preventing or slowing its rise. For instance, relating overall health care spending to specific perinatal mortality rates does not really make much sense. To examine this issue properly, spending on perinatal services should be related to perinatal mortality whilst attempting to control for other factors, such as cultural and social incentives to attend antenatal clinics and lifestyle factors such as nutrition. Consideration should also be paid to what patients want from their health services including the benefits of perinatal health services that lie beyond reductions in mortality and morbidity (Mooney, 1998). There is, moreover, the ever-present problem of ensuring that attribution of cause and effect is correct. That is, that the observable health care input is not pig-gybacking on an already declining mortality rate or coinciding with service and environmental factors that are not part of health care. These issues are further discussed later in the chapter.

In short, the use of international comparisons is naive. Therefore, it is not sur-prising that, when based on such methods, a judgement of the effective impact of health care is elusive. No matter how good the data are in the future, it always will be. It is the method that is at fault, not the data. What is required is a method which tells us, within a country, what are the costs and benefits of changing the current uses of health care resources and what are the costs and benefits of expanding or contracting the health care budget.

There is other evidence, based on changes in health care expenditures and changes in life expectancy in OECD countries, which suggests that there is a quali-tative link between relatively slow rates of growth in expenditures and both slow rates of increase in life expectancy (Wolfe, 1986; Wolfe and Gabay, 1987) and slow rates of decline in infant mortality (Maxwell, 1981). These analyses are more sophisticated than the conventional comparisons discussed above. Even so, adjustments for other 'contaminating' factors are at best very approximate and the relationship is by no means readily observable.

In summary, decisions over the appropriate level of health care expenditure require careful consideration of the relevant comparators. As Moore *et al.* (1992) state, 'The level of national health expenditures cannot be considered as too high or two low in relation either to itself or to expenditures in other countries. An assessment of the appropriateness of national health spending requires a balanc-ing of costs and benefits at the margin.' It is this latter point, that of marginal analysis, which is addressed in the next section within the context of discussing different economic approaches for dividing up those resources that are available within any given budget.

MOVING FORWARD: FROM QALY LEAGUE TABLES TO PROGRAMME BUDGETING AND MARGINAL ANALYSIS

It is clear that progress on what to spend on health care cannot be made without more precise data on the productivity of health care interventions. This requires economic evaluation in which the costs of such interventions are related to their benefits. Decision-makers can use this information to assist with making informed choices over the allocation of scarce health care resources. That is, to make choices that promote the maximisation of benefits from the resources available (i.e. allocative efficiency).

Marginal cost per quality adjusted life year (QALY) league tables have been posited as one means of addressing the goal of allocative efficiency. QALYs are measures of health status that embody both length of life and quality of life. If a marginal cost per QALY could be calculated for all existing and proposed health care interventions, a 'league table' of costs per QALY for all services could be constructed. Cost per QALY league tables indicate the number of QALYs that could be bought by spending more on existing or new health service programmes. It is implied that the way to allocate extra resources would be to buy those QALYs that are available most cheaply. Allocative efficiency is achieved by identifying where the best buys are in terms of QALY gains.

A number of challenges in the calculation and application of QALY league tables have been identified. A key issue concerning the potential of QALYs for use in decision-making concerns the extent to which the technique is adopted in health services. Relatively few studies using cost–utility analysis have been used to generate QALY league tables. Moreover, when the results have been used to generate league tables, questions have been raised over the transferability of these estimates across settings and even countries (Gerard and Mooney, 1993; Gerard *et al.*, 1999; Neumann *et al.*, 2000). QALY league tables also imply that the way to allocate extra resources would be to buy those QALYs that are available most cheaply. This is only valid if the goal of health services is to maximise health, as measured through QALYs. A number of authors have identified a range of outcomes beyond health including reassurance, information, autonomy and awareness (Mooney, 1998; Salkeld, 1998; Ryan, 1999; Gonzalez *et al.*, 2001). Detailed critiques of the QALY approach can be found in Williams (1985, 1986), Donaldson *et al.* (1988), Loomes and McKenzie (1989), Gerard and Mooney (1993) and Petrou *et al.* (1993).

The economic framework known as programme budgeting and marginal analysis (PBMA) offers another way forward. It is a somewhat cruder form of analysis. It was first used in health care by the Department of Health in England to assist it in its priority setting in the early 1970s. With the development of a focus on health outcomes internationally, PBMA has been enjoying a resurgence of interest. It has been used by numerous health authorities in the UK (Shiell *et al.*, 1993; Cohen, 1994; Craig *et al.*, 1995; Donaldson, 1995; Madden *et al.*, 1995; Twaddle and Walker, 1995; Ratcliffe *et al.*, 1996; Ruta *et al.*, 1996; Miller *et al.*, 1997; Henderson and Scott,

2001), Australia (Viney *et al.*, 1995; Newberry, 1996; Mooney *et al.*, 1997; Peacock and Edwards, 1997; Crockett *et al.*, 1999; Viney *et al.*, 2000; Haas *et al.*, 2001), New Zealand (Ashton *et al.*, 2000; Bohmer *et al.*, 2001) and more recently, in Canada (Mitton *et al.*, 2002; Mitton *et al.*, 2003).

PBMA provides a framework for making decisions about how to shift resources and realign services to achieve health improvement and other potential benefits, while recognising other objectives of a health service such as equity. It makes explicit the decisions about which services should be expanded and which contracted on the basis of what the impact of marginal resource shifts will be. PBMA provides a forum through which the information to reallocate existing resources can be considered. The idea is that by shifting resources which provide relatively low benefit to services which have higher benefit, the overall performance of the health service can be improved without an increase in budget (Newberry, 1996).

PBMA involves two stages. The first stage is the development of programme budgets. These provide an information framework to allow the examination of the relationship between resource use, activities, outputs and objectives. A key feature of this framework is that programmes are output and objective orientated rather than being focused on inputs and activities. In terms of service planning, programme budgeting is intended to answer the question 'where are we now?' The second stage is that of marginal analysis. Most decisions about the use of health care resources relate to changes in the size or scale of activities rather than whether or not an activity should receive funding at all. The emphasis is on those activities that are *marginal*. For example, if resources to a particular programme or sub-programme were to be increased, the marginal activity would be the first to be expanded. The process of evaluating marginal activities and shifting resources from those of low marginal benefit to those of high marginal benefit can be repeated until the whole programme has been evaluated. Marginal analysis therefore answers the question 'what should we change?' In practice, the process involves developing and prioritising incremental and decremental 'wish lists' (i.e. activities which should be expanded if additional resources are available, and those which would be contracted if a budget cut were imposed).

Reflecting on international experiences with PBMA, a number of insights can be gained. It is widely reported that the preparation and conduct of such exercises can be resource intensive (Bohmer *et al.*, 2001). Marginal analysis is one of the most challenging and time-consuming stages of the resource allocation process (Viney *et al.*, 1995). In terms of considering re-allocation decisions, multidisciplinary groups representing relevant health care programmes and services appear to be most useful (Viney *et al.*, 1995). Indeed, the need to engage with the relevant decision makers of various kinds at each stage of the process can be seen as an advantage of PBMA. As well, PBMA is dependent upon a strong commitment to consider and then carry through the identified resource shifts (Mitton and Donaldson, 2003).

PBMA is an approach to improving efficiency that is based largely on existing data. For some health care programmes this data is extremely limited or even non-existent. It is therefore often necessary to generate local information (Craig *et al.*, 1995). While this locally relevant data is to be preferred over data that has been imported from other settings, it may mean that health services need to invest in data collection. Finally, relevant data may come in the form of both quantitative and qualitative information. Problems with combining these different types of information into the PBMA framework have also been identified (Ashton *et al.*, 2000). It should be noted that not all of these issues are unique to PBMA. For example, the challenges associated with collecting and combining a variety of locally generated information will be faced by any 'rational' approach to priority setting that involves comparing costs and benefits. A number of useful methodological critiques of the approach have been published including Posnett and Street (1996), Ratcliffe *et al.* (1996), Jan (2000) and Mitton and Donaldson (2001).

It also may be useful to think about PBMA as not necessarily an alternative to conventional economic evaluations. PBMA can be thought of as the basic framework, through which various types of evidence can be considered within the constraint of a specific budget. The evidence which informs decision-making may be in the form of a specific outcomes data or economic evaluation. The important point for PBMA is that costs and benefits be examined explicitly, at the margin, to determine if the resource mix can be altered to improve benefits overall.

Finally, the examination of costs and benefits under approaches such as PBMA, ideally requires detailed evaluation (as advocated by Cochrane in 1972). The rigorous evaluation culture that he promoted has led to the opening of the first Cochrane Centre in Oxford (UK) in 1992 and the founding of The Cochrane Collaboration in 1993. Techniques of economic evaluation fit neatly with the concept of randomised controlled trials (RCTs) promoted by Cochrane. However, while a growing number of the studies reported by the Cochrane Collaboration include some form of economic evaluation, many do not. This is a problem that economists and their public health colleagues urgently need to address if decision-makers are to make genuinely informed resource allocation choices. The recent establishment of organisations such as The National Institute for Clinical Excellence (NICE) in the UK, building on the Australian Pharmaceutical Benefits Advisory Committee, go some way in helping to address this knowledge gap by further consolidating and generating information on the clinical and cost-effectiveness of new and existing health care interventions for the National Health Service (NHS) in England and Wales. The next critical step is to undertake some assessment of the uptake of this information as well as its impact on standards of patient care and inequities in access to treatment needs. PBMA, itself, can still survive without such organisations, however, as, in our view, its inherent approach, based on economic principles is essential for local decision-making. Indeed, in attempting to look at the whole picture of resources in a relevant area, it could be argued that PBMA is more likely to lead to relevant marginal changes than, say, NICE which, it could be argued, addresses issues piecemeal.

213

SOCIAL DETERMINANTS OF HEALTH

Another point to bear in mind in endeavouring to determine where we go from here is the fact that health care is but one input into the process by which the health of the individual is improved or maintained. In Figure 10.3, it is illustrated that income, education, genetic endowment, lifestyle, work environment, work status, housing and health care all affect an individual's stock of health. This stock of health, in turn, produces healthy time for the individual. The diagram in Figure 10.3 is a basic representation of a model relating health outcome to health inputs that was first introduced by Grossman (1970) and developed by others (Muurinen, 1982; Wagstaff, 1986). However, social science disciplines and epidemiologists would also lay legitimate claims on this area of research.

Whatever the academic property rights, in the context of health care financing, the interesting question is whether an extra amount of money spent on another input would be more productive in terms of health improvements than spending that same amount on health care. It may be that arguing for more health care resources is to the detriment of health if such resources are won at the expense of those resources being put into a more health-productive input.

Impressionistic evidence tells us that, if a major goal of public policy is health improvement, then many low-income countries would be better off implementing broader social and educational policies than in financing high-technology health care. For example, malaria is a major cause of morbidity and mortality in many low-income countries and a variety of factors both within and beyond the health

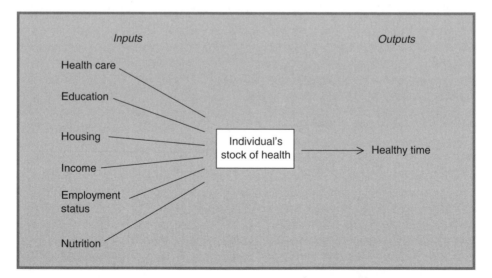

Figure 10.3 Grossman model of inputs to and outputs from health

sector determine how patients and their families cope with this illness. In Sri Lanka, Reilley *et al.* (2002) found that many families suffering from malaria did not complete treatment with anti-malarial drugs because of a lack of food to take the drugs with. Problems of food security are widespread in the developing world. They also reported that due to years of civil unrest, the roads were in very poor condition and this made travelling to health facilities extremely difficult if not impossible.

Moreover, anthropologists and other social scientists have long documented the impact of a range of social, economic and cultural factors on treatment seeking behaviour. Again, sticking with the example of malaria, evidence suggests that adherence to multiple day regimens of anti-malarials is often undermined by factors such as long duration regimens, complex dosing requirements, high cost, a poor understanding of how or why to adhere to recommended regimens and adverse side effects (Fungladda *et al.*, 1998; Bloland *et al.*, 2000; Yepez *et al.*, 2000). It has also been reported that perceptions of wellness also influence adherence particularly where there are early signs of relief and patients decide to stop taking the anti-malarial drug before the full course has been completed (McCombie, 1996). Local beliefs over the efficacy of anti-malarials are another influence of adherence. For example, in Uganda health messages have been used to inform mothers that drugs dispensed in capsule form are not necessarily dangerous (Ndyomugyenti *et al.*, 1998). They have also been used to alleviate concerns over the efficacy of chloroquine as well as its safety, in particular its alleged ability to cause abortion (Ndyomugyenti *et al.*, 1998; Reilley *et al.*, 2002).

Finally, to return to an earlier point, many of the problems of treating and preventing illnesses like malaria in developing countries are linked to broader problems of health services such as inadequate resources. Expenditure on health is highly constrained in most low-income countries by limited revenues and restrictive macroeconomic policies (Hanson *et al.*, 2002; Wiseman, 2003). In Tanzania, the annual health care expenditure is estimated to be no more than $2.50 per capita (Government of Tanzania, 2000). These examples help to highlight the dangers of failing to look for answers beyond the health sector, to acknowledge user concerns, to consider affordability and lastly, failing to investigate the impact of local beliefs and practices on health care behaviour.

Turning now to high-income countries, one does not have to look very far to find evidence of a variety of social determinants of health. The literature on this topic is vast and only a few examples will be drawn from specific literatures. For example, the evaluation of alternative ways of treating people post-myocardial infarction indicates that health care only affects survival if received very soon (within six hours) after the infarction. The earlier treatment is administered, the greater the benefit (Zapka *et al.*, 2000). Many patients do not enter the health care system that rapidly, their health is no better improved by health care than by remaining at home (Hill *et al.*, 1978; Mather *et al.*, 1978). While delay before treatment can be attributed to a variety of factors including patient delay, emergency medical service delay and hospital delay (Ho, 1991), it is the issue of patient delay that has been most closely explored in the literature. Evidence suggests that patients who delay longer typically share some combination of the following characteristics: lower incomes; older age; intermittent symptoms; fewer years of education; not recognising the importance of symptoms; living alone; transportation to the hospital by private vehicle rather than ambulance; no experience of previous cardiac problems; and fear or embarrassment about seeking help (Franzosi *et al.*, 1995; Dracup *et al.*, 1997; Leizorovicz *et al.*, 1997; McKinley *et al.*, 2000; Zapka *et al.*, 2000). The pattern of treatment seeking behaviour of patients with a history of heart problems is shown to be mixed with some patients presenting earlier (Goldberg *et al.*, 1999) and others delaying seeking help in spite of their frequent contacts with health services (Mumford *et al.*, 1999). The significance of each of these factors has been shown to vary according to the particular cultures of patients (Goff *et al.*, 1999; Goldberg *et al.*, 1999; McKinley *et al.*, 2000).

Taking a somewhat broader perspective, one can also identify positive associations between deprivation and rates of mortality and morbidity (Townsend *et al.*, 1987; Carstairs and Morris, 1989). In such studies, measures of 'deprivation' comprise aspects such as overcrowding in housing, employment status (particularly unemployment), social class and whether or not one has a car. Higher income and schooling has been shown to have a positive effect on health as well as access to health care (Grossman, 1975; Corman and Grossman, 1985; Gilmore *et al.*, 2002; Grundy and Sloggett, 2002; Wildman *et al.*, 2003). The availability of organised family planning, abortion and neonatal intensive care have been linked with lower neonatal mortality rates (Corman and Grossman, 1985). 'Good family relations' are also reported to have a protective effect against poor health (Gilmore *et al.*, 2002).

A growing number of studies have revealed that housing plays an important role in the manifestation of health inequalities. For example, lack of affordable housing has been associated with lower levels of self-reported general and mental health (Dunn *et al.*, 2002). Similarly, a lack of heated housing has been associated with higher excess winter mortality (Aylin *et al.*, 2001). Studies examining the impact of measures of social networks and social capital have shown that factors such as social exclusion and limited participation in organisations can have deleterious effects on health and well being (Bobak *et al.*, 1998; Cattell, 2001). A strong correlation has also been demonstrated between all-cause mortality and indigenous status (Wilkinson *et al.*, 2001).

It was argued at the beginning of this section that if a major goal of public policy were health improvement, then many low-income countries would be better off implementing broader social and educational policies than in financing high-technology health care. It is worth noting that a similar argument can also be levelled at many middle and high-income countries. Using cross-sectional data, a US study analysed the potential changes in mortality rates that would be associated with 10 per cent increases in some variables. It can be seen from Table 10.5 that, once again, an increase in education (represented by years of schooling) has more

Table 10.5 Percentage changes in age-specific mortality rates resulting from a 10 per cent increase in several variables

	10% increase in			
	Income	*Education*	*Cigarette consumption*	*Per capita health expenditure*
Per cent change mortality	+2.0	−2.2	+1.0	−0.65

Source: Culyer (1976).

potential for reducing mortality than does an increase in per capita health spending (Auster *et al.*, 1972). The small impact of increased spending on health care may be characteristic of many developed nations. Cigarette consumption has the expected sign, an increase leading to greater mortality. Higher income is also associated with increased mortality, suggesting that the negative effects may outweigh the positive health effects of increased income.

Decisions over the appropriate public policies for improving health are further complicated where different population groups define 'health' differently. For example, the indigenous peoples of Australia are known to define health in a much more holistic manner than conventional Western biomedical concepts. Such definitions embrace a broader set of factors including autonomy and self-determination (Kunitz, 1994; Brady, 1995). While there will always be a need (as well as a demand) for countries such as Australia to explore new health care technologies, significant gains to the welfare of the indigenous population are likely to come from beyond the health care system (McMillan, 1991; Saggers and Gray, 1991; Gracey *et al.*, 1997; Mooney *et al.*, 1998). Consequently, there is a need to take into account the relative efficiency with which different health influencing activities affect health and welfare (e.g. health services versus housing) (Mooney *et al.*, 1998). It is not enough that health services can influence health positively but that such services do so more efficiently than any alternative use of society's resources. For a useful overview of the social determinants of health see Caldwell and Santow (1989), Marmot and Wilkinson (1999) and Raphael (2000).

The 'solution' to the health and health care budget-setting problem, which can be offered by more and wider analysis of determinants of health and well-being, is many years in the future. Once again, it points us in the direction of searching for better measures of health outcome as well as evidence on the effects on health and well-being of not only health care but also investment in other health-producing activities. In determining where we go from here, it will then be possible to examine whether or not the greatest health improvements for the community will result from a larger or smaller budget for health care.

CONCLUSIONS

In analysing the major determinants of health care spending, it seems that income is the main factor: one spends what one can afford. This should not be held to be an 'iron law'; nor does it say anything about what is the 'correct' level of spending, particularly noting that global inequities on health care spending do exist. Further, while income may be the main determinant, other factors are also likely to play some role, such as the private/public financing mix and the centralisation of budgeting systems.

Regarding the appropriate level of the health care budget, little can be offered by way of evidence from economic studies on what the 'correct' level is. This is largely because there is no universally correct level. In the absence of market forces, the level which is set, or reached, will, to a large extent, depend on various cultural factors. In fact, international comparisons are naive and unhelpful. There does not seem to be any point in refining a method of comparison that does not tell us what we want to know.

The real challenge is for countries, or regionalised bodies within countries, to decide for themselves by use of appropriate economic techniques such as PBMA. This will not result in a uniform level of spending across countries but will help in deciding where increases and decreases in available resources are best targeted. This is the fundamental issue, that no matter the size of the budget overall, efforts must be made to use the available resources in the best manner possible. Relying on an approach which aids decision-makers to think at the margin about opportunity costs would certainly be a step in the right direction.

All of that said, it is also fundamentally important to remember that health care *per se* is only one input into the health of both individuals and the population. Thus, while time and resources should be put towards determining the right mix of spending within given health care budgets, continued work at a societal level is required in deciding how best to divvy up the limited resources more broadly, such as for education and housing. In principle, there is no reason that an approach like PBMA could not also be used at this level to assist in this challenging process.

CHAPTER 11

HEALTH CARE FINANCING REFORMS: WHERE NOW FOR THE VISIBLE HAND?

INTRODUCTION

It is now over ten years since the first edition of this book was published. No longer is it the case that reforms are being discussed or anticipated. Rather, the financing arrangements of many health care systems worldwide seem to be in a perpetual state of reform. The key to judging such reforms is conceptually simple and remains the same; that is whether they make things better or worse for the population at large. Our primary objective has been to show the essential role of economics in assessing performance within this climate of change. The two powerful economic criteria against which change should be assessed are, of course, efficiency and equity; the former being concerned with the need to finance services in a way that maximises the well-being of the community and the latter with access to health services for less well-off groups in need. When examined against these criteria, the economic arguments are as strong as the social and ideological arguments in favour of extensive government intervention in health care financing.

We have seen that reforms can be directed towards various levels of health care finance; micro-level changes, such as prospective payments for hospital care, or, fundamental changes (for instance the Canadian move to Medicare). Whatever the details of these reforms, the crucial economic issues that are of interest are

- How will money be raised to finance the system (and what does this mean for the nature of the financial intermediary that stands between the consumer and the provider and the principles on which the 'insurance premium' will be based)?
- What payments out-of-pocket are to be made by the consumer at the point of use? Can other forms of reliance on consumer preferences, such as medical savings accounts, be used?
- How are professional providers to be paid?
- How are institutions to be reimbursed?
- How will the 'market' be organised and to what degree will competition be used within this?

Paying due attention to the costs, benefits and equity implications of each of these is essential if informed judgements on reforms are to be made.

THE CONTRIBUTION OF ECONOMIC THEORY

The first and second parts of this book set out the economic arguments behind the inevitability that some level of government intervention in health care financing will exist and the sorts of forms it might take.

Indeed, extensive government intervention is difficult to avoid if maximisation of the community's health is an objective of health care. Rarely for any commodity do market forces work sufficiently well to produce that highly desirable outcome, maximum satisfaction at least cost to society. However, the nature of health care is such that all the basic assumptions underlying a market approach break down completely. Thus, although there are differences of opinion concerning the 'correct' balance between market forces and government intervention (evident from the diverse array – one might even say disarray – of financial arrangements that exist in health care systems around the world), the characteristics of health care make it uniquely susceptible (and, in our view, rightly so) to significant government intervention. These characteristics (the risk and uncertainty associated with contracting illness; external effects; and asymmetrical information about health care between providers and consumers combined with problems of professional licensure), make it likely that government intervention will dominate the financing of health care. The evidence on prevalence of National Health Service (NHS) and social insurance based systems (including their growth in lower income countries) bears witness to this.

Usually government finance of health care takes the form of income tax, pay-roll taxes or, sometimes, a hypothecated tax (the last of which, usually, will not cover the full costs of the system). Unevaluated methods of government finance include voucher systems, lotteries and charitable donations.

The setting of health care objectives represents an intricate piece of juggling by policy-makers to ensure that seeking too much efficiency does not counter too much equity, or vice versa. A trade-off between these two objectives is normally inevitable. This makes it important that both objectives are made explicit so that societies, or their representatives, can be well placed to judge for themselves the acceptability of trading-off some amount of the ideal level of one for some greater level of the other.

Equity itself is a difficult notion to comprehend and agree upon beyond some strong, basic understanding that some 'fair' distribution is desirable. Its pursuit in practice can be hampered by conflict between different equity definitions.

We believe that the most desirable definitions are (a) financing based on ability to pay (a progressive income-conditioned tax basis) and (b) equality of access. However, it is not possible to measure equality of access in absolute terms; rather barriers to access (e.g. geographical or time) need to be taken into account. These may only partially capture the notion of access. Even so, data on such variables may be difficult to come by and so proxy measures, particularly related to utilisation, are often used. We recognise such proxies are unsatisfactory but accept that in many instances they may be the best available. We have found considerable support in policy statements and pronouncements for our chosen definitions of equity objectives although they are by no means uncontested.

In comparison with the complexities surrounding equity objectives, efficiency definitions are uncontentious. They have been described as technical (or operational) efficiency and allocative efficiency. The appropriate 'rules' to measure and monitor them fall under the familiar auspices of economic evaluation: cost-effectiveness analysis and cost–benefit analysis.

There may be a more contentious area not on efficiency *per se* but in defining benefit. Although we have not pursued this at any length in the book, we believe that while health dominates the outputs of health care systems it does not monopolise it; there is also utility in the process of health care which, on occasions, may be more important than utility from outcome.

EMPIRICAL FINDINGS – HOW HEALTH SERVICES SHOULD BE FINANCED

Throughout the third part of this book we have reported on available evidence (and often lack of it) of the performance of different financing arrangements. This has been done in as objective a way as possible. We make no pretence at having achieved comprehensiveness as the literature is far too large for that, but feel we have reported adequately on the main published literature. Where we report crucial gaps in information (e.g. on the question of how best to pay doctors) we find it alarming that reforms can be undertaken without any prior, controlled experimentation (as in the recent UK NHS reforms as well as those of the early 1990s). Nevertheless, we feel that, due to the growth of literature assessing health care reforms, more definite conclusions can be drawn than was the case ten years ago.

Despite this, there is no unique and unambiguous overall conclusion that can be summarised easily. Inevitably, important value judgements come into play in addressing the question 'what health care financing arrangements should and should not be in place in order to operate a fair and efficient system?'

The financial intermediary

First, what should be the role of the financial intermediary that stands between the consumer and the provider? Ideally, it should provide an environment for health care providers and consumers to act efficiently and equitably. In reality, any financial intermediary is susceptible to encouraging inefficient behaviour because it breaks accountability links between those who bear the cost of health care with those who provide the benefits and those who obtain them. However, as we have seen in

Chapters 6–8, financial intermediaries, with varying degrees of success, can make attempts at re-establishing some accountability.

Government-based intermediaries seem best placed to offer a basis to cope with access problems of the sort created by unregulated health care insurance. By taking on the role of compulsory purchaser of health care insurance they can detach the basis for setting premium rates from experience of illness. Thus, such intermediaries are best placed to ensure comprehensive access to health care services or to insurance. In our view, the 'insurance premium' should be a compulsory one, set at levels according to ability to pay. However, in the event (as seems to be case, for example, in a growing number of economies that are currently in transition) the favoured health system is one with a substantial private insurance market, then it is essential that research effort goes into addressing how equity might be achieved under market solutions which aim to counter adverse selection. In particular we should watch the Australian private health insurance market closely as it experiences combining lifetime community-rated insurance premiums with personal tax rebates as one solution to this problem.

Surprisingly, government-based intermediaries may also be best placed to promote efficiency. At the level of the whole system, the collective purchasing and negotiating role provided by government agencies acts as a strong demand-side check to powerful, large and united interests on the supply side of the market.

Financing and the supply side

We further believe that the overall success of any reform to improve efficiency rests with the way in which the supply side of health care is financed, particularly the way in which doctors are paid. Given the characteristics of health care, it must be the case that ways of dealing with supply side moral hazard are easily the most influential. Despite the views of many health economists, it is not clear to us whether supplier-induced demand exists amongst doctors or, indeed, how relevant that particular concept is. Of course, doctors are better informed than consumers about the technological relationship between health care and health, and, thus, are often in the position of determining health care consumption. But, most importantly, doctors need to be given incentives to influence the amount and type of care they supply, and we know from the evidence that there are financial tools to achieve this. The hospital sector is also important as it accounts for a significant part of expenditure in any health care system. It is therefore crucial in playing an important role in not only determining the level and nature of hospital activity but also in controlling total health service costs.

Of course, more evidence on the effect of different methods of payment on doctors' performance would be preferred. A system based on fee-for-service (FFS) as the general method of payment would likely lead to problems with overuse of services. However, returning to the more general point that doctors, like other human beings, respond to incentives, fees should not be ruled out totally. There are some services which we might want to be provided on a widespread basis (e.g. preventive health services such as immunisations) for which fees may be the best form of remuneration. Thus, relating back to the key goals, fees could be part of a tightly controlled remuneration package that rewards efficient behaviour at least cost. In primary care, this might be best combined with an element of capitation, as it is good at achieving different goals. Thus, although remuneration systems have in the past often been set against one another in terms of judging which is best, it seems that 'blended systems' will achieve the best of all worlds and that many countries have learned this lesson.

Salaried payments, too, can play a part in this. Although such a mechanism may be seen as demotivating, likely leading to less utilisation as compared with fees, it is not clear whether this is good or bad. Furthermore, the salary level might be what is important. In this respect, salaries can play an important part in a 'blended' system, especially in the hospital sector and in encouraging care to be delivered to parts of the population which fees and capitation fail to reach (e.g. inner cities and remote areas).

The new GP contract in the UK is still based on the principles of blended payment, with global funds being allocated to primary care organisations through a resource allocation formula, fees for points achieved in relation to provision of particular services (e.g. for cardiovascular care), allowances to permit updating of infrastructure and the use of salaries for some GPs (NHS Confederation and British Medical Association, 2003). The important, and encouraging, point is that an array of financial mechanisms is available, and they do not have to be dichotomised, but, rather, can be used in combination to achieve policy objectives.

A note of caution, however, is that context is important, and, therefore, individual health care systems should postulate their own judgements of how well they think reforms of doctors' remuneration will work. As medical practices tend to vary socially and culturally it would not be surprising to learn of radically different remuneration packages improving efficient behaviour in different countries. For example, the social status and remuneration levels accorded Western doctors and Eastern European doctors are poles apart. Consequently, it is quite possible that, for example, a remuneration package in an Eastern European country would place greater importance on payment for 'good practice' and less on FFS remuneration than in a Western country – but that both were to work equally effectively. But regardless of social and cultural context, the key for any successful remuneration system lies in developing a better understanding of what is meant by 'good practice'. This is a recurring theme throughout the book and one which we believe should be placed high on the research agenda.

The second major element in achieving efficiency will come from financing reforms for institutions. Although costing issues are important to the financial incentives facing health care institutions, they are not of sole importance. Efficiency is about value for money. Thus, the fact that the HMO-style financial and organisational arrangement has undoubtedly been shown to achieve significant cost savings is not sufficient to assure efficiency. Indeed, the evidence points quite strongly to either selection of healthier individuals in non-randomised comparisons with FFS arrangements or reductions in quality of care in randomised comparisons with

FFS arrangements. Health care costs continue to rise unabated in the US, fuelled by mergers of providers (thus, increasing their power to charge higher rates to managed care, and other, financial intermediaries) and US consumers now selecting into higher cost plans (so as to give themselves access to a wider range of services). Thus, it seems that the managed care revolution is now dead and, if anything, it only held back cost increases temporarily. Another important lesson, here, is that market-based solutions at the level of the health care system will not achieve the cost control that seems to be so desired by US policy-makers. If too unregulated, the market will find a way round any such reforms.

Ironically, there may still be a role for market-based reforms, whereby demand is managed not through individual members of the public, but rather through some collective agency (with which the individual may have no choice over enrolment), such as a health authority or general practice. One of the tasks of these agencies is then to make the supply side compete to win funds from the agencies' budgets. Despite anecdotal views to the contrary, the evidence does show that internal markets had an impact in the publicly funded systems of countries like the UK and Sweden and that the news was not all bad. Such markets were shown to shift resources in the ways intended (e.g. out of London, UK). In the UK, general practitioner fundholding also displayed potential for achieving greater efficiencies despite inequities arising due to not all practices being covered by the scheme. It could be argued that recent reforms in the UK, away from internal markets, have placed more emphasis on providers and less on the direct involvement of GPs as purchasers, which may lead to greater inefficiencies in the future. In other words, an element of competition, which gives some power to health care purchasers is likely to be a good thing.

Another form of market-based reform in health care is that of contracting out publicly funded services to private providers. In fact, the ability to do this has existed in many countries for many years, despite recent publicity giving the impression that this is a new phenomenon. Again, the natural inclination amongst many populations would be against this. However, most of the evidence is indeterminate; although, if anything, it might be slightly weighted against private provision. Again, the important thing here is that such a reform cannot be conclusively ruled out and is available as a tool for policy-makers, although any such reform should be carefully monitored and evaluated in its context.

More generally, the relative efficiency of most reimbursement mechanisms has yet to be determined. Cost minimisation has, too frequently, been placed high on the political and administrative agendas without due attention being paid to effects on patient outcome. What should be of importance is the identification of cost reductions which can be achieved at little or no detrimental effect on patient outcome. Beyond politicians' greater concern for cost control than the health of the populations they serve, problems with health outcome measurement are largely responsible for this misguided focus on cost minimisation.

The way forward for reimbursing institutions is, we suggest, to develop the idea behind clinical budgeting. This first means, yet again, coming to terms with what is meant by 'best clinical practice' before setting reimbursement levels according to efficient modes of practice. It could be that some DRG-based tariff forms the basis of a subsequent price mechanism, but it is better if this is based on a notion of efficient, rather than average, practice. It might also be the case that some element of competition is desirable, and, as part of that, the tariff should be flexible; for example, rather than have prices based on some fixed tariff, it would seem sensible to give purchasers and providers the opportunity to negotiate 'deals' for local service provision at marginal cost, thus taking (efficient) advantage, in the sense of treating more cases from the purchaser's budget, of any spare capacity.

Financing and the demand side

The final economic issue that should be considered in assessing efficient health care financing is the question of the size of out-of-pocket payments made by consumers at the point of their consumption. We have deliberately left this issue to the end because we feel minimal responsibility should be placed on consumers.

Probably the most conclusive evidence on consumer moral hazard comes from the use of charges in the US private insurance market. Although charges help to reduce frivolous demand, the opportunity cost is high. Frivolous demand is not always easy to separate from necessary demand and low-income groups (particularly children) have been shown to be most disadvantaged by a corresponding reduction in consumption of necessary care that accompanies the introduction, or raising, of charges. Furthermore, the scale of reduced consumption suggested by published findings is contingent upon doctor behaviour since doctors' demand-inducing powers have a strong influence on consumption patterns; or, at least, it is natural for doctors simply to provide greater service intensity to those who present (i.e. those willing and able to pay the charges, and who are, therefore, less likely to be in need due to their greater wealth). It is not surprising that the countries with the greatest use if user charges also have the greatest problems with cost control. Because of both these factors, the relevance of charges to efficiency, over and above some nominal amount, must be highly contestable. With respect to equity, charges are almost inevitably bad.

Of developed countries, the US health care system is clearly still the most inequitable, both in terms of gaining access to health services and financing arrangements. Access is mostly a problem for different social groups than across urban/rural areas. Not only are basic payments regressive but gross inequities have been demonstrated in financial protection against catastrophic coverage. Lower income countries, not surprisingly given their stringent resource supply, also have serious problems with comprehensively protecting their population from the risk of ill-health. It is likely that basic payments are regressive, although it is felt by some that greater use of private health insurance by richer groups may actually contribute to equity in finance and delivery.

There is not much evidence on the recent innovation of medical savings accounts, although what evidence exists seems to indicate that they are likely to suffer from the same problems as user charges and are, therefore, unlikely to enhance efficiency or equity in health care.

Some people may believe that public financing restricts choice. We have deliberately left out this issue as we could not find any evidence to support or refute it (however 'choice' is to be defined). It is possible that private financing allows more choice, but it is equally conceivable that, because of the nature of health care, utility is gained from a situation of restricted choice, such as consumers preferring to pass on decisions to their doctors.

DETERMINING THE SIZE OF THE BUDGET

Any health care financing system will, to a large extent be culture-specific. However, within systems, debates will still go on about what the size of the health care budget should be. No such debates will be adequately resolved without more data on patient outcomes and well-being. Such data would facilitate not only comparisons of types of health care with each other but also comparisons of levels of health care spending with those of other sectors of the economy. The techniques of economic evaluation and programme budgeting and marginal analysis (PBMA) could then be used to make within-system comparisons and evaluate potential ways of shifting existing or allocating new resources, whilst analysis of determinants of health could be used to compare different sectors' contributions to health. Production of outcome data plus development of these techniques represent the most 'profitable' way forward for informed debate on health care spending. Decision-making would then not be left totally in the hands of those providing unsubstantiated arguments for health care expansion or 'cuts'.

CONCLUSIONS

The amount of evidence on potential health care reforms has mushroomed over the past ten years. Despite this, a definitive answer to the question of what an ideal health care system would look like remains elusive. Therefore, an overall, if rather depressing, conclusion must be that more evidence is required on the effects of different ways of financing health care.

It may be possible, however, to rule out (or in) specific types of financial arrangement. The main criteria for this, however, will be the objectives of the policy-maker concerned. Based on the objectives of most health care systems, it is clear that 'solutions' based on simple (even simplistic) neoclassical models which assume the existence of well-informed consumers uninfluenced by providers are very naive. Neither charges nor medical savings accounts go well with health care. Some element of competition, with public bodies acting on behalf of individual consumers, seems to have had a small positive effect, but the evidence is not strong. This does not seem to be replicated in situations of 'full blown' competition, as with managed care, in which the system still seems to find a way to increase costs at no apparent benefit in terms of population health. The key to the health care market lies on the supply side and financing reforms should be concentrated there. Such future reforms, however, can only be properly informed by adequate evaluation which in turn depends primarily on future development of: outcome measures; measures of access; incentive structures; better understanding of clinical practice variations; and use of appropriate designs which are inclusive of all relevant consequences. It is only then that the Visible Hand can be fully understood and used to guide reforms.

NOTES

1 HEALTH CARE FINANCING REFORMS: MOVING INTO THE NEW MILLENIUM

1 Social insurance means insurance operated by a government or government-approved agency, but not a private insurance company. Social insurance will usually involve funding through payroll deductions.
2 The OECD is an organisation which routinely produces data on the performance of the world's most advanced economies. They produce a lot of data, and reports, on health and health care, and so will be referred to frequently throughout the book.

2 MARKETS AND HEALTH CARE: INTRODUCING THE INVISIBLE HAND

1 Often thought of as the sum of individuals' utility (or well-being) levels. This is important, because economics is often thought of as being about maximisation of some concept of social well-being.
2 See Chapter 3 for an explanation of why 'free marketeers' accept that many public health interventions should be provided (or regulated by) governments.
3 As such, as the former UK Prime Minister, Margaret Thatcher, once said, 'there is no such thing as society!', implying that there are no community objectives.
4 Smith, despite being a Professor of Moral Philosophy, is generally regarded as one of the first economists. He, and some contemporaries, tend to be labelled 'classical' economists. More recently, economists subscribing to the school of thought which promotes the use of market mechanisms in the allocation of many goods, including health care, have become known as 'neoclassical' economists. Neoclassical economists developed and updated many of the ideas of the classical economists, but would still subscribe to many of Smith's basic insights. For a short and non-technical discussion of the development of economic thought see Whynes (1988), chapters 3 and 4.
5 Even Smith (1776) recognised the disadvantages of collusion: 'People of the same trade seldom meet together even for merriment or diversion but the conversation ends in a conspiracy against the public, or some contrivance to raise prices.' Many neoclassical economists tend not to heed the possibilities of such behaviour when espousing the virtues of 'free' markets.

6 Note the amount of government intervention in the food markets over the last few years with respect to the BSE and *E. coli* crises.

3 MARKET FAILURE IN HEALTH CARE: JUSTIFYING THE VISIBLE HAND

1 Note, it could be argued that it is more important that people have access to food relative to health care. Yet, most societies organise production and delivery of food differently than for health care. Another way of looking at this chapter is to say it is about explaining, from an economic perspective, why that is the case.

2 Only consumers themselves truly know how much anxiety, pain and suffering an illness has caused and, consequently, they may have an incentive to overstate their case when making a claim. Thus, an insurance company would never offer payment as recompense for experiencing such effects.

3 For a more precise definition of 'opportunity cost', see the section on 'efficiency' in Chapter 5.

4 Between the demise of the first Australian public insurance scheme in 1976 and the introduction of the second in 1984 there was a government-subsidised private insurance scheme. See Palmer and Short (1989) for a more detailed description.

5 Continuing the Mercedes Benz analogy, there may be an externality effect in the case of access to transport in general, though not to Mercedes Benz cars in particular. This is demonstrated to some extent by the degree of subsidisation of public transport systems in many countries. Thus, in terms of problems of access (or, in health care, adverse selection) and externalities, it could be argued that transport and health care are, more or less, similar. The main difference between transport and health care seems to be that, in many countries, the provision of a two-tiered service ('Mercedes Benz' versus 'public transport') in transport is more acceptable to the population than is a two-tiered service in health care.

6 Some public health interventions are good examples of what economists call 'public goods'. The market fails in the context of public goods because of the free rider problem. People disguise what they are willing to pay for a service that must be provided to everybody in a particular population or not be provided at all. These 'free riders' want to consume the service but let others pay for it. Given the incentive for everyone to behave in such a manner, some worthwhile public health interventions might never be funded. Examples of such interventions are clean air, clean water, water fluoridation and health-promotion campaigns in the media. Thus, there is a clear role for government intervention which is accepted by proponents of markets for health care (Logan *et al.*, 1989). This role, however, is much narrower than that which the externalities argument seeks to justify.

7 Smith's earlier work, *The Theory of Moral Sentiments*, was in the field of social philosophy rather than economics. However, he saw the contents of this work and the later *Wealth of Nations* as part of a greater whole which he intended to bring together in a third (and never completed) work on principles of law and government.

8 It should be noted at this point that, as characterised, our externality model relies on the benevolence of financially better off members of society. It may be that democratic systems lead to the election of governments mandated to take money from the rich, whether the rich like it or not. Of course, this could be used as an argument to say that, because they are achieved through the tax system, such transfers might be too great and, thus, there is

a 'cost' to the transfer not being voluntary. It is unclear what the size of the externality is and, therefore, what the amount to be paid should be.

9   Although, it seems that powerful interest groups, rather than individual consumers, manage to prevent this from happening.

10   Although, for some groups, like expectant mothers, children and older people, there seems to be little problem of defining them as being 'in need', which results in their receipt of some services on the NHS which are not available to the general population on the same terms.

11   Apologies to all doctors! The argument here is provocative so as to make a point. Of course, we recognise that there are many other factors which guide doctors' actions. All we are saying here is that doctors are human and, like other individuals in society, will, to an extent, respond to the incentives put in front of them.

12   Strictly, adverse selection is a phenomenon of private health insurance. Private health insurance did not exist to a great extent in the UK before 1944. However, in the quotations from the National Health Service policy document, there is obviously a concern about exclusion from care of certain 'needy' groups as a result of market forces and only partial coverage by the UK Government, which amounts to the same thing.

4   METHODS OF FUNDING HEALTH CARE

1   Much of the finance in these two countries actually comes from direct taxation.

2   Although, in practice, informational asymmetries may remain.

5   ECONOMIC OBJECTIVES OF HEALTH CARE

1   Note that the provision of opportunity is a supply-side phenomenon rather than relying on the demand-side (via the burden placed on the consumer) to achieve the equity objective.

2   Note that this does not mean that inequalities can not be reduced. This still requires a definition of 'health inequalities' and, furthermore, clarification of the scale of reduction in inequalities to be pursued.

6   COUNTERING CONSUMER MORAL HAZARD

1   These are typically defined as the balance of its costs and benefits to users in monetary terms (McPake, 1993).

7   COUNTERING DOCTOR MORAL HAZARD

1   In fact, although registration of doctors in these countries actually commenced in the mid-19th Century, it was not until the early 20th Century that unqualified practitioners, or 'quacks', were effectively prevented from practising by law (Peterson, 1978; Allen, 1982).

2   It is thought that one of the main proponents of HMOs in the UK, Professor Alain Enthoven of Stanford University, provided the stimulus to the UK reforms, when he reviewed the UK health care system in the mid-1980s (Enthoven, 1985). In a more recent monograph, he attributes the idea for that aspect of the reforms known as GP fundholding, to Alan Maynard (Professor of Economics at the University of York) (Enthoven, 1999).

8   COUNTERING MORAL HAZARD IN THE HOSPITAL SECTOR

1   Perfect agency would require doctors to weight equally the patient's benefit and the hospital's financial interests. As Evans (1984) has pointed out, this would also require the doctor to be a 'perfect schizophrenic'!
2   The point about supplier-induced demand and the theory of Ellis and McGuire (1986) demonstrate that, partly contrary to our earlier assertions, some theories about the response of individual actors (in this case, doctors) to reimbursement mechanisms can also be brought to bear when predicting how institutions (like hospitals) might respond to different mechanisms.
3   Of course, the incorrect classification may have been the earlier code. Either way, it is difficult to justify reimbursing hospitals for 'upcoding'.
4   The marginal cost, in this context, would be the cost of admitting one more patient. With spare capacity, staffing and other costs are unlikely to be affected by the admission one more patient. However, average cost data would include these staffing and other costs. Therefore, the marginal cost is likely to be less than the average. The most competitive price for hospital care is one which reflects marginal cost.

9   ACHIEVING EQUITY

1   Negative Kakwani values represent regressivity and positive values progressivity. The details can be found in Wagstaff *et al.*, 1989; Wagstaff *et al.*, 1999a and Wagstaff and Van Doorslaer, 2000.
2   Like the Kakwani index, the measure of redistributive effect is negative for pro-rich and positive for pro-poor (see van Doorslaer *et al.*, 1999)

10   FUTURE CONSIDERATIONS: SETTING THE HEALTH CARE BUDGET

1   Luxury goods are those for which a percentage increase in income (in this case, national income) leads to a greater percentage increase in the amount of the good consumed (in this case, health care). The value of income elasticity for a luxury good is therefore greater than 1.

REFERENCES

A National Health Service (1944) Cmnd 6502. London: HMSO.

Aaron HA and Schwartz WB (1984) *The Painful Prescription*. Washington, DC: Brookings Institute.

Abel-Smith B (1986) Funding health for all – is insurance the answer? *World Health Forum* 7: 3–11.

Abel-Smith B and Dua A (1989) Community-financing in developing countries: the potential for the health sector. *Health Policy and Planning* 3: 95–108.

Acheson D (1998) *Independent inquiry into inequalities in health.* London: TSO.

Adams CE, Kramer S and Wilson M (1995) Home health quality outcomes; fee-for-service versus health maintenance organization enrolees. *JONA* 25(11): 39–45.

Akin J (1988) Health insurance in developing countries: experience and prospects. In: Health Care Financing: Regional Seminar in Health Care Financing, 27 July–3 August 1987, Manila, Philippines Asian Development Bank, Manila; Economic Development Institute of the World Bank; East-West Center, Honolulu.

Alberta Health and Wellness (1999) *Policy Statement on the Delivery of Surgical Services.* Alberta Health and Wellness, Edmonton.

Allen J (1982) Octavius Beale reconsidered: infanticide, babyfarming and abortion in NSW in the 1930s. In: *What Rough Beast? The State and Social Order in Australian History* (Sydney Labour History Groups, ed.), Sydney: George Allen and Unwin.

Almond P (2001) What is consumerism and has it had an impact on health visiting provision? A literature review. *Journal of Advanced Nursing* 35: 893–901.

Alter DA, Naylor D, Austin P and Tu JV (1999a) Effects of socioeconomic status on access to invasive cardiac procedures and on mortality after acute myorcardial infarction. *New England Journal of Medicine* 341 (18): 1359–67.

Alter DA, Basinski AS, Cohen EA and Naylor CD (1999b) Fairness in the coronary angiography queue. *Canadian Medical Association Journal* 5 Oct., 161(7): 813–17.

Alter DA, Naylor CD, Austin PC, Chant BT and Tu JV (2003) Geography and service supply do not explain socioeconomic gradients in angiography use after acute myocardial infarction. *Canadian Medical Association Journal* 4 Feb., 168(3): 261–4.

Altman DE and Levitt L (2002) The sad history of health care cost containment as told in one chart. *Health Affairs–Web Exclusive*, W83.

American College of Physicians and American Society of Internal Medicine (2000) No health insurance? It's enough to make you sick. Philadelphia: American College of Physicians – *American Society of Internal Medicine*.

Andaleeb SS (2000) Public and private hospitals in Bangladesh: service quality and predictors of hospital choice. *Health Policy Plan* 15(1): 95–102.

Andersen T and Mooney G (1990) *The Challenges of Medical Practice Variations. Basingstoke*: Macmillan Press.

Anderson GF and Poullier JP (1999) Health Spending, access and outcomes: trends in industrialised countries. *Health Affairs* 18(3): 178–92.

Archibald G and Donaldson D (1976) Paternalism and Prices. In *Resource Allocation and Economic Policy* (Allingham MaBM, ed.), London: Macmillan.

Arnold P and Schlenker T (1992) The impact of health care financing on childhood immunization practices. *American Journal of Diseases in Children* 146: 728–32.

Arrow KJ (1963) Uncertainty and the welfare economics of medical care. *American Economic Review* LIII (5): 941–67.

Ashby JL and Greene TF (1993) Implications of a global budget for facility-based health spending. *Inquiry* 30(4): 362–71.

Ashton T, Cumming J and Devlin N. (2000) Priority-setting in New Zealand: Translating principles into practice. *Journal of Health Services & Research Policy* 5(3): 170–5.

Ashton T (1991) Personal Communication.

Asian Development Bank, Manila (1988) Health Care Financing: Regional Seminar in Health Care Financing, 27 July–3 August 1987, Manila, Philippines. Asian Development Bank, Manila; Economic Development Institute of the World Bank; East-West Center, Honolulu.

Audibert M and Mathonnat J (2000) Cost recovery in Mauritania: initial lessons. *Health Policy and Planning* 15(1): 66–75.

Audit Commission (1995) *A Price on Their Heads: Measuring Management Costs in NHS Trusts.* Audit Commission Bulletin, May 1995, London: HMSO.

Auster R *et al.* (1972) The production of health: an exploratory study. In *Essays in the Economics of Health and Medical Care* (Fuchs VR, ed.), New York: National Bureau of Economics Research, Columbia University Press.

Australia, Budget Statements (1989) *Budget Statements 1988–89.* Budget Paper No. 1. Canberra, Australian Government Publishing Service.

Ayanian JZ, Weissman EC, Schneider JA, Ginsburg JA and Zaslavsky AM (2000) Unmet health needs of uninsured adults in the United States. *Journal of American Medical Association* 284(16): 2061–9.

Aylin P, Morris S, Wakefield J, Grossinho A, Harup L and Elliott P (2001) Temperature, housing, deprivation and their relationship to excess winter mortality in Great Britain, 1986–1996. *International Journal of Epidemiology* 30 Oct (5): 1100–8.

Badgett J and Rabalais G (1997) Prepaid capitation versus fee-for-service reimbursement in a Medicaid population. *American Journal of Managed Care* 3: 277–82.

Bailit H, Newhouse J, Brook R, Duan N, Goldberg G, Hanley J, Kamberg C, Spolsky V, Black A and Lohr K (1985) Does more generous dental insurance coverage improve oral health? *Journal of the American Dental Association* 110: 701–77.

Baines DL and Whynes DK (1996) Selection bias in GP fundholding. *Health Economics* 5: 129–40.

Baines DL, Tolley KH and Whynes DK (1997a) *Prescribing budgets and fundholding in General Practice.* London: Office of Health Economics.

Baines DL, Brigham P, Phillips DR, Tolley KH and Whynes DK (1997b) GP fundholding and prescribing in UK general practice: evidence from two rural, English Family Health Services Authorities. *Public Health* 111(5): 321–5.

Baker DW, Shapiro MF and Schur CL (2000) Health insurance and access to care for symptomatic conditions. *Arch Intern med.* 8 May, 160(9): 1269–74.

Bamezai A, Zwanziger J, Melnick GA and Mann JM (1999) Price competition and hospital cost growth in the United States (1989–1994). *Health Economics* 8(3): 233–43.

References

Barer M, Evans R, Hertzman C and Lomas J (1987) Aging and health care utilization: New evidence on old fallacies. Social Science and Medicine 24(10): 851–62.

Barer M, Evans R and Labelle R (1988) Fee controls as cost control: evidence from the frozen North. *Milbank Quarterly* 66: 1–64.

Barer ML, Evans RG and Stoddart GL (1979) *Controlling Health Care Costs by Direct Charges to Patients: Snare or Delusion?* Ontario Economic Council Occasional Paper No. 10. Toronto: Ontario Economics Council.

Barr MD (2001) Medical savings accounts in Singapore: a critical enquiry. *Journal of Health Politics, Policy and Law* 26: 709–26.

Barr N (1998) Towards a 'third way': rebalancing the role of the welfare state. *New Economy* 4: 71–6.

Barros P (1998) The black box of health care expenditure growth determinants. *Health Economics* 7(6): 533–44.

Beck R (1974) The effects of co-payment on the poor. *Journal of Human Resources* 9: 129–42.

Becker E and Sloan FA (1985) Hospital ownership and performance. *Economic Inquiry* 23: 21–36.

Benyoussef A and Wessen AF (1974) Utilization of health services in developing countries – Tunisia, *Social Science & Medicine,* May, 8(5): 287–304.

Berki SE and Ashcraft M (1980) HMO enrollment: who gains what and why? A review of the literature. *Milbank Memorial Fund Quarterly* 58: 588–632.

Berki SE, Ashcraft M, Penchansky R and Fortus R (1977) Enrollment choice in a multi-HMO setting: the roles of health risk, financial vulnerability, and access to care. *Medical Care* 15: 95–114.

Bijker N, Rutgers EJ, Peterse JL, Fentiman IS, Julien JP, Duchateau L *et al.* (2001) Variations in diagnostic and therapeutic procedures in a multicentre, randomized clinical trial (EPRTC 10853) investigating breast-conserving treatment for DCIS. *European Journal of Surgical Oncology* 27: 135–40.

Billinghurst B and Whitfield M (1993) Why do patients change their general practitioner? A postal questionnaire study of patients in Avon. *British Journal of General Practice* 43: 336–8.

Birch S (1986) Increasing patient charges in the National Health Service: a method of privatising primary health care. *Journal of Social Policy* 15: 163–84.

Birch S (1989) Hypothesis: charges to patients impair the quality of dental care for elderly people. *Age Ageing* 18: 136–40.

Bischof R and Nash D (1996) Managed care. Past, present and future. *Managed Care and Office Practice* 80: 225–44.

Black Report (1980) *Inequalities in Health: Report of a Research Working Group.* London: Department of Health and Social Security.

Blaxter M (1984) Equity and consultation rates in general practice. *British Medical Journal* 288: 1963–7.

Blendon RJ, Benson JM, Brodie M, Altman DE, Rowland D. Neuman P and Matt J (1997) Voters and health care in the 1996 election. *Journal of the American Medical Association,* 277: 1253–8.

Blewett N (1988) Opening address to the Public Health Association of Australia and New Zealand Conference, Sydney, August 1987. *Community Health Studies* 12: 106–11.

Bloland PB, Ettling M and Meek S (2000) Combination therapy for malaria in Africa: hype or hope? *Bulletin of the World Health Organization* 78(12): 1378–88.

Bloom BS and Fendrick AM (1987) Waiting for care. Queuing and resource allocation. *Medical Care* 25: 131–9.

Blumberg MS (1980) Health status and health care use by type of private health coverage. *Milbank Memorial Fund Quarterly* 58: 633–55.

Bobak M, Pikhart H, Hertzman C and Rose R. Marmot (1998) *Socioeconomic factors, perceived control and self-reported health in Russia.* A cross-sectional survey. *Social Science and Medicine* July, 47(2): 269–79.

Bohmer P, Pain C, Watt A, Abernethy P and Sceats J (2001) Maximising health gain within - available resources in the New Zealand public health system. *Health Policy* 55(1): 37–50.

Bond MT, Heshizer BP and Hrivnak MW (1996) Medical savings accounts: why do they work? *Benefits Quarterly,* second quarter: 78–83.

Bornstein BH, Marcus D and Cassidy W (2000) Choosing a doctor: an exploratory study of factors influencing patients' choice of a primary care doctor. *Journal of Evaluating Clinical Practitioners* Aug., 6(3): 255–62.

Bovbjerg RR, Hadley J, Pohl MB and Rockmore M (2002) Medicaid coverage for the working uninsured: the role of state policy. *Health Affairs* (Millwood). Nov.–Dec., 21(6): 231–43.

Bradshaw D (1998) Health for all – monitoring equity. In Health systems Trust (ed.) *South African Health Review 1998.* Durban: Health Systems Trust.

Brady, M (1995) WHO defines health? Implications of differing definitions on discourse and practice in Aboriginal health. In Robinson G (ed.) Aboriginal Health: Social and Cultural Transitions. *Proceedings of a Conference at the Northern Territory University Darwin, September, Darwin: NTU Press.*

Braithwaite J, Hindle D, Phelan PD and Hanson R (1998) Casemix funding in Australia. *Medical Journal of Australia* 168: 558–62.

Brook RH, Ware JE Jr, Rogers WH, Keeler EB, Davies AR, Donald CA, Goldberg GA, Lohr KN, Masthay PC and Newhouse JP (1983) Does free care improve adults' health? Results from a randomized controlled trial. *New England Journal of Medicine* 309: 1426–34.

Broomberg J (1994) Managing the health care market in developing countries: prospects and problems. *Health Policy and Planning* 9: 237–51.

Broyles RW, Manga P, Binder DA, Angus DE and Charette A (1983) The use of physician services under a national health insurance scheme. An examination of the Canada Health Survey. *Medical Care* 21: 1037–54.

Buchanan JL and Cretin S (1986) Risk selection of families electing HMO membership. *Medical Care* 24: 39–51.

Burns LR (1991) Differences in access and quality of care across HMO types. *Health Services Management Research* 4(1): 32–44.

Burstrom B (2002) Increasing inequalities in health care utilization across income groups in Sweden during the 1990s? *Health Policy* 62: 117–29.

Caldwell, J and Santow, G (1989) Selected Readings in the *Cultural, Social and Behavioural Determinants of Health. Health Transition Series, No.1.* Health Transition Centre, Australian National University.

Calnan M and Gabe J (2001) From consumerism to partnership? Britain's national health service at the turn of the century. *International Journal of Health Services* 31: 119–31.

Carey T, Weis K and Homer C (1990) Prepaid versus traditional Medicaid plans: Effects on preventive health care. *Journal of Clinical Epidemiology* 43: 1213–20.

Carr-Hill RA, Sheldon TA, Smith P, Martin S, Peacock S and Hardman G (1994) Allocating resources to health authorities; development of method for small area analysis of use of impatient services. *British Medical Journal* 309 (961): 1046–9.

Carrasquillo O, Himmelsteing DU, Woolhandler S and Bor DH (1999) Trends in health insurance coverage, 1989–1997. *International Journal of Health Services* 29(3): 467–83.

References

Carrin G and Vereecke M (1992) Strategies for Health Care Finance in Developing Countries with a *Focus on Community Financing in Sub-Saharan Africa*. Basingstoke: Macmillan Press.

Carroll NV and Erwin WG (1987) Patient shifting as a response to Medicare Prospective Payment. *Medical Care* 25: 1161–7.

Carstairs V and Morris R (1989) Deprivation: explaining differences in mortality between Scotland and England and Wales. *British Medical Journal* 299: 886–9.

Catalano R, Libby A, Snowden L and Evans Cuellar A (2000) The effect of capitated financing on mental health services for children and youth: The Colorado experience. *American Journal of Public Health* 90: 1861–5.

Cattell V (2001) Poor people, poor places, and poor health: the mediating role of social networks and social capital. *Social Science & Medicine* May, 52(10): 1501–16.

Cella DF, Orav EJ, Kornblith AB *et al.* (1991) Socioeconomic status and cancer survival. *Journal of Clinical Oncology* 9: 1500–9.

Chaix-Couturier C, Durand-Zaleski I, Jolly D and Durieux P (2000) Effects of financial incentives on medical practice: results from a systematic review of the literature and methodological issues. *International Journal for Quality in Health Care* 12: 133–42.

Chawla M and Ellis R (2000) The impact of financing and quality changes on health care in Niger. *Health Policy and Planning* 15(1): 76–84.

Chase C, Chernew M, Cowen M, Kirking D and Smith D (2000) Pharmaceutical cost growth under capitation: A case study. *Health Affairs* 19: 266–76.

Cheng SH and Chiang TL (1997) The effect of universal health insurance on health care utilisation in Taiwan: results from a natural experiment. *Journal of the American Medical Association* 278: 89–93.

Cheng TM (2003) Taiwan's new national health insurance program: genesis and experience so far. *Health Affairs* (Millwoood). May–June, 22(3): 61–76.

Cherkin DC, Deyo RA, Loeser JD, Bush T and Waddell G (1994) An international comparison of back surgery rates. *Spine* 19: 1201–6.

Churchill L (1999) The United States health care system under managed care. *Health Care Analysis* 7: 393–411.

Cichon M, Yamabana H, Normand C, Newbrander W, Weber A and Preker A (1999) *Modelling in health care finance*. Geneva: International Labour Office.

Clement JP (1997) Dynamic cost shifting in hospitals: evidence from the 1980s and 1990s. *Inquiry* 34(4): 340–50.

Cochrane AL (1972) *Effectiveness and Efficiency: Random Reflections in Health Services*. London: Nuffield Provincial Hospital Trust.

Coffey E, Moscovice I, Finch M, Christianson J and Lurie N (1995) Capitated Medicaid and the process of care of elderly Hypertensives and Diabetics: Results from a randomized trial. *The American Journal of Medicine* 98: 536.

Cohen D (1994) Marginal analysis in practice: an alternative to needs assessment for contracting health care. *British Medical Journal* 309: 781–5.

Coleman EA, Kramer AM, Kowalsky JC, Eckhof D, Lin M, Hester EJ, Morgenstern N and Steiner JF (2000) A comparison of functional outcomes after hip fracture in group/staff HMOs and fee-for-service systems. *Effective Clinical Practice* 4: 229–39.

Collins E and Klein R (1980) Equity and the NHS: self-reported morbidity, access, and primary care. *British Medical Journal* 281: 1111–15.

Commons M and McGuire TG (1997) Some economics of performance-based contracting for substance-abuse services. In Egerston JA, Fox DM and Leshner AI (eds) *Treating Drug Abusers Effectively*. Massachussets: Blackwell.

Conrad D, Noren J, Marcus-Smith M, Ramsey S, Kirz H, Wickizer T *et al.* (1996) Physician compensation models in medical group practice. *Journal of Ambulatory Care Management* 19: 18–27.

Constance B, Messmer PL, Gyurko CC, Domagala S, Franklin C, Eads TS, Harshman KS and Layne MK (2000) Hospital ownership, performance and outcomes: assessing the state of the science. *Journal of Nursing Administration* 30(5): 227–40.

Constitucao da Republica Portuguesa (1982) Lisbon: Rei dos Livros.

Cooper MH and Culyer AJ (1971) An economic survey of the nature and intent of the British National Health Service. *Social Science and Medicine* 5: 1–13.

Corman H and Grossman M (1985) Determinants of neonatal mortality rates in the U.S. A reduced form model. *Journal of Health Economics* 4: 213–36.

Coulam RF and Gaumer GL (1991) Medicare's prospective payment system: A critical appraisal. *Health Care Financing Review* 13 (Annual Supplement): 45–77.

Coulter A and Bradlow J (1993) Effect of NHS reforms of general practitioners' referral patterns. *British Medical Journal* 306: 433–7.

Coulter A, McPherson K and Vessey M (1988) Do British women undergo too many or too few hysterectomies? *Social Science and Medicine* 27: 987–94.

Council on Ethical and Judicial Affairs (1990) Black–white disparities in health care. *Journal of the American Medical Association* 263: 2344–6.

Coyte PC, Wright JG, Hawker GA, Bombardier C, Dittus RS, Paul JE, Freund DA and Ho E (1994) Waiting times for knee-replacement surgery in the United States and Ontario. *New England Journal of Medicine* 331(16): 1068–71.

Craig N, Parkin D and Gerard K (1995) Clearing the fog on the Tyne: programme budgeting in Newcastle and North Tyneside Health Authority. *Health Policy* 33: 107–25.

Creese A (1991) User charges for health care: a review of recent experience. *Health Policy and Planning* 6(4): 309–19.

Creese A (1997) User fees. They don't reduce costs, and they increase inequity. *British Medical Journal* 315: 202–3.

Creese A and Bennett S (1997) Rural risk sharing strategies. In Schieber GJ (ed.) *Innovations in Health Care Financing: Proceedings of the World Bank Conference, March, 1997.* World Bank Discussion Paper No. 365, Washington: World Bank.

Crockett A, Cranston J, Moss J, Scown P, Mooney G and Alpers J (1999) Program budgeting and marginal analysis: a case study in chronic airflow limitation. *Australia Health Review* 22(3): 65–77.

Cromwell J and Mitchell JB (1986) Physician-induced demand for surgery. *Journal of Health Economics* 5: 293–313.

Cruz C and Zurita B (1993) The public private mix – the case of Mexico. In *Report of the Workshop on Public/Private Mix for Health Care in Developing Countries. Health Economics and Financing Programme.* Health Policy Unit, Department of Public Health and Policy, London School of Hygiene and Tropical Medicine, UK.

Csillag C (2001) New Danish government announces proposals to reduce waiting lists. *The Lancet* 358: 1973.

Cubellis J (1997) *Selective Contracting and Hospital Quality under Managed Care*: An Empirical Analysis of Network Open-Heart Surgery Hospital in California over Time. University of California, Irvine.

Cuellar AE, Libby A and Snowden L (2001) How capitated mental health care affects utilization by youth in the juvenile justice and child welfare systems. *Mental Health Services Research* 3: 61–72.

References

Cullis JG and West P (1979) *The Economics of Health.* Oxford: Martin Robertson.

Cullis JG and Jones PR (1985) National Health Service waiting lists. A discussion of competing explanations and a policy proposal. *Journal of Health Economics* 4: 119–35.

Cullis JG, Jones PR and Popper C (2000) Waiting lists and medical treatment: analysis and policies. In Culyer AJ and Newhouse JP (eds) *Handbook of Health Economics, Volume I.* London: Elsevier Science B.V., 2000.

Culyer AJ (1971) The nature of the commodity health care and its efficient allocation. *Oxford Economic Papers* 23: 189–211.

Culyer AJ (1976) *Need and the National Health Service: Economic and Social Choice.* London: Martin Robertson.

Culyer AJ (1985) *Economics.* Oxford: Basil Blackwell.

Culyer AJ (1986) *The Withering of the Welfare State and Whither the Welfare State?* 1985 Woodward Lectures in Economics. Vancouver: University of British Columbia.

Culyer AJ (1988) *Health Expenditure in Canada.* Toronto: Canadian Tax Foundation.

Culyer AJ (1989) Cost containment in Europe. *Health Care Financing Review.* Annual supplement 21–32.

Culyer AJ (1991) The normative economics of health care finance and provision. In McGuire A, Fenn P, Mayhew K, eds. *Providing Health Care: The Economics of Alternative Systems of Finance and Delivery.* Oxford: Oxford University Press.

Culyer AJ and Cullis JG (1976) Some economics of hospital waiting lists. *Journal of Social Policy* 5: 239–64.

Culyer AJ and Simpson H (1980) Externalities models and health: a look back over the last twenty years. *Economic Record* 56: 222–30.

Culyer AJ, Donaldson C and Gerard K (1988) Financial aspects of health services: Drawing on experience. 3. London: Institute of Health Services Management.

Culyer AJ, Maynard A and Williams A (1981) Alternative systems of health care provision: an essay on motes and beams. In *A New Approach to the Economics of Health Care* (Olsen M, ed.), Washington, DC: American Enterprise Institute.

Cunningham PH, Grossman JM, St Peter RF and Lesser CS (1999) Managed care and physicians' provision of charity care. *Journal of American Medical Association* Mar. 24–31.

Cunningham R and Sherlock DB (2002) Bounceback: Blues thrive as markets cool towards HMOs. *Health Affairs* 21: 24–38.

Currie G, Donaldson C and Lu M (2003) What does Canada profit from the for-profit debate? *Canadian Public Policy* 29: 227–51.

Currie J, Gruber J and Fischer M (1995) Physician payments and infant mortality: evidence from Medicaid fee policy. *American Economic Review Papers and Proceedings, Incentives and the Demand for Health Services* 106–11.

Davey Smith G, Bartley M and Blane D (1990) The Black Report on socioeconomic inequalities in health 10 years on. *British Medical Journal* 310: 373–7.

Davies P and Carrin G. (2001) Risk-pooling-necessary but not sufficient. *Bull World Health Organ* 79(7): 587.

Davis D and Taylor-Vaisey A (1997) Translating guidelines into practice. A systematic review of theoretic concepts, practical experience and research evidence in the adoption of clinical practice guidelines. *Canadian Medical Association Journal* 157: 408–16.

Davis K and Russell LB (1972) The substitution of hospital outpatient care for inpatient care. *Review of Economics and Statistics* 54: 109–20.

de Bethune V (1989) The influence of an abrupt price increase on health services utilisation: evidence from Zaire, *Health Policy and Planning* 4: 76–81.

238

Dearden B (1991) First welfare state at the end of the road. *Health Services Journal* 101: 15.

Debrock L and Arnould R (1992) Utilization control in HMOs. *Quarterly Review of Economics and Finance* 32: 31–53.

Deeble J (1982) Unscrambling the omelet: public and private health care financing in Australia. In MaLachlan G, Maynard A, eds. *The Public/Private Mix for Health: The Relevance and Effects of Change* London: Nuffield Provinicial Hospitals Trust.

Deeble JS and Smith LR (2000) Cost containment in the Australian health care system – an unexpected success. *Cah Socio Dem Med* 40: 95–112.

Delcheva E, Balabanova B and McKee M (1997) Under-the-counter payments for heath care: evidence from Bulgaria. *Health Policy* 42: 89–100.

Dellana SA and Glascoff DW (2001) The impact of health insurance plan type on satisfaction with health care. *Health Care Management Review* 26(2): 33–46.

Department of Health (2001) *New Award Scheme: Rewarding Commitment and Excellence in the NHS.* London: Department of Health

Department of Health and Social Security (1976) *Sharing Resources for Health in England.* HMSO: London. Report of the Resource Allocation Working Party.

Devereux S (1999) Targeting transfers. Innovative solutions to familiar problems. *IDS Bulletin* 30(2): 61–74.

Di Matteo L and Di Matteo R. (1998) Evidence on the determinants of Canadian provincial government health expenditures: 1965–1991. *Journal of Health Economics* 17(2): 211–28.

Diderichsen F. Varde E and Whitehead M (1997) Resource allocation to health authorities: the quest for an equitable formula in Britain and Sweden. *British Medical Journal* Oct. 4, 315(7112): 875–8.

Diop F, Yazbeck A and Bitran R (1995) The impact of alternative cost recovery schemes on access and equity in Niger. *Health Policy and Planning* 10(3): 223–40.

Directorate General for Research and Documentation (1988) The health systems of European Community countries. Series No. 12. Luxemburg, Environment, Public Health and Consumer Protection Services.

Dismuke CE and Sena V (1999) Has DRG payment influenced the technical efficiency and productivity of diagnostic technologies in Portuguese public hospitals? An empirical analysis using parametric and non-parametric methods. *Health-Care-Management-Science* 2(2): 107–16.

Dixon J and Glennerster H (1995) What do we know about fundholding in general practice. *British Medical Journal* Sep. 16, 311(7007): 727–30.

Docteur E, Suppanz H and Wood J (2003) *The US Health System: An Assessment and Prospective Directions for Reform.* OECD Economics Department Working Papers No. 350.

Donaldson C (1995) Economics, public health and health care purchasing: reinventing the wheel? *Health Policy* 33: 79–90.

Donaldson C and Gerard K (1989a) Paying general practitioners: shedding light on the review of health services. *Journal of the Royal College of General Practitioners* 39: 114–17.

Donaldson C and Gerard K (1989b) Countering moral hazard in public and private health care systems: a review of recent evidence. *Journal of Social Policy* 18: 235–51.

Donaldson C and Gerard K (1991) Minding our Ps and Qs? Financial incentives for efficient hospital behaviour. *Health Policy* 17: 51–76.

Donaldson C and Gerard K (1993) *Economics of Health Care Financing: the Visible Hand.* London: Macmillan.

Donaldson C, Mapp T, Ryan M and Curtin K (1996) Estimating the economic benefits of avoiding food-borne risk: is 'willingness to pay' feasible? *Epidemiology and Infection* 116: 285–94.

239

References

Donaldson C and Magnussen J (1992) DRGs: The road to hospital efficiency? *Health Policy* 21: 47–64.

Donaldson C and Mooney G (1997) The new NHS in a global context: is it taking us where we want to be? In Anand P and McGuire A (eds) *Changes in Health Care: Reflections on the NHS Internal Market*. London: Macmillan.

Donaldson C, Atkinson A, Bond J and Wright K (1988) Should QALYs be programme-specific? *Journal of Health Economics* 7: 239–57.

Donaldson C, Lloyd P and Lupton D (1991) Primary health care consumerism amongst elderly Australians. *Age Ageing* 20: 280–6.

Doescher MP, Franks P, Banthin JS and Clancy CM (2000) Supplemental insurance and mortality in elderly Americans: findings from a national cohort. *Archives of Family Medicine* 9: 251–7.

Dor A and van der Gaag J (1988) *The Demand for Medical Care in Developing Countries, Quantity Rationing in Rural Cote d'Ivoire, Living Standards Measurement Survey* Working Paper No. 35. Washington, DC: World Bank.

Dowd BE, Johnson AN and Madson RA (1986) Inpatient length of stay in Twin Cities health plans. *Medical Care* 24: 694–710.

Dowling B (1997) Effect of fundholding on waiting times: data base study. *British Medical Journal* 315: 290–2.

Dranove D (1988) Pricing by non-profit institutions. The case of hospital cost-shifting. *Journal of Health Economics* 7: 47–57.

Dranove D and White WD (1994) Recent theory and evidence on competition in hospital markets. *Journal-of-Economics-and-Management-Strategy* 3(1): 169–209.

Draper D, Kahn KL, Reinisch EJ, Sherwood MJ, Carney MF, Kosecoff J, Keeler EB, Rogers WH, Savitt H and Allen H (1990) Studying the effects of the DRG-based prospective payment system on quality of care. Design, sampling, and fieldwork. *Journal of the American Medical Association* 264: 1956–61.

Draper DA, Hurley RE, Lesser CS and Strunk BC (2002) The changing face of managed care. *Health Affairs* 21: 11–23.

Dror DM (2001) Reinsurance of health insurance for the informal sector. *Bulletin of the World Health Organization* 79(7): 672–80.

Dukes MN and Lunde I (1981) The regulatory control of non-steroidal anti-inflammatory agents. *European Journal of Clinical Pharmacology* 19: 3–10.

Dunlop S, Coyte PC and McIssac (2003) Socio-economic status and the utilisation of physicians' service results from the Canadian National Population Health Survey. *Social Science and Medicine* 51(1): 123–33.

Dunn JR, (2002) Housing and inequalities in health: a study of socioeconomic dimensions of housing and self reported health from a survey of Vancouver residents. *Journal of Epidemiology & Community Health*, Sep, 56(9): 671–81.

Durieux P, Chaix-Couturier C, Durand-Zaleski I and Ravaud P (2000) From clinical recommendations to mandatory practice. *International Journal of Technology Assessment in Health Care* 16: 969–75.

Durieux P, Gaillac B, Giraudeau B, Doumenc M and Ravaud P (2000) Despite financial penalties, French physicians' knowledge of regulatory practice guidelines is poor. *Archives of Family Medicine* 9: 418.

Dusheiko M, Gravelle H and Jacob, R (2003) *The effect of practice budgets on patient waiting times: allowing for selection bias*. Discussion Papers in Economics, 2003/15, University of York.

Edlefsen K, Mandelson M, McIntosh M, Andersen M, Wagner E and Urban N (1999) Prostate-specific antigen for prostate cancer screening. Do physician characteristics affect its use? *American Journal of Preventive Medicine* 17: 87–90.

Eggers P (1980) Risk differential between Medicare beneficiaries enrolled and not enrolled in an HMO. *Health Care Financing Review* 1: 91–9.

Ellis RP and McGuire TG (1986) Provider behaviour under prospective reimbursement. Cost sharing and supply. *Journal of Health Economics* 5: 129–51.

Elofsson S, Unden AL and Krakau I (1998) Patient charges – a hinderance to financially and psychologically disadvantaged groups seeking care. *Social Science and Medicine* 46: 1375–80.

Emery JCH, Auld C and Lu M (1999) *Paying for Physician Services in Canada: The Institutional, Historical and Policy Contexts.* Institute of Health Economics Working Paper, Edmonton.

Ensor T and Savelyena L (1998) Informal payments for health care in the former Soviet Union: some evidence from Kazakstan. *Health Policy and Planning* 13 (1): 41–9.

Ensor T and Thompson R (1998) Health insurance as a catalyst to change in former communist countries? *Health Policy* 43: 203–18.

Enthoven A (1980) *Health plan: the Only Practical Solution to the Soaring cost of Medical Care.* Reading, MA: Addison-Wesley.

Enthoven A (1985) *Reflections on Management in the National Health Service: An American Looks at Incentives to Efficiency* in Health Service Management in the UK. London: Nuffield Provincial Hospitals Trust.

Enthoven A (1989) NHS review. Words from the source: an interview with Alain Enthoven. Interview by Robert Smith. *British Medical Journal* 298: 1166–8.

Enthoven A and Kronick R (1989a) Consumer choice health plan for the 1990s. Universal health insurance in a system designed to promote quality and economy. *New England Journal of Medicine* 320: 94–101.

Enthoven A and Kronick R (1989b) A consumer-choice health plan for the 1990s. Universal health insurance in a system designed to promote quality and economy (2). *New England Journal of Medicine* 320: 94–101.

Enthoven A (1999) *In Pursuit of an Improving National Health Service.* London: Nuffield Trust.

Epstein AM, Stern RS and Weissman JS (1990) Do the poor cost more? A multi-hospital study of patients' socioeconomic status and use of hospital resources. *New England Journal of Medicine* 322: 1122–8.

Escarce J, Kapur K, Joyce G and Van Vorst K (2001) Medical care expenditures under gatekeeper and point-of-service arrangements. *Health Services Research* 36: 1037–57.

Esworth M (2003) The Acheson report: the aftermath. In Oliver A and Exworthy M (ed.) *Health inequalities: Evidence, Policy and Implementations.* London: Nuffield Trust, pp. 15–21.

European Commission (2001) Healthcare: Commission proposes three common EU objectives for healthcare and care for the elderly – access for all, high quality financial sustainability. *Employment and Social Affairs*, Dec., 245.

European Observatory on Health Care (1998) Health Care Systems in Transition – Russian Federation. *European Observatory on Health Care Systems.*

European Observatory on Health Care (1999a) Health Care Systems in Transition – Hungary. *European Observatory on Health Care Systems.*

European Observatory on Health Care (1999b) Health Care Systems in Transition – Poland. *European Observatory on Health Care Systems.*

European Observatory on Health Care (2000) Health Care Systems in Transition – Czech Republic *European Observatory on Health Care Systems.*

References

European Observatory on Health Care Systems (2002) *Health Care Systems in Eight Countries: Trends and Challenges*. London School of Economics and Political Science.

Evans RG (1974) Supplier-induced demand: empirical evidence and implications. In Perlman M (ed.) *The Economics of Health and Medical Care*. New York: John Wiley and Sons.

Evans RG (1982) Health care in Canada: patterns of funding and regulation. In *The Public/Private Mix for Health: The Relevance and Effects of Change* McLachlan G, Maynard A, (eds). London: Nuffield Provincial Hospitals Trust.

Evans RG (1984) *Strained Mercy: The Economics of Canadian Medical Care*. Toronto: Butterworths.

Evans RG (1986) Find the levers, find the courage: lessons from cost containment in North America. *Journal of Health, Politics, Policy and Law* 114: 585–615.

Evans RG (1987) Public health insurance: the collective purchase of individual care. *Health Policy* 7: 115–34.

Evans RG (1990a) Tension, compression, and shear: directions, stresses, and outcomes of health care cost control. *Journal of Health Politics Policy and Law* 15: 101–28.

Evans RG (1990b) The dog in the night-time: Medical practice variations and health policy. In Macmillan Press (ed.) *The Challenge of Medical Practice Variations*. London.

Evans RG (1997) Going for the gold: the redistributive agenda behind market-based health care reform. *Journal of Health Politics, Policy & Law* 22: 427–65.

Evans RG (2000) Canada. *Journal of Health Politics, Policy & Law* 25: 889–97.

Evans RG, Barer ML and Stoddart GL (1993) *User Fees For Health Care: Why a Bad Idea Keeps Coming Back*. Toronto: CIAR Program in Population Health (Working Paper No. 26).

Evans RG, Lomas J, Barer ML, Labelle RJ, Fooks C, Stoddart GL, Anderson GM, Feeny D, Gafni A and Torrance GW (1989) Controlling health expenditures – the Canadian reality. *New England Journal of Medicine* 320: 571–7.

Evans RW (1993) Organ transplantation and the inevitable debate as to what constitutes a basic health care benefit. *Clinical Transplantation*, 359–91.

Every N, Cannon C, Granger C, Moliterno D, Aguirre F, Talley D *et al.* (1998) Influence of insurance type on the use of procedures, medications and hospital outcome in patients with unstable Angina: Results from the GUARANTEE Registry. *Journal of the American College of Cardiology* 32: 387–92.

Experton B, Ozminkowski RJ, Pearlman DN, Li Z and Thompson S (1999) How does managed care manage the frail elderly? *American Journal of Preventive Medicine* 16(3): 163–72.

Fahs MC (1992) Physician response to the United Mineworkers' cost-sharing program: the other side of the coin. *Health Services Research* 27: 25–45.

Fairbrother G, Hanson K, Friedman S and Butts G (1999) The impact of physician bonuses, enhanced fees and feedback on childhood immunization coverage rates. *American Journal of Public Health* 89: 171–5.

Fallon M. (1988) The doctors in excess. *The Guardian* 17 February 1988.

Farley PJ (1985) Who are the underinsured? *Milbank Memorial Fund Quarterly* 63: 476–503.

Feasby TE, Quan H and Ghali WA (2001) Geographic variation in the rate of carotid endarterectomy in Canada. *Stroke* 32: 2417–22.

Feldstein M (1977) The high cost of hospitals – what to do about it. *Public Interest* 48: 40.

Ferrall C, Gregory A and Tholl W (1998) Endogenous work hours and practice patterns of Canadian physicians. *The American Journal of Medicine* 31: 1–27.

Fisher CR (1987) Impact of the prospective payment system on physician charges under Medicare. *Health Care Financing Review* 8: 101–3.

Fitzgerald JF, Fagan LF, Tierney WM and Dittus RS (1987) Changing patterns of hip fracture care before and after implementation of the prospective payment system. *Journal of the American Medical Association* 258: 218–21.

Flood A, Fremont A, Jin K, Bott D, Ding J and Parker R (1998) Public policy and managerial impact section. *Health Services Research* 33: 79–99.

Flores G. Fuentes-Afflick E, Barbot O, Carter-Pokras O, Claudio L, Lara M, McLaurin JA, Pachter L, Ramos-Gomez FJ, Mendoza F, Valdex RB, Villarruel AM, Zambrana RE, Greenberg R and Weitzman M (2002) The health of Latino children: urgent priorities, unanswered questions, and a research agenda. *Journal of American Medical Association* Jul. 3, 288(1): 82–90.

Foot M (1973) *Aneurin Bevan: a Biography, 1945–1960, Volume II.* London: David-Poynter.

Foxman B, Valdez RB, Lohr KN, Goldberg GA, Newhouse JP and Brook RH (1987) The effect of cost sharing on the use of antibiotics in ambulatory care: results from a population-based randomized controlled trial. *Journal of Chronic Disease* 40: 429–37.

Francome C and Savage W (1993) Caesarian section in Britain and the United States, 12 % or 14%: is either the right rate? *Social Science and Medicine* 37: 1199–1218.

Frank RG, Salkever DS and Mullann F (1990) Hospital ownership and the care of uninsured and Medicaid patients: findings from the National Hospital Discharge Survey 1979–1984. *Health Policy* 14: 1–11.

Franzosi MG, Negri E, La-Vecchia C and Tognoni G (1995) Attributable risks for nonfatal myocardial infarction in Italy. GISSI_EFRIM investigators.Gruppo Italiano per lo Studio della Sopravvivenza nell'Infarto Miocardico. Epidemiologia dei Fattori di Rischio dell'Infarto Miocardioco. *Preventive Medicine* Nov., 24(6): 603–9.

Freund D and Hurley R (1995). Medicaid managed care: Contribution to issues of health reform. *Annual Review Public Health* 16: 473–95.

Fuchs VR (1978) The supply of surgeons and the demand for operations. *Journal of Human Resources* 13 (Supplement): 35–56.

Fuchs VR and Hahn JS (1990) How does Canada do it? A comparison of expenditures for physicians' services in the United States and Canada. *New England Journal of Medicine* 323: 884–90.

Fungladda W *et al.* (1998) Compliance with artesunate and quinine + tetracycline treatment of uncomplicated malaria in Thailand. *Bulletin of the World Health Organization* 76 (Supplement 1): 59–66.

Gabel J, Levitt L, Rickreign J *et al.* (2000) Job-based health insurance in 2000: premiums rise sharply while coverage grows. *Health Affairs* (Millwood) 19(5): 144–51.

Gaffney D, Pollock A, Price D and Shaoul J (1999) PFI in the NHS – is there an economic case? *British Medical Journal* 319: 116–19.

Gama R, Nightingale P, Broughton P, Peters M, Ratcliffe J, Bradby G *et al.* (1991) Modifying the request behaviour of clinicians. *Journal of Clinical Pathology* 45: 248–9.

Gao J, Qian J, Tang S, Eriksson BO and Blas E (2002) Health equity in transition from planned to market economy in China. *Health Policy and Planning* 17 (Supplement) 20–9.

Gardner J (1995) Medical savings accounts make waves. *Modern Healthcare* 25 (9): 57.

Garrick DW, Luft HS, Gardner LB, Morrison EM, Barrett M, O'Neil A and Harvey B (1990) Services and charges by PPO physicians for PPO and indemnity patients. An episode of care comparison. *Medical Care* 28: 894–906.

Gaskin DJ and Hadley J (1997) The impact of HMO penetration on the rate of hospital cost inflation, 1985–1993. *Inquiry* 34: 205–16.

References

Gaumer G (1986) Medicare patient outcomes and hospital organisational mission. In Institute of Medicine, *For-profit Enterprise in Health Care*. Washington, DC: National Academy Press.

Geest S, Macwan'Gi M, Kamwanga J, Mulikelela D, Mazimba A and Mwangelwa M (2000) User fees and drugs: what did the health reforms in Zambia achieve? *Health Policy and Planning* 15(1): 59–65.

George B, Harris A and Mitchell A (2001) Cost-effectiveness analysis and the consistency of decision making. *Pharmocoeconomics* 19: 1103–9.

Gerard, K and Mooney, G (1993) QALY league tables: handle with care. *Health Economics* 2(1): 59–64.

Gerard, K, Smoker, I and Seymour, J (1999) Raising the quality of cost-utility analyses: lessons learnt and still to learn. *Health Policy* 46(3): 217–38.

Gerdtham UG, Jonsson B, MacFarlan M and Oxley H (1988) The determinants of health expenditure in the OECD countries: a pooled data analysis. *Developments in Health and Public Policy* 6: 113–34.

Gerdtham U, Sogaard J, Andersson F and Jonsson B (1992) An econometric analysis of health care expenditure: a cross-section study of OECD countries. *Journal of Health Economics* 11(1): 63–84.

Gertler P and van der Gaag J (1990) *The Willingness to Pay for Medical Care*. Baltimore: John Hopkins University Press.

Getchell WS, Larsen GC, Morris CD and McAnulty JH (2000) A comparison of medicare fee-for-service and a group-model HMO in the inpatient management and long-term survival of elderly individuals with syncope. *The American Journal of Managed Care* 6: 1089–98.

Getzen TE (2000) Forecasting health expenditures: short medium and long (long) term. *Journal of Health Care Finance* 26(3): 56–72.

Giammanco MD (1999) The short-term response of hospitals to the introduction of the DRG based prospective payment system: some evidence from Italy. *Giornale-degli-Economisti-e-Annali-di-Economia* 58(1): 27–62.

Gibbins FJ, Sen I, Vaz FS and Bose S (1988) Clinical budgeting and drug management on long-stay geriatric wards. *Age Ageing* 17: 328–32.

Gillett J, Hutchison B and Birch S (2001) Capitation and primary care in Canada: financial incentives and the evolution of health service organizations. *International Journal of Health Services* 31: 583–603.

Gilmore AB, McKee M and Rose R (2002) Determinants of and inequalities in self-perceived health in Ukraine, *Social Science & Medicine*, Dec., 55(12): 2177–88.

Gilson L (1997) The lessons of user fee experience in Africa, *Health Policy and Planning* 12(4): 273–85.

Gilson L and Mills A (1995) Health sector reforms in sub-Saharan Africa: lessons of the last 10 years. In Berman P (ed.) *Health Sector Reform in Developing Countries. Making Health Development Sustainable*. Boston: Harvard University Press, pp. 277–316.

Gilson L, Russell S and Buse K (1995) The political economy of user fees with targeting: developing equitable health financing policy. *Journal of International Development*, 7(3): 369–401.

Ginsburg PB (1988) Public insurance programs: Medicare and Medicaid. In Frech HI (ed.) *Health Care in America: the Political Economy of Hospitals and Health Insurance*. San Francisco: Pacific Research Institute for Public Policy.

Giuffrida, A, Gosden, T, Forland, F, Kristiansen, IS, Sutton, M, Leese, B, Pedersen, L and Sutton, M (2002) *Target Payments in Primary Care: Effects on Professional Practice and Health Care Outcomes* (Cochrane review). The Cochrane Library Issue 1. Oxford:Update Software. (Ref Type: Electronic Citation).

Giuliani G, Selke G and Garattini L (1998) The German experience in reference pricing. *Health Policy* 44: 73–85.

Glassman A, Reich M, Laserson K and Rojas F (1999) Political analysis of health reform in the Dominican Republic. *Health Policy and Planning* 14(2): 115–26.

Glennerster H, Hills J and Travers T (2000) *Paying for Health Care, Housing and Education.* Oxford: Oxford University Press.

Globerman S, Hodges H and Vining A (2002) Canadian and the United States' health care systems performance and governance: elements of convergence. *Applied Health Economics and Health Policy* 1(2): 25–38.

Goddard M, Mannian R and Smith P (2000) Enhancing performance in health care: a theoretical perspective on agency and the role of information. *Health Economics* 9: 95–107.

Goddard M and Smith P (2001) Equity for access to health care services: theory and evidence from the UK. *Social Science and Medicine* Nov., 53(9): 1149–62.

Goetzel R, Anderson D, Whitmer R, Ozminkowski R, Dunn R and Wasserman J (1998) The relationship between modifiable health risks and health care expenditures. *Journal of Occupational and Environmental Medicine* 40(10): 843–54.

Goff DC, Feldman HA, McGovern PG, Goldberg RH, Simons-Morton DG, Cornell CE, Osganian SK, Cooper LS and Hedges JR (1999) Prehospital delay in patients hospitalised with heart attack symptoms in the Unites States: the REACT trial Rapid Early Action for Coronary Treatment (REACT) Study Group. *American Heart Journal* Dec., 138(6 Pt 1): 1046–57.

Gold MR, Mittler J, Aizer A, Lyons B and Schoen C (2001) Health Insurance Expansion through States in a Pluralistic System. *Journal of Health Politics, Policy & Law* 26: 581–615.

Goldberg RJ, Steg PG, Sadiq I, Granger CB, Jackson EA, Budaj A, Brieger D, Avezum A and Goodman S (1999) Extent of, and factors associated with, delay to hospital presentation in patients with acute coronary disease (the GRACE registry). *American Journal of Cardiology* Apr. 1, 89(7): 791–6.

Goldman DP (1995) Managed care as a public cost-containment mechanism. *RAND Journal of Economics* 26(2): 277–95.

Goldman DP, Hosek SD, Dixon LS and Sloss EM (1995) The effects of benefit design and managed care on health care costs. *Journal of Heath Economics* 14: 401–18.

Goldsmith M (1988) Do vouchers hold the key to the funding dilemma? *Health Services Journal* 98: 78.

Gonzalez-Block MA, Sandiford P, Ruiz, JA and Rovira J (2001) Beyond health gain: the range of health system benefits expressed by social groups in Mexico and Central America. *Social Science and Medicine* 52(10): 1537–50.

Goodwin N, Mays N, McLeod H, Malbon G and Raftery J (1998) Evaluation of total purchasing pilots in England and Scotland and implications for primary care groups in England: personal interviews and analysis of routine data. *British Medical Journal* 317: 256–9.

Gornick ME, Eggers PW, Reilly TW, Mentnech RM, Fitterman LK, Kucken LE and Vladeck BC (1996) Effects of race and income on mortality and use of services among Medicare beneficiaries. *New England Journal of Medicine* Sep. 12, 335(110): 791–9.

Gosden T, Pedersen L and Torgerson D (1999) How should we pay doctors? A systematic review of salary payments and their effect on doctor behaviour. *Quarterly Journal of Medicine* 92: 55.

Gosden T, Forland F, Kristiansen I, Sutton M, Leese B, Giuffrida A *et al.* (2002) Capitation, salary, fee-for-service and mixed systems of payment: effects on the behaviour of primary care physicians. *The Cochrane Library.*

References

Gottschalk P, Wolfe and Haveman R (1989) Health care financing in the US, UK and Netherlands: distributional consequences. *Changes in Revenue Structures*. Proceedings of the 42nd Congress of the International Institute of Public Finance, Athens 351–73.

Government of Tanzania (January 2000). *Guidelines for the Preparation of the Medium Term Plan and Expenditure Framework, 2000/01 – 2002/03*. Issued by the President's Office, Planning Commission and the Ministry of Finance Mimeographed Document.

Gracey M, Williams P and Houston S (1997) Environmental health conditions in remote and rural aboriginal communities in Western Australia. *Australian and New Zealand Journal of Public Health* 21(5): 511–8.

Gramm P (1994) Why we need medical savings accounts. *New England Journal of Medicine* 330(24): 1732–3.

Gratzer D (1999) *Code Blue: Revising Canada's Health Care System*. Toronto: ECW Press.

Gray B (2001) Do Medicaid physician fees for prenatal services affect birth outcomes? *Journal of Health Economics* 20: 571–90.

Green D (1986) *Which Doctor?* London: Institute of Economic Affairs.

Greß S, Groenewegen P, Kerssens J, Braun B and Wasem J (2002) Free choice of sickness funds in regulated competition: evidence from Germany and the Netherlands. *Health Policy* 60: 235–54.

Greenspan AM, Kay HR, Berger BC, Greenberg RM, Greenspon AJ and Gaughan MJ (1988) Incidence of unwarranted implantation of permanent cardiac pacemakers in a large medical population. *New England Journal of Medicine* 318: 158–63.

Griffin C (1992) Welfare gains from user charges for government health services. *Health Policy and Planning* 7(2): 177–80.

Grimaldi PL (1996) Is a medical savings account in your future? *Nursing Management* 27 (5): 14–16.

Grimshaw J and Russell I (1993) Effect of clinical guidelines on medical practice: a systematic review of salary payments and their effect on doctor behaviour. *Quarterly Journal of Medicine* 92: 55.

Grimshaw JM, Thomas RE, Maclennan G, Fraser C, Ramsay CR, Vale L, Whitty P, Eccles MP, Matowe L, Shirran E, Wensing M, Dijkstra R and Donaldson C (2003) Effectiveness and efficiency of guideline dissemination and implementation strategies. Health Technol Assess.

Grivell AR, Forgie HJ, Fraser CG and Berry MN (1981) Effect of feedback to clinical staff of information on clinical biochemistry requesting patterns. *Clinical Chemistry* 27: 1717–20.

Grol R, Mokkink H and Schellevis F (1988) The effects of peer review in general practice. *Journal of the Royal College of General Practitioners* 38: 10–13.

Grootendorst P and Holbrook A (1999) Evaluating the impact of reference-based pricing. *Canadian Medical Association Journal* 161: 273–4.

Gross DJ, Alecxih L, Gibson MJ, Corea J, Caplan C and Brangan N. (1999) Out-of-pocket health spending by poor and near-poorly elderly Medicate beneficiaries. *Health Service Research* Apr., 34(1 Pt 2): 241–54.

Grossman M (1970) *The Demand for Health: a Theoretical and Empirical Investigation*. National Bureau of Economic Research Occasional Paper No 119. New York: Columbia University Press.

Grossman M (1975) The correlation between health and schooling. In Terleck N, (ed.) *Household Production and Consumption*. New York: National Bureau of Economic Research.

Gruber J, Kim J and Mayzlin D (1999) Physician fees and procedure intensity: the case of cesarean delivery. *Journal of Health Economics* 18: 490.

Grundy E and Sloggett A (2002) Health inequalities in the older population: the role of personal capital, social resources and socio-economic circumstances. *Social Science & Medicine* Mar., 56(5): 935–47.

Grytten J and Sorensen R (2001) Type of contract and supplier-induced demand for primary physicians in Norway. *Journal of Health Economics* 20: 379–93.

Grytten J, Carlsen F and Skau I (2001) The income effect and supplier induced demand. Evidence from primary physician services in Norway. *Applied Economics* 33: 1455–67.

Grytten J, Rongen G and Sorensen R (1995) Can a public health care system achieve equity? The Norwegian experience. *Medical Care* 33, (9): 938–51.

Guterman S and Dobson A (1986) Impact of the Medicare prospective payment system for hospitals. *Health Care Financing Review* 7: 97–114.

Haas M, Viney R, Kristensen E, Pain C and Foulds K (2001) Using programme budgeting and marginal analysis to assist population based strategic planning for coronary heart disease. *Health Policy 2001* 55(3): 173–86.

Haile PA and Stein RM (2002) Managed care incentives and inpatient complications. *Journal of Economics and Management Strategy* 11: 37–79.

Hakansson S (1994) New ways of financing and organizing health care in Sweden. *International Journal Health Planning & Management* 9: 103–24.

Hakansson S, Majnoni d'Intignano B, Roberts J and Zollner H (1988) *The Leningrad Experiment in Health Care Management 1988*. Report of a visit to the USSR. SSR/MPBN 501. Copenhagen: World Health Organisation Report.

Hall J (1991) *Equity, Access and Health*. Sydney: Department of Public Health, University of Sydney, PhD thesis.

Hamilton BH (1999) HMO selection and Medicare costs: Bayesian MCMC estimation of a robust panel data tobit model with survival. *Health Economics* Aug., 8(5): 403–14.

Hamilton H and Bramley-Harker RE (1999) The impact of the NHS reforms on queues and surgical outcomes in England: evidence from hip fracture patients. *The Economic Journal* 109: 437–62.

Hamilton BH, Hamilton VH and Mayo NE (1996) What are the costs of queuing for hip fracture surgery in Canada? *Journal of Health Economics* 15: 161–85.

Hamilton BH, Ho V and Goldman DP (2000) Queuing for surgery: is the U.S. or Canada worse off? *The Review of Economics and Statistics* 82(2): 297–308.

Hanson, K., Hanson Kara, Goodman Catherine, Lines Jo, Meek Sylvia, Bradley David, Mills Anne. (2002) *The Economics of Malaria Control*. Discussion Paper for the Health Economics and Financing Programme, London School of Hygiene and Tropical Medicine, 2002.

Harris BL, Stergachis A and Reid DI (1990). The effect of drug copayments on utilisation and cost of pharmaceuticals in a Health Maintenance Organisation. *Medical Care* 28: 908–17.

Harris JE (1977) The internal organisation of hospitals: some economic implications. *Bell Journal of Economics* 8: 467–82.

Harris K, Schultz J and Feldman R (2002) Measuring consumer perceptions of quality differences among competing health benefit plans. *Journal of Health Economics* 21: 1–17.

Harrison MI and Calltorp J (2000) The reorientation of market-oriented reforms in Swedish health-care. *Health Policy* 50: 219–40.

Hayward RA, Shapiro MF, Freeman HE and Corey CR (1988) Inequities in health services among insured Americans. Do working-age adults have less access to medical care than the elderly? *New England Journal of Medicine* 318: 1507–12.

Health Care Financing Administration (1989) *International Comparison of Health Care Financing and Delivery: Data and Perspectives*. Health Care Financing Review Annual Supplement.

References

Health Targets and Implementation (Health for All) Committee (1988) Health for All Australians. Canberra: Australian Government Publishing Service.

Hecht R, Overholt C and Holmberg H (1993) Improving the implementation of cost recovery: lessons from Zimbabwe. *Health Policy* 25: 213–42.

Heffner J (2001) Altering physician behavior to improve clinical performance. *Topics in Health Information Management* 22: 1–9.

Hellander I, Himmelstein DU, Woolhandler S and Wolfe S (1994) Health care paper chase, 1993 – the cost to the nation, the states and the District of Columbia. *International Journal of Health Services* 24: 1–9.

Heller PS (1982) A model of the demand for medical and health services in Peninsular Malaysia. *Social Science & Medicine* 16: 267–84.

Hellinger F (1995) Selection bias in HMOs and PPOs: A review of the evidence. *Inquiry* 32: 135–42.

Helms L, Newhouse JP and Phelps CE (1978) Co-payments and the demand for medical care: the California Medicare experience. *Bell Journal of Economics* 9: 192–208.

Hemenway D, Killen A, Cashman SB, Parks CL and Bicknell WJ (1990) Physicians' responses to financial incentives. Evidence from a for-profit ambulatory care center. *New England Journal of Medicine* 322: 1059–63.

Henderson LR and Scott A (2001) The costs of caring for stroke patients in a GP-led community hospital: an application of programme budgeting and marginal analysis. *Health Social Care Community* 9(4): 244–54.

Henke K-D, Murray M and Ade C (1994) Global budgeting in Germany: Lessons for the United States. *Health Affairs* 13: 7.

Her Majesty's Government (1999) *The Health Act*. The Stationary Office, London.

Herzlinger R and Krasker W (1987) Who profits from non-profits. *Harvard Business Review* 93–106.

Hern JEC (1994) What should be done about merit awards? Merit awards – the case for change. *British Medical Journal* 308: 973–4.

Herzlinger RE and Krasker WS (1987) Who profits from non-profits. *Harvard Business Review* 93–106.

Hickson GB, Altemeier WA and Perrin JM (1987) Physician reimbursement by salary or fee-for-service: effect on physician practice behavior in a randomized prospective study. *Pediatrics* 80: 344–50.

Hill JD, Hampton JR and Mitchell JR (1978) A randomised trial of home-versus-hospital management for patients with suspected myocardial infarction. *Lancet* 1: 837–41.

Hillman AL, Pauly MV and Kerstein JJ (1989) How do financial incentives affect physicians' clinical decisions and the financial performance of health maintenance organizations? *New England Journal of Medicine* 321: 86–92.

Himmelstein DU and Woolhandler S (1986) Cost without benefit. Administrative waste in U.S. health care. *New England Journal of Medicine* 314: 441–5.

Himmelstein DU and Woolhandler S (1989) A national health program for the United States. A physicians' proposal. *New England Journal of Medicine* 320: 102–8.

Himmelstein DU, Lewontin JP and Woolhandler S (1996) Who administers? Who cares? Medical administrative and clinical employment in the United States and Canada. *American Journal of Public Health* 86: 172–8.

Hindle D, Acuin L and Valera M (2001) Health insurance in the Phillippines: bold policies and socio-economic realities. *Australian Health Review* 24(2): 96–111.

Hitiris T and Posnett J (1992) The determinants and effects of health expenditure in developed countries. *Journal of Health Economics* 11(2): 173–181.

Hjertqvist J (2002) *User fees for health care in Sweden: a two-tier threat or tool for solidarity?* Atlantic Institute for Market Studies, Health Care Commentary Number 6, Halifax, Nova Scotia.

Ho MT (1991) Delays in the treatment of acute myocardial infarction: an overview. *Heart & Lung,* Sep., 20(5 Pt 2): 566–70.

Ho V, Hamilton B and Roos L. (2000) Multiple approaches to assessing the effects of delays for hip fracture patients in the United States and Canada. *Health Services Research* 34(7): 1499–518.

Hopkins J (1999) Financial incentives for ambulatory care performance improvement. *Journal on Quality Improvement* 25: 223–38.

Hopkins S and Cumming J (2001) The impact of changes in private health expenditure on New Zealand households. *Health Policy* 58: 215–29.

Howie J, Heaney D and Maxwell M (1994) Evaluating care of patients reporting back pain in fundholding practices. *British Medical Journal* 309: 705–10.

Hoyer G (1985) Trangsinnleggesber og trangsretensjon i psykiatriske institusjoner – en sam mentignrng av regelverk og praksis i de skemdincenyke land. *Nordisk Psykrorisk Trdsskritt* 29: 147–57.

Hsiao W (1995a) Colombia health system reform. In *Ahsr and Fhsr Annual meeting Abstract Book* 12: 120–1.

Hsiao W (1995b) Medical savings accounts: lessons from Singapore. *Health Affairs* 14(2): 260–6.

Hu S, Chen W, Cheng X, Chen K, Zhou H, Wang L (2001) Pharmaceutical cost-containment policy: experiences in Shanghai, China. *Health Policy and Planning* 16: 4–9.

Hughes D (1993) General practitioners and the new contract: promoting better health through financial incentives. *Health Policy* 25: 39–50.

Hughes D and Yule B (1992) The effect of per-item fees on the behaviour of general practitioners. *Journal of Health Economics* 11: 413–37.

Hurley J (2000) Medical savings accounts: approach with caution. *Journal of Health Services Research and Policy* 5(3): 130–2.

Hurley J, Lomas J and Goldsmith L (1997) Physician responses to global physician expenditure budgets in Canada: A common property perspective. *The Millbank Quarterly* 75: 343–64.

Huskins WC, Ba-Thike K, Festin MR, Limpongsanurak S, Lumbiganon P, Peedicayil A *et al.* (2001) An international survey of practice variation in the use of antibiotic prophylaxis in cesarian section. *International Journal of Gynaecology and Obstetrics* 73: 141–5.

Hutchinson J and Foley R (1999) Method of physician remuneration and rates of antibiotic prescription. *Canadian Medical Association Journal* 160: 1013–177.

Hutchison B, Birch S, Hurley J, Lomas J and Fawne S-D (1996) Do physician-payment mechanisms affect hospital utilization? A study of health service organisations in Ontario. *Canadian Medical Association Journal* 154: 653–61.

Illich I (1976) *Limits to Medicine. Medical Nemesis: The Expropriation of Health.* London: Marian Boyers.

Indulski JA, Smolen MM and Wlodarczyz C (1989) *Some economic aspects of the Polish NHS reform project.* Barcelona, Sept. Paper presented to the First European conference on Health Economics.

References

International Forum on Common Access to Health Services (2003) Programme statement, Jan. 2003. Stockholm: International Forum on Common Access to Health Services.

Irwin WG, Mills KA and Steele K (1986) Effect on prescribing of the limited list in a computerised group practice. *British Medical Journal* 293: 857–9.

Isakova L, Zelckovich R and Frid E (1995) Health insurance in Russia – the Kuzbass experience. *Health Policy* 31: 157–69.

Italian Ministry of Justice (1978) *Legge 838: Institutione del Sernzio Sanitario.* Supplement to Tazzotta Ufficcale. 298 December 1978, Rome.

Iversen T and Luras H (2000) The effect of capitation on GP's referral decision. *Health Economics* 9: 199–210.

Jack W (2000) *Health Insurance Reform in Four Latin American Countries. Theory and Practice.* Policy Research Working Paper 2492. The World Bank Development Research Group, Public Economics. Ref Type: Report.

Jan S (2002) Institutional considerations in priority setting: Transactions cost perspective on PBMA. *Health Economics* 9(7): 631–41.

Jan S, Mooney G, Ryan M, Bruggemann K and Alexander K (2000). The use of conjoint analysis to elicit community preferences in public health research: a case study. *Australian and NewZealand Journal of Public Health* 24: 64–70.

Jonsson B (1989) What can Americans learn from Europeans? *Health Care Financing Review* Spec. No: 79–93.

Josephson G and Karcz A (1997) The impact of physician economic incentives on admission rates of patients with ambulatory sensitive conditions: An analysis comparing two managed care structures and indemnity insurance. *The American Journal of Managed Care* 3: 49–56.

Jowett M, Contoyannis P and Vinh ND (2003) The impact of public voluntary health insurance on private health expenditures in Vietnam. *Social Science and Medicine* Jan., 56(2): 333–42.

Juba DA, Lave JR, and Shaddy J (1980) An analysis of the choice of health benefits plans. *Inquiry* 17: 62–71.

Kahn KL, Keeler EB, Sherwood MJ, Rogers WH, Draper D, Bentow SS, Reinisch EJ, Rubenstein LV, Kosecoff J and Brook RH (1990a) Comparing outcomes of care before and after implementation of the DRG-based prospective payment system. *Journal of the American Medical Association* 264: 1984–88.

Kahn KL, Rogers WH, Rubenstein LV, Sherwood MJ, Reinisch EJ, Keeler EB, Draper D, Kosecoff J and Brook RH (1990b) Measuring quality of care with explicit process criteria before and after implementation of the DRG-based prospective payment system. *Journal of the American Medical Association* 264: 1969–73.

Kamke K (1998) The German health care system and health care reform. *Health Policy* 43: 171–94.

Kamper-Jorgensen F (2001) *The Danish government programme on public health and health promotion 1999–2008.* A case study. Policy Learning Curve Series Number 5. Brussels: World Health Organization Europe and European Centre for Health Policy.

Kanavos P and Mossialos E (1999) International comparisons of health care expenditures: what we know and what we do not know. *Journal of Health Services and Research Policy* 4(2): 122–6.

Kapral MK, Wang H, Mamdani M and Tu JV (2002) Effect of socioeconomic status on treatment and mortality after stroke. *Stroke* Jan., 33(1): 268–73.

Kapur K, Young A, Murata D, Sullivan G and Koegel P (1999) The economic impact of capitated care for high utilizers of public mental health services: The Los Angeles PARTNERS program experience. *The Journal of Behavioural Health Services & Research* 26: 416–29.

Kawabata K, Xu K and Carrin G (2002) Preventing impoverishment through protection against catastrophic health expenditure. *Bull World Health Organisation* 80(8): 612.

Keeler EB and Rolph JE (1988) The demand for episodes of treatment in the Health Insurance Experiment. *Journal of Health Economics* 7: 337–67.

Keeler EB, Brook RH, Goldberg GA, Kamberg CJ and Newhouse JP (1985) How free care reduced hypertension in the health insurance experiment. *Journal of the American Medical Association* 254: 1926–31.

Keeler EB, Malkin JD, Goldman DP and Buchanan JL (1996) Can medical savings accounts for the non-elderly reduce health care costs? *Journal of the American Medical Association* 275 (21): 1666–71.

Kemper P, Reschovsky JD and Tu HT (1999) Do HMOs make a difference? Summary and implications. *Inquiry* 36. 419–25.

Kerr D, Malcolm L, Schousboe J and Pimm F (1996) Successful implementation of laboratory budget holding by Pegasus Medical Group. *New Zealand Medical Journal* 109: 334–7.

Kessler DP and McClellan MB (2000) Is hospital competition socially wasteful? *Quarterly-Journal-of-Economics* 115(2): 577–615.

Kinder K (2001) Assessing the impact of payment method and practice settings on German physicians' practice patterns. *Journal of Ambulatory Care Management* 24: 11–18.

Kleiman E (1974) The determinants of national outlay on health. In Perlman M (ed.) *The Economics of Medical Care*. New York: Macmillan.

Klinkman M, Gorenflo D and Ritsema T (1997) The effects of insurance coverage on the quality of prenatal care. *Archives of Family Medicine* 6: 557–66.

Koivusalo M (1999) Decentralisation and equity of healthcare provision in Finland. *British Medical Journal* 318: 1198–1200.

Kominski GF and Long SH (1997) Medicare's disproportionate share adjustment and the cost of low-income patients. *Journal of Health Economics* Apr., 16(2): 177–90.

Kosecoff J, Kahn KL, Rogers WH, Reinisch EJ, Sherwood MJ, Rubenstein LV, Draper D, Roth CP, Chew C and Brook RH (1990) Prospective payment system and impairment at discharge. The 'quicker-and-sicker' story revisited. *Journal of the American Medical Association* 264: 1980–83.

Kouides R, Bennett N, Lewis B, Cappuccio J, Barker W and LaForce FM (1998) Performance-based physician reimbursement and influenza immunization rates in the elderly. The primary-care physicians of Monroe County. *American Journal of Preventive Medicine* 14: 89–95.

Kralewski J, Rich E, Feldman R, Dowd B, Berhnardt T, Johnson C et al. (2000) The effects of medical group practice and physician payment methods on costs of care. *Health Services Research* 35: 591–613.

Kramer A, Kowalsky J, Lin M, Grigsby J, Hughes R and Steiner J (2000) Outcome and utilization differences for older persons with stroke in HMO and Fee-for-service systems. *Journal of the American Geriatrics Society* 48: 726–34.

Krasnik A, Groenewegen PP, Pedersen PA, von Scholten P, Mooney G, Gottschau A, Flierman HA and Damsgaard MT (1990) Changing remuneration systems: effects on activity in general practice. *British Medical Journal* 300: 1698–701.

Krieble TA (2000) New Zealand. *Journal of Health Politics, Policy & Law* 25: 925–30.

Kristiansen IS (1989) Personal communication.

Kristiansen I and Holtedahl K (1993) Effect of the remuneration system on the general practitioner's choice between surgery consultations and home visits. *Journal of Epidemiology and Community Health* 47: 481–4.

References

Kristiansen IS and Pedersen KM (2000) *Helsevesenet I De Nordiske Land: Er likhetene større enn ulikhetene?* (in English: *Health Care in the Nordic Countries – Are the similarities greater than the differences?*). Tidsskr Nor Lægeforen 2000; 120: 2023–9 (Medline referenced paper).

Ku L and Matani S (2001) Left out: immigrants' access to health care and insurance. *Health Affairs* Jan.–Feb., 20(1): 247–56.

Kunitz, S. (1994) *Disease and Social Diversity. The European Impact on the Health of Non-Europeans*. New York: Oxford University Press.

Kwon S (1997) Payment systems for providers in health insurance markets. *Journal of Risk and Uncertainty* 64: 155–73.

Laffont JJ and Tirole J (1993) *A Theory of Incentives in Procurement and Regulation*. Cambridge, MA: MIT Press.

Langa K and Sussman E (1993) The effect of cost-containment policies on rates of coronary revascularization in California. *The New England Journal of Medicine* 329: 1784–89.

Le Grand J (1978) The distribution of public expenditure: the case of health care. *Economica* 45: 125–42.

Le Grand J (1982) *The Strategy of Equality*. London: George, Allen and Unwin.

Le Grand J (2002) Further tales from the British National Health Service. *Health Affairs* 21: 116–28.

Leavey R, Wilkin D and Metcalfe DH (1989) NHS review. Consumerism and general practice. *British Medical Journal* 298: 737–9.

Lee JC (2003) Health care reform in South Korea: success or failure? *American Journal of Public Health*, Jan., 93(1): 48–51.

Lee JS and Tollen L (2002) How low can you go? The impact of reduced benefits and increased cost sharing. *Health Affairs (Web exclusive)*: W229–W241.

Lee-Feldstein A, Feldstein P, Buchmueller T and Katterhagen G (2001) Breast cancer outcomes among older women. HMO, Fee-for-service and delivery system comparisons. *Journal of General Internal Medicine* 16: 189–99.

Lees DS (1961) *Health Through Choice*. Hobart Paper 14, London: Institute of Economic Affairs.

Lees DS (1962) The logic of the British National Health Service. *Journal of Law and Economics* 5: 111–18.

Leibowitz A, Buchanan J and Mann J (1992) A randomized trial to evaluate the effectiveness of a Medicaid HMO. *Journal of Health Economics* 11: 235–57.

Leizorovicz A, Haugh, MC, Mercier C and Boissel JP (1997) Pre-hospital and hospital time delays in thrombolytic treatment in patients with suspected acute myocardial infarction. Analysis of data from the EMIP study. European Myocardial Infarction Study. *European Heart Journal* 18(2): 248–53.

Leu R (1986) The public/private mix and institutional health care costs. In (Culyer A, Jonsson B (eds)) *Public and Private Health Services: Complementaries and Conflicts*. Oxford: Basil Blackwell.

Lewin LS, Derzon RA and Margulies R (1981) Investor-owneds and nonprofits differ in economic performance. *Hospitals: Journals of the American Hospital Association* 55: 52–8.

Lewin LS, Eckels TJ and Miller LB (1988) Setting the record straight. The provision of uncompensated care by not-for-profit hospitals. *New England Journal of Medicine* 318: 1212–15.

Lexchin J (2002) Effects of restrictive formularies in the ambulatory care setting. *The American Journal of Managed Care* 8: 69–76.

Liaropoulous L and Tragakes E (1998) Public/private financing in the Greek health care system: implications for equity. *Health Policy* 43: 153–69.

Lindsay CM (1980) *National Health Issues: the British experience.* Welwyn: Roche Laboratories.

Linna M (2000) Health care financing reform and the productivity change in Finnish hospitals. *Journal of Health Care Finance* 26: 83–100.

Litvack J and Bodart C (1993) User fees plus quality equals improved access to health care: results of a field experiment in Cameroon. *Social Science and Medicine* 37(3): 369–83.

Liu Y, Hsiao WC, Li Q, Liu X and Ren M (1995) Transformation of China's rural health care financing. *Social Science Medicine* Oct., 41(8): 1085–93.

Loft A and Mooney G (1989) Trying to judge what is best medical practice. *International Journal of Health Planning and Management* 4: 159–66.

Logan J, Green D and Woodfield A (1989) *Healthy Competition.* Sydney: Centre for Independent Studies.

Lohr KN, Brook RH, Kamberg CJ, Goldberg GA, Leibowitz A, Keesey J, Reboussin D and Newhouse JP (1986) Use of medical care in the Rand Health Insurance Experiment. Diagnosis- and service-specific analyses in a randomized controlled trial. *Medical Care* 24: S1–87.

Longman New Universal Dictionary (1982) Harlow: Longman Group Limited.

Loomes G and McKenzie L (1989) The use of QALYs in health care decision making. *Social Science & Medicine* 28: 299–308.

Louis DZ, Yuen EJ, Braga M, Cicchetti A, Rabinowitz C, Laine C *et al.* (1999) Impact of a DRG-based hospital financing system on quality and outcomes of care in Italy. *Health Services Research* 34(1 Pt 2): 405–15.

Lowry M (1978) Variations between paediatricians in the treatment of childhood asthma. *Paediatric Reviews and Communications* 1: 55–65.

Lu, M (1999) Separating the 'True Effect' from 'Gaming' in incentive-based contracts in health care. *Journal of Economics & Management Strategy* 8(3): 383–432.

Lu M and Donaldson C (2000) Performance-based contracts and provider efficiency. *Disease management and health outcomes* 7(3): 127–37.

Lu M, Ma CA and Yuan L (2002) Risk selection and matching in performance-based contracting. *Health Economics* May 12(5): 339–54.

Lupton D (1997) Consumerism, reflexivity and the medical encounter. *Social Science and Medicine* 45: 373–81.

Lupton D, Donaldson C and Lloyd P (1991) Caveat emptor or blissful ignorance? Patients and the consumerist ethos. *Social Science & Medicine* 33: 559–68.

Lurie N, Christianson J, Finch M and Moscovice I (1994) The effects of capitation on health and function status of the Medicaid elderly. *Annals of Internal Medicine* 120: 506–11.

Lurie N, Moscovice I, Finch M, Christianson J and Popkin M (1992) Does capitation affect the health of the chronically mentally ill? *Journal of the American Medical Association* 267: 3300–4.

Lynch M, (1998) Financial incentives and primary care provision in Britain: do general practitioners maximise their income. *Development in Health Economics and Public Policy* 6: 191–210.

Mackillop WJ, Zhou Y and Quirt CF (1995) A comparison of delays in the treatment of cancer with radiation in Canada and the United States. *International Journal of Radiation Oncology* 32: 531–9.

Madden L, Hussey R, Mooney G and Church E (1995) Public health and economics in tandem: programme budgeting, marginal analysis and priority setting in practice. *Health Policy* 33: 161–8.

References

Magnussen J and Solstad K (1994) Case-based hospital financing: the case of Norway. *Health Policy* 27: 23–36.

Mandeblatt J, Andrews H, Kerner J, Zauber A and Burnett W (1991) Determinants of late stage diagnosis of breast cancer and cervical cancer: the impact of age, race, social class and hospital type. *American Journal of Public Health* 81: 646–9.

Manga P, Broyles RW and Angus DE (1987) The determinants of hospital utilization under a universal public insurance program in Canada. *Medical Care* 25: 658–70.

Manning W, Liu C-F, Stoner T, Gray D, Lurie N, Popkin M *et al.* (1999) Outcomes for Medicaid beneficiaries with Schizophrenia under a prepaid mental health carve-out. *Journal of Behavioural Health Services & Research* 26: 442–50.

Manning WG, Leibowitz A, Goldberg GA, Rogers WH and Newhouse JP (1984) A controlled trial of the effect of a prepaid group practice on use of services. *New England Journal of Medicine* 310: 1505–10.

Manning WG, Newhouse JP, Duan N, Keeler EB, Leibowitz A and Marquis MS (1987) Health insurance and the demand for medical care: evidence from a randomized experiment. *American Economic Review* 77: 251–77.

Margolis H (1982) *Selfishness, Altruism and Rationality.* Cambridge: Cambridge University Press.

Mariam DH (2003) Indigenous social insurance as an alternative financing mechanism for health care in Ethiopia (the case of elders). *Social Science Medicine* 56(8): 1719–26.

Marmot M and Wilkinson RG (1999) *Social Determinants of Health.* Oxford University Press, Oxford.

Massaro TA and Wong Y (1995) Positive experience with medical savings accounts in Singapore. *Health Affairs* 14(2): 267–72.

Mastilica M and Bozikov J (1999) Out-of-pocket payments for health care in Croatia: implications for equity. *Croatian Medical Journal* 40(2): 152–9.

Mather HG, Morgan DC, Pearson NG, Read KL, Shaw DB, Steed GR, Thorne MG, Lawrence CJ and Riley IS (1976) Myocardial infarction: a comparison between home and hospital care for patients. *British Medical Journal* 1: 925–9.

Matisonn S (2000) *Medical Savings Accounts in South Africa.* Policy Report No. 234. Dallas: National Center for Policy Analysis.

Maxwell R (1981) *Health and Wealth.* Lexington, MA: Lexington Books.

Maynard A and Tingle R (1975) The objectives and performance of the mental health services in England and Wales in the 1960s. *Journal of Social Policy* 4: 151–68.

Maynard A, Marinker M and Gray DP (1986) The doctor, the patient, and their contract. III. Alternative contracts: are they viable? *British Medical Journal* 292: 1438–40.

Maynard A (1994) Can competition enhance efficiency in health care? Lessons from the reform of the U.K. National Health Service. *Social Science and Medicine* 39(10): 1438–45.

Maynard A (2003). Hidden costs of 'dangerous' GP contract. *Health Services Journal*, Nov. 6: 19.

Maynard A and Bloor K (1996) Introducing a market into the United Kingdom's National Health Service. *New England Journal of Medicine*, 334: 604–8.

McClelland A (1991) *In Fair Health? Equity and the Health System.* Background Paper No. 3. Canberra: National Health Strategy Unit.

McCombie SC (1996) Treatment seeking for malaria: a review of recent research. *Social Science and Medicine* 43: 933–45.

McGrail M, Tsai S and Bernacki E (1995) A comprehensive initiative to manage the incidence and cost of occupational injury and illness. *Journal of Occupational and Environmental Medicine* 37: 1263–8.

McGuire A and Hughes D (2003) The economics of the hospital: issues of asymmetry and uncertainty as they affect hospital reimbursement. In Scott A, Maynard A and Elliott R (eds) *Advances on Health Economics*. Wiley: Chichester.

McGuire A, Henderson T and Mooney G (1988) *The Economics of Health Care: An Introductory Text*. London: Routledge and Kegan Paul.

McIntyre D, Doherty J and Gilson L (2003) A tale of two visions: the changing fortunes of Social Health Insurance in South Africa. *Health Policy Plan*, Mar., 18(1): 47–58.

McIntyre D, Muirhead D and Gilson L (2002) Geographic patterns of deprivation in South Africa: informing health equity analyses and public resource allocation strategies. *Health Policy Plan*, Dec., 17 (Supplement): 30–9.

McIsaac W, Goel V and Naylor D (1997) Socio-economic status and visits to physicians by adults in Ontario Canada. *Journal of Health Services Research and Policy* 2(2): 94–102.

McKinley S, Moser DK and Dracup K (2000) Treatment-seeking behaviour for acute myocardial infarction symptoms in North America and Australia. *Heart-Lung*, July–Aug., 29(4): 237–47.

McLachlan G and Maynard A (1982) The public/private mix in health care: The emerging lessons. In *The Public/Private Mix in Health Care: The Relevance and Effects of Change*. (McLachlan G and Maynard A, eds), London: Nuffield Provincial Hospitals Trust.

McLaughlin CG (1988) The effect of HMOs on overall hospital expenses: is anything left after correcting for simultaneity and selectivity? *Health Services Research* 23: 421–41.

McMenamin I and Timonen V (2002) Poland's health reform: politics, markets and informal payments. *Journal of Social Policy* 31(1): 103–18.

McMillan SJ (1991) Food and nutrition policy issues in remote aboriginal communities: lessons from Arnhem Land. *Australia Journal of Public Health* 15(4): 281–5.

McPake B (1993) User charges for health services in developing countries: a review of the economic literature. *Social Science and Medicine* 36(11): 1397–1405.

McPake B (2000) Reforms to financing systems in poor countries. In Mills A (ed.) *Reforming Health Sectors*. London: Keagan Paul International.

McPherson K, Strong PM, Epstein A and Jones L (1981) Regional variations in the use of common surgical procedures: within and between England and Wales, Canada and the United States of America. *Social Science & Medicine* 15: 273–88.

McPherson K, Wennberg JE, Hovind OB and Clifford P (1982) Small-area variations in the use of common surgical procedures: an international comparison of New England, England, and Norway. *New England Journal of Medicine* 307: 1310–14.

Meden T, St John-Larkin C, Hermes D, Sommerschield S. MSJournal of American Medical Association (2002) Relationship between travel distance and utilization of breast cancer treatment in rural northern Michigan. *Journal of the American Medical Association* Jan. 2, 287(1): 111.

Meerabeau L (1998) Consumerism and health care: the example of fertility treatment. *Journal of Advanced Nursing* 27: 721–29.

Meerding WJ, Bonneux L, Polder JJ, Koopmanschap MA and van der Maas PJ (1998) Demographic and epidemiological determinants of healthcare costs in Netherlands: cost of illness study. *British Medical Journal* 317(7151): 111–15.

Melnick GA, Zwanziger J (1988) Hospital behavior under competition and cost-containment policies. The California experience, 1980 to 1985. *Journal of the American Medical Association* 260: 2669–75.

Menke TJ, Ashton CM, Petersen NJ and Wolinsky FD (1998) Impact of an all-inclusive diagnosis-related group payment system on inpatient utilization. *Medical Care* 36(8): 1126–37.

References

Miller P, Parkin D, Craig N, Lewis D and Gerard K (1997) Less fog on the Tyne? Programme budgeting in Newcastle and North Tyneside. *Health Policy* 40: 217–29.

Miller RH and Luft HS (1994) Managed care plan performance since 1980: a literature analysis. *Journal of the American Medical Association* 271(19): 1512–19.

Miller RH and Luft HS (1997) Does managed care lead to better or worse quality of care? *Health Affairs* 16(5): 7–25.

Miller RH and Luft HS (2002) HMO plan performance update: an analysis of the literature, 1997–2001. *Health Affairs* 21: 63–86.

Mills A (2000) Fashions, passions and common sense. In Mills A (ed.) *Reforming Health Sectors*. London: Keagan Paul International.

Mills A, Bennett S and Russell S (2001) *The Challenge of Health Sector Reform*. Hampshire: Macmillan.

Ministerio do Sanidad y Consumo (1989) *The Spanish Health Care System: Highlights*. Madrid.

Ministry of Health, Ethiopia (1984) Financial planning for health care development in Ethiopia. *World Health Statistics Quarterly* 37: 421–7.

Ministry of Health and Social Affairs (Sweden) (2001) *Towards public health on equal terms*. Fact sheet no.3 March 2001. Ministry of health and Social Affairs, Stockholm.

Ministry of Social Affairs and Health (Finland) (2001) *Government resolution on the Health 2015 public health programme*. Publications of the Ministry of Social affairs and Health: Helsinki.

Mitton C, Donaldson C, Halma L and Gall N (2002) Setting priorities and allocating resources in regional health authorities: a report from two pilot exercises using program budgeting and marginal analysis. *Healthcare Management* Forum 15(1): 39.

Mitton C and Donaldson C (2001) Twenty-five years of program budgeting and marginal analysis in the health sector, 1974–99. *Journal of Health Services Research and Policy* 6(4): 239–48.

Mitton C and Donaldson C (2003) Setting priorities and allocating resources in health regions: lessons from a project evaluating program budgeting and marginal analysis (PBMA). *Health Policy* 64: 335–48.

Mitton C, Patten S, Waldner H and Donaldson C (2003) Priority setting in health authorities: a novel approach to a historical activity. *Social Science and Medicine* 57: 1653–63.

Mobley LR (1998). Effects of selective contracting on hospital efficiency, costs and accessibility. *Health Economics* 7(3): 247–61.

Mooney G (1987a) What does equity in health mean? *World Health Statistics Quarterly* 40: 296–303.

Mooney G (1994) *Key Issues in Health Economics*. New York: Harvester Wheatsheaf.

Mooney G (1996) And now for vertical equity? Some concerns arising from aboriginal health in Australia. *Health Economics*, Mar.–Apr., 5(2): 99–103.

Mooney G (1998) Beyond health outcomes: the benefits of health care. *Health Care Analysis* June, 6(2): 99–105.

Mooney G, Haas M, Viney R and Cooper L (1997) *Linking Health Outcomes to Priority Setting, Planning and Resource Allocation*. NSW, Australia: Center for Health Economics Research and Evaluation.

Mooney G, Jan S and Wiseman V (1998) *Equity and Aboriginal and Torres Strait Islander Health Services*. Report to the Office of Aboriginal and Torres Strait Islander Health Services, Department of Health and Family Services.

Mooney G, Jan S and Wiseman V (2002) Staking a claim for claims: a case study of resource allocation in Australian Aboriginal health care. *Social Science Medicine* June, 54(11): 1657–67.

Mooney GH (1987b) *Equity and Efficiency: an Inevitable or Unethical Conflict?* Sydney, Paper presented to the First Conference of the Public Health Association of Australia and New Zealand.

Moore GT (1991) Let's provide primary care to all uninsured Americans – now! *Journal of the American Medical Association* 265: 2108–09.

Moore WJ, Newman RJ and Fheili M (1992) Measuring the relationship between income and NBES. *Health Care Financing Review* 14(1): 133–9.

Morgan M, Mays N and Holland WW (1987) Can hospital use be a measure of need for health care? *Journal of Epidemiology and Community Health* 41: 269–274.

Morgan RO, Virnig BA, DeVito CA and Persily NA (1997) The Medicare HMO revolving door-the healthy go in and the sick go out. *New England Journal of Medicine* July 17, 337(3): 169–75.

Morris AL, Roos LL, Brazauskas R and Bedard D (1990) Managing scarce services. A waiting list approach to cardiac catheterization. *Medical Care* 28: 784–92.

Morrisey MA (1995) Movies and myths: hospital cost shifting. *Business-Economics* 30(2): 22-25.

Morrisey MA (2001) Competition in hospital and health insurance markets: a review and research agenda. *Health Services Research* 36(1 Pt 2): 191 221.

Morrisey MA, Sloan FA and Valvona J (1988) Medicare prospective payment and posthospital transfers to subacute care. *Medical Care* 26: 685–698.

Moser WL (1987) The evolution of health care delivery in American industry. *Geneva Papers on Risk and Insurance* 12, 45: 297–307.

Mosquera M, Zapata Y, Lee K, Arango C and Varela A (2001) Strengthening user participation through health sector reform in Columbia: a study of institutional change and social representation. *Health Policy and Planning* 16 (Suppl. 2): 52–60.

Moss N (1998) Resource allocation to health authorities. Expenditure on private health care must be taken into account. *British Medical Journal* Mar. 21, 316(7135): 939–40.

Mossialos E and Thomson S (2003) *User charges and voluntary health insurance – Implications for equity of access.* Paper prepared for the Swedish Ministry of Health and Social Affairs. January. http://www.social.regenerigen.se/forum/pdf/user_charges_and_voluntary_health_insurance.pdf

Mukamel DB, Zwanziger J and Tomaszewski KJ (2001) HMO penetration, competition, and risk-adjusted hospital mortality. *Health Serv Res* 36(6 Pt 1): 1019–35.

Mumford AD, Warr KV, Owen SJ and Fraser AG (1999) Delays by patients in seeking treatment for acute chest pain: implications for achieving earlier thrombolysis. *Postgraduate Medical Journal* Feb., 75(880): 90–5.

Murray J, Greenfield S, Kaplan S and Yano E (1992) Ambulatory testing for capitation and fee-for-service patients in the same practice setting. *Medical Care* 30: 252–61.

Musgrove P (1986) Measurement of equity in health. *World Health Statistics Quarterly* 39: 325–35.

Musgrove P (2003) Judging health systems: reflections on WHO's methods. *Lancet* May 24, 361(9371): 1817–20.

Mushlin AI, Panzer RJ, Black ER, Greenland P and Regenstreif DI (1988). Quality of care during a community-wide experiment in prospective payment to hospitals. *Medical Care* 26: 1081–91.

Muurinen JM (1982) Demand for health: a generalised Grossman model. *Journal of Health Economics* 1: 5–28.

Mwabu G and Mwangi W (1986) Health care financing in Kenya: a simulation of welfare effects of user fees. *Social Science and Medicine* 22(7): 763–7.

257

References

Mwabu G, Mwanzia J and Liambila W (1995) User charges in government health facilities in Kenya: effect on attendance and revenue. *Health Policy and Planning* 10(2): 164–70.

Narine L, Senathirajah M and Smith T (1999) Evaluating reference-based pricing: initial findings and prospects. *Canadian Medical Association Journal* 161: 286–8.

National Forum on Health (1997) *Canada Health Action: Building on the Legacy.* Final Report of the National Forum on Health, Ottawa.

Navarro V (1989) Why some countries have national health insurance, others have national health services, and the U.S. has neither. *Social Science & Medicine* 28: 887–98.

Naylor CD (1991) A different view of queues in Ontario. *Health Affairs,* Fall: 111–28.

Naylor CD, Levinton CM, Wheeler S and Hunter L (1993) Queuing for coronary surgery during severe supply-demand mismatch in a Canadian referral centre: a case study of implicit rationing. *Social Science and Medicine* 37: 61–7.

Ndyomugyenyti R, Neema S and Magnussen P (1998) The use of formal and informal services for antenatal care and malaria treatment in rural Uganda. *Health Policy and Planning* 13(1): 94–102.

Needham A, Brown M and Freeborn S (1988) Introduction and audit of a general practice antibiotic formulary. *Journal of the Royal College of General Practitioners* 38: 166–7.

Needleman J, Lamphere J and Chollet D (1999) Uncompensated care and hospital conversions in Florida. *Health Affiliated (Millwood),* July–Aug., 18(4): 125–33.

Neumann PJ, Stone PW, Chapman RH, Sandberg EA and Bell CM (2000) The quality of reporting in published cost-utility analyses. *Annals of Internal Medicine* 132(12): 964–72.

Newacheck PW (1988) Access to ambulatory care for poor persons. *Health Services Research* 23: 401–19.

Newberry G (1996) *Setting health priorities: The use of programme budgeting and marginal analysis by the Central Coast AHS.* Central Coast Area Health Service.

Newbrander W, Collins D and Gilson L (2001) *User Fees for Health Services: Guidelines for Protecting the Poor.* Boston: Management Sciences for health.

Newhouse JP (1974) A design for health insurance experiment. *Inquiry* 16: 5–27.

Newhouse JP (1975) Development and allocation of medical care resources: Medico-economics approach. In *Development and allocation of resources – Proceedings of 29th World Medical Assembly,* Tokyo: Japan Medical Association.

Newhouse JP (1977) Medical-care expenditure: a cross-national survey. *Journal of Human Resources* 12: 115–25.

Newhouse JP (2002) Medicare. In Frankel JA and Orszag PR (eds) *American Policy in the 1990s.* MIT Press: Cambridge, MA.

Newhouse JP and Byrne DJ (1988) Did Medicare's prospective payments system cause length of stay to fall? *Journal of Health Economics* 7: 413–16.

Newhouse JP and the Insurance Experiment Group (1993) *Free for All? Lessons from the RAND Health Insurance Experiment.* Cambridge: Harvard University Press.

Newhouse JP and Phelps C (1974) *On having your cake and eating it too: economic problems in estimating the demand for health service.* R.-1149-NC. Santa Monica, California: Rand Corporation.

Newhouse JP, Manning WG, Morris C, Orr L, Duan N *et al.* (1981) Some interim results from a controlled trial of cost sharing in health insurance. *New England Journal of Medicine* 305: 1501–7.

New Zealand Ministry of Health (2000) *The New Zealand Health Strategy.* Wellington: Ministry of Health Manatu Hauora.

NHS Confederation and British Medical Association (2003) *The New GMS Contract, 2003: Investing in General Practice.* London: NHS Confederation and BMA.

NSW Department of Health (1999) *Resource Distribution Formula Technical Paper 1998 99 Revision.* Sydney: NSW Department of Health.

Nolan B (1993) Economic incentives health status and health services utilisation. *Journal of Health Economics* 12: 151–69.

Nolan B and Turbat V (1993) *Cost Recovery in Public Health Services in Sub-Saharan Africa.* Economic Development Institute, Human Resources Division, Washington.

North of England Study of Standards and Performance in General Practice (1990) *Final Report: Volume III – The Effects of Setting and Implementing Clinical Standards.* Report No. 40. Health Care Research Unit. University of Newcastle upon Tyne.

Noterman J, Criel B, Kegels G and Isu K (1995) A prepayment scheme for hospital care in the Masisi district in Zaire: a critical evaluation. *Social Science and Medicine* 40(7): 919–30.

Nuiri N and Tregakes F (2002) *Health Care Systems in Transition* – Albania. European Observatory on Health Care Systems.

Oberlander J (1998) Remaking Medicare: the voucher myth. *International Journal of Health Services* 28: 29–46.

O'Connell JM (1996) The relationship between health expenditures and the age structure of the population in OECD countries. *Health Economics* 5(6): 573–8.

O'Donnell O and Propper C (1989) *Equity and the Distribution of National Health Service Resources. Discussion Paper WSP/45.* London, Suntory Toyota International Centre for Economics and Related Studies, London School of Economics.

Oleske D, Branca M, Schmidt J, Ferguson R and Linn E (1998) A comparison of capitated and fee-for-service Medicaid reimbursement methods on pregnancy outcomes. *Health Services Research* 33: 55–73.

Organisation for Economic Cooperation and Development (1985) Measuring health care, 1060–1983, expenditure, costs and performance. Paris: OECD.

Organisation for Economic Cooperation and Development (1987) *Financing and delivering health care: a comparative analysis of OECD countries.* Paris: Social Policy Studies No. 4.

Ozanne L (1996) How will medical savings accounts effect medical spending? *Inquiry* 33(3): 225–36.

Palmer G and Short S (1989) *Health Care and Public Policy: an Australian Analysis.* Melbourne: Macmillan.

Pan American Health Organisation (1998) *Health in the Americas,* 1998 edition. PAHO, Washington DC.

Parker D and Knoppenberg R (1991) *Community Cost-sharing and Participation: A Review of the Issues.* UNICEF: Bamako Initiative Technical Report Series.

Parkin D, McGuire A and Yule B (1987) Aggregate health care expenditures and national income. Is health care a luxury good? *Journal of Health Economics* June, 6(2): 109–27.

Pattison RV and Katz HM (1983) Investor-owned hospitals and health care costs. *New England Journal of Medicine* 309: 370–2.

Pauly MV (1968) The economics of moral hazard. *American Economic Review* 58: 531–57.

Peacock S and Edwards D (1997) *Setting Priorities in South Australian Community Health: The Mental Health Program Budget.* Melbourne: Center for Health Program Evaluation, Monash University.

Pearce M and Begg E (1992) A review of limited lists and formularies: Are they cost-effective? *Pharmocoeconomics* 1: 191–202.

Pector E (2000) How patients really choose their doctors. *Medical Economics* 154–7.

Peebles R (1992) Preferred provider organizations. *American College of Surgeons Bulletin* 77: 31–48.

References

Pereira J (1989) *What does Equity in Health mean?* Discussion Paper 61. York, Centre for Health Economics.

Perneger TV, Etter JF and Rougemont A (1996) Switching Swiss enrolees from indemnity health insurance to managed care: the effect on health status and satisfaction with care. *American Journal of Public Health* 86(3): 388–93.

Petchey R (1995) General practitioner fundholding: weighing the evidence. *Lancet* 346: 1139–42.

Peterson M (1978) *The Medical Profession in Mid-Victorian England.* California: University of California Press.

Petrou S, Malek M and Davey PG (1993) The reliability of cost-utility estimates in cost-per-QALY league tables. *Pharmacoeconomics* 3(5): 345–53.

Phelps CE (1986) Induced demand-can we ever know its extent? *Journal of Health Economics* 5: 355–65.

Phelps CE and Newhouse J (1974) *Coinsurance and the demand for medical services.* Santa Monica, Ca: Rand Corporation.

Pina DL (1998) Medicaid a beneficiaries' experiences in HMO and fee-for-service health care. *Journal of Health Care Poor Underserved* Nov., 9(4): 433–48.

Plaza B, Barona A and Hearst N (2001) Managed competition for the poor or poorly managed competition? Lessons from the Colombian health reform experience. *Health Policy and Planning* 16 (Suppl. 2): 44–51.

Polikowski M and Santos-Eggimann B (2002) How comprehensive are the basic packages of health services. An international comparison of six health insurance systems. *Journal of Health Services Research and Policy* 7(3): 133–42.

Popkin M, Lurie N, Manning W, Harman J, Callies A, Gray D *et al.* (1998) Changes in the process of care for Medicaid patients with Schizophrenia in Utah's Prepaid Mental Health Plan. *Psychiatric Services* 49: 518–23.

Porell FW and Turner WM (1990) Biased selection under an experimental enrolment and marketing Medicare HMO broker. *Medical Care* 28: 604–15.

Posnett J and Street A (1996) Programme budgeting and marginal analysis: an approach to priority setting in need of refinement. *Journal of Health Services Research and Policy* 1(3): 147–53.

Potter C and Porter J (1989) American perceptions of the British National Health Service: five myths. *Journal of Health Politics Policy and Law* 14: 341–65.

Poullier J-P and Sandier S (2000) France. *Journal of Health Politics, Policy & Law* 25: 899–905.

Preker AS, Carrin G, Dror D *et al.* (2002) Effectiveness of community health financing in meeting the cost of illness. *Bulletin of the World Health Organization* 80(2): 143–50.

Price D (2000) Capital planning and the private finance initiative: cost minimisation or health care planning? *Critical Public Health* 10: 71–81.

Propper C (1996) Market Structure and Prices: The Responses of Hospitals in the UK National Health Service to Competition. *Journal-of-Public-Economics* 61(3): 307–35.

Propper C and Soderlund N (1998) Competition in the NHS internal market: an overview of its effects on hospital prices and costs. *Health Economics* 7(3): 187–97.

Propper C, Burgess S and Green K (2004) Competition and quality: evidence from the NHS internal market 1991–1999. *Journal-of-Public-Economics*, 88: 1247–72.

Propper C, Wilson D and Soderlund N (1998) The effects of regulation and competition in the NHS internal market: the case of general practice fundholder prices. *Journal of Health Economics* 17: 645–73.

Province of Alberta (1994) *Regional Health Authorities Act: Chapter R-9.07.* Queen's Printer for Alberta.

Puig-Junoy J (1999) Managing risk selection incentives in health sector reforms. *International Journal Health Planning & Management* 14: 287–311.

Quam L (1989) Post-war American health care: The many costs of market failure. *Oxford Review of Economic Policy* 5: 113–23.

Quan H, Lafreniere R and Johnson D (2002) Health service costs for patients in the waiting list. *Canadian Journal of Surgery* 45: 34–22.

Rabinowitz HK and Paynter NP. MSJournal of American Medical Association (2002) The rural vs urban practice decision. *Journal of American Medical Association* Jan.2, 287(1): 113.

Rabinowitz JK, Diamond JJ, Markham FW and Hazelwood CE (1999) A program to increase the number of family physicians in rural and underserved areas: impact after 22 years. *Journal of American Medical Association* Jan. 20, 281(3): 255–60.

Ranson K (2002) Reduction of catastrophic health care expenditures by a community-based health insurance scheme in Gujarat, India current experiences and challenges. *Bulletin of the WHO* 80(8): 613–21.

Raphael D (2000) Health inequities in the United States: prospects and solutions. *Journal of Public Health and Policy* 21(4): 394–427.

Ratcliffe J, Donaldson C and Macphee S (1996) Programme budgeting and marginal analysis: a case study of maternity services. *Journal of Public Health Medicine* 18(2): 175–82.

Rawls J (1971) *A Theory of Justice*. Cambridge, MA: Harvard University Press.

Reddy S and Vandemoortele J (1986) *User Financing of Basic Social Services, a Review of Theoretical Arguments and Empirical Evidence*. Working Paper, Office of Evaluation, Policy and Planning, UNICEF, New York.

Redmon DP and Yakoboski PJ (1995) The nominal and real effects of hospital global budgets in France. *Inquiry* 32(2): 174–83.

Reilley B, Abeyasinghe and Pakianathar, MV (2002) Barriers to prompt and effective treatment of malaria in northern Sri Lanka. *Tropical Medicine and International Health* 7(9): 744–49.

Reinhardt U (1978) Parkinson's law and the demand for physicians, services (comments of F Sloan and R Feldman, 'Competition among physicians'). In Greenberg W (ed.) *Competition in the Health Care Sector: Past, Present and Future*. Aspen: Germantown, MD.

Relman AS (1983) The Rand health insurance study: is cost sharing dangerous to your health? *New England Journal of Medicine* 309: 1453.

Reschovsky JD, Kemper P and Tu H (2000) Does type of health insurance affect health care use and assessments of care among the privately insured? *Health Services Research* 35(1): 220–37.

Retchin S and Brown B (1990) The quality of ambulatory care in Medicare health maintenance organizations. *American Journal of Public Health* 80: 411–15.

Retchin SM, Brown RS, Yeh S-C J, Chu D and Moreno L (1997) Outcomes of stroke patients in medicare fee for service and managed care. *Journal of the American Medical Association* 278(2): 119–24.

Reuveni H, Sheizaf B, Elhayany A, Sheef M, Limoni Y, Scharff S and Peled R (2002) The effect of drug co-payment policy on the purchase of prescription drugs for children with infections in the community. *Health Policy* 62: 1–13.

Rice TH (1983) The impact of changing medicare reimbursement rates on physician-induced demand. *Medical Care* 21: 803–15.

Rice TH and Labelle RJ (1989) Do physicians induce demand for medical services? *Journal of Health Politics Policy and Law* 14: 587–600.

References

Richardson J (1987) Ownership and regulation in the health care sector. In *Privatisation: An Australian Perspective*. Sydney: Australian Professional Publications.

Richardson J, Wildman J and Robertson IK (2003) A critique of the World Health Organisation's evaluation of health system performance. *Health Economics* May, 12(5): 355–66.

Riordan J (2001) New approach to the consultant contract: this offers a clearer relationship between workload and reward. *British Medical Journal* 322: 502–03.

Ritchie L, Bissett A, Russell D, Leslie V and Thomson I (1992) Primary and preschool immunisation in Grampian: progress and the 1990 contract. *British Medical Journal* 304: 816–19.

Roberts J (2000) Spurious regression problems in the determinants of health care expenditure: a comment on hitiris. *Applied Economics Letters* 7(5): 279–83.

Robinson J (2001) Theory and practice in the design of physician payment incentives. *The Millbank Quarterly* 79(2): 149–77.

Robinson JC (1991) HMO market penetration and hospital cost inflation in California. *Journal of American Medical Association* 266(19): 2719–723.

Robinson JC (1996) Administered Pricing and Vertical Integration in the Hospital Industry. *Journal-of-Law-and-Economics* 39(1): 357–78.

Robinson JC (2002) Renewed emphasis on consumer cost-sharing in health insurance benefit design. *Health Affairs (Web exclusive)* W130–54.

Robinson JC and Luft HS (1988) Competition, regulation, and hospital costs, 1982 to 1986. *Journal of the American Medical Association* 260: 2676–81.

Romanow Commission (2002) Building on Values. *The Future of Health Care in Canada. Commission on the Future of Health Care in Canada*. Final Report, Nov. 2002, Saskatoon.

Ron A (1999) NGOs in community health insurance schemes: examples from Guatemala and the Philippines. *Social Science and Medicine* 48: 939–50.

Roos LL, Fisher ES, Sharp SM, Newhouse JP, Anderson G and Bubolz TA (1990) Postsurgical mortality in Manitoba and New England. *Journal of the American Medical Association* 263: 2453–458.

Rosenthal TC and Fox C (2000) Access to health care for the rural elderly. *Journal of the American Medical Association* 25; 284(16): 203–06.

Rosenthal T, Horwitz M, Snyder G and O'Connor J (1996) Medicaid primary care services in New York State: Partial capitation versus full capitation. *Journal of Family Practice* 42: 362–68.

Routh S, Thwin AA, Kane TT and Hel Baqui A (2000) User fees for family planning methods: an analysis of payment behaviour among urban contraceptors in Bangladesh. *Journal of Health Population and Nutrition* Sept., 18(2): 69–78.

Rubenstein LV, Kahn KL, Reinisch EJ, Sherwood MJ, Rogers WH, Kamberg C, Draper D and Brook RH (1990) Changes in quality of care for five diseases measured by implicit review, 1981 to 1986. *Journal of the American Medical Association* 264: 1974–9.

Russell LB and Manning CL (1989) The effect of prospective payment on Medicare expenditures. *New England Journal of Medicine* 320: 439–44.

Ruta D, Donaldson C and Gilray I (1996) Economics, public health and health care purchasing: the Tayside experience of programme budgeting and marginal analysis. *Journal of Health Services Research and Policy* 1(4): 185–93.

Ryan M (1999) Using conjoint analysis to take account of patient preferences and go beyond health outcomes: an application to in vitro fertilisation. *Social Science and Medicine* 48(4): 535–46.

Sager MA, Easterling DV, Kindig DA and Anderson OW (1989) Changes in the location of death after passage of Medicare's prospective payment system. A national study. *New England Journal of Medicine* 320: 433–9.

Saggers S and Gray D (1991) *Aboriginal Health and Society*, NSW: Allen and Unwin.

Salisbury CJ (1989) How do people choose their doctor? *British Medical Journal* 299: 608–10.

Salkeld G (1998) What are the benefits of preventive health care? *Health Care Analysis* 6(2): 106–12.

Saltman RB and von Otter C (1995) Vouchers in planned markets. In Saltman RB and von Otter C (eds) *Implementing Planned Markets in Health Care*. Buckingham. Open University Press.

Samuels B, Diamond G, Mahrer P and Denton T (2000) Intensity of Antianginal therapy in patients referred for Coronary Angiography: A comparison of fee-for-service and health maintenance organization therapeutic strategies. *Clinical Cardiology* 23: 165–70.

Schaefer E and Reschovsky JD (2002) Are HMO enrollees healthier than others? Results from a community tracking study. *Health Affairs* 21: 249–58.

Schauffler HH and McMenamin S (2001) Assessing PPO performance on prevention and population health. *Medical Care Research and Review* 58(Supp. 1): 112–36.

Schlenker R, Shaughnessy P and Hittle D (1995) Patient-level cost of home health care under capitated and fee-for-service payment. *Inquiry* 32: 252–70.

Schneeweiss S, Soumerai S, Glynn R, Maclure M, Dormuth C and Walker A (2002) Impact of reference-based pricing for angiotensin-converting enzyme inhibitors on drug utilization. *Canadian Medical Association Journal* 166: 737–45.

Schneider EC, Zaslavsky AM and Epstein AM (2002) Racial disparities in the quality of care for enrolees in medicare managed care. *Journal of American Medical Association* Mar 13; 287(10): 1288–940.

Schoen C, Davis K, DesRoches C, Donelan K and Blendon R (2000) Health insurance markets and income inequality: findings from an international health policy survey. *Health Policy* 51: 67–85.

Schoenman J, Evans W and Schur C (1997) Primary care case management for Medicaid recipients: Evaluation of the Maryland access to care program. *Inquiry* 34: 155–70.

Scholkopf M (2000) The Hospital Sector in Germany: An Overview. *World Hospitals and Health Services* 36: 13–18.

Schroeder SA (2001) Prospects for expanding health insurance coverage. *Northern England Journal of Medicine* 15 Mar, 344(11). 847–52.

Schwartz WB and Aaron HJ (1984) Rationing hospital care. Lessons from Britain. *New England Journal of Medicine* 310: 52–6.

Scott A and Farrar S (2003) Incentives in health care. In Scott A, Maynard A and Elliott R (eds) *Advances in Health Care*. Chichester: John Wiley and Sons.

Secretaries of State (1989) *Funding Contracts for Health Services*. Working Paper 2. London: HMSO.

Secretaries of State for Health, Scotland Wales and N. Ireland (1989) *Working for Patients*. London: HMSO.

Segouin C and Thayer C (1999) The French prescription for health care reform. *International. Journal Health Planning & Management* 14: 313–27.

Sen A (1977) Rational fools: a critique of the behavioural foundations of economic theory. *Philosophy and Public Affairs* 6: 317–44.

Sen A (2002) Why health equity? *Health Economics* Dec., 11(8): 659–66.

Senior ML, Williams H and Higgs G (2003) Morbidity, deprivation and drug prescribing: factors affecting variations in prescribing between doctors' practices. *Health Place* 9(4): 281–9.

References

Shaughnessy P, Schlenker R and Hittle D (1994) Home health care outcomes under capitated and fee-for-service payment. *Health Care Financing Review* 16: 187–222.

Sheils JF (1995) Why MSAs increase costs. *Health Affairs* 15: 241.

Shaw RP and Griffin C (1995) *Financing Health care in Sub-Saharan Africa Through User Fees and Insurance.* Washington, DC: World Bank.

Sheiman I (1995) New methods of financing and managing health care in the Russian Federation. *Health Policy* 32: 167–80.

Sheldon TA, Smith GD and Befan G (1993) Weighting in the dark: resource allocation in the new NHS. *British Medical Journal,* Mar. 27, 306(6881): 835–39.

Shiell A and Hall J. (1993) *Advancing health in NSW: planning in an economic framework.* Sydney: CHERE.

Shiels JF (1995) Why MSAs increase costs? *Health Affairs* 15: 241.

Shiller RJ (2000) *Irrational Exuberance.* Princeton, NJ: Princeton University Press.

Short PF and Banthin JS (1995) New estimates of the underinsured younger than 65 years. *Journal of American Medical Association* 274(16): 1302–306.

Shortell S, Zazzali J, Burns L, Alexander J, Gillies R, Budetti P *et al.* (2001) Implementing Evidence-Based Medicine. *Medical Care* 39: I62–78.

Shortt SE and Shaw RA (2003) Equity in Canadian health care: does socioeconomic status affect waiting times for elective surgery? Canadian Medical Association Journal 168(4): 413–16.

Silverman EM, Skinner JS and Fisher ES (1999) The association between for-profit hospital ownership and increased Medicare spending. *New England Journal of Medicine* 341(6): 420–6.

Siu AL, Sonnenberg FA, Manning WG, Goldberg GA, Bloomfield ES, Newhouse JP and Brook RH (1986) Inappropriate use of hospitals in a randomized trial of health insurance plans. *New England Journal of Medicine* 315: 1259–66.

Sketris I and Hill S (1998) The Australian national publicly subsidized Pharmaceutical Benefits Scheme: Any lessons for Canada? *Canadian Journal of Clinical Pharmacology* 5: 111–18.

Skidelsky R (1996) *Beyond the Welfare State.* London: Social Market Foundation.

Skinner A (1986) Introduction. In Smith A (ed.) *An Inquiry into the Nature and Causes of the Wealth of Nations.* Hardmondsworth: Penguin.

Sloan FA and Vraciu R (1983) Investor-owned and not-for-profit hospitals: addressing some issues. *Health Affairs* 2: 25–37.

Sloan FA (1998) *Hospital Ownership and Cost and Quality of Care: Is There a Dime's Worth of Difference?* National Bureau of Economic Research Working Paper: 6706, August 1998.

Smith A (1759) *The Theory of Moral Sentiments.* London: Strachan & Cadell.

Smith A (1776) *An Inquiry into the Nature and Causes of the Wealth of Nations.* Harmondsworth: London: Penguin Classics.

Smith DG (1997) The effects of preferred provider organizations on health care use and costs. *Inquiry* 34: 278–87.

Smith GD, Bartley M and Blane D (1990) The Black report on socioeconomic inequalities in health 10 years on. *British Medical Journal* 301: 373–7.

Smith PC (2002) Performance management in British health care: will it deliver? *Health Affairs* 21: 103–13.

Smith P, Sheldon TA, Carr-Hill RA, Martin S, Peacock S and Hardman G (1994) Allocating resources to health authorities: results and policy implications of small area analysis of use of inpatient services. *British Medical Journal* Oct. 22, 309(6961): 1050–4.

Smith T (1985) Limited lists of drugs: lessons from abroad. *British Medical Journal* 290: 532 34.

Solanki G, Schauffler HH and Miller LS (2000) The direct and indirect effects of cost-sharing on the use of preventive services. *Health Services Research* 34: 1331–350.

Sommersguter-Reichmann M (2000) The impact of the Austrian hospital financing reform on hospital productivity: empirical evidence on efficiency and technology changes using a non-parametric input-based Malmquist approach. *Health Care Management Science* 3: 309–21.

Sorensen R and Grytten J (2000) Contract design for primary care physicians: Physician location and practice behaviour in small communities. *Health Care Management Science* 3: 151–57.

Stano M (1985) An analysis of the evidence on competition in the physician services market. *Journal of Health Economics* 4: 197–211.

Stanton B and Clemens J (1989) User fees for health care in developing countries: a case study of Bangladesh. *Social Science & Medicine* 29: 1199–205.

Starr A, Furnary A, Grunkemeier G, He G-W and Ahmad A (2002) Surgery for acquired heart disease. Is referral source a risk factor for coronary surgery? Health maintenance organization versus fee-for-service system. *The Journal of Thoracic and Cardiovascular Surgery* 111: 708–17.

Streshthaputra N and Indaratna K (2001) *The Universal Coverage Policy of Thailand: An Introduction.* Paper prepared for the Asia-Pacific Health Economics Network, 19 July 2001.

Sullivan K (2001) On the 'efficiency' of managed care plans. *International Journal of Health Services* 31(1): 55–65.

Suwandono A, Gani A, Purwani S, Blas E and Brugha R (2001) Cost recovery beds in public hospitals in Indonesia. *Health Policy and Planning*, 16(Suppl. 2): 10–18.

Tamblyn R, Laprise R, Hanley JA, Abrahamowicz M, Scott S, Mayo N, Hurley J, Grad R, Latimer E, Perreault R, McLeaod P, Huang A, Larochelle P and Mallet L (2001) Adverse effects associated with prescription drug cost-sharing among poor and elderly persons. *Journal of the American Medical Association* 285: 2328–329.

Tambour M and Rehnberg C (1997) *Internal Markets and Performance in Swedish Health Care.* Stockholm School of Economics, Working Paper No. 161, March 1997.

Tangcharoensathien V, Tantivess S, Teerawattananon Y, Auamkul N and Jongudoumsuk P. (2002) Universal coverage and its impact on reproductive health services in Thailand. *Reproduction Health Matters.* Nov, 10(20): 59–69.

Taroni F, Guerra R and D'Ambrosio M (1998) The Health Care Reform in Italy: Transition or Turmoil. *Journal of Health and Human Services Administration* 20: 396–422.

ten Have H (1988) Ethics and economics in health care: a medical philosopher's view. In Mooney G and McGuire A (eds) *Medical Ethics and Economics in Health Care.* Oxford: Oxford Medical Publications.

Thomas EJ, Orav EJ and Brennan TA (2000) Hospital ownership and preventable adverse events. *International Journal of Health Services* 30(4): 745–61.

Thomas L, McColl E, Cullum N, Rousseau N, Soutter J and Steen N (1998) Effect of clinical guidelines in nursing, midwifery, and the therapies: a systematic review of evaluations. *Quality in Health Care* 7: 183–91.

Thomas S, Killingsworth J and Acharya S (1998) User fees, self-selection and the poor in Bangladesh. *Health Policy and Planning* 13(1): 50–58.

Thomason J, Mulou N and Bass C (1994) User charges for rural health services in Papua New Guinea. *Social Science and Medicine* 39(8): 1105–115.

265

References

Thorpe KE (1992) Inside the black box of administrative costs. *Health Affairs* 11(2): 41–55.

Thorpe KE and Florence CS (1999) Why are workers uninsured? Employer-sponsored health insurance in 1997. *Health Affairs* (Millwood) 18 (2): 213–18.

Thorpe KE, Siegel JE and Dailey T (1989) Including the poor: the fiscal impacts of Medicaid expansion. *Journal of the American Medical Association* 261: 1003–7.

Titmuss R (1970) *The Gift Relationship: From Human Blood to Social Policy* London: Allen and Unwin.

Tobias J (1994) In defence of merit awards. *British Medical Journal* 308: 974–75.

Tokita T, Chino T and Kitaki H (2000) Healthcare expenditure and the major determinants in Japan. Hitotsubashi *Journal of Economics* 41(1): 1–16.

Tollman S, Schopper D and Torres A (1990) Health maintenance organisations in developing countries: what can we expect? *Health Policy and Planning* 5: 149–69.

Tountas Y, Karnaki P and Pavi E (2002) Reforming the reform: the Greek national health system in transition. *Health Policy* 62: 15–29.

Townsend P, Phillimore P and Beattie A (1987) *Health and Deprivation: Inequalities and the North.* London: Croom Helm.

Trevino FM, Moyer ME, Valdez RB and Stroup-Benham CA (1991) Health insurance coverage and utilization of health services by Mexican Americans, mainland Puerto Ricans, and Cuban Americans. *Journal of the American Medical Association* 265: 233–37.

Tu F, Tokunaga S, Deng ZL and Nobutomo K (2002) Analysis of hospital charges for cerebral infraction stroke inpatients in Beijing, People's Republic of China. *Health Policy* 59: 243–56.

Tussing AD and Wojtowycz MA (1986) Physician-induced demand by Irish GPs. *Social Science & Medicine* 23: 851–60.

Twaddle A (1996) Health system reform – toward a framework for international comparisons. *Social Science and Medicine* 43: 637–54.

Twaddle S, Walker A. (1995) Programme budgeting and marginal analysis: application within programmes to assist purchasing in Greater Glasgow Health Board. *Health Policy* 33: 91–105.

Twigg J (1999) Regional variation in Russian medical insurance: lessons from Moscow and Nizhny Novgorod. *Health & Place* 5: 235–45.

Tymowska K (2001) Health care under transformation in Poland. *Health Policy* 56: 85–98.

Udvarhelyi I, Jennison K, Phillips R and Epstein A (1991) Comparison of the quality of ambulatory care for fee-for-service and prepaid patients. *Annals of Internal Medicine* 115: 400.

UK Department of Health (1997) *The New NMS: Modern, Dependable.* London: UK Department of Health.

UK Department of Health (2003) *Resource allocation: Weighted Capitation Formula.* London: Department of Health.

United Nations Development Program (2002) *Human Development Report 2002: Representing Democracy in a Fragmented World.* New York: Oxford University Press.

University of Minnesota Center for Health Services Research (1987) *Comparison of Utilization Rates and Satisfaction with Services According to Types of Coverage.* Minneapolis: University of Minnesota.

US Congress, Office of Technology Assessment (1995) *Hospital Financing in Seven Countries,* OTA-BP-H-148. Washington DC: US Government Printing Office.

US Employee Benefits Research Institute (1997) Sources of Health Insurance and Characteristics of the Uninsured: Analysis of the March 1997 Current Population Survey. *EBRI Issue Brief* No. 192, December 1997. Washington DC: EBRI.

Valdez RB (1986) *The Effects of Cost-sharing on the Health of Children.* Santa Monica, CA: The Rand Corporation.

van de Ven W and Rutten F (1994) Managed competition in the Netherlands: lessons from five years of health care reform. *Australian Health Review* 17: 9–27.

van de Ven WMM (1989) *A Future for Competitive Health Care in the Netherlands*. Occasional Paper No. 9. University of York, Centre for Health Economics.

Van Der Geest S, Macwan'gi M, Kamwanga J, Mulikelela D, Mazimba A and Mwangelwa M (2000) User fees and drugs: what did the health reforms in Zambia achieve? *Health Policy and Planning* 15(1): 59–65.

Van Der Geest S, Macwan'gi M, Kamwanga J, Mulikelela D, Mazimba A and Mwangelwa M (2000) User fees and drugs: what did the health reforms in Zambia achieve? *Health Policy and Planning* 15: 59–65.

Van Der Heever, AM (1998) Private sector health reform in South Africa. *Health Economics* 7: 281–89.

Van Dis J. MSJournal of American Medical Association (2002) Where we live: health care in rural vs urban America. *Journal of American Medical Association* 2 Jan., 287(1): 108.

Van Doorslaer, Wagstaff A, van der Burg H, Christiansen T, Citoni G, Di Biase R, Gerdtham U, Gerfin G, Gross L, Häkkinen U, John J, Johnson P, Klavus J, Lachaud C, Lauritsen J, Leu R, Nolan B, Perán E, Pereira J, Propper C, Puffer F, Rochaix L, Rodriguez M, Schellhorn M, Sundeberg G and Winkelhake O (1999) The redistributive effect of health care financing in 12 OECD countries, *Journal of Health Economics*, 18: 291–313.

van Doorslaer E and Schut FT (2000) Belgium and the Netherlands revisited. *Journal of Health Politics, Policy and Law* 25: 875–87.

van Doorslaer E, Wagstaff A, van der Burg H, Christianses T, De Graeve D, Duchensne I, Gerdtham U, Gerfin M, Geurts J, Gross L, Häkkinen U, John J, Klavus J, Leu R, Noland B, Donnell I, Propper C, Puffer F, Schellhorn M, Sundberg G and Winkelhake I (2000) Equity and the delivery of health care in Europe. *Journal of Health Economics* 19: 553–83.

van Dulmen A (2000) Physician reimbursement and the medical encounter: An observational study in Dutch pediatrics. *Clinical Pediatrics* 39(10): 591–601.

Vayda E (1973) A comparison of surgical rates in Canada and in England and Wales. *New England Journal of Medicine* 289: 1224–29.

Vayda E, Barnsley JM, Mindell WR and Cardillo B (1984) Five-year study of surgical rates in Ontario's counties. *Canadian Medical Association Journal* 131: 111–15.

Vayda E, Mindell WR and Rutkow IM (1982) A decade of surgery in Canada, England and Wales, and the United States. *Archives of Surgery* 117: 846–53.

Vernon S, Heckel V and Jackson G (1995) Medical outcomes of care for breast cancer among health maintenance organization and fee-for-service patients. *Clinical Cancer Research* 1: 179–84.

Vernon S, Hughes J and Heckel V (1990) HMO versus fee for service practice: a four-year retrospective analysis of colorectal cancer diagnosis and treatment. Is there a difference in quality of care? *In Advances in Cancer Control: Screening and Prevention Research*, pp. 341–50. Engstrom P, Rimer B and Mortenson L (eds). Wiley-Liss: Inc., New York.

Verrilli DK and Zuckerman S. (1996) Preferred provider organizations and physician fees. *Health Care Financing Review* 17(3): 161–70.

Viney R, Haas M and De Abreu LR (2000) A practical approach to planning health services: using PBMA. *Australian Health Review* 23(3): 10–19.

Viney R, Haas M and Mooney G (1995) Program budgeting and marginal analysis: a guide to resource allocation. *NSW Public Health Bulletin* 6(4): 29–32.

References

Waddington C and Enyimayew K (1990) A Price to Pay, Part 2: the impact of user charges in the Ashanti-Akim Region of Ghana. *International Journal of Health Planning and Management* 4: 17–47.

Wagner EH and Bledsoe T (1990) The Rand Health Insurance Experiment and HMOs. *Medical Care* 28: 191–200.

Wagstaff A (1986) The demand for health: theory and applications. *Journal of Epidemiology and Community Health* 40: 1–11.

Wagstaff A (2002) Reflections on and alternative to WHO's fairness of financial contribution index. *Journal of Health Economics* Mar. 11(2): 103–15.

Wagstaff A and van Doorsler E (2000) Equity in health care financing and delivery, In AJ Culyer and JP Newhouse (eds) *Handbook of Health Economics*, North Holland: 1803–82.

Wagstaff A, van Doorsler E and Paci P (1989) Equity in the finance and delivery of health care: some tentative cross-country comparisons. *Oxford Review of Economic Policy* 5: 89–112.

Wagstaff A, Doorslaer van E, Burg van der H, Calonge S, Christiansen T, Citoni G *et al.* (1999a). Equity in the finance of health care: some further international comparisons. *Journal of Health Economics* 18: 263–90.

Wagstaff, A, van Doorslaer E *et al.* (1999b) Redistributive effect, progressivity and differential tax treatment: personal income taxes in twelve OECD countries. *Journal of Public Economics* 72: 73–98.

Waller D, Agass M, Mant D, Coulter A and Fuller A and Jones L (1990) Health checks in general practice: another example of inverse care? *British Medical Journal* 300: 1115–18.

Ward M, Lubeck D and Leigh J (1998) Long-term health outcomes of patients with Rheumatoid Arthritis treated in managed care and fee-for-service practice settings. *Rheumatology* 25: 641–49.

Ware JE Jr., Brook RH, Rogers WH, Keeler EB, Davies AR, Sherbourne CD, Goldberg GA, Camp P and Newhouse JP (1986) Comparison of health outcomes at a health maintenance organisation with those of fee-for-service care. *Lancet* 1: 1017–22.

Ware JE, Bayliss MS, Rogers WH, Kosinski M and Tarlov AR (1996) Differences in 4-year health outcomes for elderly and poor, chronically ill patients treated in HMO and fee-for-service systems. *Journal of the American Medical Association* 276(13): 1039–47.

Warner R and Huxley P (1998) Outcome for people with Schizophrenia before and after Medicaid capitation at a community agency in Colorado. *Psychiatric Services* 49: 802–7.

Watt JM, Derzon RA, Renn SC, Schramm CJ, Hahn JS and Pillari GD (1986) The comparative economic performance of investor-owned chain and not-for-profit hospitals. *New England Journal of Medicine* 314: 89–96.

Weisbrod BA (1978) Comment on MV Pauly. *Competition in the health care sector. Proceedings of a conference sponsored by Bureau of Economics, Federal Trade Commission.* Greenberg W (ed). Germanstown, Aspen Systems.

Weissman JS, Dryfoos P and London K (1999) Income levels of bad-debt and free-care patients in Massachusetts hospitals. *Health Affairs* (Millwood) Jul.–Aug., 18(4): 156–66.

Wells KB, Rogers WH, Davis LM, Kahn K, Norquist G, Keeler E *et al.* (1993) Quality of care for hospitalized depressed elderly patients before and after implementation of the Medicare Prospective Payment System. *American Journal of Psychiatry* 150(12): 1799–805.

Wensing M, van der Weijden T and Grol R (1998) Implementing guidelines and innovations in general practice: which interventions are effective? *British Journal of General Practice* 48: 991–97.

West P (1981) Theoretical and practical equity in the National Health Service in England. *Social Science & Medicine* 15c: 117–22.

White J (1995) *Competing Solutions: American Health Care Proposals and International Experience*. Washington DC: Brookings Institution.

Whitehead M (1988) *The Health Divide*. London: Penguin.

Whynes D (1983) *Invitation to Economics*. Oxford: Basil Blackwell.

Whynes DK, Baines DL and Tolley KH (1997a) GP fundholding and the costs of prescribing: further results. *Journal of Public Health Medicine* 19: 18–22.

Whynes DK, Heron T and Avery AJ (1997b) Prescribing cost savings by GP fundholders: long-term or short-term? *Health Economics* 6: 209–11.

Wickings I, Childs T, Coles J and Wheatcroft C (1985) *Experiments using PACTs in Southend and Oldham HAs. A Final Report to the DHSS of the PACTs Projects at Southend HA and Oldham HA, 1979–1985*. London: CASPE Research, King Edward's Hospital Fund.

Wildavsky A (1977) Doing better and feeling worse: the political pathology of health policy. *Daedalus* 106: 105–24.

Wildman J (2003) Income related inequalities in mental health in Great Britain: analysing the causes of health inequality over time. *Journal of Health Economics* Mar. 22(2): 295–312.

Wilensky GR (1988) Filling the gaps in health insurance: impact on competition. *Health Affairs* (Millwood) 7: 133–49.

Wilensky GR and Rossiter LF (1983) The relative importance of physician-induced demand in the demand for medical care. *Milbank Memorial Fund Quarterly* 61: 252–77.

Wilkinson D, Ryan P and Hiller J (2001) Variation in mortality rates in Australia: correlation with Indigenous status, remoteness and socio-economic deprivation. *Journal of Public Health Medicine* Mar., 23(1): 74–7.

Willcox S (2001) Promoting private health insurance in Australia. *Health Affairs* (Millwood) May–Jun., 20(3): 152–61.

Williams A (1985) Economics of coronary artery bypass grafting. *British Medical Journal* 291: 326–29.

Williams A (1986) The cost-benefit approach to the evaluation of intensive care units. *In The ICU – a cost-benefit study* (Reis Miranda D and Langrehr D, eds), Amsterdam: Elsevier.

Williams A (1988) Health economics: the end of clinical freedom? *British Medical Journal* 297: 1183–186.

Williams A (1998) Primeval health economics in Britain: a personal retrospect of the pre-HESG period. *Health Economics* (Suppl.): 53–9.

Williams A (2001) Science or marketing at WHO? A commentary on 'World Health 2000'. *Health Economics* 10: 93–100.

Williams J, Petchey R, Gosden T, Leese B and Sibbald B (2001) A profile of PMS salaried GP contracts and their impact on recruitment. *Family Practice* 18: 283–7.

Willis C (1993) *Means Testing in Cost Recovery of Health Services in Developing Countries, Phase I: review of concepts and literature, and Preliminary Field Work Design*. Bethesda: Abt Associates Inc.

Wilson R, Buchan I and Walley T (1995) Alterations in prescribing by general practitioner fundholders: an observational study. *British Medical Journal* 311: 1347–50.

Winslow CM, Kosecoff JB, Chassin M, Kanouse DE and Brook RH (1988a) The appropriateness of performing coronary artery bypass surgery. *Journal of the American Medical Association* 260: 505–09.

Winslow CM, Solomon DH, Chassin MR, Kosecoff J, Merrick NJ and Brook RH (1988b) The appropriateness of carotid endarterectomy. *New England Journal of Medicine* 318: 721–7.

269

References

Wiseman, V (2003) *Interventions to improve the effectiveness and cost-effectiveness of malaria treatment.* Report to the Institute of Medicine of the National Academies, Washington, DC.

Wolfe B and Gabay M (1987) Health status and medical expenditures: more evidence of a link. *Social Science & Medicine* 25: 883–8.

Wolfe BL (1986) Health status and medical expenditures: is there a link? *Social Science & Medicine* 22: 993–9.

Wolfe PR and Moran DW (1993) Global budgeting in the OECD countries. *Health Care Financ Rev* 14(3): 55–76.

Woolhandler S and Himmelstein DU (1991) The deteriorating administrative efficiency of the U.S. health care system. *New England Journal of Medicine* 324: 1253–8.

Woolhandler S and Himmelstein DU (1997) Costs of care and administration at for-profit and other hospitals in the United States. *New England Journal of Medicine* 336: 769–4.

Wordsworth S, Donaldson C and Scott A (1996) *Can We Afford the NHS?* London: Institute for Public Policy Research.

World Bank (1996) *Cost Sharing: Towards Sustainable Health Care in Sub-Saharan Africa.* Africa Region. Report Number 63, May 1996.

World Health Organisation (1982) *Plan of action implementing the Global Strategy for Health for All.* Geneva: World Health Organisation.

World Health Organisation (1985) *Targets for all: targets in support of the European regional strategy for health for all.* Copenhagen: WHO Regional Office for Europe.

World Health Organization (1999) *World Health Report 1999 – Making a Difference.* Geneva: World Health Organization.

World Health Organization (2000) *The World Health Report 2000. Health Systems.* Geneva: World Health Organisation.

Wouters AV (1990) The cost of acute outpatient primary care in a preferred provider organization. *Medical Care* 28: 573–85.

Wyszewianski L (1986) Families with catastrophic health care expenditures. *Health Services Research* 21: 617–34.

Xiao J, Lee A, Vemuri SR and Beaver C (2000) An assessment of the effects of casemix funding on hospital utilisation: a Northern Territory perspective. *Australian Health Review* 23(1): 122–36.

Xu K, Evans DV, Kawabata K, Zeramdini R, Klavus J and Murray CJ (2003) Household catastrophic health expenditure: a multicountry analysis. *Lancet*, 12 July 362(9378): 111–17.

Yelin EH, Criswell LA and Feigenbaum PG (1996) Health care utilization and outcomes among persons with rheumatoid arthritis in fee-for-service and prepaid group practice settings. *Journal of the American Medical Association* 276(13): 1048–53.

Yelin EH, Shearn MA and Epstein WV (1986) Health outcomes for a chronic disease in prepaid group practice and fee for service settings. The case of rheumatoid arthritis. *Medical Care* 24: 236–47.

Yepez, M et al. (2000) The factors associated with noncompliance with antimalarial treatment in Ecuadorian patients. *Revista Cubana de Medicina Tropical* 52: 81–9.

Yip W and Hsiao W (1997) Medical savings accounts: lessons from China. *Health Affairs* 16(6): 244–51.

Yoder RA (1989) Are people willing and able to pay for health services? *Social Science & Medicine* 29: 35–42.

Young AF and Dobson AJ (2003) The decline in bulk-billing and increase in out-of-pocket costs for general practice consultations in rural areas of Australia, 1995–2001. *Medical Journal of Australia* 178(3): 122–6.

Young AF, Dobson AJ and Byles JE (2001) Determinants of general practitioner use among women in Australia. *Social Science and Medicine* 53(12): 1641–51.

Young GJ, Desai KR and Van Deusen Lukas C (1997) Does the sale of nonprofit hospitals threaten health care for the poor? *Health Affairs* (Millwood), Jan.–Feb., 16(1): 137–41.

Yule BF, Fordyce ID, Bond CM and Taylor RJ (1988) *The 'Limited List' in general practice: implications for the costs and effectiveness of prescribing*. Discussion Paper No. 01/88, 1988. Health Economics Research Unit, University of Aberdeen.

Zapka JG, Oakes JM, Simons-Morton DG, Mann NC, Goldbert R, Sellers DE, Estabrook B, Gilliland J, Linares AC, Benhamin-Garner R and McGovern P (2000) Missed opportunities to impact fast response to AMI symptoms. Patient Education Counselling 2000, Apr., 40(1): 67–82.

Zelder M (2000) *Spend more, wait less? The myth of underfunded Medicare in Canada*. Vancouver: Fraser Institute.

Zwanziger J and Auerbach RR (1991) Evaluating PPO performance using prior expenditure data. *Medical Care* 29: 142–51.

Zwanziger J, Kravitz RL, Hosek SD, Hart K, Sloss EM, Sullivan O, Kallich JD and Goldman DP (2000a) Providing managed care options for a large population: Evaluating the CHAMPUS reform initiative. *Military Medicine* 165: 403–10.

Zwanziger J and Melnick GA (1988) The effects of hospital competition and the Medicare PPS program on hospital cost behaviour in California. *Journal of Health Economics* 7: 301–20.

Zwanziger J, Melnick GA, Mann J, Simonson L (1994a) How hospitals practice cost containment with selective contracting and the Medicare Prospective Payment System. *Medi Care* 32(11): 1153–62.

Zwanziger J, Melnick GA and Bamezai A (1994b) Costs and price competition in California Hospitals, 1980–1990. *Health Affairs* 13(4): 118–26.

Zwanziger J, Melnick GA and Bamezai A (2000a) Can cost shifting continue in a price competitive environment? *Health Economics* 9(3): 211–6.

Zwanziger J, Melnick GA and Bamezai A (2000b) The effect of selective contracting on hospital costs and revenues. *Health Services Research* 35(4): 849–67.

Zweifel P (2000) Switzerland. *Journal of Health Politics, Policy & Law* 25: 938–44.

Zweifel P, Felder S and Meiers M (1999) Ageing of population and health care expenditure: a red herring? *Health Economics* 8(6): 485–96.

INDEX